SWEET REASON

Sweet Reason pulls off the impossible: it provides a fun-to-read but also competent introduction to logic. Students in any discipline will find the text to be an intriguing first course in logical theory.

J.C. Beall, University of Connecticut and University of Otago

Introductory logic books are a dime a dozen. But this one's different. No, really. With a unique combination of philosophical nous, paradox, humor, and – often provocative – exercises, it teaches the elements of both formal logic and critical reasoning. And it shows logic as a living, breathing, evolving, stimulating, subject. If you don't want to get interested in logic, don't use this book.

Graham Priest, City University of New York Graduate Center

This extraordinary book, refined over the years in a very successful course at Smith College, is unique in scope among introductory logic texts, beginning with critical thinking, moving through a first-rate treatment of standard propositional and predicate logic, and introducing students along the way to a variety of more advanced topics, including modal logic, many-valued logics, set theory, cardinal and ordinal arithmetic, the logic of probability, and the logic of paradox.

John Horty, University of Maryland

James M. Henle, Jay L. Garfield and Thomas Tymoczko

illustrated by Emily Altreuter

Sweet Reason

A FIELD GUIDE TO MODERN LOGIC Second Edition

WILEY-BLACKWELL

A John Wiley & Sons, Ltd., Publication

This edition first published 2011
© 2012 John Wiley & Sons Inc.

Wiley-Blackwell is an imprint of John Wiley & Sons, formed by the merger of Wiley's global Scientific, Technical and Medical business with Blackwell Publishing.

Registered Office
John Wiley & Sons Ltd, The Atrium, Southern Gate, Chichester, West Sussex, PO19 8SQ, United Kingdom

Editorial Offices
350 Main Street, Malden, MA 02148-5020, USA
9600 Garsington Road, Oxford, OX4 2DQ, UK
The Atrium, Southern Gate, Chichester, West Sussex, PO19 8SQ, UK

For details of our global editorial offices, for customer services, and for information about how to apply for permission to reuse the copyright material in this book please see our website at www.wiley.com/wiley-blackwell.

The right of James M. Henle, Jay L. Garfield and Thomas Tymoczko to be identified as the authors of this work has been asserted in accordance with the UK Copyright, Designs and Patents Act 1988.

Library of Congress Cataloging-in-Publication Data

Henle, James M.
Sweet reason : a field guide to modern logic / James M. Henle, Jay L. Garfield, Thomas Tymoczko ; with illustrations by Emily Altreuter. – 2nd ed.
    p.   cm.
  Thomas Tymoczko listed first of prev. ed.
  Includes bibliographical references and index.
  ISBN 978-1-4443-3715-0 (pbk.)
1. Logic, Modern–20th century.   I. Garfield, Jay L., 1955–   II. Tymoczko, Thomas.   III. Title.
  BC38.T86 2011
  160–dc22

                                                2011015191

A catalogue record for this book is available from the British Library.

This book is published in the following electronic formats: ePDFs 9781118078631; ePub 9781118078686

Set in 10/13pt Minion by SPi Publisher Services, Pondicherry, India
Printed and bound in Singapore by Fabulous Printers Pte Ltd

1   2011

To those taught us Logic, Gene Kleinberg,
Nuel D Belnap, Jr and Hilary Putnam

Contents

Preface

This is an unusual introductory logic text. It teaches beginning students to understand logic not as a fixed body of knowledge or set of techniques, but as an active field of inquiry and intellectual controversy. We provide students with the tools to explore the nature of inference, the subtleties of language, and to test the bounds of rationality. This is a book designed to begin the education of logicians.

Sweet Reason goes deeper into the philosophy and applications of logic than standard texts. It is also more fun to read and more enjoyable to teach. We focus on the paradoxes at the heart of philosophical logic and the puzzles at the heart of mathematical logic. There are stories, there are entertainments, there are characters.

We present all the usual topics in first-order predicate logic. We also offer a unique and especially clean approach to analytic reading, writing and debate. The two areas, "formal" and "informal" logic, are thoroughly integrated in the text, each illustrating and informing the other.

We contextualize our presentation in the history and philosophy of logic, allowing us to introduce a variety of extensions to basic logic that take students to areas of exciting contemporary research: many-valued logic, modal logic, for example, and probability. Every chapter addresses both formal logic and critical thinking, as well as the philosophy of logic and its applications. Students learn more logic, enjoy it more and develop a deeper appreciation for logical inquiry through this integrated treatment of the discipline, and through exposure to controversy in the field.

Sweet Reason is ambitious but approachable and attainable. Novice logicians—that is, first-semester first-year students—do as well as philosophy majors and pre-law students. The mix of light and serious draws them in. The mix of formal and informal keeps them centered.

Not everything we teach fits within these covers. Our website contains a wealth of supplemental material, ranging from examples and exercises, to puzzles and curios, to extended discussions of history, philosophy, and mathematics. There are essays on religion, poetry, time travel, the tax code, and much more. Whenever a topic in the book is explored more deeply on the website, we place this logo in the margin of the text.

The website (**sweetreason2ed.com**) is constantly being updated, and will keep the volume current.

Problems of greater difficulty are specially marked:

1.   (Ordinary problem)

2!   (Hard problem)

3!!   (Really hard problem)

4!!!   (Absurdly hard problem)

This second edition of *Sweet Reason* is a wholesale revision of the first, reflecting our own (Jim's and Jay's) evolving pedagogy. We think that students and teachers alike will find it clearer and more enjoyable. We owe a lot to our late colleague Tom whose absence in this enterprise we feel keenly.

Colleagues near and far contributed much to the shape and content of this edition: Howard Adelman, Lee Bowie, Jill DeVilliers, Keith Devlin, Ruth Eberle, Lawry Finsen, Randy Frost, Michael Henle, Fred Hoffman, Murray Kiteley, Roman Kossak, Joe O'Rourke, Judy Roitman, Bob Roos, Lee Sallows, Dan Velleman, Stan Wagon, Marlene Wong, and Andrzej Zarach.

We are especially grateful for the support of students past and present, especially Gina Cooke, Kira Hylton, Marti McCausland, Cathy Weir, Theresa Huang, Julia Wu, Caroline Sluyter and all who cut their logical teeth on primitive versions of "Buffalo buffalo buffalo," "*The Digestor's Digest*," and "Obscure British Novels of 1873."

The second edition owes an incalculable debt to a talented team of student editors: Sarah Bolts, Ekaterina Eydelnaut, Caroline Fox, Emily Garvey, Penka Kovacheva, Juan Li, Sally Moen, and Katherine Peterson. Their many contributions include numerous problems, illustrations, and intelligent review.

We would like to salute here the late Jerry Lyons, our first editor and constant counsel. Perhaps there would have been a second edition, but without his encouragement and enthusiasm there wouldn't have been a first.

Tom Tymoczko died in 1995 after a short illness. He was a remarkable philosopher who made important contributions to the philosophies of mind, epistemology, language, and especially the philosophy of mathematics. His work compelled attention for a variety of reasons. He combined an appreciation for the unchanging nature of his subjects with a sharp understanding of their mutability. His insight into mathematical practice could almost be described as hip. His ideas were clear and he wrote about them with great clarity. As colleague and friend, we miss him.

Jim Henle and Jay Garfield
June 2010

How critical is Logic? I will tell you. In every corner of the known universe, you will find either the presence of logical arguments or, more significantly, the absence. (V. K. Samadar)

What Is Logic?

That's hard to say.

Logic is about relationships among statements, about the abstract structure of statements, and about the nature of arguments. A logic is an attempt to understand when one statement follows from other statements, and why. Logic is not a settled body of knowledge, but a domain of inquiry, in which we encounter different logics for different purposes, and debates among logicians about the nature of these logics and their relative merits.

We're going to show you a number of logics and introduce you to some of the challenges logic provides. You will encounter unfamiliar and sometimes perplexing ideas. You will learn a set of techniques for thinking and writing, and will gain a deeper appreciation of structure. You will think and write more clearly. You will debate more effectively.

You're also going to have a lot of fun. Some of the deepest ideas of logic appeared first as paradoxes, some of them thousands of years ago. There is a great synergy between logical puzzles and logical insight. And there is pleasure in logic. The most powerful logical ideas are also the most enchanting, the most beautiful.

So, what *is* logic?

We'll talk about that again at the end.

Sweet Reason: A Field Guide To Modern Logic, Second Edition. Jim Henle, Jay L. Garfield, Thomas Tymoczko and Emily Altreuter.
© 2012 John Wiley & Sons Inc. Published 2012 by John Wiley & Sons Inc.

Chapter One

First, a word about this chapter. Let's say you're going to learn to swim. You're 5 years old and a little afraid of the water. Your swimming teacher tells you not to be afraid, and picks you up and throws you into the pool!

You immediately start thrashing about with your arms and legs. You're really scared, but after a few seconds, you notice that you're not drowning, you're keeping your head above water. In a few more seconds, you've made your way to the side of the pool and you're hanging on to the edge trying to figure out what happened.

You didn't drown because everyone is born with swimming reflexes and instincts. When your teacher threw you in, those reflexes took command and saved you. Now that it's over, you're not as frightened of the water. You've been in the middle of the pool and survived.

This chapter is a little like that first swimming lesson. You may never have studied logic, but you do, in fact, know quite a bit. If you didn't, you could hardly speak, let alone make your way in the world.

We're going to throw everything at you. You'll be surprised at how easy it is to understand the symbols. It's easy because the logical ideas represented by the symbols are basic ideas that you've worked with all your life.

Logic can seem scary at first. If you don't know what they mean, strange symbols

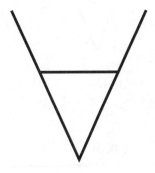

Sweet Reason: A Field Guide To Modern Logic, Second Edition. Jim Henle, Jay L. Garfield, Thomas Tymoczko and Emily Altreuter.
© 2012 John Wiley & Sons Inc. Published 2012 by John Wiley & Sons Inc.

can appear frightening . . .

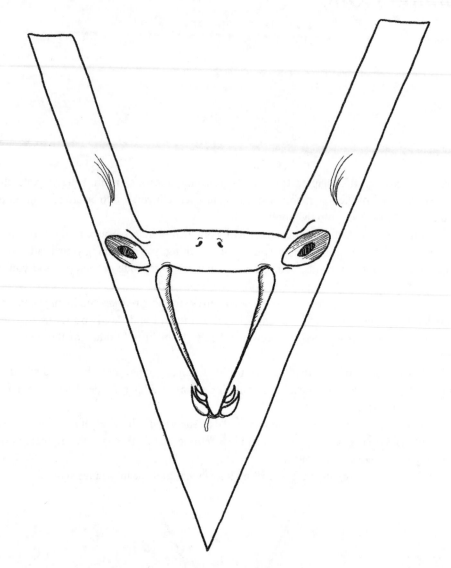

But don't panic. The "∀" symbol just means "everything." You'll see how it works in a moment. It's not as mean as it looks.

1.1   Introducing Formal Logic

There was only one catch and that was Catch 22, which specified that a concern for one's own safety in the face of dangers that were real and immediate was the process of a rational mind. Orr was crazy and could be grounded. All he had to do was ask; and as soon as he did, he would no longer be crazy and would have to fly more missions. Orr would be crazy to fly more missions and sane if he didn't, but if he was sane he had to fly them. If he flew them he was crazy and didn't have to but if he didn't want to he was sane and had to. (Joseph Heller, *Catch-22*)

We begin with connectives, the logical operations that link sentences to each other. We don't have many connectives; they're all familiar to you. You know them as "and", "or", "not", "if ... then", and "if and only if". Connectives allow us to create complex statements from simple statements. Suppose A and B are statements. Then we'll use

$$A \wedge B$$

to say that both A and B are true. We'll use

$$A \vee B$$

to mean that at least one of A, B is true (A is true or B is true or both are true). We'll use

$$\neg A$$

to mean that A is *not* true. We'll use

$$A \Rightarrow B$$

to mean that if A is true then so is B. And finally we'll use

$$A \Leftrightarrow B$$

to mean that A is true if and only if B is true, that is, A and B have the same truth value.

Let's say we have these statements:

P: George is late to the meeting.
Q: The meeting is in Detroit.
R: George brings a casserole.

Example

How do we say that either George will be late or he'll bring a casserole?
Answer:

$$P \vee R$$

Example

What does $Q \Rightarrow P$ mean?
Answer: If the meeting is in Detroit then George will be late.

Example

Represent the following with symbols: The meeting is in Detroit and either George doesn't bring a casserole or George is late.

Answer: $Q \wedge (\neg R \vee P)$ Note the use of parentheses here. We'll say more about this later.

| **Exercises** | **Introducing Formal Logic** | Odd-numbered solutions begin on page 350 |

Translate the following sentences using P, Q, and R from above.

1. George is late and the meeting is in Detroit.
2. If the meeting is in Detroit, then George brings a casserole.
3. Either George is late or he does not bring a casserole.
4. George brings a casserole if and only if the meeting is in Detroit.
5. If George does not bring a casserole, he is not late.
6. If the meeting is in Detroit then George brings a casserole, and if George brings a casserole then he is late.

7. The meeting is in Detroit if and only if both George is late and he doesn't bring a casserole.
8. The meeting is in Detroit, and either George is late or he brings a casserole.

Determine the meaning of each of the following sentences.

9. $P \vee R$
10. $R \wedge \neg Q$
11. $Q \Rightarrow P$
12. $R \Leftrightarrow \neg Q$
13. $\neg P \vee (\neg Q \wedge R)$
14. $P \wedge (Q \vee R)$
15. $R \wedge (Q \Rightarrow P)$
16. $Q \vee (\neg P \Leftrightarrow R)$

The Greek philosopher Epimenides is credited with formulating a paradox that has stimulated some of the most important advances in logic from the classical period right up to yesterday afternoon (we guarantee this, no matter when you are reading these words). He, a Cretan, put it this way:

All Cretans are Liars.

Since Epimenides was a Cretan, he was asserting that he is a liar, meaning that what he says is false. So it's false that all Cretans are liars. So maybe he's not a liar. So what he is saying is true? So he is a liar! So it's false! So it's true! Paradox!

The paradox isn't perfect. Epimenides might be a liar, but some Cretans (not Epimenides) could be truth-tellers. But we can refine it.

This sentence is false.

Is it true? If so, then, since what it says is that it's false, it must be a false sentence. But then it must be true. But then it must be false! And so on.

This is the paradox of the Liar. For all its simplicity, it is very deep. Can it be resolved? In the history of logic there have been many proposals . . .

1.2   Constants and Relations

Please accept my resignation. I don't want to belong to any club that will accept me as a member. (Groucho Marx)

We can express more delicate ideas if we set up some symbols to represent individuals and other symbols to represent properties and relations. We'll use some lower case letters to refer to people.

> *a* refers to Jim Henle (a logician)
> *b* refers to Oprah
> *c* refers to Tom Tymoczko (another logician)
> *d* refers to Aristotle (a philosopher, scientist, and logician)
> *e* refers to Hillary Clinton
> *f* refers to Jay Garfield (yet another logician)

We'll use some upper case letters to express particular properties and relationships.

We'll use W to say that something is female. We'll write Wb to mean that Oprah is female. We'll use G similarly to say that something is male.

We'll use M to say that two individuals are married. If we write Mdc, for example, then we are saying that Tom Tymoczko and Aristotle are married.

We'll use P to represent a relationship among three individuals. P will say that the first two individuals are the natural parents of the third. That is, if we write $Pbcd$ then we are saying that Oprahand Tom begat Ari (when you've had a little more logic, you can call Aristotle "Ari," too).

Finally, we'll use $=$ to say that two individuals are identical. If we write $e = a$ then we are saying that Hillary Clinton is Jim Henle.

Example

How can we say that both Tom and Jay are male?

Answer: $Gc \land Gf$.

Example

What does $Mec \Rightarrow We$ mean?

Answer: If Hillary and Tom are married to each other, then Hillary is female.

Exercises   **Constants and Relations**

Odd-numbered
solutions
begin on page 350

Write English sentences that express the meanings of these formulas.

1. Wc
2. Mea
3. $d = f$
4. $Pacb$
5. $Pcab$
6. $Pabc$
7. $Wa \wedge Ga$
8. $Ge \Rightarrow \neg Med$

Using only the symbols that have been introduced, write formulas that express the meanings of these sentences.

9. Hillary Clinton is married to Aristotle.
10. Aristotle is male.
11. Aristotle is married to Hillary Clinton.
12. Jim Henle is Oprah
13. Aristotle and Jay Garfield are the parents of Hillary Clinton.
14. Jim Henle is male and Tom Tymoczko is female.
15. Jay Garfield is not married to Jim Henle.
16. If Oprah and Hillary are married then Oprah is male.

The remaining problems concern the following map:

We'll use Nxy to mean that x shares a border with y at more than just a point. For example, Ngh is true because regions g and h are neighbors, but Nkh is false because k and h touch only at the corner. Furthermore, no region will be considered a neighbor of itself.
True or false?

17. Nej
18. $\neg Nah$
19. $Nkh \vee Nhe$
20. $Nbd \wedge Nbc$
21. Ngg
22. $(Ncf \wedge Njf) \wedge \neg Ncj$
23! $\neg Nij \Leftrightarrow \neg Nde$
24! $\neg Nge \Rightarrow (Nag \vee Ngh)$

"During the First World War he [Ernest Harrison] was a naval officer and shaved his mustache. On visiting Cambridge, the Master (not recognizing him) asked him at a dinner whether he was related to 'our dear Ernest Harrison.' Adopting a certain philosophical view of relations (repudiated by Russell) he replied: No."
—J. E. Littlewood, *A Mathematician's Miscellany*

1.3 Quantifiers and Variables

If you call a tail a leg, how many legs has a dog? Five? No, calling a tail a leg don't make *it a leg.* (Abraham Lincoln)

If we say, "Everyone loves ice cream," we aren't talking about anyone in particular. We're making a universal statement. We have logical notation for that. Let's say that Cx means x loves ice cream. Using the individuals of the previous section, Cb would mean that Oprahloves ice cream. Then

$$\forall x Cx$$

means "for all x, x loves ice cream." The "$\forall x$" is a way of discussing all individuals at once.

If we say, "Someone loves ice cream" we again are not talking about a particular person. We're making what we call an existential statement, a statement that something of some kind exists. There's a way to say this in our primitive logical language:

$$\exists x Cx.$$

It means "there is an x such that x loves ice cream."

The x is a variable. It doesn't stand for anyone in particular. If we use a different variable, y, the meaning is the same. Both $\forall x Cx$ and $\forall y Cy$ mean the same thing (they mean that everyone loves ice cream).

Example

How can we say that Hillary is married?
Answer: We say that there is someone who is married to Hillary , that is,

$$\exists x Mxe.$$

Equivalently, we can say $\exists x Mex$, there is someone to whom Hillary is married.

Example

What does $\forall y(Myb \Rightarrow Gy)$ mean?

Answer: It says that every y is such that if y is married to Oprah then y is male. More simply, it says that all of Oprah's spouses are male.

Exercises   Quantifiers and Variables

Odd-numbered
solutions
begin on page 350

Translate each of the following predicate statements into English using the predicate language from the previous section (see chart below).

1. $\forall x Mxa$
2. $\exists y Mya$
3. $\neg \forall y Pbfy$
4. $\forall x Mbx \vee \exists y \neg Mby$
5. $\exists x(Mxd \wedge Mxb)$
6. $\forall z((z = e) \Rightarrow Wz)$
7. $\neg Gd \Rightarrow \neg \exists y Gy$
8. $\forall x(Mxa \Rightarrow Wx)$

a	Jim Henle
b	Oprah
c	Tom Tymoczko
d	Aristotle (aka Ari)
e	Hillary Clinton
f	Jay Garfield
Wx	x is female.
Gx	x is male.
Mxy	x is married to y.
$Pxyz$	x and y are the parents of z.

Translate each of the following sentences into symbolic notation.

9. Either everyone is female or everyone is male.
10. Everyone is either female or male.
11. If Tom Tymoczko is married to someone, then Tom is male.
12. Jay is a bachelor.
13. Hillary is not married to herself.

14. Jim is everyone's mother.
15. Aristotle is married to someone female, or there is a woman who is not married to Aristotle.

16! Hillary is a grandparent.

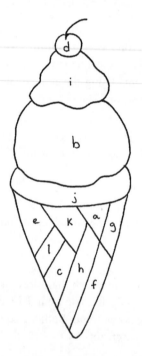

Remember that we use Nxy to mean x is a neighbor of y and that no region is next to itself. In each of the following, x stands for one of the regions in the ice cream cone above. Find x such that the statement is true.

17. Nxd
18. $Nxi \wedge Nxj$

19. $Nxf \wedge \neg Nxc$
20. $Nxe \wedge (Nxi \vee Nxh)$
21. $Nxb \wedge Nxa$
22. $Nxj \wedge Nxh \wedge \neg Nxg$

23. $Nxe \wedge \neg Nxk$
24. $Nxg \wedge \neg \exists y(Nxy \wedge Nyg)$
25. $\exists y \forall z(Nyx \wedge (Nzx \Rightarrow z = y))$
26. $\forall y(Nxy \Rightarrow Nyb)$

Have you been thinking about the paradox of the Liar? If it keeps you up at night, you have a future in logic.

One proposal to resolve the paradox is this: Perhaps the Liar sentence is neither true nor false. Maybe it has no truth-value at all, or some third, weird truth-value, like "deviant." Then, one might say, there is no paradox. The sentence is just deviant.

But consider the Strengthened Liar paradox:

This sentence is not true.

It's clear that if this sentence is true, we are once again landed into paradox, and that if it is false it's paradoxical as well. Does calling it deviant, or saying that it has no truth value, help?

No. Suppose that it has no truth value, or that it's deviant. Then it's not true, right? But that's what it says! So it *is* true! But it says that it's not! So it is! So it isn't! Back to square one.

1.4   Introducing Informal Logic

An autocrat's a ruler that does what th' people wants an' takes th' blame f'r it. A constitootional ixicutive, Hinnissy, is a ruler that does as he dam pleases an' blames th' people. (Finley Peter Dunne)

You're a first year student. You arrived two weeks ago at Sophist College, the ivy-draped liberal arts institution you dreamed of for years. Two weeks, but you're still floating on air. The academic atmosphere . . . the intellectual giants who are your professors . . . the imposing architecture . . . the excitement of campus life . . . the opportunities you see ahead . . . the challenge of the courses you've just begun . . . everything is as new and as thrilling as you had hoped.

Above all, you're in awe of the older students. They're so confident, so accomplished, so wise, so *cynical*. Well, I suppose there's nothing great about being cynical, except that you have to know a lot to be cynical, don't you? In any case, you relish those bull sessions that last until three in the morning . . . that's where it's at, that's where the world really unfolds, that's where . . .

But then one night the whole wonderful picture collapses. The discussion is about China. You just read that morning about the tight rein the government keeps on people. All you say is, "What they need is some democracy. If they would only let the people rule," and then Cathy jumps on you. Cathy, the junior you admired for her quickness, her assurance – and she seemed to like you.

"What's so terrific about democracy?" she asks. "In a democracy, the people choose, but they make terrible choices. They get freedom in the Balkans and the first thing they do is start shooting at each other. They get the vote in Iraq and they have a civil war.

"We have democracy, right? Well how great is that? We don't protect the environment, our schools are rotten, and we're in debt up to our eyeballs. If democracy is so wonderful, how come only 23 percent of the people vote here?"

You try to cut in. "But democracy has made us the most powerful, the most envied —" But she runs right over you!

"Oh, brother. We're powerful and envied because we're rich, not because of our campaign commercials. And all we do is abuse that power. And anyhow, we don't really have democracy. You know about Washington, D.C.? One of the biggest cities in the country, and they don't have self-government or representation in Congress. Why? Because it's a black city and we're all racists.

"Look at all the democracies in South America: all bankrupt. The only country down there with its act together is Chile, and it took a dictator, Pinochet, to put it on the road to recovery. You know what H.L. Mencken said? He called democracy the form of government that believes that the people know what they want and they deserve to get it – good and hard!"

You're devastated. Your deepest beliefs are in ruins! You can't say a thing because . . . well . . . everything she's saying sort of makes sense. But you still believe in democracy! You know it's right! But then, what's wrong with her arguments? What do you say?

You need to know how to argue!

There are good reasons for learning the art of argument.

First of all, you want to be able to defend your point of view. You want to persuade others. This is certainly true if you're right. And maybe it's useful even if you're wrong.

Secondly, and more nobly, you want to find out what is actually true. There is, perhaps, no better way to get to the bottom of things than to argue. When two skilled debaters engage, the best argument prevails. More often than not the winner is the truth.

Finally, the ability to argue represents power. If you can marshall your thoughts, arrange them in a logical order, and explain them clearly, people will pay attention. If your arguments are understandable and persuasive, you will be influential. *Your* issues, *your* perspectives, *your* proposals will take center stage.

In this book we'll teach you how to argue. We'll do it in stages. We'll start by showing you how to take apart an argument such as Cathy's, diagram it, and attack it. Then we'll show you how to construct your own argument, diagram it, and write it.

* * * * * * * * * * * *

A word about Cathy. She's sort of unpleasant. Unfortunately, she appears throughout this book; she insisted on it.

But responding to her is a good logical exercise. What's her point, anyway? We'll come back to this, but first we'll think more generally about the task of identifying conclusions.

1.5 Conclusions

Joe DiMaggio might have hit in 56 consecutive games, a seemingly unrivaled record, but he never won 33,277 arguments in a row, like Ted Williams, the undisputed champion of contentiousness. (David Halberstam, *The Teammates*)

The first step in tackling an argument is identifying the conclusion. This is more difficult than it sounds. You would think that anyone going to the trouble of making an argument would make sure we got the point. But that isn't always the case.

Writing is difficult. Writing arguments is especially difficult (as you will soon see). It's not surprising that it's often done poorly. That makes reading arguments a challenge. The key, and it is the key in formal logic too, is language. Unfortunately, while it is easy to say, "I would like to argue that . . ." or "My conclusion is . . ." that is too simple for most writers.

Consider the following three letters to the editor of *The New York Times*, May 11, 2005, responding to a column by Thomas Friedman arguing for an economic boycott of Iran and North Korea if they don't terminate their nuclear programs:

It is disturbing that Thomas L. Friedman seems to suggest that the world's most powerful countries (or groups of countries) should simply starve their opponents into submission.

First, it would be a blatant violation of international human rights principles. Second, such measures would mostly harm those people (civilians) who have the least power to do anything about the situation in their respective countries.

Surely Mr. Friedman does not believe that the leaders of Iran and North Korea are incapable of securing the necessities of life for themselves and their own families, and they have already demonstrated that they care little for the rest of their populations.

Jessica Crutcher

This is pretty simple. The writer is opposed to a boycott. But note that this conclusion is not explicitly stated. We have to figure that out from the list of negative effects of a boycott.

If China pressured North Korea to cease its weapons program by saying to Kim Jong Il, "You will shut down your nuclear weapons program and put all your reactors under international inspection, or we will turn off your lights, cut off your heat and put your whole country on a diet," perhaps the United States should insist that China do just that, lest we stop all our imports and bring its production machine to a grinding halt.

Lisa Calef

This letter is clearly in favor a boycott, though again it is not stated as such; instead the writer urges that the United States boycott China if China doesn't boycott North Korea.

Thomas L. Friedman is correct: there is a lot more that China and the European Union could do to deter both North Korea and Iran in their nuclear ambitions. But let us not underestimate the main attraction of obtaining such weapons: your enemies will think twice about attacking you.

Terry Phelps

This third letter is a little puzzling. What exactly is the conclusion? Should we boycott the countries? Would that address their motivation?

And what do you suppose is Cathy's conclusion in the previous section? She starts out attacking democracy. But then she complains that we don't have democracy and seems to think that's bad. Then she goes back to slamming democracy. This is one of the reasons Cathy is so hard to deal with – she jumps from one attack to another.

The best answer is that Cathy is arguing that democracy is not a good form of government. We'll begin rebutting arguments, starting with this one, in Chapter Three.

Exercises   Conclusions

Odd-numbered
solutions
begin on page 350

The conclusion can appear anywhere in the argument, or nowhere. A good place to look for it, though, is at the beginning and at the end. A well-written argument is likely to state it in both places. Look for key words, "therefore", "so", "hence", and "consequently."

Find the conclusions of the following arguments.

1. If we have the picnic on Sunday, David can't make it. We have to have it before exam period starts on Tuesday. The later the picnic is the better, so let's make it Monday.

2. I think the solution is to raise the tax on gasoline. If gas were more expensive, people would conserve. That would reduce emissions. And the government would collect money that could be used to clean up oil spills.

3. Doug is a dog only if he plays fetch. Doug is a cat. If Doug is a cat, then he's not a dog. So Doug does not play fetch.

4. There is no real difference between classical and popular music, and it is easy to see why. Everybody agrees that jazz is popular music, but it is also classical. After all, classical music is the music that represents the highest and most distinctive music produced by a culture, the music that endures and is passed from generation to generation, and in the performance and

composition of which virtuosity is demonstrated. But jazz plays this role in African-American culture. So jazz is classical music. Therefore, since it is also popular music, there is no real difference.

5. Should we legalize marijuana? Should we make it easier for people to poison themselves? Should we provide amnesty for drug-dealers? Should we give society's blessing to a degenerate, degrading practice?

6. Should we keep drug use illegal? Should we use the army and navy to attack drug dealers? Should we glamorize a destructive habit? Should we jack up the price of drugs so that addicts kill to get high? Should we enrich South American drug-dealing terrorists?

7. The economy is crashing right now because of oil prices. The cost of gasoline is at a historic high. So raising the tax on gas would be a big mistake. It would make it impossible for small businesses to operate.

8. Censorship of speech is never justified. Speech itself never harms anybody; at most the actions inspired by it cause harm, and they can be prohibited. If speech is censored, valuable ideas will be lost to the public and individuals will be prevented from expressing their own ideas and values. Now, pornography is a kind of speech. Consequently pornography should never be censored. Now, some people might be offended by pornography, but their own emotional reaction is their problem, and should not count against the rights of others.

1.6   Dialects of Logic

Histories make men wise; poets, witty; the mathematics, subtle; natural philosophy, deep; moral philosophy, grave; logic and rhetoric, able to contend. (Francis Bacon)

Each chapter of this book will begin with sections on formal logic, followed by sections on informal logic. Each chapter will end with a section on one of the many different logics, formal and informal, that are part of the history of logic and part of current research in logic.

> **A Typical Chapter**
> Some formal logic
> Some related informal logic
> A logic variant

In this first chapter, the logic variant is quite tame. We thought we'd tell you about some alternate notation for the basic connectives – notation which we *won't* use but which other writers may and which you might encounter elsewhere. Knowing that the odd symbols are just alternate notation for the same ideas will help you avoid confusion. It will also help to keep you aware of the difference between symbols and what symbols stand for.

And

Many logicians, especially philosophical logicians, use & instead of ∧. Indeed, the first edition of *Sweet Reason* used this symbol. Other logicians have used the letter K, a single dot · , ∩, u, or have simply written "*P* and *Q*" as *PQ*.

Or

There is unanimity today for the wedge, "∨" Still, in the history of logic, ∪, +, A, and even × have been used for "or".

Not

It is quite common to use ∼ for not. Other notations include - , N, ⇁, and placing a line or a ∼ above the statement letter.

If . . . then

You will see ⊃ in many logic books. You will also see differently shaped arrows, →, −− >, =>. In the distant past, C, and ⊃ have also been used.

If and only if

The symbol, ≡, is frequently used in place of ⇔. In the past, ↔, ∼, E, and ⊃⊂ have been used.

"If and only if" is often abbreviated **iff**. This is so handy we'll use it too. When you see "iff" it will always mean "if and only if."

That's all for now. You'll see some of these symbols in different contexts later in this book, sometimes to explain, sometimes to entertain, and in one case, to tease.

Quiz

To test your aptitude for studying logic

For each of the statements below, answer either true or false:

1. My answer to statement 2 is different from my answer to this statement.
2. My answer to statement 3 is the same as my answer to this statement.
3. Wow! This book is off to an amazing start! What a great read! These guys Jim, Jay, and Tom are AWESOME! I'll bet this wins a Pulitzer or a Nobel or an Oscar, or whatever it is they give to obscure texts in logic! I can't wait to find out what happens in the next chapter! I want to sit here and read the whole thing right now! Wow!

You may grade the quiz yourself. After you have completed writing your answers, ask yourself whether each answer is correct. For example, suppose you answer:

1. T
2. F
3. F

then the answer to statement 1 is correct (because your answer to 2 is different from your answer to 1). But your answer to 2 is incorrect (your answer to 3 is the same as your answer to 2 but you wrote 'F'). *Your own judgment is perfectly acceptable in deciding whether you have answered statement 3 correctly.*

It is possible to get a perfect score on this quiz.

Chapter Two

Sweet Reason focuses on two areas of logic: formal logic and what we are calling informal logic. The first deals with logic in the context of formal language, where statements are abstract and are often without determinate meaning.

$$P \wedge Q \qquad \forall x(Ax \vee Bx) \qquad (J \Rightarrow K) \Rightarrow (M \Rightarrow N) \qquad C \Leftrightarrow \exists y \exists z Hyz$$

The second deals with logic in the context of natural language, in this book, English. Here, statements are more often concrete and meaningful.

Today is Tuesday. My dog has fleas. Life is really, really strange.

There are good reasons to study formal logic. The very abstractness of formal language allows us to see logical issues clearly. Natural language is full of ambiguity and vagueness. Formal languages streamline, clarify, and simplify.

There is also good reason to study informal logic. Natural languages, like English, after all, are important human tools. We use them to understand the world, to communicate our understanding, to interact, to influence people, and to have an impact on events. Logic can help us to do all of this more effectively, and can help us to understand these aspects of our lives.

The two areas of logic are different but they're intimately connected. Formal language is abstracted from natural language. The choices made, for instance, in the definitions of $\vee$, $\wedge$, $\Rightarrow$ are based on the meaning of words in English. The world of people and events and the English language are reality checks on formal logic.

Formal logic, on the other hand, reveals the meaning and structure in natural language that words often obscure. It reveals the abstract skeletons of arguments and statements that enable them to be meaningful in the first place.

Nowhere is this connection between the formal and the informal clearer than in the question of inference. That is the focus of this chapter.

Sweet Reason: A Field Guide To Modern Logic, Second Edition. Jim Henle, Jay L. Garfield, Thomas Tymoczko and Emily Altreuter.
© 2012 John Wiley & Sons Inc. Published 2012 by John Wiley & Sons Inc.

2.1 Formal Inference

Why is this thus? What is the reason for this thusness? (Artemus Ward)

Logic is about what follows from what; it's about how to construct and understand arguments, about the relation between language and the world, and about how to tell a good argument from a bad one. We'll get to all of this, but let's begin by introducing a few terms. Some of these are technical terms in logic, and have meanings that are different from those they have in ordinary speech.

An argument is **valid** if and only if it's impossible for its premises to be true and its conclusion false. Another way to put this is to say that an argument is valid iff[1] the truth of the premises guarantee the truth of the conclusion. The premises are the reasons given in support of a conclusion. The conclusion is what we derive from the premises.

Example

$$P$$
$$\frac{Q}{\therefore P \wedge Q}$$

The premises of the argument are the statements above the line, P and Q; the conclusion is the statement below the line, $P \wedge Q$. The dots, $\therefore$, mean "therefore".

Is it possible for the premises of this argument to be true and the conclusion false? Absolutely not. If P and Q are true, so is $P \wedge Q$. This is a valid argument.

Example

$$\frac{P \vee Q}{\therefore P}$$

Is it possible for the premises of this argument to be true and the conclusion false? Indeed it is. In our formal language P and Q are independent statements. It's possible for P to be false and Q true. In that case, the premise, $P \vee Q$, is true while the conclusion, P, is false. This is an invalid argument.

The case where P is false and Q is true is a **counterexample**. It's an example of a situation where the premises are true and the conclusion is false. A counterexample shows conclusively that an argument is invalid.

Example

$$P$$
$$\frac{P \Rightarrow Q}{\therefore Q}$$

---

[1] Remember, this is "if and only if" (p.16).

Is it possible for the premises of this argument to be true and the conclusion false? Let's see. If the premises are true, then P is true. If the conclusion is false, then Q is false. But if P is true and Q is false, then $P \Rightarrow Q$ is false; $P \Rightarrow Q$ promises that if P is true then Q will be true. Thus it's not possible for the premises to be true and the conclusion false. This is a valid argument. It's so fundamental it has a name, *modus ponens*.

Example

$\exists x Px$

$\underline{\exists x Qx}$

$\therefore \exists x(Px \wedge Qx)$

Is it possible for the premises to be true and the conclusion false? The first premise says that something has property P. The second one says that something has property Q. The conclusion says that something has both property P and property Q.

This is a nice example where the real world and English can be helpful. Think of possible meanings for P and Q. Suppose Px means that x is human and that Qx means that x is a tree. Then on the planet Earth, $\exists x Px$ is true; there is a human. Also, $\exists x Qx$ is true; there is a tree. But the conclusion, $\exists x(Px \wedge Qx)$ is false. Nothing on Earth is both a human and a tree. This argument is invalid.

Again, giving the particular meanings to Px and Qx creates a counterexample which shows that the argument is invalid.

Exercises   Formal Inference

Odd-numbered solutions begin on page 351

Decide, for each argument below, whether it is valid or invalid. For any invalid argument, find a counterexample.

1. $\dfrac{P \vee Q}{\therefore P}$

2. $\dfrac{P \Leftrightarrow Q}{\therefore P}$

3. $\dfrac{P \wedge Q}{\therefore P \vee Q}$

4. $\dfrac{\neg\neg P}{\therefore P}$

5. $\dfrac{P \Rightarrow Q}{\therefore P}$

6. $\dfrac{P \Rightarrow Q}{\therefore Q}$

7. $\dfrac{\neg(P \Leftrightarrow Q)}{Q}$ $\;\therefore P$

8. $\dfrac{P \Rightarrow Q}{\therefore Q \Rightarrow P}$

9. $\dfrac{\forall x Px}{\therefore Pa}$

10. $\dfrac{\forall x(Px \wedge Qx)}{\therefore Qb}$

11. $\dfrac{\exists x Px}{\therefore Pa}$

12. $\dfrac{\exists x(Px \wedge Qx)}{\therefore Qb}$

Let's call an expression *autological* if it applies truly to itself, and *heterological* if it does not. The word, "short," for instance, applies truly to "short" ("short" is a short word) and so "short" is autological. "Long", however, is not long, and so "long" is heterological. "English" is autological because "English" is English, but "French" is heterological, because "French" is not French. It's easy to see that every expression is either heterological or autological, and that none can be both. Now here's the question: Is "heterological" heterological?

If "heterological" is heterological, then clearly it applies truly to itself. Thus, "heterological" is autological and not heterlogical. On the other hand, if "heterological" is autological, i.e., not heterological, then it doesn't apply truly to itself and so it's heterological and not autological.

This paradox is due to Kurt Grelling and Leonard Nelson. "Heterological" is heterological if and only if it isn't! What's going on here?

2.2 Informal Inference

The purpose of writing is to inflate weak ideas, obscure pure reasoning, and inhibit clarity. With a little practice, writing can be an intimidating and impenetrable fog! (Calvin (Bill Watterson))

We have a definition of validity for formal logic. It's important, so we'll repeat it.

An argument is

Valid   Iff the conclusion is true whenever the premises are true.
Invalid Iff it's possible for the premises to be true and the conclusion false.

Arguments in English are more difficult to evaluate. We can do this most successfully when we can identify the formal argument inside. Consider this argument:

> All dogs are mammals.
> McLeod is a dog. (This is true.)
> ∴ McLeod is a mammal.

This seems pretty reasonable. The fact that all dogs are mammals and that McLeod is a dog guarantees that McLeod is a mammal. It can't be otherwise if those premises are true. Now consider this argument:

$$\frac{\begin{array}{l}\text{All dogs are human.}\\ \text{McLeod is a dog.}\end{array}}{\therefore \text{McLeod is human.}}$$

Strange! The first premise is false! And yet, if all dogs really were human and if McLeod was a dog, wouldn't he be human? Indeed, the form of this argument is the same as the form of the first argument. We might write it as:

$$\frac{\begin{array}{l}\text{All } A \text{ are } B.\\ s \text{ is an } A.\end{array}}{\therefore s \text{ is a } B.}$$

This is the underlying form. The only differences between the two arguments are the meanings of *A*, *B*, and *s*. And the form is valid. It is impossible, no matter what meanings we attach to *A*, *B*, and *s* to make the premises true and the conclusion false. Notice that in the first argument the premises and the conclusion are true. In the second, not all the premises are true and the conclusion is false. But this doesn't violate the definition of validity which says that *if* the premises are true the conclusion must be true. There is no requirement if not all the premises are true.

$$\frac{\begin{array}{l}\text{All dogs are human.}\\ \text{Jay is a dog. (False.)}\end{array}}{\therefore \text{Jay is human.}}$$

This is a third argument with the same underlying form. Note that here too the conditions of validity are satisfied.

Now we'll give you something invalid.

$$\frac{\begin{array}{l}\text{Some dogs are mammals.}\\ \text{McLeod is a dog.}\end{array}}{\therefore \text{McLeod is a mammal.}}$$

To see why this is invalid, look at the underlying form.

$$\frac{\begin{array}{l}\text{Some } P \text{ are } Q.\\ d \text{ is a } P.\end{array}}{\therefore d \text{ is a } Q.}$$

Can we find a counterexample? Can we make, by a clever choice of meanings for *P*, *Q* and *d*, the premises true and the conclusion false? We can.

$$\frac{\begin{array}{l}\text{Some humans are female.}\\ \text{Jim Henle is a human. (True.)}\end{array}}{\therefore \text{Jim Henle is female. (False.)}}$$

This argument form has sold a lot of snake oil.

> Many hard-working people who tried Jay's snake oil found it changed their lives!
> You're a hard-working person!
> ∴ This snake oil will change your life!

Now here's another invalid argument:

> Everyone who voted Republican wore red.
> My mom wore red.
> ∴ She voted Republican.

This argument form is especially common and pernicious. It's called **affirming the consequent**. Here's a counterexample:

> All birds have wings.
> A Boeing 747 has wings.
> ∴ A Boeing 747 is a bird.

Enough said? No argument of this form should ever convince you of anything. Again, it's a common advertising trick:

> If you're hip, you wear Calvins.
> You wear Calvins.
> ∴ Hey, you are SO hip!

Here's the point in this discussion: If an argument form is invalid, you can show that by coming up with a counterexample. You haven't yet learned to show that an argument is *valid*, but that will come.

One last bit of terminology. Obviously, while we care about argument form, truth is nice, too. So, we have a special name for valid arguments all of whose premises are true. These are **sound** arguments. It follows that the conclusion of a sound argument is always true.

An argument is

Valid   Iff the conclusion is true whenever the premises are true.
Invalid   Iff it's possible for the premises to be true and the conclusion false.
Sound   Iff it's valid and the premises are true.

Exercises   Informal Inference

Odd-numbered
solutions
begin on page 351

For each argument, decide whether it is valid or invalid. If it is invalid, find a counterexample.

1.

   All pies are delicious.
   Rhubarb pie is a pie.

   ∴ Rhubarb pie is delicious.

2.

   Pope Benedict XVI is pope.
   The pope is infallible.
   If one is infallible then everything one says is true.

   ∴ Everything Pope Benedict XVI says is true.

3.

   If Georgia goes to college she learns logic.
   Georgia does not go to college.

   ∴ Georgia does not learn logic.

4.

   All college graduates are powerful and successful.
   Hillary Clinton is powerful and successful.

   ∴ Hillary Clinton is a college graduate.

5.

   Everyone loves logic.
   If Jim loves logic, he is not bald.

   ∴ Jim is not bald.

6.

   If Leroy is a flippet then he minks.

   ∴ Leroy minks.

7.

   Edward chirs if and only if he does not wix.
   Edward does not wix.

   ∴ Edward chirs.

8.

   If Oprah goes to the ball then if the prince is there she will dance with him.
   Oprah goes to the ball and the prince is there.

   ∴ Oprah dances with the prince.

9.

   We go to war or we have peace.
   We do not have peace.
   If we send an ambassador then we do not go to war.

   ∴ We don't send an ambassador.

10.

   You go abroad if you have a high GPA.

   ∴ You go abroad only if you have a high GPA.

11!

   If everyone reads the book, then everyone passes the course.
   If everyone passes the course, the teacher is happy.
   If the teacher is happy, she brings us cupcakes.
   John doesn't read the book.

   ∴ The teacher doesn't bring us cupcakes.

12.

   If you do drugs, you drop out of school.
   If you drop out of school then you have to work in McDonald's until you die.
   Alberta works at McDonald's until she dies.

   ∴ Alberta does drugs.

There are only a finite number of English words (about 500 000). Consequently there are only a finite number of grammatical phrases in English using fewer than twenty words. But there are infinitely many natural numbers $(1, 2, 3, \ldots)$. Many phrases in English of fewer than twenty words describe natural numbers, such as "the sum of three and four," or "the highest number to which Jay ever counted plus the highest number to which Jim ever counted," or "the square root of one trillion." But there are only finitely many of these phrases. So there must be many numbers which are not described by any phrase with fewer than twenty words.

Now consider the smallest number not describable by an English phrase of fewer than twenty words. That's a number. And we just described it with an English phrase of fewer than twenty words!

This paradox was invented by G. G. Berry, a friend of Bertrand Russell.

2.3   Diagramming Arguments

All generalizations are dangerous, even this one. (Alexandre Dumas)

If an argument is well-written and if we have read it correctly, then we should have a picture in our mind of the logic of the argument. We're going to represent the logic of arguments with diagrams.

It's raining so I'm not going to the library.

The conclusion is that I'm not going to the library. The reason is that it's raining. We'll diagram this as follows:

We place the conclusion at the bottom. In general, if statement A supports statement B, we'll put A above B and draw an arrow from A to B.

We aren't talking about valid arguments here, or even good arguments. We're simply diagramming what we think the author intended. In the next two chapters we'll start attacking arguments. When we do, we'll use what we've learned about validity.

Now here's a different argument:

It's raining and I have plenty of books to read so I'm not going to the library.

There are two reasons for not going to the library. The reasons are independent; neither one depends on the other. That is, either reason would be a reason on its own, even without the other. We diagram it like this:

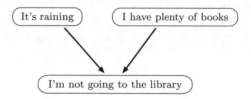

Now a third argument.

It's raining and I don't have an umbrella so I'm not going to the library.

This time the reasons aren't independent, they work together. Neither by itself is a reason for not going to the library – if it were raining and I did have an umbrella, I'd go. And if it weren't raining, I'd go. But taken together – rain and no umbrella – they provide a reason. We diagram the argument this way:

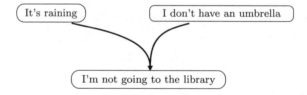

Here's a more complicated argument:

Nancy will make a terrific chair of the entertainment committee. She spent a year on the housing committee so she knows all the administrative officers. She has great people skills. And she just got a new laptop.

Let's make a list of the statements:

a. Nancy will make a terrific chair.
b. Nancy spent a year on housing.
c. Nancy knows all the administrative officers.
d. Nancy has great people skills.
e. Nancy has a new laptop.

The conclusion is clear; it's **a**. How do the other statements fit it? It's pretty clear that **d** and **e** support **a** independently. What about **b** and **c**? At first it seems that **b** supports **a**, but looking a little closer, we see that **b** supports **c** which in turn supports **a**. Then here's our diagram:

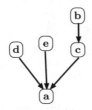

Bear in mind as you diagram **What** you are doing and **Why**.

What. What you're doing is representing graphically the intent of the arguer. If the argument is silly, your diagram will be silly. That's as it should be.

Why. You're diagramming the argument so that you can understand it. That may be because you endorse it, or it may be because you want to attack it; but even if you want to attack it, you must understand it. The diagram can be a way to improve and defend an argument, or it can be a blueprint for attacking it.

Are we ready to tackle Cathy's argument from Chapter One? Here's a list of her statements:

a. In a democracy, the people choose, but they make terrible choices.
b. They get freedom in the Balkans and the first thing they do is start shooting at each other.
c. They get the vote in Iraq and they have a civil war.
d. We have democracy.
e. We don't protect the environment.
f. Our schools are rotten.
g. We're in debt up to our eyeballs.
h. Only 23 percent of the people vote here.
i. We're powerful and envied because we're rich.
j. We abuse our power.
k. We don't really have democracy.
l. Washington is one of the biggest cities in the country.
m. Washington doesn't have self-government or representation in Congress.
n. Washington is a Black city.
o. We're all racists.
p. The South American democracies are bankrupt.
q. Chile isn't bankrupt.
r. Pinochet is a dictator.
s. Pinochet set Chile on the road to recovery.
t. H.L. Mencken dumped on democracy.

That's quite a lot.

Let's call the conclusion we found in Chapter One, that democracy is bad, **u**.

u. Democracy is bad.

It's best to work backwards from the conclusion. What are Cathy's reasons? The first is **a**, that people behave badly.

Cathy defends **a** with two examples: **b**, they fight in the Balkans, and **c**, they go to war in Iraq.

Next, Cathy gives the United States as an example (**d**) and lists our faults. Let's take the first, that we don't protect the environment (**e**). How do we diagram that? Is it like this?

No, it's not. Cathy doesn't say that **e** follows from **d**. She also doesn't say that **d** follows from **e**. But both statements are important. Is it like this?

No again. **d** and **e** don't independently support **u**. Democracy isn't bad just because the United States is a democracy! It's bad because the United States is an example of a democracy that doesn't protect the environment. **d** and **e** work together.

Cathy lists other faults of our democracy, **f**, **g**, and **h**. All of them need **d**. We could diagram it like this.

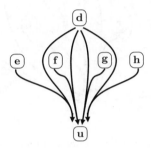

What about **i** and **j**? They don't seem to be part of the argument. Cathy was just in a bad mood.

Then Cathy claims that we aren't actually a democracy. But if the United States isn't a democracy, then its sins (**e**, **f**, **g**, and **h**) aren't sins of democracy. This actually hurts Cathy's argument. We should skip it.[2] We'll skip **k**, **l**, **m**, **n**, and **o**.

How do we deal with South America? Cathy is saying that dictatorship there has been better than democracy. Cathy uses **r**, **s**, and **q** to argue that dictators are ok. She doesn't say this, but this has to be her reasoning. Then that and **p** support the conclusion.

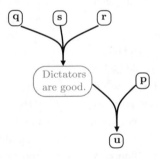

We put "Dictators are good" in gray because it was unstated.

And Mencken? The quote is witty, but it proves nothing. Still, it's likely Cathy intended us to take it as evidence democracy is bad, so let's include it. Altogether we have:

---

2 We won't include it in the diagram, but when we attack the argument, we can point out this flaw in her reasoning.

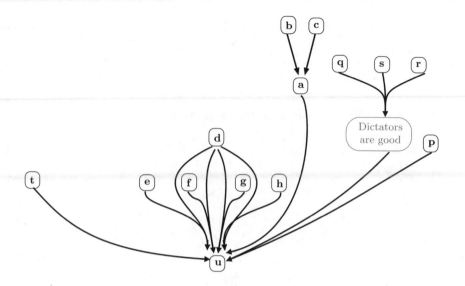

And that's it. We still don't know whether her argument is any *good*, but at least we know what it *is*.

Exercises   Diagramming Arguments

Odd-numbered
solutions
begin on page 351

Diagram the following arguments:

1. There is no God. Here's why: If God exists, then God is everywhere. If God is everywhere, then God is in my nose. If God is in my nose, then I can feel it. But I can't feel it.

2. God exists. By definition, God is perfection, God is the most perfect being. If God did not exist, He would be less than perfect, He would lack something that the humblest creature on earth possesses. Thus by definition, God exists.

3. Dogs are more intelligent than cats. On test after test, dogs have shown their ability to solve tasks more surely and more swiftly than cats. Dogs are more loving than cats. Dogs are more loyal to their owners. Dogs come when they are called; few cats do. Your dog will love you no matter what. If you forget to pay your taxes, your dog will still be your friend. Cats, on the other hand, care only about mealtimes. Yes, they will sit in your lap and purr, but only on their terms. And cats will scratch and bite if they are only slightly inconvenienced. It's no contest; dogs are better pets than cats.

4. Cats are more intelligent than dogs. On test after test, cats have shown their ability to solve tasks more surely and more swiftly than dogs. Cats are cleaner than dogs. They are almost immediately house-trained. There is more satisfaction in owning a cat. Dogs are blindly affectionate. You don't have to earn a dog's love. There is no sense of accomplishment in its

affection. You can be a serial killer and still have a loyal dog. Cats are discriminating. If a cat sits in your lap and purrs the love is meaningful; it's a sign of your worth. It's no contest; cats are better pets than dogs.

5. There is no real difference between classical and popular music, and it is easy to see why. Everybody agrees that jazz is popular music, but it is also classical. After all, classical music is the music that represents the highest and most distinctive music produced by a culture, the music that endures and is passed from generation to generation, and in the performance and composition of which virtuosity is demonstrated. But jazz plays this role in African-American culture. So jazz is classical music. So, since it is also popular music, there is no real difference.

6. Censorship of speech is never justified. Speech itself never harms anybody; at most the actions inspired by it cause harm, and they can be prohibited. If speech is censored, valuable ideas will be lost to the public and individuals will be prevented from expressing their own ideas and values. Some people might be offended by some speech, such as pornography, but their own emotional reaction is their problem, and should not count against the rights of others. Now, pornography is a kind of speech. So pornography should never be censored.

7. It is a fundamental human right to earn a living. So anyone has a right to use whatever talents he or she has to earn a living as long as he or she is not being coerced. Many people are capable of earning a living through prostitution, and are willing to do so. So these people have a fundamental right to engage in prostitution. No state can legally deprive people of fundamental human rights. So, no state can legally ban prostitution.

8. Cathy has breakfast

"Hi, Cathy! Join us for breakfast?"

Jennifer and her friend Wei had just started to eat. Full of excitement at the prospect of the classes ahead, Jenn flashed a cheerful smile at the drowsy junior.

"What's that stuff you're eating? It looks like Meow Mix."

"Cheerios! Breakfast of Champions! Or is that Count Chocula?" Wei's mastery of third millennium American culture had some gaps.

"Oh, brother! You're in big trouble. Cheerios are wrong, wrong, wrong!" As Cathy approached, Jennifer moved to the far end of the table.

"Sugar. It's got sugar in it. Sugar is bad for you."

Wei picked up her spoon.

"Sugar in the blood means your body has to counterattack with insulin. That drives down your blood sugar so you get hungry before your eleven-o'clock class. It's bad!"

Wei put down her spoon.

"Salt. Cheerios has more salt per ounce than potato chips. Salt is bad for you. It gives you high blood pressure. Would you pour milk on a bowl of potato chips and eat it for breakfast? Gimme a break!"

Wei got up to go.

"They also have this real dumb shape."

Diagram Cathy's argument.

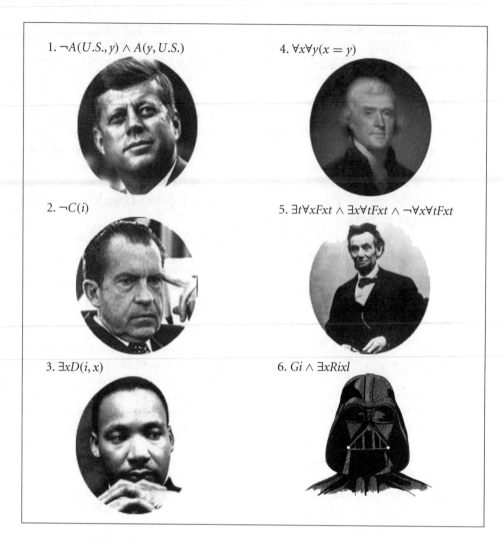

1. $\neg A(U.S., y) \land A(y, U.S.)$

4. $\forall x \forall y (x = y)$

2. $\neg C(i)$

5. $\exists t \forall x F x t \land \exists x \forall t F x t \land \neg \forall x \forall t F x t$

3. $\exists x D(i, x)$

6. $Gi \land \exists x Rixl$

2.4   Saying No

What part of
No
don't you understand?

(Anonymous)

Negation is an elementary logical operation, perhaps the most important. Despite that, we will see that understanding negation is not as straightforward as it might appear.

One statement is the **negation** of another statement if it's impossible for the two statements to be true at the same time and impossible for them both to be false at the same time.

That is, if one is true, the other is false, and vice versa. For example, what is the negation of the following compound statement?

Mei-ling is at home and the sun is shining.

An answer often given is "Mei-ling is not at home and the sun is not shining." This is *wrong*: Although the statements can't be true simultaneously, it is possible for them to be false simultaneously. It could happen, for example, that it's a sunny day and Mei-ling is not at home.

To find the correct answer, imagine that you are in a court of law and you must prove that the statement "Mei-ling is at home and the sun is shining" is false. What do you have to do? It would be sufficient to show that Mei-ling is not at home. It would also be sufficient to show that the sun is not shining. Either one alone would work, although, of course, both together do, too. In short, you must show either that Mei-ling is not at home or that the sun is not shining. This actually tells us the correct answer:

Either Mei-ling is not at home or the sun is not shining.

In the next chapter we'll look at this in formal logic and see the same phenomenon. Here's another example:

Every student has weird ideas.

What would you have to do to disprove this? All you have to do is find one student who doesn't have weird ideas. The negation, then, is the following:

Some student does not have weird ideas.

or

There is a student who has no weird ideas.

Informally, "negation" is often confused with "opposite." For instance, the opposite of "Every student has weird ideas" might be "No student has weird ideas." That is definitely *not* the negation. If some students have weird ideas and some don't, then both "Every student has weird ideas" and "No student has weird ideas" are false.

Exercises   Saying No

Odd-numbered solutions begin on page 352

Find negations for the following statements. Your answers should be in colloquial English. Furthermore, do not simply place "It is not true that" in front of the statement. This would work of course – it would produce a correct negation – but it's too easy (for the readers of *Sweet Reason*). You're asked here to think about what the statement means and to compose a negation based on the meaning.

1. Jim Henle is bald.
2. Tom and Jim are bald.
3. Jay is bald and Jim is bald.
4. Either Wally or Jay is a rock star.
5. Either Wally is a rock star or Jay is a rock star.
6. Martha is married and George is married.
7. Martha and George are married.
8. All mollusks are female.
9. There is a male mollusk.
10. Some popsicles are ambidexterous.
11. No geology majors are amphibious.
12. No math majors are extraterrestrials and all philosophy majors are extraterrestrials.

13. *The Digestor's Digest* is a weekly newspaper devoted to reports on food for the benefit of consumers. Each issue carries product reviews by the *Digest* staff. The first issue is devoted to breakfast. Unfortunately, for financial reasons the *Digest* must print advertisements as well. The situation is made worse by the fact that the advertisers make their ads look as much like articles as possible. To help readers tell the ads from the articles, the *Digest* requires that every sentence in every ad be false. A page may contain two ads, two articles, or one of each. Since every sentence in every article is true, it should be easy to tell them apart. Or should it?

The Digestor's Digest

Vol. I, No. 1

Scientists Report

Grittibits is good for you! Among all breakfast cereals on the market, Grittibits has the most protein. This is not an advertisement!

Scientists Report

Wheezies is good for you! Among all breakfast cereals on the market, Wheezies has the most protein. This is the only ad on this page!

What can you say about these two pieces?

Protagoras was a fifth-century B.C. Greek philosopher, one of the first Sophists. There is a story that he had a student of rhetoric, Euathlus. Euathlus was training to speak at court and agreed to pay Protagoras as soon as he had won his first case.

At the end of his training, Euathlus did not seek cases nor speak in court. Finally, believing he would never be paid, Protagoras sued Euathlus for payment.

But how could the court rule? It couldn't rule in favor of Protagoras because Euathlus had not yet won a case. But if it ruled in favor of Euathlus, then Euathlus would indeed have won a case and should pay!

2.5 Metalogic

I remain convinced that obstinate addiction to ordinary language in our private thoughts is one of the main obstacles to progress in philosophy. (Bertrand Russell)

We've thrown a few paradoxes at you – the Liar, the Strengthened Liar, Grelling's paradox, Berry's paradox, and the Quiz at the end of Chapter One. There are more coming. We give paradoxes for an important reason. Paradox lies at the heart of logic. Attempting to deal with them leads us deeper into logic. Many of the paradoxes you will encounter in this book are the subject of intense debate among logicians; some have been around for thousands of years, and there is as yet no consensus regarding what to say about them.

There's a common theme running through the paradoxes we have shown you so far: self-reference. In each one, something refers to itself. Trying to understand and reason with statements of this sort seems to get us in trouble. Should we forbid self-referential statements?

The philosopher and logician Bertrand Russell thought this was the problem and he devised a method for dealing with it. His suggestion goes roughly like this: The English language is not one language, but many. The core is a language we could call **Basic English**, or **Benglish**, for short. Benglish is all of English except that in Benglish, we can't talk about sentences in Benglish. In Benglish, self-reference is not allowed. We can say:

Snow is white.

But we can't say anything about the truth of "Snow is white." If we want to say:

"Snow is white." is true.

we need **Metabenglish**. Metabenglish is Benglish except that now we're allowed to talk about sentences in Benglish. The sentence, "'Snow is white' is true." is in Metabenglish. That last sentence, by the way:

The sentence, "'Snow is white' is true" is in Metabenglish.

isn't in Benglish or in Metabenglish. In Metabenglish we also forbid self-reference. The sentence discusses sentences in Metabenglish. It must be in *Metametabenglish*. Hold it! "It must be in *Metametabenglish*." must be in Metametametabenglish! And *that* sentence … !

The hierarchy goes on infinitely.

Russell suggests the following rule. We can only apply "true" in one language to sentences of a lower level in the meta-hierarchy. Since "Snow is white" is in Benglish, I can say that "Snow is white is true." in Metabenglish, where "true" means Metabenglish-true. And I can say that *that* sentence is true in Metametabenglish by saying:

"'Snow is white' is Metabenglish true" is Metametabenglish true.

Where does this get us? The Liar sentence (even in the strengthened form) is then simply ungrammatical nonsense. It might *look* like a sensible sentence, but it's just word-junk, because the words "is false" or "is not true" would have to be in the same level of English as the sentence to which they apply, since they are in that very sentence. But that violates the rule. So we have legislated the Liar out of existence.

All the meta extensions of Benglish are in English, so you're actually fluent in an infinite number of languages. And the Liar is not true in any meta-language (since it's ungrammatical.) In triumph, we can say *the Liar sentence is meaningless in all meta-languages.*

Great!

But … uh-oh. In what language can we write the following?

"The Liar sentence is meaningless in all meta-languages."

We can't write it in Metabenglish, because it talks about Metametabenglish and up. Not in Metametabenglish, either. Nor in Metametametabenglish … ! In other words, we may have triumphed, but we're unable to express that triumph! The "solution" is, by its own lights, inexpressible. So it is either no solution at all – or it's wrong.

Note! The logo in the margin is a sign that there is more on this subject on the *Sweet Reason* website. See

sweetreason2ed.com

Chapter Three

In Chapters One and Two we gave you a rich and complex logical language. We asked you to read it and write it more or less intuitively. Now we're going to go back and take up just the simplest part, Basic Sentential, and work with it carefully.

In Sentential, basic logical statements will be no more complicated than a single letter. We will put aside, until Chapter Six, the fine structure of constants, variables, relations, and quantifiers. A sentence like "Joan is female" will not be represented as Fj, but rather just as A. "All fish bite" won't be $\forall x(Fx \Rightarrow Bx)$ but just B. "Joan is female and not all fish bite" will then be $A \wedge \neg B$.

If logic is an X-ray machine revealing the structure of arguments and sentences, then we are temporarily turning the power down. For now, we'll focus on gross, large-scale structure – on the bones; no soft tissue. We'll get inside clauses in Chapter Six.

3.1   Basic Sentential

I feel that controversies can never be finished, nor silence imposed upon the Sects, unless we give up complicated reasoning in favor of simple calculation, words of vague and uncertain meaning in favor of fixed symbols...When controversies arise, there will be no more necessity of disputation between two philsophers than between two accountants. Nothing will be needed but that they should take pen in hand, sit down with their counting tables and (having summoned a friend, if they like) say to one another: Let us calculate. (G.W. Leibniz)

In Sentential, statements are joined together by the connectives representing the English words **and, or, not** and **if...then**. Note that we call $\neg$ (not) a "connective" even though it doesn't appear to connect anything. We could say, perhaps, that it connects a sentence to Nothing. In logic, Nothing is Something – more on that in Chapter Seven.

Sweet Reason: A Field Guide To Modern Logic, Second Edition. Jim Henle, Jay L. Garfield, Thomas Tymoczko and Emily Altreuter.
© 2012 John Wiley & Sons Inc. Published 2012 by John Wiley & Sons Inc.

When we connect statements in Basic Sentential using a connective, the truth value of the resulting complex statement is determined just by the truth value of its parts. ("Truth value" is just a general name for such things as **true** and **false**). The **negation symbol**, ¬, is especially simple. Any statement beginning with ¬ is a **negation**. If A is a true statement, then ¬A is false; if A is false, then ¬A is true.

We can summarize the story of negation in a table as follows:

A	¬A
T	F
F	T

The table has two lines because a statement A can have only two different truth values in basic logic. The table shows the truth value of ¬A for every possible value of A. Note that the table captures the essence of negation as we discussed in Section 2.4. A statement and its negation always have opposite truth values.

We can give similar tables, **truth tables**, for the other connectives ∧, ∨, ⇒, and ⇔. The table for ∧ is easy. This is the **conjunction symbol**, the symbol for "and". The conjunction $A ∧ B$ is true iff both **conjuncts** (A, B) are true.

A	B	$A ∧ B$
T	T	T
T	F	F
F	T	F
F	F	F

The table has four lines because there are four possible combinations of truth values of A and B: TT, TF, FT, and FF. The table shows the truth value of $A ∧ B$ for all possible values of A and B. If the symbol for conjunction seems odd to you, use the fact that it's the letter "A" without the cross-bar,

$$∧ \ A$$

with "A" standing for "And."

The "vee," ∨, is the **disjunction symbol**, the symbol for "or." $A ∨ B$ means that at least one of the **disjuncts** (A, B) is true.

A	B	$A ∨ B$
T	T	T
T	F	T
F	T	T
F	F	F

What you need to remember about ∨ is that it means "either one or the other *or both*" (this is the **inclusive** or). This or does *not* mean "one or the other but not both" (that use is the **exclusive** or). We'll introduce a symbol for the exclusive or later.

The symbol for disjunction is an upside-down conjunction. If you've studied Latin, you can associate it with the letter "v"—the word for "or" in Latin is *vel*.

∨ Vel

Notice that the meanings of ∧ and ∨ in the truth tables correspond with the informal understanding we used in Chapter One. Nothing has changed.

The **conditional** is symbolized by ⇒. It means "if ... then," and it has a (possibly) perplexing truth table.

A	B	A ⇒ B
T	T	T
T	F	F
F	T	T
F	F	T

The table is designed, in part, so that we may reason:

If *A* and *A* ⇒ *B* are both true, then *B* must also be true.

That reasoning is valid because the only time when the premises (*A* and *A* ⇒ *B*) are both true is the top line, and on the top line *B* is also true.

And notice that *A* ⇒ *B* is true whenever *B*, the **consequent**, is true. It's also true whenever *A*, the **antecedent**, is false. According to the truth table, the compound statement

Tuskegee is in France ⇒ Tuskegee is in Africa

counts as true because "Tuskegee is in France" is false; Tuskegee is in Alabama.

Think of *A* ⇒ *B* as a promise. It promises that *B* will be true if *A* is. The promise should be judged "innocent unless proven guilty", that is, it's true unless the promise is broken. The promise is broken when *A* is true and *B* is false. Suppose Jay says:

If it rains, then I carry my umbrella.

When would you be able to call him a liar?

Suppose first that the antecedent clause ("It rains") is true. And suppose the consequent ("I carry my umbrella") is also true. Then Jay has spoken the truth.

Suppose again that the antecedent is true but now the consequent is false – it's raining and he has no umbrella. He can then be convicted of speaking falsely.

These are the first two lines of the truth table.

Now, suppose that the antecedent is false: it's sunny. Suppose he is carrying his umbrella, perhaps to ward off the sun. Is he a liar? No. He only said that he would carry his umbrella if it's raining. He said *nothing* at all about what he would or would not do in the sun.

Similarly, suppose that both clauses are false: It is sunny and he has no umbrella. You surely can't call him a liar. So in these last two cases, we give the conditional the benefit of the doubt and mark it *True*.

These account for the last two lines of the truth table.

Some students hear "If A then B" and are ready to conclude that B must be true (and A as well). The temptation is easy to understand. In everyday speech, we often utter sentences of the form "If A then B" because we take it that A is true, and indicate that therefore B is true. Often we don't care about the conditional unless A is true.

But note that we can assert a conditional when we don't know whether the antecedent is true, and when we don't know whether the consequent is true. All we know is the conditional, as in "If the team plays well, they will win," or "If you don't pay your taxes you'll go to jail." Even if you know the conditional to be true, you can infer neither the truth of the antecedent nor the truth of the consequent. Beware the confusion!

Heads up!

Don't confuse $\Rightarrow$ with $\wedge$!

The last truth table is simple. The **biconditional** $A \Leftrightarrow B$ is true iff the truth values of A and B are the same.

A	B	$A \Leftrightarrow B$
T	T	T
T	F	F
F	T	F
F	F	T

Also in our language are parentheses, '(' and ')'. We'll get quite specific about them in Chapter Five but for the moment we'll be informal. Their purpose is to avoid ambiguity. Sometimes they are critical. The statements, $\neg P \wedge Q$ and $\neg(P \wedge Q)$ are quite different. But sometimes parentheses are unnecessary. The statements $P \wedge Q$ and $(P \wedge Q)$ are entirely the same.

And remember the umbrella sentence. It will help you with $\Rightarrow$. Just ask yourself, "When can I call someone who utters the umbrella sentence a liar?"

Exercises   Basic Sentential

Odd-numbered solutions begin on page 352

Consider R to be a true statement and S to be false. Find the truth values of the following statements:

1. $S \Rightarrow R$
2. $\neg R \Rightarrow \neg S$
3. $R \vee (S \wedge R)$
4. $(S \wedge R) \vee S$
5. $R \Rightarrow (R \Rightarrow \neg R)$
6. $R \Leftrightarrow (R \vee S)$
7. $\neg R \wedge \neg(S \Rightarrow \neg R)$
8. $\neg(S \Rightarrow \neg R) \Leftrightarrow \neg(R \Rightarrow \neg S)$
9. Match each statement in the left column with a statement in the right column that has exactly the same meaning.

$$P \vee Q \qquad \neg P \Rightarrow Q$$
$$P \wedge Q \qquad (P \Rightarrow Q) \wedge (Q \Rightarrow P)$$
$$P \Rightarrow Q \qquad \neg(\neg P \vee \neg Q)$$
$$P \Leftrightarrow Q \qquad \neg P \vee Q$$

10. Match each statement in the left column with a statement in the right column that has exactly the same meaning.

$$\neg(P \vee Q) \quad P \Rightarrow \neg Q$$
$$\neg(P \wedge Q) \quad (P \Rightarrow \neg Q) \wedge (\neg Q \Rightarrow P)$$
$$\neg(P \Rightarrow Q) \quad P \wedge \neg Q$$
$$\neg(P \Leftrightarrow Q) \quad \neg P \wedge \neg Q$$

CrossLogic puzzles

Example

Place a "*T*" or "*F*" in each box.

Across
1. ¬(2 Down)
3. 2 Down ∧ 1 Across

Down
1. Different from 1 Across
2. 2 Down

Solution: The clue for 1 Across says that it's the negation, cell-by-cell, of 2 Down. That means that if we put a "*T*" in the upper left corner, then the upper right corner must be an "*F*." And then since the upper right corner is an "*F*", then the lower right corner will have to be a "*T*." Altogether, we can see that we'll have either $\begin{array}{|c|c|}\hline {}^1T & {}^2F \\\hline {}^3{} & T \\\hline\end{array}$ or $\begin{array}{|c|c|}\hline {}^1F & {}^2T \\\hline {}^3{} & F \\\hline\end{array}$

The clue for 1 Down says is that 1 Down and 1 Across are different in at least one cell. That means we'll have either $\begin{array}{|c|c|}\hline {}^1T & {}^2F \\\hline {}^3T & T \\\hline\end{array}$ or $\begin{array}{|c|c|}\hline {}^1F & {}^2T \\\hline {}^3F & F \\\hline\end{array}$.

The clue for 3 Across allows us to solve the puzzle. Since 2 Down and 1 Across are different, we must get '*F*' when we ∧ them (we ∧ these cell by cell, that is, *TF* ∧ *FT* is *FF*). Thus the answer must be $\begin{array}{|c|c|}\hline {}^1F & {}^2T \\\hline {}^3F & F \\\hline\end{array}$

11.

Across
1. 1 Down ∨ 1 Across

Down
1. 1 Down ⇒ 1 Across

12.

Across
1. ¬(3 Across ∧¬(1 Across))
3. ¬(1 Down)

Down
1. ¬¬(1 Down)
2. ¬¬(1 Across)

13.

Across
1. ¬(2 Down)
4. Different from 5 Across
5. ¬¬(3 Down)

Down
1. (3 Down) ⇒ (1 Across)
2. (1 Down) ∧ ¬(3 Down)
3. (1 Down) ∧ (5 Across)

1	2	3
4		
5		

Parmenides was a Greek philosopher of the fifth century BC who held that change is an illusion. Zeno of Elea was a disciple of Parmenides. Zeno defended Parmenides by finding apparent contradictions in our understanding of motion. These contradictions are known today as Zeno's "paradoxes of motion." Here is one, the Arrow.

An arrow is at rest if it is in one and only one place. At every instant, an arrow is in one and only one place. So at every instant a flying arrow is at rest. Thus an arrow cannot move.

3.2   Truth Tables

If your parents never had children, chances are . . . neither will you. (Dick Cavett)

Expressions in Basic Sentential can be completely analyzed with truth tables.

Example

$(\neg P \lor Q) \Rightarrow (Q \land P)$

The truth or falsity of this depends entirely on the truth or falsity of P and Q. To make a truth table for this formula, we start with a table of possibilities for P and Q.

P	Q	(	$\neg$	P	$\lor$	Q	)	$\Rightarrow$	(	Q	$\land$	P	)
T	T												
T	F												
F	T												
F	F												

Now we fill in the values for P and Q.

P	Q	(	$\neg$	P	$\lor$	Q	)	$\Rightarrow$	(	Q	$\land$	P	)
T	T			T		T				T		T	
T	F			T		F				F		T	
F	T			F		T				T		F	
F	F			F		F				F		F	

Now we can fill in the truth value of ¬P.

P	Q	(	¬	P	∨	Q	)	⇒	(	Q	∧	P	)
T	T		**F**	T		T				T		T	
T	F		**F**	T		F				F		T	
F	T		**T**	F		T				T		F	
F	F		**T**	F		F				F		F	

And then the truth value of Q ∧ P.

P	Q	(	¬	P	∨	Q	)	⇒	(	Q	∧	P	)
T	T		F			T				T	**T**	T	
T	F		F			F				F	**F**	T	
F	T		T			T				T	**F**	F	
F	F		T			F				F	**F**	F	

Then the truth value of ¬P ∨ Q.

P	Q	(	¬	P	∨	Q	)	⇒	(	Q	∧	P	)
T	T		F		**T**	T					T		
T	F		F		**F**	F					F		
F	T		T		**T**	T					F		
F	F		T		**T**	F					F		

And finally the truth value of (¬P ∨ Q) ⇒ (Q ∧ P).

P	Q	(	¬	P	∨	Q	)	⇒	(	Q	∧	P	)
T	T				T			**T**			T		
T	F				F			**T**			F		
F	T				T			**F**			F		
F	F				T			**F**			F		

The way we filled in the table reflects the structure of the formula. The formula is a conditional. It's composed of two smaller formulas.

$$(\neg P \vee Q) \Rightarrow (Q \wedge P)$$

$$\neg P \vee Q \qquad\qquad Q \wedge P$$

The first of the two formulas is composed of two even smaller formulas.

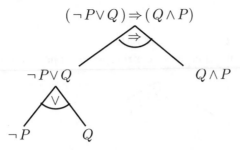

We can follow all the branches of this diagram down until we've broken the formula up into its component parts.

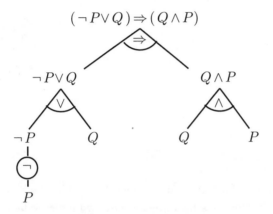

We call this a **syntactic tree**. It's traditional to draw them this way. Think of the lines going down as "roots" (if you think of them as branches you'll worry about the tree being upside-down). Notice that the tree and the letters at the bottom give you all the information you need about the formula.

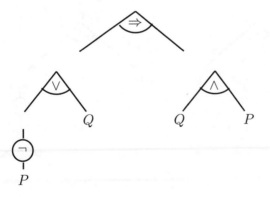

From the tree you can reconstruct the formula.

Now to fill in the truth table, we start with the roots of the tree, filling in the truth values of the letters at the bottom, then move upward.

Example

Find the truth table of $(Q \Leftrightarrow R) \vee (P \Rightarrow \neg(Q \wedge \neg R))$.

Before we construct the table, let's work through one line of it using the syntactic tree.

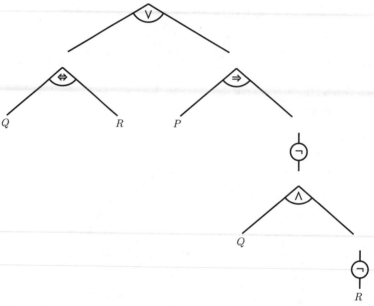

Let's take the top row of the truth table, where P, Q and R are all T (true). Constructing the truth table simply consists of replacing the letters with their values (in this case T) and moving up the tree.

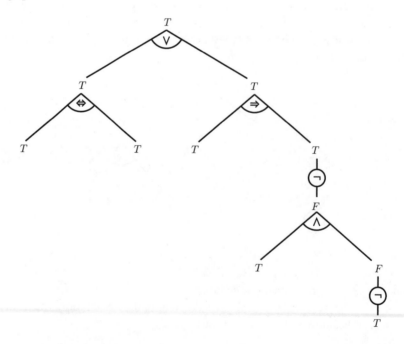

Now we have three letters to deal with. The truth table will have 8 rows because there are 8 possible truth values for P, Q, and R. Think of it this way: with just P and Q there are four possibilities.

P	Q
T	T
T	F
F	T
F	F

For each of these possibilities R could be either true or false.

P	Q	R
T	T	T
		F
T	F	T
		F
F	T	T
		F
F	F	T
		F

This gives eight possibilities altogether.

P	Q	R
T	T	T
T	T	F
T	F	T
T	F	F
F	T	T
F	T	F
F	F	T
F	F	F

A truth table for a sentence with one letter has 2 lines. A truth table for a sentence with two letters has 4 lines. A truth table for a sentence three letters has 8 lines. There's a pattern here. For a sentence or argument with n letters, you will need 2^n lines in your truth table.

Filling in the truth table, we again proceed by stages. First the letters themselves,

P	Q	R	(Q	⇔ R)	∨ (P	⇒ ¬ (Q	∧ ¬ R))
T	T	T	T	T	T	T	T
T	T	F	T	F	T	T	F
T	F	T	F	T	T	F	T
T	F	F	F	F	T	F	F
F	T	T	T	T	F	T	T
F	T	F	T	F	F	T	F
F	F	T	F	T	F	F	T
F	F	F	F	F	F	F	F

then ¬R,

P	Q	R	(	Q	⇔	R	)	∨	(	P	⇒	¬	(	Q	∧	¬	R	)	)
T	T	T		T		T				T				T		**F**	T		
T	T	F		T		F				T				T		**T**	F		
T	F	T		F		T				T				F		**F**	T		
T	F	F		F		F				T				F		**T**	F		
F	T	T		T		T				F				T		**F**	T		
F	T	F		T		F				F				T		**T**	F		
F	F	T		F		T				F				F		**F**	T		
F	F	F		F		F				F				F		**T**	F		

then Q ∧ ¬R,

P	Q	R	(	Q	⇔	R	)	∨	(	P	⇒	¬	(	Q	∧	¬	R	)	)
T	T	T		T		T				T				T	**F**	F			
T	T	F		T		F				T				T	**T**	T			
T	F	T		F		T				T				F	**F**	F			
T	F	F		F		F				T				F	**F**	T			
F	T	T		T		T				F				T	**F**	F			
F	T	F		T		F				F				T	**T**	T			
F	F	T		F		T				F				F	**F**	F			
F	F	F		F		F				F				F	**F**	T			

then Q ⇔ R,

P	Q	R	(	Q	⇔	R	)	∨	(	P	⇒	¬	(	Q	∧	¬	R	)	)
T	T	T		T	**T**	T				T				F					
T	T	F		T	**F**	F				T				T					
T	F	T		F	**F**	T				T				F					
T	F	F		F	**T**	F				T				F					
F	T	T		T	**T**	T				F				F					
F	T	F		T	**F**	F				F				T					
F	F	T		F	**F**	T				F				F					
F	F	F		F	**T**	F				F				F					

then ¬(Q ∧ ¬R),

P	Q	R	(	Q	⇔	R	)	∨	(	P	⇒	¬	(	Q	∧	¬	R	)	)
T	T	T			T					T		**T**			F				
T	T	F			F					T		**F**			T				
T	F	T			F					T		**T**			F				
T	F	F			T					T		**T**			F				
F	T	T			T					F		**T**			F				
F	T	F			F					F		**F**			T				
F	F	T			F					F		**T**			F				
F	F	F			T					F		**T**			F				

then $P \Rightarrow \neg(Q \wedge \neg R)$,

P	Q	R	(Q ⇔ R) ∨ (P ⇒ ¬ (Q ∧ ¬ R))
T	T	T	T T **T** T
T	T	F	F T **F** F
T	F	T	F T **T** T
T	F	F	T T **T** T
F	T	T	T F **T** T
F	T	F	F F **T** F
F	F	T	F F **T** T
F	F	F	T F **T** T

and finally $(Q \Leftrightarrow R) \vee (P \Rightarrow \neg(Q \wedge \neg R))$.

P	Q	R	(Q ⇔ R)	∨	(P ⇒ ¬ (Q ∧ ¬ R))
T	T	T	T	**T**	T
T	T	F	F	**F**	F
T	F	T	F	**T**	T
T	F	F	T	**T**	T
F	T	T	T	**T**	T
F	T	F	F	**T**	T
F	F	T	F	**T**	T
F	F	F	T	**T**	T

Exercises   **Truth Tables**

Odd-numbered
solutions
begin on page 352

Compose truth tables for the following formulas:

1. $(Q \Rightarrow R) \wedge R$
2. $P \vee (Q \Leftrightarrow P)$
3. $(P \vee \neg Q) \Rightarrow Q$
4. $\neg(Q \wedge R) \vee (R \Leftrightarrow Q)$
5. $P \Rightarrow (Q \vee R)$
6. $(P \wedge R) \vee (\neg P \Rightarrow Q)$
7. $\neg(P \vee Q) \Leftrightarrow (R \Rightarrow \neg S)$
8. $R \Rightarrow ((P \vee S) \wedge (Q \Leftrightarrow R))$

The symbol for exclusive "or" is $\veebar$. Recall, this is the "or" which is false if the two disjuncts are both true. Here is the truth table:

P	Q	P ⊻ Q
T	T	F
T	F	T
F	T	T
F	F	F

Find truth tables for these:

9. $P \veebar P$
10. $\neg P \veebar Q$
11. $(P \veebar Q) \vee (P \Leftrightarrow Q)$
12. $(P \veebar Q) \vee R$

Bertrand Russell was one of the most influential philosophers and mathematicians of the twentieth century. His fame rests on his many contributions: essays, books, most especially his monumental work with Alfred North Whitehead, *Principia Mathematica*. If he had done none of this, however, he would live forever for a small piece of conversation at a dinner.

The story is that Russell was dining with a group of people and discussing the principles of logic. He explained that from a contradictory proposition one can prove anything. One member of the party thought this was outrageous. He challenged the idea but said he would be convinced if Russell could take the proposition "0 = 1" and prove that he, Russell, was the Pope.

Russell considered this briefly, and then said something like, "If 0 = 1, then by adding 1 to both sides, we have 1 = 2. I and the Pope are two, therefore I and the Pope are one."

3.3   English to Sentential

He thought he saw an Argument
That proved he was the Pope:
He looked again, and found it was
A Bar of Mottled Soap.

(Lewis Carroll, *Sylvie and Bruno*)

Basic Sentential is a formal language. It follows precise rules (we'll get them in Chapter Five). When we translate from English to Sentential, we're formalizing what we say. There are minuses and plusses to this. Basic Sentential is more primitive then English, so when we translate, we lose detail. On the other hand, we highlight structure.

For a given sentence, there may be several ways to translate it, depending on what details are important to the translator. For example, if one is formalizing "Calvin is a little brat," then whether one translates this as P (for "Calvin is a little brat") or as $Q \land R$ (for "Calvin is little" and "Calvin is a brat") depends on what is important in the argument in which it occurs. If the words "brat" and "little" occur only in that sentence, then it's reasonable to translate "Calvin is a little brat" either way; the only difference will be in appearance. One translation of the argument will have $Q \land R$ wherever the other has P, but otherwise the two will be identical.

On the other hand, if the sentence is in an argument which includes the statement "Calvin is a brat" or "Calvin is not a brat," then clearly $Q \land R$ is the better choice because it distinguishes a clause identifying Calvin as little and a clause identifying Calvin as a brat. By translating "Calvin is a brat" as R and "Calvin is not a brat" as $\neg R$, we reveal the logical connections.

The point is that formalization – or translation – is neither automatic nor mechanical. It requires practice and a little thought. Let's deal with each connective separately.

¬

This is negation. It signals that what follows is false. That can be tricky. Granted that "Tom is male" is to be formalized as P, which of the English statements could you formalize as $\neg P$?

Tom is not male.
It's not true that Tom is male.
It's not the case that Tom is male.
That's not male (said of Tom).
Tom is female.

The first four statements can be translated as $\neg P$. But even if no male is female and everything is one or the other, it seems stretching things to consider "Tom is female" as $\neg P$. It would be much better to formalize the latter by some new letter Q and, if you insist, to introduce a new premise such as "Tom is female if and only if Tom is not male," or $Q \Leftrightarrow \neg P$. The advantage of this approach is that everything is explicit and aboveboard. At least it allows the possibility of a challenge to the premise $Q \Leftrightarrow \neg P$ (perhaps Tom is a car [neither male nor female] or a hermaphrodite [both male and female]). Formalizing "Tom is female" by $\neg P$ rules out such challenges rather arbitrarily.

∧

We use conjunction to formalize quite a few English constructions: "P and Q," "both P and Q," "P, but Q," "P, however Q," "P, moreover Q," "P, furthermore Q,"

Most of these are clear but consider "P, but Q." We grant that the English "but" certainly means something different from the English "and," but if you attend only to truth values, you'll see that they amount to the same thing. "She's rich, but she's honest" is true in only one case: when she's rich and honest.

Not every use of "and" is conjunction, though. In "Calvin and Hobbes are buddies," the "and" cannot be represented by ∧.

Another case in point is supplied by negation. "Tom is not male" is the negation of "Tom is male"; "Calvin is not a brat" is the negation of "Calvin is a brat." But don't for a moment think that "S is not G" is always the negation of "S is G." "Tom and Jim are not bald" is not the negation of "Tom and Jim are bald"(remember Section 2.4). The proper negation of "Tom and Jim are bald" is "Either Tom or Jim is not bald." "All readers of this book are not female" does not negate "All readers of this book are female." What does negate it is "Some readers of this book are not female."

∨

We use disjunction to formalize "P or Q," "either P or Q," and "P unless Q."

That $P \vee Q$ can translate "P unless Q" certainly seems strange. Let's analyze this carefully. Consider "You won't go on the field trip unless you have a note from a parent." Here P is "the kid doesn't go" and Q is "the kid has a note."

It's clear that if the kid doesn't have a note and the teacher doesn't let the kid go on the trip, then the teacher spoke truthfully.

kid doesn't go	kid has note	kid doesn't go unless kid has note
T	T	
T	F	**T**
F	T	
F	F	

Suppose the kid doesn't have a note but goes on the trip. Then clearly the teacher spoke falsely.

kid doesn't go	kid has note	kid doesn't go unless kid has note
T	T	
T	F	T
F	T	
F	F	**F**

But what if the kid has a note, but there's a big snowstorm and the trip is cancelled? You can't say the teacher lied. The kid had a note but didn't go; nobody went. The teacher spoke truthfully.

kid doesn't go	kid has note	kid doesn't go unless kid has note
T	T	**T**
T	F	T
F	T	
F	F	F

And finally, if the kid has a note and goes on the trip, the teacher spoke truthfully.

kid doesn't go	kid has note	kid doesn't go unless kid has note
T	T	T
T	F	T
F	T	**T**
F	F	F

Notice that the pattern of T's and F's we get is the pattern for disjunction (see page 38).

Some readers will want to translate "*P* unless *Q*" as $\neg Q \Rightarrow P$ (if his car doesn't break down, he'll come) or $\neg P \Rightarrow Q$ (if he doesn't come then it must be that his car broke down). Well in fact *those readers would be absolutely correct.* These three sentences, though they look different, have identical meaning. And they have the same truth tables.

$$P \vee Q \quad \neg Q \Rightarrow P \quad \neg P \Rightarrow Q.$$

But some readers will *still* have trouble with "*P* unless *Q*" when both *P* and *Q* are true. They want to say that "T unless T" is F. For those readers we have one more argument. Suppose the teacher said, "You won't go on the field trip unless you have a note from a parent. Also, you won't go if you don't have $3 lunch money." That certainly sounds reasonable. But suppose the kid brings $3 and forgets the note. What can the teacher do? If the kid is allowed to go, then the first sentence is false. If the kid is not allowed to go, then (if you insist that "T unless T" is F) the second sentence is false. In other words no matter what, the teacher spoke falsely!

We use the biconditional for "*P* if and only if *Q*," "*P* iff *Q*," "*P* is a necessary and sufficient condition of *Q*," and "*P* is equivalent to *Q*."

We use the conditional to translate "if *P* then *Q*," "if *P*, *Q*," "*Q*, if *P*," "*P* only if *Q*," "*P* is a sufficient condition of *Q*," and "*Q* is a necessary condition of *P*."

The first two are obvious. You should also be able to see the third as just another way of expressing the second.

For "*P* only if *Q*," think about what it says. It says that if you know *P* happens, then you know that *Q* happens. That's $P \Rightarrow Q$. What's confusing is that *Q* might happen before *P*. But $\Rightarrow$ is not about time, it's about logical connection. For example, "My car will make it to San Diego only if I get a tune-up," is saying that *if* the car makes it to San Diego *then* it must be that I got the car a tune-up. San Diego $\Rightarrow$ tune-up.

Here's another way to think of it. The double-arrow statement, $P \Leftrightarrow Q$ means "if and only if," that is, it says "*P* if *Q*" and "*P* only if *Q*." The "*P* if *Q*" is $Q \Rightarrow P$ and the "*P* only if *Q*" is $Q \Leftarrow P$ or $P \Rightarrow Q$.

$$P \Leftrightarrow Q$$

$$Q \Rightarrow P \qquad P \Rightarrow Q$$

$$\text{if } Q \text{ then } P \qquad \text{if } P \text{ then } Q$$

$$P, \text{ if } Q \qquad P \text{ only if } Q$$

$$P \text{ if and only if } Q$$

The definition of $\Rightarrow$ is different from many ordinary uses of "if … then." One ordinary use is called the **contrary-to-fact** conditional or the **subjunctive** conditional because its verbs are often in the subjunctive mood. The statement

If Tuskegee *were* in France, then Tuskegee *would be* in Africa,

understood as subjunctive, is false because France is not in Africa; it's in Europe. A true subjunctive statement is

> If Tuskegee *were* in France, then Tuskegee *would be* in Europe.

Our ⇒ is not meant to capture the subjunctive conditional. It represents a different, more basic meaning of "if . . . then," one that logicians call the **material conditional**. For us,

> Tuskegee is in France ⇒ Tuskegee is in Africa,

is true. It's true because both the antecedent and the consequent are false—see the last line of the truth table for ⇒.

"If . . . then" turns out to have several different meanings in English, and not all of them can be captured in Basic Sentential. In fact, logicians have struggled and argued a great deal throughout the history of logic regarding the best ways to represent the various meaning of "if . . . then" in English, and this is still a topic of logical research. For now we'll be content with our ⇒ as the material conditional. Later on we'll explore more sophisticated approaches to "if . . . then." Until then, remember Jay's umbrella.

It may also help you to keep in mind that $A \Rightarrow B$ says the same thing as $\neg A \vee B$ (either not A or B), no more, no less. To see this, think about when $\neg A \vee B$ is false. It's false only when both $\neg A$ and B are false, in other words, when A is true and B is false. That's also the only time that $A \Rightarrow B$ is false.

Heads Up!

The tricky ones:

P but Q	$P \wedge Q$
P unless Q	$P \vee Q$
P only if Q	$P \Rightarrow Q$

Terms		
$\neg P$	negation	
$P \wedge Q$	conjunction	P and Q are conjuncts
$P \vee Q$	disjunction	P and Q are disjuncts
$P \Rightarrow Q$	conditional	P is the antecedent; Q is the consequent
$P \Leftrightarrow Q$	biconditional	

Exercises   English to Sentential

Odd-numbered
solutions
begin on page 353

Translate the following arguments into Basic Sentential. For fun, take a guess with each argument – is it valid?

1. If I am hungry, I eat cereal. If I eat cereal, I have milk. However, I am not hungry, so I will not have milk.
2. I will either grow up to be president or become a screenwriter. In order to become a screenwriter, though, I've got to be good at writing. I must admit that I'm not particularly good at writing. Therefore, I will grow up to be president.
3. Zeus either divorces Hera or is annoyed by her. If Zeus divorces her, then he runs off with a younger woman. If Zeus is annoyed with her, then he runs off with a younger woman. So either way, Zeus runs off with a younger woman.
4. If Rocky the squirrel can read, he lives in the bushes. If Rocky can read, he escaped from NIMH. Rocky lives in the bushes, so he must have escaped from NIMH.
5. If I don't have logic today, it must be Monday. Today is Wednesday. So I have logic today.

6. Either I love logic or I'm obsessed with it. (I just can't decide!) If I love logic, then I will major in it. I'm totally obsessed with logic. So, it follows that I won't major in it.
7. All men love to be scratched behind the ears. Hobbes is a man. Therefore, Hobbes loves to be scratched behind the ears.
8. Mrs White did it and she did it either with the wrench or with the rope. But she did it with the rope if and only if the murder was committed in the study. The murder was committed in the hall. Therefore, Mrs White did it and she did it with the wrench.
9. If the world is round then I can sail around it if I have a boat. I have a boat but I don't sail around the world. Thus, the world is not round.
10. If drugs are legalized, then there will be more money to treat addicts, there will be less drug-related crime, and the mob will lose its main source of income. Without the source of money, the mob will wither away and die. It is clear, then, that drugs will never be legalized, since the mob will never die.

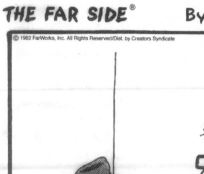

"Well, I dunno. ... Okay, sounds good to me."

3.4   Negating Statements

> *The Nothing Nots.* (Martin Heidegger)

In section 2.4 we looked at negating sentences in English. This was your introduction to negation so it was probably a little strange.

Example

Mei-ling is at home and the sun is shining.

   We said that the negation of this was not "Mei-ling is not at home and the sun is not shining," but rather

> *Either Mei-ling is not at home or the sun is not shining.*

Let's use the tools of this chapter to check this. First, we formalize the original statement to

$$M \wedge S$$

where M stands for "Mei-ling is at home" and S stands for "the sun is shining." Next, we formalize "Mei-ling is not at home and the sun is not shining" as

$$\neg M \wedge \neg S$$

and "Either Mei-ling is not at home or the sun is not shining" as

$$\neg M \vee \neg S.$$

Now let's look at the truth tables of these statements.

M	S	M	∧	S	¬	M	∧	¬	S	¬	M	∨	¬	S
T	T	T	T	T	F	T	F	F	T	F	T	F	F	T
T	F	T	F	F	F	T	F	T	F	F	T	T	T	F
F	T	F	F	T	T	F	F	F	T	T	F	T	F	T
F	F	F	F	F	T	F	T	T	F	T	F	T	T	F

Now if we compare them,

M	S	M	∧	S	¬	M	∧	¬	S	¬	M	∨	¬	S
T	T		T				F					F		
T	F		F				F					T		
F	T		F				F					T		
F	F		F				T					T		

we can see that indeed $\neg M \vee \neg S$ and $M \wedge S$ are negations; when one is true the other is false and vice-versa. Notice that the negation of a conjunction turns out to be a disjunction.

Example

Either Wally or Mavis is a rock star.

We can formalize this as $W \vee M$. Informally, to deny that either Wally or Mavis is a rock star is to say that neither is a rock star. That's $\neg W \wedge \neg M$. The truth table agrees.

W	M	W	∨	M	¬	W	∧	¬	M
T	T	T	T	T	F	T	F	F	T
T	F	T	T	F	F	T	F	T	F
F	T	F	T	T	T	F	F	F	T
F	F	F	F	F	T	F	T	T	F

Notice that the negation of a disjunction turns out to be a conjunction.

Example

Either Lucinda and Jake both go to the movie or Jake stays home.

We can formalize this as

$$(L \wedge J) \vee \neg J,$$

where L stands for "Lucinda goes to the movie" and J stands for "Jake goes to the movie" (we're taking "Jake stays home" as "Jake doesn't go to the movie"). Using the ideas of the last two examples, we might reason that since this is a disjunction, its negation is a conjunction,

$$\neg(L \wedge J) \wedge \neg\neg J,$$

that is,

$$\neg(L \wedge J) \wedge J.$$

And the first conjunct, $\neg(L \wedge J)$, is the negation of a conjunction, so it should be the disjunction of negations,

$$(\neg L \vee \neg J) \wedge J.$$

We can stop there, but look what this is saying. It says that at least one of them stays home ($\neg L \vee \neg J$) but Jake goes. That means Lucinda stays home and Jake goes, that is,

$$\neg L \wedge J.$$

The reader can check this with truth tables.

Exercises   Negating Statements

Odd-numbered
solutions
begin on page 353

Find the negations of these statements:

1. Smedley had three potstickers because she didn't think they had spinach.
2. Unless you give me a million dollars in small bills, I won't go to your party.
3. Jay is bald and either Mabel is not bald or Susan is bald.
4. Either Wally is a rock star or Mavis and Jasper are both rock stars.
5. Martha is married and George is married and Frank is upset.
6. Either Greenfield wins and Rosewood wins or both lose.
7. The picnic is Sunday unless it rains.
8. Either Martha is single or else both Martha and George are married.
9! She will win if and only if her opponent is Rhett.

Another CrossLogic puzzle

10.

Across

1. (1 Across)∨(1 Across)
4. (3 Down)∨¬(4 Across)
5. Different from 3 Down

Down

1. (1 Across) ∧ (2 Down)
2. Different from 1 Down
3. (3 Down)∨(3 Down)

1	2	3
4		
5		

The "paradox" of the barber

There is a village with one barber. This barber cuts the hair of those and only those who don't cut their own hair.

Who cuts the barber's hair?

Let's say the barber is a woman (so we don't have a problem with pronouns). Then she cuts her hair if and only if she is one of the people who don't cut their own hair. In other words, she cuts her hair if and only if she doesn't cut her own hair.

This sounds like another paradox, but it's not; there is a simple resolution. Think about it. The answer is on page 353.

3.5   Rebutting Premises

> *"I can lick you!"*
> *"I'd like to see you try it."*
> *"Well, I can do it."*
> *"No you can't either."*
> *"Yes I can."*
> *"No you can't."*
> *"I can."*
> *"You can't."*
> *"Can!"*
> *"Can't!"*
> *An uncomfortable pause. Then Tom said:*
> *"What's your name?"*
>
> (Mark Twain, *Tom Sawyer*)

Here is an argument diagram.

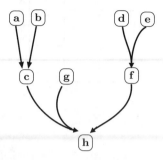

How do we attack it?

There are two sorts of attacks that make sense. One is to attack the premises. The premises of an argument are the statements at the top of the diagram, the statements that aren't supported by other statements. The argument depends on these statements. If they fall, the argument falls. In the argument above, the premises are **a**, **b**, **d**, **e**, and **g**.

The other way to attack an argument is to attack the arrows, the lines of support. The two sorts of attacks are quite different. Consider this argument:

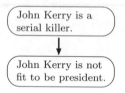

There's nothing wrong with the logic. The problem is the premise. In your rebuttal you should argue that John Kerry is not a serial killer. But consider this argument:

Now it's the logic that's at fault. The premise is unassailable. But the inference—if you're a veteran then you shouldn't be president – is terrible and you can say so.

In this chapter we'll concentrate on attacking premises. We'll take up attacking arrows in the next chapter.

Of course, you usually can't bring down all the premises, but sometimes just a few will do serious damage. Take the argument at the top of the section. If you rebut premise **d**, then you have also killed statement **f**, since the only justification for **f** is the combined efforts of **d** and **e**.

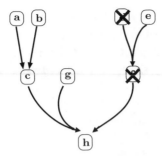

Note that rebutting **a** doesn't kill **c** since **a** and **b** work independently.

A closer look at the first argument shows that successful attacks on **d** and **g** completely torpedo the argument. Nothing is left!

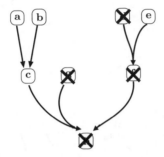

You may be wondering, "What about attacking statements other than premises? Can I attack **c** in the argument above?"

Our answer is, "Don't do it!" Here's why. If **c** is not true, then there must be something else wrong. We have **a** supporting **c**. If **c** is false then either **a** is false or the arrow from **a** to **c** is invalid. In the first case you attack the premise **a**. In the second case you attack the arrow. Either is much better than attacking **c**. This way you get to the heart of the matter. And of course the same is true with **b**: either **b** is false or else the arrow from **b** to **c** is invalid.

> **Heads Up!**
>
> Never attack intermediate statements; attack only premises and inferences. And don't forget, premises are the statements at the top of your diagram, the statements that aren't supported by other statements.

If you can only attack premises, does that mean you can't attack the conclusion? *You bet it does.* There is a difference between rebutting an argument and arguing for a contrary position (counterarguing) and you must do the former before you can begin the latter, or you end up talking past your opponent. Indeed, you may agree with a conclusion and still find much fault in the argument. (On the other hand, you can't, or shouldn't, find an argument sound and still disagree with the conclusion!) We'll begin the discussion of constructing your own argument in Chapter Seven.

Now let's attack some premises. Let's tackle Cathy's argument. We'll ignore statements **i**, **j**, **k**, **l**, **m**, **n**, and **o** (see page 29), since they don't lead to the conclusion.

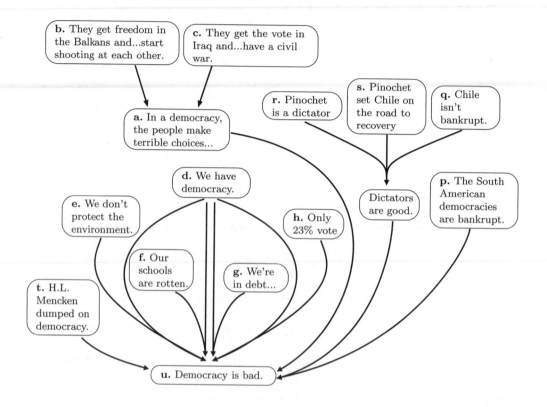

The premises are **b**, **c**, **d**, **e**, **f**, **g**, **h**, **p**, **q**, **r**, **s**, and **t**. Which can we attack?

What about **b**? Rebutting premises is very much like negating statements. **b** is a conjunction, $F \wedge S$. The negation of this is $\neg(F \wedge S)$ which is the same as $\neg F \vee \neg S$ (check this!). That means to attack **b** you only need to show that either F is false (they didn't get freedom) or S is false (they didn't start shooting). You'll have to do some research. It's true that they started shooting, but not everyone participated. And before the wars with Croatia and Bosnia, Slovenia seceded peacefully from Yugoslavia, no shooting.

Statement **c** may be more difficult to rebut.

And let's leave **d** alone.

But we can certainly rebut **e**. The United States does quite a bit to protect the environment. There are lapses, but the Clean Air Act, the Superfund Act, the Endangered Species Act, and so on all work to maintain and improve the environment.

Notice that rebutting premises isn't simple. It's not enough, for example, to say simply that **e** is false. If it were that easy, that's all anyone would do and no one would pay attention.

Heads up!

It's not enough to contradict a statement. You must do more than simply say that the statement is false. This convinces no one. You must provide evidence.

Heads up!

And it's totally useless to say, "Premise **x** has no support!" Premises *always* have no support; that's the definition of a premise. If a premise needs support, then the premise is questionable and you should be able to explain why it could be, or is, false.

What about **f** – can we defend our schools? A little research will help here. Our schools may not be the best in the world but they're still excellent. What percentage of Nobel prizes go to Americans?

How many voted in the last election (premise **h**)? I think you can nail Cathy on this one. She just made up that figure. I think her gym locker number is 23. By the way, did *you* vote?

Statement **p** is vulnerable. Only Argentina came close to bankruptcy and it's now in pretty good shape.

Finally, **r** and **t** seem pretty secure.

Well. What do we have?

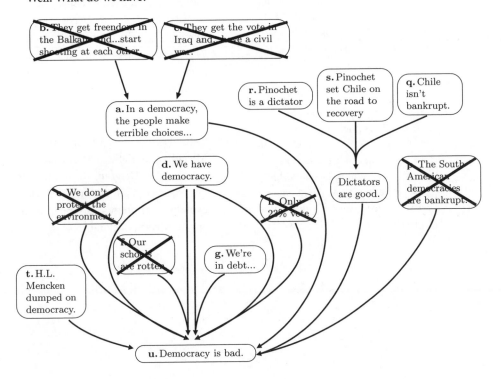

Not bad! But we're not finished, either. Some lines of argument remain unrefuted. The fact that some of her arguments for the conclusion are bad doesn't mean they all are. You might defend a conclusion with a sound argument and an unsound one. Refuting the unsound one does not impugn the sound one.

Exercises   Rebutting Premises

Odd-numbered solutions begin on page 354

For problems 1–7, rebut the arguments in the exercises for Section 2.3 (page 30) by attacking at least some of the premises.

8.

Cathy works out

"Gosh, that's really disgusting!" Miriam and Katie stood in the doorway of the living room, staring in horror and envy at Cathy, who was asleep on the sofa. Her head rested on an enormous bag of popcorn. Bags of chips were snuggled under each arm. At their words she sat up suddenly, sending waves of snack food across the floor.

"Oh hell. It's the children." With sociopathic calm, she focussed on the two first-year students standing awkwardly at attention.

"Disgusting?" she sneered, *"I'll give you disgusting. You guys have been running again, right?* That's *disgusting!"*

"I meant no disrespect Cathy," began Miriam, who now, at least, meant no disrespect. *"We were running for our health!"*

"Then you're in big trouble. Running is bad for your knees, bad for your kidneys, bad for your ankles. You'll be cripples at 30."

"Well, I don't know about that," said Katie, adjusting her sweatband, *"but I have to keep in shape! I don't want to put on the freshman 50!"*

"Then don't eat so much! That's the problem with Americans. They eat most of the world's food. Then when they're stuffed, they jiggle and jog to make room for more. Peasants starve so you can sweat!"

That silenced Miriam who, despite a substantial breakfast, was very hungry. Katie made one more attempt.

"This has nothing to do with anybody else, Cathy. Exercise is self-improvement. I want to become a better person!"

"Very humble! But what sounds like humility, is really vanity. Me! Me! Me! That's what you're saying. Your exercise is no more noble than cosmetic surgery." Cathy paused, then added, *"Vanity's a* SIN, *you know."*

Cathy is rebutting an argument by Miriam and Katie that it's good to get physical. Diagram this argument. For each of Cathy's three rebuttals, explain what premise or line of inference Cathy is attacking.

Imagine the great warrior Achilles in a race against a tortoise. Since Achilles is the faster runner, we give the tortoise a head start.

Can Achilles overtake the tortoise? To pass the tortoise, Achilles must first make up for the head start. But by the time he's covered that distance, the tortoise has moved ahead further.

Achilles must therefore make up that distance. But once Achilles has done that, the tortoise has moved again.

However many times this happens, the tortoise is always ahead. Achilles will never catch up to the tortoise! This is the most famous of Zeno's paradoxes of motion.

3.6   Computer Logic

Computers are like Old Testament gods; lots of rules and no mercy. (Joseph Campbell)

Communication inside a digital computer takes the form of streams of impulses. These impulses are of two kinds, which we can call yes and no, on and off, or true and false. Usually they are represented as 1 and 0.

These streams are manipulated when they pass through **gates**. For example, the *not* gate

takes a stream and changes all the 0s to 1s and all the 1s to 0s:

There are several gates that take two input streams and produce one output stream. The *or* gate

is one. Whenever two streams enter, it checks to see if either one is a 1. If so, then it outputs a 1; otherwise, it outputs a 0.

Before

After

Another is the *and* gate.

This outputs a 1 if and only if both streams have a 1:

Before

After

At this point, you may see the connection to Sentential. The *or* gate, for example, has its own "truth table":

Input 1	Input 2	*or* Gate Output
1	1	1
1	0	1
0	1	1
0	0	0

which looks exactly like the truth table for the connective ∨. The "1" corresponds to T, true, and the "0" corresponds to F, false.

We don't need a gate to correspond to ⇒ because we can construct a circuit that will have the same effect. Recall that ¬P ∨ Q and P ⇒ Q have the same truth tables. We can then use a *not* and an *or* gate to create a *conditional* gate:

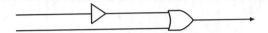

These gates are the computational heart of a computer. Theoretically, any machine or organism with these gates and with some sort of accessible memory can compute.

Exercises   Computer Logic

Odd-numbered solutions begin on page 354

What comes out of the following circuits when the streams 101001 and 110101 enter? How would you describe the action of the circuits in terms of our logical connectives?

1.

2.

3.

4.

Design a circuit to function in the same way as each statement.

5. $(P \wedge Q) \vee R$
6. $P \wedge \neg(Q \vee \neg P)$
7. $P \vee \neg P$ (Is the result what you would expect?)
8! $P \Leftrightarrow Q$
9! $P \vee Q$

We've invented a new logic gate. We call it the "smiley face" gate and it works like this:

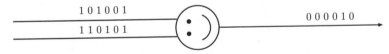

10!! Using only smiley face gates, construct a logic diagram that works just like a NOT gate.

11!!! Using only smiley face gates, construct a logic diagram that works just like an AND gate.

12. The Smiley face gate corresponds to a connective. What is the truth table for $P \odot Q$?

13. Remember, every statement in an article is true; every statement in an ad is false. What can you say about the pieces in this edition?

The Digestor's Digest

Vol. I, No. 2

Great News!

For those of you who need a high-fiber breakfast, the new cereal, Honey Hemp, has more than all others combined. In addition, three years of testing now shows conclusively that it can be eaten under laboratory conditions. The other item on this page is an advertisement.

Great News!

For those of you who need a high-fiber breakfast, the new cereal, Sani-Bran, has more than all others combined. In addition, three years of testing now shows conclusively that it can, with appropriate equipment, be eaten. This report is just as correct as the other on this page.

Chapter Four

In this chapter we'll go deeper into Sentential, focussing on entailment – what follows from what?

4.1 Validity

For you of your sweet reason gave me rest
From yearning, from desire, from potent pain (Dante Gabriel Rosetti)

This is so important we're going to say it again.

An argument is
Valid   iff the conclusion is true whenever the premises are true.
Invalid   iff it's possible for the premises to be true and the conclusion false.

In Chapter Two we looked at arguments intuitively. We suggested that readers might manage simple arguments with common sense. Now, with Basic Sentential and truth tables, we can be precise. Truth tables can tell us exactly when an argument is valid or invalid.

Example

Is $A \vee B$ valid?
   $\neg B$
   ─────────
   $\therefore A$

To decide we create a joint truth table containing both the premises and the conclusion.

Sweet Reason: A Field Guide To Modern Logic, Second Edition. Jim Henle, Jay L. Garfield, Thomas Tymoczko and Emily Altreuter.
© 2012 John Wiley & Sons Inc. Published 2012 by John Wiley & Sons Inc.

	A	B	PREMISES $A \vee B$	$\neg B$	CONCLUSION A
1.	T	T	T	F	T
2.	T	F	T	T	T
3.	F	T	T	F	F
4.	F	F	F	T	F

We want to know whether there are any lines of the table on which all of the premises are true and the conclusion is false. If there is such a line, that would show that it's possible for the premises to be true and the conclusion false. That would mean that the argument is *invalid*.

In the table, there is only one line where both premises are true, line 2. And in this line the conclusion is also true. That means it is indeed impossible for the premises to be true and the conclusion false. The truth table shows all possible situations. Thus the argument is *valid*.

This particular argument is called the **disjunctive syllogism,** by the way. It plays an interesting role in our story; we'll see it again.

Example

Is $A \Rightarrow B$ valid?
$$\neg A$$
$$\therefore \neg B$$

First, the truth table:

	A	B	PREMISES $A \Rightarrow B$	$\neg A$	CONCLUSION $\neg B$
1.	T	T	T	F	F
2.	T	F	F	F	T
3.	F	T	T	T	F
4.	F	F	T	T	T

In this table there are two lines where both premises are true, lines 3 and 4. In one of them, line 3, the conclusion is false. That means it is possible for the premises to be true and the conclusion false. Thus this argument is *invalid*.

This particular argument is called **denying the antecedent,** by the way, and it will be of considerable interest to us later. It's a favorite of political advertisers.

Example

Is $P \Leftrightarrow \neg Q$ valid?
$$P \vee \neg R$$
$$R \Leftrightarrow Q$$
$$\therefore P$$

Here is the truth table, which needs 8 rows because we have three sentence letters:

	P	Q	R	PREMISES $P \Leftrightarrow \neg Q$	$P \vee \neg R$	$R \Leftrightarrow Q$	CONCLUSION P
1.	T	T	T	F	T	T	T
2.	T	T	F	F	T	F	T
3.	T	F	T	T	T	F	T
4.	T	F	F	T	T	T	T
5.	F	T	T	T	F	T	F
6.	F	T	F	T	T	F	F
7.	F	F	T	F	F	F	F
8.	F	F	F	F	T	T	F

There is only one line where all three premises are true, line 4. In this line the conclusion is true, so the argument is valid.

Heads up!

It's easy to get confused about validity. Students sometimes spot a line like this in a truth table

PREMISES		CONCLUSION
T	T	T

and decide that the argument is valid. *That's not enough evidence.* The problem is that there might *also* be a line such as this

PREMISES		CONCLUSION
T	T	F

showing that the argument is *invalid*. Watch out!

Exercises   Validity

Odd-numbered solutions begin on page 355

Test these arguments for validity:

1. "Affirming the Consequent"

    $P \Rightarrow Q$

    Q

    $\therefore P$

2. "Explosion"

    $H \wedge \neg H$

    $\therefore J$

3. $Q \Rightarrow R$
    $R \Rightarrow S$
    $\therefore Q \Rightarrow S$

4. $S \Rightarrow (Q \Rightarrow R)$
    $S \wedge Q$
    $\therefore R$

5. $Q \vee P$
    $\neg R \vee \neg P$
    $R \Rightarrow \neg Q$
    $\therefore R$

6. $P \Leftrightarrow Q$
    $\neg(P \wedge Q)$
    $\therefore \neg P \wedge Q$

In Chapter Three we asked you to formalize these arguments and then guess which are valid. Now we ask you to determine validity carefully using truth tables.

7. I will either grow up to be president or become a screenwriter. In order to become a screenwriter, though, I've got to be good at writing. I must admit that I'm not particularly good at writing. Therefore, I will grow up to be president.

8. If Rocky the squirrel can read, he lives in the bushes. If Rocky can read, he escaped from NIMH. Rocky lives in the bushes, so he must have escaped from NIMH.

9. Either I love logic or I'm obsessed with it. (I just can't decide!) If I love logic, then I will major in it. I'm totally obsessed with logic. So, it follows that I won't major in it.

10. Mrs White did it and she did it either with the wrench or with the rope. But she did it with the rope if and only if the murder was committed in the study. The murder was committed in the hall. Therefore, Mrs White did it and she did it with the wrench.

11. If the world is round then I can sail around it if I have a boat. I have a boat but I don't sail around the world. Thus, the world is not round.

12. If drugs are legalized, then there will be more money to treat addicts, there will be less drug-related crime, and the mob will lose its main source of income. Without the source of money, the mob will wither away and die. It is clear, then, that drugs will never be legalized, since the mob will never die.

13. The object of this next exercise is to create valid arguments that are "economical," that is they are valid, and all of the premises are necessary. The conclusion of all the arguments will be *B*. Choose premises and conclusions from the following eight wffs to form as many economical, valid arguments as you can:

    $B \Rightarrow W \quad N \quad \neg M \Rightarrow \neg B \quad \neg S$

    $M \quad \neg B \Rightarrow S \quad W \quad N \Rightarrow B$

14. Choose premises and conclusions from the following eight wffs to form as many economical, valid arguments as you can. The conclusion of all of the arguments should be $\neg B$.

    $B \Rightarrow W \quad \neg N \quad \neg L \Rightarrow B \quad \neg G$

    $L \quad \neg B \vee G \quad \neg W \quad N \Rightarrow B$

The English word "Buffalo" is a logical curiosity. On the one hand, it's a noun denoting any individual animal of a certain species, as in "Look at that buffalo trample Sidney!" It's also a plural noun, denoting any group of animals of that species, as in "Look at those buffalo trample Sidney!" On the other hand, the word "buffalo" is also a transitive verb meaning roughly "to intimidate or confuse," as in "That campaign speech completely buffaloed me." More than that, "buffalo" is a plural verb; thus "Campaign speeches always buffalo me" is a well-formed English sentence.

Since "buffalo" is both a plural noun and a plural transitive verb, the following sentence, though strange, is entirely grammatical and meaningful: "Buffalo buffalo buffalo."

Because of other peculiarities of English, any transitive verb can be used with its object deleted, as in "Tom eats" or "Jim buffaloes." Hence "Buffalo buffalo" is perfectly grammatical. Additionally, in the imperative mood, the understood subject "you" can be deleted, as in "Eat!" or "Buffalo!"

Thus, "Buffalo!" "Buffalo buffalo." and "Buffalo buffalo buffalo." are all grammatical, meaningful English sentences.

What about four 'buffalo's? Is that possible? See Chapter Five.

4.2   The Logic of English

Get your fresh-picked ifs, ands and buts. (Norton Juster, *The Phantom Tollbooth*)

Basic Sentential is an artificial, formal language, meant to capture some, but not all, of the logical structure of sentences and arguments in natural languages. Natural languages, and the things we do with them, are complex and unruly, and we must always be modest about how much meaning and inference we can capture with a simple logic. But we should not despair of capturing a lot that is interesting and useful, even when it might appear that we have failed. Consider the following sentence:

Mel got bored and left the party.

We would write this in Basic Sentential as

$$B \wedge L.$$

But, you might say, the English "and" here clearly means more. It means that he got bored and then left the party (because he was bored, probably), and the Basic Sentential representation omits the important order of the events. After all,

Mel left the party and got bored.

has a very different ring to it. In setting up Basic Sentential, we made choices. One choice we made was to formalize "and" in a very limited way. Given that we wanted a definition that could be captured in a simple truth table (the one on page 38) the choice was easy.

The case for "or," however, is not so clear. Let's say that your waitperson says to you:

You can have fries or a salad with that.

In Basic Sentential, she said

$$F \lor S,$$

which, as you now know, is true when either one or both of F and S are true. So, you say, "I'll have both then," and the waitperson glowers at you. It does seem that "or" in English in this case means one or the other, but *not* both, and that Basic Sentential gets this wrong. You might be tempted to say, "Jim, Jay, and Tom: you thought you had a choice between

A	B	$A \lor B$		A	B	$A \lor B$
T	T	T		T	T	F
T	F	T	and	T	F	T
F	T	T		F	T	T
F	F	F		F	F	F

but you didn't really have a choice. Logically $\lor$ must be the exclusive 'or' ($P \lor Q$ is false if P and Q are true)."

But we did have a choice, and a beautiful analysis by the philosopher Paul Grice explains why. Grice shows how we can tell whether a meaning is logically forced or a matter of context. The trick, he says, is to try to contradict it. If the meaning is logically forced, the contradiction will be jarring. It will seem wrong, even crazy. But if the meaning is a matter of context, then it can easily be contradicted.

Example

"Today is Jan's birthday and she had toast for breakfast."
I think we all believe we are logically forced by this statement to believe that today is Jan's birthday. Now let's try to contradict it. Suppose someone said,

"Today is Jan's birthday and she had toast for breakfast, but actually today isn't her birthday,"

we would look at them as if they were out of their mind. That's evidence of logical content.

Now suppose we apply this to "or".

Example

"You can have fries or a salad with that."
Let's contradict this. Suppose we said,

"You can have fries or a salad with that, and actually you can have both if you want."

That doesn't sound bad at all. That means that exclusion is not part of the logical content of "or". We did have a choice.[1]

Example

"Mel got bored and left the party."
We can also use Gricean analysis on this. How does this sound?

Mel got bored and left the party, but not necessarily in that order.

It sounds fine. Logically, the sentence does not require one act to precede the other.

Let's take up one more quarrel, the conditional.

Example

"If P then Q."
Many students take this form to mean that P is true and that is why Q is true too. Is this part of the logical content of "if ... then"?
In a word, no. Consider:

If I had the dough, I'd buy a lexus. But I don't have the dough, so I won't.

This seems most reasonable.

---

[1]   And there is a good reason for the choice we made. You'll be seeing it soon!

A RESOLVE.
Cousin Kate: "NOW THAT YOU ARE WELL OFF, CHARLIE, YOU MUSTN'T LET THEM SAY OF YOU,
'A FOOL AND HIS MONEY ARE SOON PARTED.'"
Cousin Charles: "NO, YOU BET I WON'T. I'LL SHOW THEM THAT I AM AN EXCEPTION TO THE
RULE."

4.3   Negating Conditionals

It's not denial. I'm just selective about the reality I accept. (Bill Watterson)

By now you should be comfortable with the fact that the negation of a conjunction,

> *Jim and Jay are rock stars.* $\qquad\qquad P \wedge Q$

is a disjunction

> *Either Jim isn't a rock star or Jay isn't a rock star.* $\qquad \neg P \vee \neg Q$

and the negation of a disjunction,

> *Either I'm crazy or that's a pink elephant.* $P \lor Q$

is a conjunction.

> *I'm not crazy and that's not a pink elephant.* $\neg P \land \neg Q$

This very neat fact is one reason that we chose $\lor$ to be the inclusive "or".
The negation of a biconditional,

> *Harriet will go if and only if Gloria goes.* $P \Leftrightarrow Q$

may be less familiar, but it still makes intuitive sense. It's another biconditional,

> *Harriet will go if and only if Gloria doesn't go.* $P \Leftrightarrow \neg Q$

After all, $P \Leftrightarrow Q$ says P and Q have the same truth value. $P \Leftrightarrow \neg Q$ says that P and $\neg Q$
have the same truth value, that is, that P and Q have *different* truth values.
What is less intuitive is the negation of the conditional.

> *If you know the answer, you will write it down.* $P \Rightarrow Q$

> **If you know the negation of that sentence, write it down.**

Now let's puzzle it out.
The negation of $P \Rightarrow Q$ should have the opposite truth table.

P	Q	$P \Rightarrow Q$	??
T	T	T	F
T	F	F	T
F	T	T	F
F	F	T	F

The mystery statement is true only when P is true and Q is false.

P	Q	$P \Rightarrow Q$	??
T	T	T	F
T	**F**	**F**	**T**
F	T	T	F
F	F	T	F

It's easy to find a statement with that truth table. It's $P \land \neg Q$.

P	Q	$P \Rightarrow Q$	$P \land \neg Q$
T	T	T	F
T	F	F	T
F	T	T	F
F	F	T	F

You know the answer but you won't write it down. $P \wedge \neg Q$

But of course. $P \Rightarrow Q$ is a promise, remember? It promises that if P is true, Q will be true. The negation of $P \Rightarrow Q$, then, is the broken promise. P was true, but Q, which you promised, is false.

Remember also the umbrella in Chapter Three. Jay said that if it rains, he carries his umbrella. That's a conditional, $P \Rightarrow Q$. We asked when we could say he was lying. The answer was that the only time we could say he was lying was if it was raining *and* he didn't carry his umbrella. That's a conjunction, $P \wedge \neg Q$.

Note that the analysis in this section is nothing more than what your intuition tells you. Did you laugh at the cartoon on page 76? Then you already understood the negation of a conditional. Charles insisted the sentence

"If Charles is a fool he will soon be parted from his money."

would be false. You knew exactly what that meant.

Exercises   Negating Conditionals

Odd-numbered solutions begin on page 355

Find the negations of these statements in Sentential:

1. $P \Rightarrow \neg Q$
2. $(P \wedge Q) \Rightarrow R$
3. $P \Rightarrow (Q \vee R)$
4. $P \Rightarrow (R \wedge S)$
5. $(P \Rightarrow R) \Rightarrow S$
6. $P \Rightarrow (R \Rightarrow S)$
7. $P \Rightarrow (R \Leftrightarrow S)$
8. $(A \Rightarrow B) \wedge (B \Rightarrow A)$

Find the negations of these statements in English:

9. If you don't get me a cup of coffee then you don't love me.
10. If this is Tuesday then I have logic class.
11. If I fail logic then either I take it again next year or I change my major to modern dance.
12. If I finish the paper tonight and tomorrow is a sunny day then I'll play ultimate.
13. I'm going to law school only if I can scrape together tuition money.
14. If the department will give me credit only if I pass then I'll study, I guess.
15. I'll pay for dinner but only if you buy the movie tickets.
16. I'll pay for dinner if you buy the movie tickets.

17. With arrows, join some of the statements below to support the conclusion at the bottom. *Note: Not all the statements can be used to support the conclusion.*

If I brush my teeth after every meal, then my teeth are pearly white.

I keep a toothbrush on a string around my neck.

If I don't have time, then I don't brush my teeth after every meal.

My breath does not make strong men faint.

I have time to brush my teeth after every meal.

If I don't brush my teeth after every meal, my breath makes strong men faint.

My teeth are pearly white.

If I keep a toothbrush on a string around my neck, then I brush my teeth after every meal.

Conclusion: I brush my teeth after every meal.

18. With arrows, join some of the statements below to support the conclusion at the bottom. *Note: Not all the statements can be used to support the conclusion.*

If I brush my teeth after every meal, then my teeth are pearly white.

I don't keep a toothbrush on a string around my neck.

If I don't floss after every meal, then I brush after every meal.

I don't eat garlic pop tarts.

I floss my teeth after every meal.

I don't brush my teeth after every meal unless I eat garlic pop tarts.

My teeth are not pearly white.

If I keep a toothbrush on a string around my neck, then I brush my teeth after every meal.

Conclusion: I don't brush my teeth after every meal.

> **Warning**
> A special feature of this book is the Surprise Examination. The exam is printed on one page, and is identified by the title "Surprise Examination." The title is apt. *The exam will come as a surprise.* By this we mean that is impossible for you to know before you turn the page and see the exam what page it will be on.
>   Study hard and be prepared for the
>
> *Surprise Examination!*

4.4   Rebutting Inferences

If you give me six lines written by the most honest man, I will find something in them to hang him. (Cardinal Richelieu)

In Chapter Two we attacked arguments by challenging premises. Now we'll challenge the lines of inference, the arrows. This is trickier.

Example

We all want cancer cured. Therefore we should increase government funding for cancer research.

Here's the diagram:

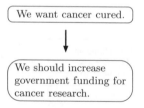

The arrows in an argument diagram are not always formal arguments, but the principles behind them are the same. Think of the inference above as a conditional,

We want cancer cured $\Rightarrow$ We should increase funding.

In the last section we saw that the negation of this is

We do want cancer cured $\wedge \neg$ We should increase funding.

That's essentially what we have to do when rebutting this arrow. We have to argue that even if we accept the premise (that we all want cancer cured) that is not enough to accept the conclusion (that we should increase funding).

We could argue that right now the medical community has all the support it can use. We could also argue that logically the arrow can't be valid. If it were, then we should keep increasing government funding until we no longer want cancer to be cured, which of course is silly.

Finally, we could show that the arrow is unjustified by presenting a parallel argument, an argument with the same form but one where the premise is obviously true and the conclusion obviously false. We could say, for example, that we all want Cynthia to enjoy her birthday, but that doesn't mean she should have government funding.

Here's a more complex example.

Example

We have no other choice. We must raise taxes. If we don't raise taxes, there will be a huge budget deficit. A deficit will mean our children will be saddled with an enormous debt to pay. There are other reasons for raising taxes. If we raise taxes, we'll have more money to spend on social programs. Some of our social programs badly need additional funds. Finally, no less an authority than Buckfunster Miller, last year's Nobel Prize winner in economics, recommends raising taxes.

Here's the diagram with the arrows labelled:

a. If we don't ... huge budget deficit.
b. A deficit will mean our children will be saddled with an enormous debt to pay.
c. If we raise taxes, we'll have more money to spend on social programs.
d. Some social programs need additional funds.
e. Miller recommends raising taxes.
f. We must raise taxes.

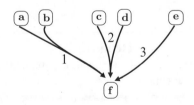

Can we attack the arrow #1? Can we say, for example, that there are other ways to keep the deficit down, such as reducing spending on the military?

No, we can't. That wouldn't be attacking the arrow, that would be attacking the premise, "If we don't raise taxes, there will be a huge budget deficit." Instead, we have to argue that even if there is a huge deficit we will not be in great difficulty. We could argue, for example that this country has had a debt for most of its history and that as a percentage of GDP the debt is not large.

Can we attack arrow #2?

Yes indeed. A logical error is being committed here. The argument is

$$\begin{array}{l} \text{We raise taxes} \Rightarrow \text{we get money.} \\ \underline{\text{We need money.}} \\ \therefore \text{We should raise taxes.} \end{array}$$

There is an unstated premise, that if doing something gets you something you need then you should do it. But is that true? What if we take the logical form of the argument,

$$\begin{array}{l} \text{We do X} \Rightarrow \text{we get money.} \\ \underline{\text{We need money.}} \\ \therefore \text{We should do X.} \end{array}$$

and replace "X" with "rob a bank"? When we do this, we get a counter-example, an argument with exactly the same form,

$$\begin{array}{l} \text{We rob a bank} \Rightarrow \text{we get money.} \\ \underline{\text{We need money.}} \\ \therefore \text{We should rob a bank.} \end{array}$$

where the premises are true but the conclusion is false. Without the unstated premise it resembles the invalid argument we met in Chapter Two,

$$\begin{array}{l} P \Rightarrow Q \\ \underline{\quad Q \quad} \\ \therefore P \end{array}$$

affirming the consequent (see page 23).

Heads up!

Rebuttal by counter-example is a powerful technique but you must use it correctly. You must match the logical form of the argument *exactly*.

Finally, can we attack arrow #3?

Perhaps. Economists don't always agree. There's a good chance that on any issue you can find Nobel laureates on different sides. Consequently, the authority of one prize winner is of little consequence by itself.

The issue of rebutting helps us with one peculiar diagramming issue:

Example

Suppose in an argument we assert that most hoddahoos are fobular and in support of this we argue that hoddahoos A, B, C, and D are all fobular. How do we diagram this?

First try:

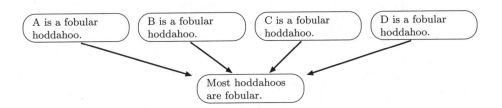

There is a problem with this, though. The argument may be reasonable, but the diagram is not. Every inference can be attacked easily (one example of a fobular hoddahoo hardly tells us that *most* hoddahoos are fobular).

Second try:

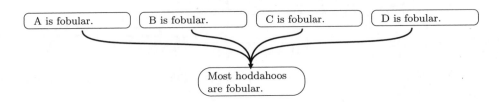

This works.

Note again that the arrows in these informal argument diagrams, while related to the formal ⇒, are qualitatively different. Four examples of fobular hoddahoos may not prove that most hoddahoos are fobular. For one thing, it's not clear what "most" means. But even if we wanted to claim that over 70% of hoddahoos are fobular, four examples probably wouldn't suffice. Of course, if there are only five hoddahoos four fobular ones are very good evidence. But if there are millions of hoddahoos ...

The question of how much certainty a few examples gives belongs to inductive logic. This is a huge field, encompassing deep areas of philosophy and mathematics. It's really beyond the scope of this book but we'll give you an idea of it all in Chapters Seven and Eight.

Now let's take on Cathy. Here's her argument again, with the arrows labelled:

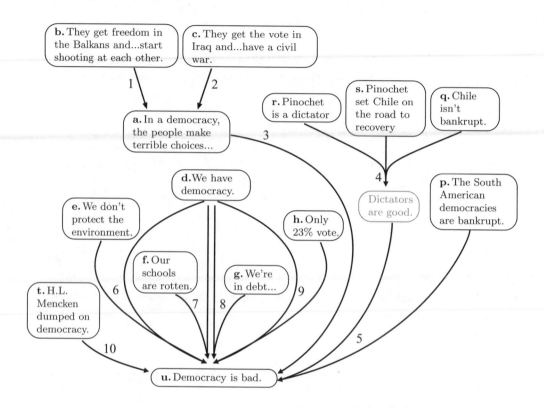

As before, we'll ignore the parts of the argument that do not support the conclusion **u**. Here's our analysis:

#1 Statement **a** is a universal statement, while **b** is just one example. One example is not enough. Otherwise you could say that birds don't fly. I just saw a penguin and it can't fly.

#2 This is similar to #1. Now Cathy might argue that **b** and **c** work together, that the diagram should look like:

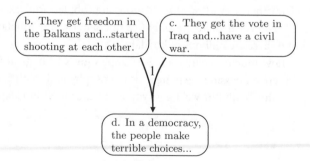

Then, of course, the argument is a little stronger, but the arrow can still be refuted by citing examples of countries that gained democracy and remained peaceful: East Germany, Poland, Hungary, Romania, Bulgaria, Lithuania, Latvia, Estonia, and so on.

#6–#8 The best way to rebut these would be to show that other forms of govenment have similar failures. Eastern Europe and the Soviet Union under communism failed to protect the environment. The schools in China under Mao were deliberately weakened. The economies of military dictatorships in South America were deeply in debt.

#9 This is a little different from the last three. We can't rebut this by citing dictatorships where no one votes since that's not a critical part of the process. Instead you could argue that the lack of excitement in voting is a measure of how satisfied American citizens are with their government. That's the real reason for democracy – not good government, but popular government.

#10 Mencken sneers at democracy, but what one person says is hardly an argument. Democracy has many supporters. You could construct a similar argument with a supporter of democracy concluding that democracy is good. Then you would have an argument having the same form as #10. Since they have the same form they must either be both valid or both invalid. If they're valid, then the conclusions are true. But the conclusions can't both be true. Thus, they are both invalid.

Here's the argument diagram again, with our rebuttals from this and the previous chapter noted.

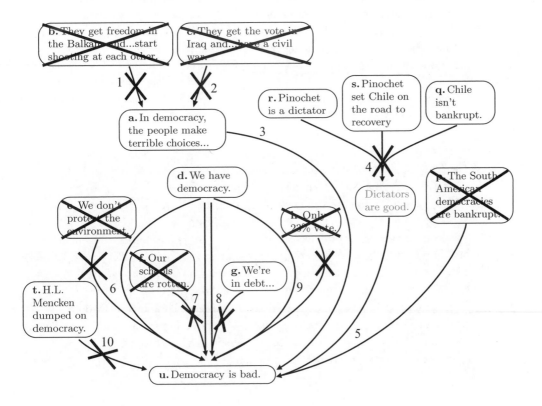

Odd-numbered
solutions
begin on page 356

Exercises   Rebutting Inferences

For problems 1–7, rebut the arguments in the exercises for Section 2.3 (page 30) by attacking the inferences, where possible.

8.

Cathy goes to war

In Italy for thirty years under the Borgias they had warfare, terror, murder, bloodshed, but they produced Michelangelo, Leonardo da Vinci, and the Renaissance. In Switzerland, they had brotherly love, they had five hundred years of democracy and peace. And what did they produce? The cuckoo-clock.

– Orson Welles, contributed to the script of *The Third Man*

Here is Cathy again, in a holiday mood. Diagram her argument (conclusion: war is better than peace). Label the inferences and attack as many of them as you can.

Somebody was playing Christmas carols. It was an evening in December, and most of the first-year students were decorating a tree, when Maud breezed in.

"Hey!" she said. "Peace on earth!"

Cathy, who had been scowling in the corner for the past twenty minutes, snorted. "Baloney! Veggie baloney! Peace is the pits! Peace is stagnation. Peace is boring. In peace, the problems of the world only get worse." Cathy grinned as everyone looked at her in astonishment.

"War may be hell, but it's progress. In war, the economy booms because everybody is working to make weapons and feed the troops. War forces important advances in science and technology. War inspires great music, art, and literature. In war, things get done!"

"But people die!" began Jennifer, who hadn't seen her family in three months and was beginning to wonder if an Eastern liberal arts college was a mistake.

"Yeah, and another problem with peace is overpopulation," Cathy sneered.

"Look, when we build a monument to somebody, that means that person is a hero, right? Well, we don't build monuments to peacemakers, so they're bums!"

There is a classic thought experiment concerning infinity called *Hilbert's Hotel*, the invention of mathematician David Hilbert.

Imagine a hotel with an infinite number of rooms. The rooms are numbered 1, 2, 3, ... The hotel is also full; there's a guest in each room.

Now a traveler arrives and needs a room. The hotel is full! But does the manager turn him away? She doesn't. She asks the person in room 1 to move to room 2, the person in room 2 to move to room 3, the person in room 3 to move to room 4, and so on. The movement is done simultaneously: all the guests step out of their rooms, then all move to the door of the next room, then all move into their new room.

Everyone has a room to sleep in and room #1 is now empty, ready for the traveler.

Are you wondering what happens to the person in the last room? There is no last room. Next to any room n is the next room, $n + 1$.

If another traveler arrives, the manager could repeat the procedure. But what if an infinitely long tour bus arrives with an infinite number of travelers? Can they all be accomodated? The answer is in Chapter Five.

4.5   The Logic of Sets

Everything You Always Wanted to Know About Sets*

*But Were Afraid to Ask

Anonymous

We assume that you are familiar with the concept of a set as a collection of objects. There are many ways to picture sets, but perhaps the simplest is with circles or blobs on a page. Such pictures are called **Venn diagrams** for their inventor, John Venn. For example, if A is the set of letters in the word "mother" and B is the set of letters in the word "father," we can draw

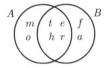

That is, $A = \{m, o, t, h, e, r\}$ and $B = \{f, a, t, h, e, r\}$. The **union** of A and B, written $A \cup B$, is the set of letters that are in either set:

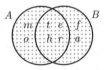

so $A \cup B = \{m, o, t, h, e, r, f, a\}$. The **intersection** of A and B, written $A \cap B$, is the set of letters that are in both sets:

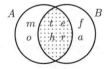

so $A \cap B = \{t, h, e, r\}$. The **complement** of A, which we will write as A^c, consists of all things that are not in A:

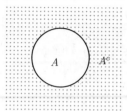

Actually, there are lots of things that aren't in A: the letter j, the letter z, but also Marcel Proust, the People's Republic of China, and all the members of the 1946 Boston Red Sox. Usually, though, we limit ourselves to some category. In this case, letters of the alphabet seem appropriate. Thus

$$A^c = \{a, b, c, d, f, g, i, j, k, l, n, p, q, s, u, v, w, x, y, z\}$$

There's a nice connection between this notation and our symbolic language. Let P and Q be propositions. Let p be the set of situations where P is true and q be the set of situations where Q is true:

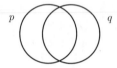

Now, what is the set of situations where $P \lor Q$ is true? The answer is $p \cup q$:

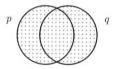

What about the situations where $P \land Q$ is true? It's $p \cap q$.

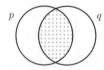

And the set of situations where $\neg P$ is true is p^c.

Example

We learned in Chapter Three that the negation of a conjunction is a disjunction and vice-versa. These are known as **DeMorgan's laws** after Augustus DeMorgan. We can verify that $\neg(P \wedge Q)$ and $\neg P \vee \neg Q$ are the same by looking at the equivalent Venn diagrams.

We'll compare the diagrams for $(p \cap q)^c$ and $p^c \cup q^c$. For the first, we take $p \cap q$,

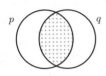 then take the complement.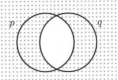

For the second, we look at the complements of p and q,

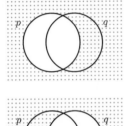 and take their union,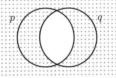

getting exactly the same diagram.

Finally, how do we interpret $P \Rightarrow Q$? What that statement means is that every situation where P is true is a situation where Q is true, that is, the set p is contained in the set q. We say in this case that p is a **subset** of q and we write

$$p \subseteq q$$

The line underneath $\subset$ helps us to remember that p and q might be equal.

Heads up!

You can remember which logical symbols correspond to which set symbols just by looking at them. Note the similarities

$$\vee \qquad \cup,$$

and

$$\wedge \qquad \cap.$$

This is yet another reason why we chose the inclusive or for $\vee$.

Example

Here is a problem that we can tackle using Venn diagrams. Out of a total of 73 students, 31 have signed up for a course in Aristotle, 17 have signed up for both Plato and Aristotle, and 12 have failed to sign up for either. How many signed up for Plato? To solve this problem, we can draw a Venn diagram as follows:

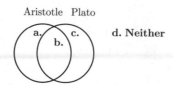

The problem says that there are 31 students in regions **a** and **b** combined and 17 students in region **b**. Putting this information together we have

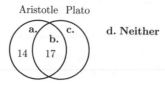

The problem tells us that there are 12 students in region **d**.

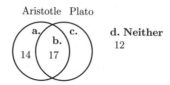

Altogether there are 73 students. By a little subtraction, we find that there are 30 students in region **c**. Finally, the answer we seek is the number in **b** and **c** together, or 47.

There's one last set to tell you about. It's the **empty set**, the set that has nothing in it. It's surprisingly important. We can write it as

$$\{\,\}$$

but it's also common to write:

$$\emptyset.$$

You'll see it later.

Exercises   The Logic of Sets

Odd-numbered solutions begin on page 356

Use the following information to answer questions 1–5.

In 1991, it rained on 57 days and snowed on 14 days, and on 280 days the sun came out for at least a while. There was no precipitation on 301 days. Whenever it snowed, the sun failed to come out, and there were only 3 days of both rain and sun. It's not a leap year. Use a diagram to answer the questions.

1. How many dry, sunny days were there?
2. How many dry, cloudy days were there?
3. On how many days was there rain or snow, but no sun?
4. On how many days was there just rain?
5. The same weather statistics were true in 1992. What change did that make?

Use the following information to answer questions 6–12 below.

You are thinking of running for the city council. You are especially cynical and have no firmly held opinions, and so you have decided to take positions on three major issues that will give you the greatest advantage during the election. You make the reasonable assumption that voters who agree with you on at least two of the three issues will vote for you. The three issues are:

(1) Should the city turn the high school into a mall?
(2) Should the city sell the mineral rights to downtown?
(3) Should there be term limits for meter maids?

A diagram is helpful for classifying the voters:

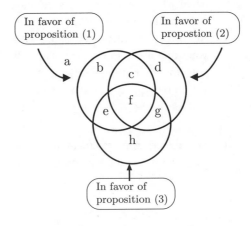

6. If you oppose proposition (1) and support (2) and (3), voters in which regions of the diagram will agree with you completely?
7. If you support proposition (2) and oppose (1) and (3), voters in which regions of the diagram will agree with you completely?
8. How many different combinations of positions are there?
9. Polls show that 48% favor proposition (1), 45% favor proposition (2), and 49% favor proposition (3). We also know that 19% favor both (1) and (2), 19% favor both (2) and (3), and 21% favor both (1) and (3). Finally, 4% favor all three. What percentage of the population fall into each of the eight regions?
10. What combination of positions is held by the most voters?
11. What combination of positions is held by the fewest voters?

12. Assume your opponent chooses as her platform the combination of position held by the most voters and suppose you choose the combination: In favor of (1) and (2), opposed to (3). Who will win? Assume that voters who agree with you on more issues than agree with your opponent will vote for you; that voters who agree with your opponent more than you will vote for your opponent; and those who agree equally with the two of you will stay home.

13. A majority of the voters opposes each proposition. But that's not the most popular combination (as you discovered in problem 11). If one candidate takes the most popular combination of positions and the other follows the majority on each issue, who will win and how does the voting go?

14. How many different positions would there be if there were four issues?

15! Can you draw circles (or any other shape) to show four sets with all possibilities represented?

16. Remember, every statement in an article is true; every statement in an ad is false. What can you say about the pieces in this edition?

The Digestor's Digest

Vol. I, No. 3

In Taste Tests

The latest laboratory tests show that the ever-popular Choco-lumps is the best-tasting cereal of all!

In Taste Tests

The latest laboratory tests show that Chem-treats is *not* the best-tasting cereal. Chem-treats did, however, place second behind Flaky Corns. Actually, it placed third behind Flaky Corns and Tastiturf.

Chapter Five

5.1 Well-formed Formulas

*One cannot escape the feeling that these mathematical formulae have an indepen-
dent existence and an intelligence of their own, that they are wiser than we are, wiser
even than their discoverers, that we get more out of them than was originally put into
them.* (Heinrich Hertz)

We began by talking about logic informally. Very slowly, we've been tightening the screws.
Now it's time to get serious about grammar.

Grammar is central to Basic Sentential. Grammar was present at the birth of the language. Grammar defines the language. Grammar connects form to meaning. And grammar
enables us to reason about Sentential in ways that would be impossible with a natural
language like English. Indeed, grammar distinguishes symbolic languages from natural
languages. You could say that a major goal of linguistics is to discover comprehensive
grammatical rules for natural languages.

What we mean by "grammar" here is a complete description of what combinations of
symbols are to be meaningful formulas of Basic Sentential, what are called **well-formed
formulas**, or **wffs** for short. Our strategy is based on diagrams such as the one that appeared
on page 45. We were analyzing the formula, $((\neg P \vee Q) \Rightarrow (Q \wedge P))$, and we broke it down
like this:

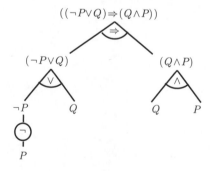

Sweet Reason: A Field Guide To Modern Logic, Second Edition. Jim Henle, Jay L. Garfield, Thomas Tymoczko and Emily Altreuter.
© 2012 John Wiley & Sons Inc. Published 2012 by John Wiley & Sons Inc.

The idea is that a string of symbols is a wff if and only if it's possible to break it down this way. If it can't, then it isn't a wff.

Our definition has three clauses. We'll start by defining the simplest wffs, the letters at the bottom of the diagram. Then we'll legislate how more complex wffs can be made. That's two clauses. There's one more clause. We'll tell you about that at the end. Here we go:

> 1. Any capital letter, *A*, *B*, etc., is a wff of Basic Sentential except for *T* and *F* (so we don't get confused with *True* and *False*). Also, just in case we need more letters and we've run out, we allow $A_1, A_2, \ldots, B_1, B_2, \ldots$ and so on.

That first clause is the **base clause**. It gives us something definite to build on. In practice, we won't use the subscripts. We have them just in case. They're just like the roman numerals that appear in families which like to reuse names: John D. Rockefeller III, for example, or Henry VIII.

The next clause is the **recursion clause**. It tells us how, given some wffs, we may create longer wffs.

> 2. If $\mathcal{A}$ and $\mathcal{B}$ are wffs of Basic Sentential then
>
>   a. $\neg\mathcal{A}$
>   b. $(\mathcal{A} \wedge \mathcal{B})$
>   c. $(\mathcal{A} \vee \mathcal{B})$
>   d. $(\mathcal{A} \Rightarrow \mathcal{B})$
>   e. $(\mathcal{A} \Leftrightarrow \mathcal{B})$
>
>   are also wffs of Basic Sentential.

We're using $\mathcal{A}$ and $\mathcal{B}$ to stand for any wff of Basic Sentential. We're using script letters so you understand we don't mean *A* and *B*, the sentence letters. $\mathcal{A}$ can be $(P \wedge Q)$, for example, or $((H \Rightarrow \neg A) \vee Q)$, or of course, *A*.

The last clause is the **closure clause**. It closes the door.

> 3. The only strings of symbols that are wffs are those justified by the base clause and the recursion clause.

Let's see how this works on the wff in the diagram, $((\neg P \vee Q) \Rightarrow (Q \wedge P))$: First we note that *P* and *Q* are wffs. Why? Because of clause 1; *P* and *Q* are both sentence letters.

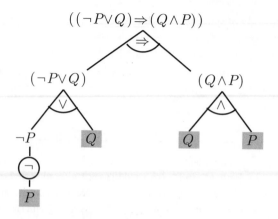

Next, we note that $(Q \wedge P)$ is a wff. Why? Since Q and P are wffs, part b of clause 2 says that $(Q \wedge P)$ is a wff. We're using $\mathcal{A}$ to stand for Q and $\mathcal{B}$ to stand for P.

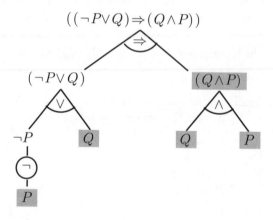

Now we claim that $\neg P$ is a wff. Why? Since P is a wff, part a of clause 2 says that $\neg P$ is a wff. Now we're using $\mathcal{A}$ to stand for P.

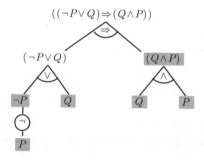

Next we claim that $(\neg P \vee Q)$ is a wff. Why? Since $\neg P$ and Q are wffs, part c of clause 2 says that $(\neg P \vee Q)$ is a wff. We're using $\mathcal{A}$ to stand for $\neg P$ and $\mathcal{B}$ to stand for Q. Note that we couldn't let $\mathcal{A}$ stand for $\neg P$ until we had established that $\neg P$ is a wff; clause 2 only applies to known wffs.

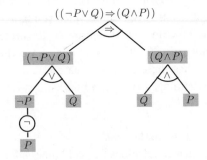

Finally, we can say that $((\neg P \vee Q) \Rightarrow (Q \wedge P))$ is a wff by part d of clause 2. Since $(\neg P \vee Q)$ and $(Q \wedge P)$ are wffs, clause 2 says that $((\neg P \vee Q) \Rightarrow (Q \wedge P))$ is a wff. We're using $\mathcal{A}$ to stand for $(\neg P \vee Q)$ and $\mathcal{B}$ to stand for $(Q \wedge P)$.

You can see why clause 2 is called the *recursion* clause. It *recurs* over and over!

Example

Is $P \wedge Q \vee R$ a wff?

It is not; clause 2 demands parentheses. The fact that this is not a well-formed formula is reflected by the fact that it's not clear how you would constuct a syntactic tree for it.

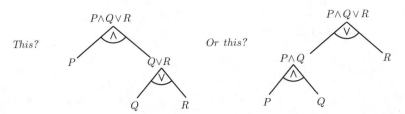

It's the difference between $(P \wedge (Q \vee R))$ and $((P \wedge Q) \vee R)$ – both genuine wffs. The two statements have different truth tables. If, for example, P is false and R is true, the first wff is false and the second wff is true.

The issue of parentheses in Sentential is mirrored in English. The sentence, "She went to her office and picked up Samantha or bought the paper." is ambiguous. Is it $(P \wedge (Q \vee R))$ or $((P \wedge Q) \vee R)$? There are parentheses, in effect, in English. To mean $(P \wedge (Q \vee R))$ we could say,

She went to her office and either picked up Samantha or bought the paper.

To mean $((P \wedge Q) \vee R)$ we could say,

Either she went to her office and picked up Samantha or she bought the paper.

We're being rigid, now, about parentheses in Sentential. Later we'll relax. For some wffs parentheses are needed to avoid ambiguity, for example, $\neg(A \vee B)$. For others, they're unnecessary, for example, $(A \wedge (B \wedge C))$. You'll get a feel for the difference. It's important that you know how to be rigid so that you can be when you have to.

We hope you appreciate how tidy our definition is. It's finite, just three clauses. But it defines an infinite number of wffs. It's an example of a **recursive definition**. In general, a recursive definition has three clauses, a base clause, a recursion clause, and a closure clause. If we were defining, say, what a mizzleplop is, the definition would have the form:

1. We give you explicitly a few mizzleplops.
2. We tell you how to get new mizzleplops from old mizzleplops.
3. We tell you that's all the mizzleplops you're going to get.

The first clause gets you started. The second keeps you going. If you like, you can think of the third clause as something the lawyers insisted on to make sure nothing weird sneaks in.

Did you notice a resemblance between recursive definitions and the self-referential paradoxes of Chapters One and Two? They're all examples of what we are going to call in this book "reflectivity". In each case, the whole is reflected inside itself. In "This sentence is not true", the whole is reflected in the words "This sentence". In the recursive definition of Basic Sentential, "wff" is being used to define "wff"; the whole is reflected inside itself.

Both the paradox and the definition are reflective. Reflectivity is a theme that courses through logic. Here's a little story:

> Sometime in the 1950s, a boy was given an electric set by his parents. The set included a light-sensitive switch. When exposed to light, the switch switched; when the light was turned off, it switched back.
>
> The boy played with the set for a while and then had an idea. He created an electric circuit with a light and the light-sensitive switch. He arranged it so that if the light was on, the circuit would be broken and the light would be off; and if the light were off, the circuit would be closed and the light would be on. The light was on if and only if it was off. It was the electrical version of the Liar.
>
> There were two consequences to this. One was that the light in the circuit turned on and off incredibly fast, fluttering until the boy took out the battery. The second result was that the boy, Gene Kleinberg, grew up to be a logician.

The paradox and the definition are both reflective but there's an important difference. In the first, you're caught in an endless cycle:

… so the sentence is true so the sentence is false so the sentence is true so the sentence is false …

It's like what you see when you are between two mirrors.

But in the definition, the cycle ends doesn't go on forever, it ends.

$((P \land Q) \Rightarrow R)$ is a wff because $(P \land Q)$ and R are wffs because P, Q and R are wffs.

It's like a set of Russian dolls.

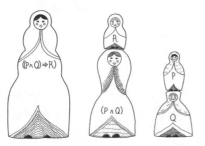

We conclude with the definition of wff in brief:

Basic Sentential

1. Capital letters (except T and F) are wffs.
2. If $\mathcal{A}$ and $\mathcal{B}$ are wffs, then so are $\neg \mathcal{A}$, $(\mathcal{A} \land \mathcal{B})$, $(\mathcal{A} \lor \mathcal{B})$, $(\mathcal{A} \Rightarrow \mathcal{B})$, and $(\mathcal{A} \Leftrightarrow \mathcal{B})$.
3. That's all the wffs.

Exercises   **Well-formed Formulas**

Odd-numbered
solutions
begin on page 356

Determine which of the following are wffs in our strict version of Sentential:

1. $Q \lor R$
2. $(A \Rightarrow B) \land (C \Rightarrow \neg B)$
3. $(G \land (\neg H))$
4. $((R \land S) \Rightarrow (S \lor U))$
5. $((P \lor Q) \land (Q \Rightarrow S)) \Rightarrow N$
6. $((A \land \neg B) \Rightarrow (\neg C \land D))$

Show how to use the recursive definition to build the following wffs:

7. $(M \land N)$
8. $(C \Rightarrow D)$
9. $((A \land B) \Rightarrow C)$
10. $(\neg U \Rightarrow \neg\neg W)$
11. $((\neg X \land Y) \lor Z)$
12. $((P \lor Q) \Rightarrow (\neg R \land S))$
13. I think you know what "ancestor" means, but have you ever thought about how to define it? Write a recursive definition of "ancestor of mine" as follows:
    a. Write the base clause.
    b. Write the recursion clause.
    c. Write the closure clause.

14. Informally, we could say that a "Bacon colleague" is someone who made a film with Kevin Bacon, or someone who made a film with someone who made a film with Kevin Bacon, or someone who made a film with someone who made a film with someone who made a film with Kevin Bacon, etc., etc. Write a recursive definition of "Bacon colleague" as follows:
    a. Write the base clause.
    b. Write the recursion clause.
    c. Write the closure clause.

We have a new language we call *Arizona*. The symbols consist of:

Dingbats: ◇, ♣◇,

Hotdogs: ♡, ♠.

The rules for forming wffs in Arizona are:

> 1. Any dingbat is a wff.
> 2. If $\mathcal{A}$ and $\mathcal{B}$ are wffs, then so are: $h\mathcal{AB}$ and $\mathcal{A}h\mathcal{B}$, where h is a hotdog.
> 3. There are no other wffs.

Decide which of the following are wffs of Arizona.

15. ◇
16. ♣
17. ♡◇
18. ♡♣◇
19. ♠◇♣◇
20. ♡◇♠◇♡◇
21. ♣◇♠◇♠◇♠♣◇
22. ♣◇♠◇♠◇♠♣◇♠◇♠◇♠♣
23. ♣◇♠◇♠◇♠♣◇♠◇♠◇♠♣♡
24. ♣◇♠◇♠◇♠♣◇♠◇♠◇♠♣♡
25! ♡♡◇♠◇♡◇♠
26! ◇♠◇♡♡◇♠◇◇
27. Why is this language called "Arizona"?

There is special property of English that allows for longer "buffalo" sentences (see p. 73 for what a buffalo sentence is). In relative clauses introduced by the word "that," the "that" can be omitted if it is the object of the clause. Here's an example.

"Dogs that kids like bark."

In this case, "that" refers to "dogs" and "dogs" is the object of the clause (kids like dogs). With "that" omitted, the sentence still makes sense and has the same meaning:

"Dogs kids like bark."

That means that the sentence, "Buffalo that buffalo buffalo buffalo" can be shortened to "Buffalo buffalo buffalo buffalo."

For clarity, we can replace "buffalo" with "bison" when we use it as a noun, and replace "buffalo" with "intimidate" when we use it as a verb. With this in mind, we can add commas and rewrite "Buffalo buffalo buffalo buffalo" as "Bison, (that) bison intimidate, intimidate."

This is a deep psychological truth. Bullying in the prairie has the same underlying cause as bullying on the playground.

What about five "buffalo"s? Is that possible? See Chapter Six.

5.2   The Shortcut Method

Traditional science is all about finding shortcuts. (Rudy Rucker)

The method of truth tables will always tell us whether an argument form is valid in Basic Sentential. But it can sometimes be cumbersome. It's easy when we only have two sentence letters to consider; we have only four lines on our truth table. But if we have three letters then there are eight lines. With five letters we have thirty-two lines. Wouldn't it be nice to have a shortcut? It would, and here it is.

The basic idea of the shortcut method is this: We test an argument form to see whether we can find an assignment of truth-values to the sentence letters that makes the conclusion false and all of the premises true. If we succeed, if we can find such an assignment (essentially, a line in the truth table), then the argument is invalid. If we do not succeed and if we can show that we *must* fail, then the argument is valid, since then it would be impossible to make the premises true and the conclusion false.

Example

> If the economy is good then the president is competent.
> If the president is incompetent then the markets will be in turmoil.
> The economy is not good and the markets are in turmoil.
> ∴ The president is incompetent.

First, we formalize this as

$$E \Rightarrow P$$
$$\neg P \Rightarrow M$$
$$\neg E \wedge M$$
$$\overline{\qquad\qquad}$$
$$\therefore \neg P$$

Now let's start with the conclusion. To make it false, we clearly must make P true.

$$E \Rightarrow P^{(\text{True})}$$
$$\neg P^{(\text{True})} \Rightarrow M$$
$$\neg E \wedge M$$
$$\overline{\neg P^{(\text{True})}} \qquad \text{False}$$

Notice that we automatically have that the first premise is true.

$$E \Rightarrow P^{(\text{True})} \qquad\qquad \text{True}$$
$$\neg P^{(\text{True})} \Rightarrow M$$
$$\neg E \wedge M$$
$$\overline{\neg P^{(\text{True})}} \qquad\qquad \text{False}$$

Actually, since $\neg P$ is false, the second premise is also true.

$$E \Rightarrow P^{(\text{True})} \qquad\qquad \text{True}$$
$$\neg P^{(\text{True})} \Rightarrow M \qquad\qquad \text{True}$$
$$\neg E \wedge M$$
$$\overline{\neg P^{(\text{True})}} \qquad\qquad \text{False}$$

To make the third premise true, we need to make E false and M true. That's easy.

$$E^{(\text{False})} \Rightarrow P^{(\text{True})} \qquad\qquad \text{True}$$
$$\neg P^{(\text{True})} \Rightarrow M^{(\text{True})} \qquad\qquad \text{True}$$
$$\neg E^{(\text{False})} \wedge M^{(\text{True})} \qquad\qquad \text{True}$$
$$\overline{\neg P^{(\text{True})}} \qquad\qquad\qquad\quad \text{False}$$

We've succeeded in making all the premises true and the conclusion false. This is an invalid argument.

Example

>   Al will cook unless Bill does.
>   But Bill only cooks if Cathy comes to dinner.
>   Neither Cathy nor Doris will come to dinner if Edith comes.
>   Edith is coming.
> _____
> $\therefore$ So Al will cook.

We formalize this as

$$A \lor B$$
$$B \Rightarrow C$$
$$E \Rightarrow \neg(C \lor D)$$
$$E$$
$$\overline{}$$
$$\therefore A$$

Notice that this argument form has five sentence letters and so would require 32 lines in a truth table! But the shortcut method works quickly.

Can we make the conclusion false? We can. We can do it by making A false.

$$A^{(\text{False})} \lor B$$
$$B \Rightarrow C$$
$$E \Rightarrow \neg(C \lor D)$$
$$E$$
$$\overline{A^{(\text{False})}} \qquad \qquad \textbf{False}$$

Now, we try to make the premises true.

The first premise is a disjunction. Since we've already made A false, the only way to make $A \lor B$ true is to make B true. So that's what we do.

$$A^{(\text{False})} \lor B^{(\text{True})} \qquad \qquad \textbf{True}$$
$$B^{(\text{True})} \Rightarrow C$$
$$E \Rightarrow \neg(C \lor D)$$
$$E$$
$$\overline{A^{(\text{False})}} \qquad \qquad \textbf{False}$$

To make the second premise true, we have to make C true. We do this.

$$A^{(\text{False})} \lor B^{(\text{True})} \qquad \qquad \textbf{True}$$
$$B^{(\text{True})} \Rightarrow C^{(\text{True})} \qquad \qquad \textbf{True}$$
$$E \Rightarrow \neg(C^{(\text{True})} \lor D)$$
$$E$$
$$\overline{A^{(\text{False})}} \qquad \qquad \textbf{False}$$

So far, so good. And it's clear now that we must make *E* true (to make the last premise true).

$$A^{\text{(False)}} \lor B^{\text{(True)}} \qquad\qquad \text{True}$$
$$B^{\text{(True)}} \Rightarrow C^{\text{(True)}} \qquad\qquad \text{True}$$
$$E^{\text{(True)}} \Rightarrow \neg(C^{\text{(True)}} \lor D)$$
$$\underline{E^{\text{(True)}}} \qquad\qquad\qquad\qquad\quad \text{True}$$
$$A^{\text{(False)}} \qquad\qquad\qquad\qquad\quad \text{False}$$

One premise to go, the fourth. To make that true we have to make the consequent true. To do that, we have to make $C \lor D$ false. But that can't be done! No matter what we make *D*, $C \lor D$ is true because *C* is true. We're stuck!

At every stage we assigned truth values to letters because we *had to* in order to make the conclusion false and the premises true. Doing what had to be done, we were still unable to make the conclusion false and the premises true. That means the argument is *valid*.

Example

> Fred will buy a new car if Gretchen wants one.
> Helen will buy a motorcycle if Fred buys a new car.
> Irene told me that Helen is getting a motorcycle.
> If Irene tells me that Helen is getting a motorcycle, Helen will get one.
> ∴ Fred will get the new car and Gretchen wants it.

First, we formalize:

$$G \Rightarrow F$$
$$F \Rightarrow H$$
$$I$$
$$\underline{I \Rightarrow H}$$
$$\therefore F \land G$$

Now, we want to make the conclusion false and the premises true. The conclusion is a conjunction, and so could be false if either conjunct is false. Hmmm… that's a problem. If we make *F* false and *G* true and find we can't make the premises all true, then we have to come back and try *F* true and *G* false. And if we still can't make the premises true, we need to try both false. Remember, to show that the argument is valid, we need to show that there is *no possibility* of making the premises true and the conclusion false. We have to explore every avenue. That's a lot of work. It might be easier, though, if we try starting the shortcut method with a premise instead of the conclusion.

Let's look instead at the third premise. That's simple. To make that true, *I* has to be true. We substitute.

$$G \Rightarrow F$$
$$F \Rightarrow H$$
$$I^{\text{(True)}} \qquad\qquad\qquad \text{True}$$
$$\underline{I^{\text{(True)}} \Rightarrow H}$$
$$F \land G$$

Now we see that to make the last premise true, we have to make H true.

$$G \Rightarrow F$$
$$F \Rightarrow H^{(\text{True})}$$
$$I^{(\text{True})} \qquad\qquad \text{True}$$
$$\underline{I^{(\text{True})} \Rightarrow H^{(\text{True})} \qquad\qquad \text{True}}$$
$$F \wedge G$$

Hey that's good! We accidentally made the second premise true. No matter what truth value F has, $F \Rightarrow H$ is true because H is true.

$$G \Rightarrow F$$
$$F \Rightarrow H^{(\text{True})} \qquad\qquad \text{True}$$
$$I^{(\text{True})} \qquad\qquad \text{True}$$
$$\underline{I^{(\text{True})} \Rightarrow H^{(\text{True})} \qquad\qquad \text{True}}$$
$$F \wedge G$$

All we need to do now is make the first premise true and the conclusion false. There are several ways we could do this. The easiest is to make G false. That simultaneously makes the first premise true and the conclusion false.

$$G^{(\text{False})} \Rightarrow F \qquad\qquad \text{True}$$
$$F \Rightarrow H^{(\text{True})} \qquad\qquad \text{True}$$
$$I^{(\text{True})} \qquad\qquad \text{True}$$
$$\underline{I^{(\text{True})} \Rightarrow H^{(\text{True})} \qquad\qquad \text{True}}$$
$$F \wedge G^{(\text{False})} \qquad\qquad \text{False}$$

That does it! We've made all the premises true and the conclusion false. That means the argument is invalid.

Exercises   The Shortcut Method

Odd-numbered solutions begin on page 356

Test each of these argument forms for validity. If invalid, find a counter-example.

1.
$$P \Rightarrow Q$$
$$\underline{Q \Rightarrow R}$$
$$\therefore R \vee \neg P$$

2.
$$Q \vee R$$
$$\underline{P \wedge \neg R}$$
$$\therefore P \Rightarrow Q$$

3.
$$(A \vee B) \Rightarrow C$$
$$A \Leftrightarrow D$$
$$\underline{B \vee (\neg A \vee C)}$$
$$\therefore C \vee D$$

4.
$$(P \vee \neg P) \Rightarrow Q$$
$$\neg R \Rightarrow \neg P$$
$$\underline{R \wedge \neg Q}$$
$$\therefore Q$$

5. $(A \land \neg B) \lor \neg (C \Rightarrow A)$
      $C \lor \neg A$
      $\neg A \Rightarrow B$
      $B \lor (A \Rightarrow C)$
      _____
      $\therefore \neg A$

6. $Q \Rightarrow P$
      $(R \lor S) \lor W$
      $U \Leftrightarrow \neg Q$
      $(R \land U) \Rightarrow P$
      $W \Rightarrow (R \lor P)$
      _____
      $\therefore (\neg P \land W) \Rightarrow (P \lor \neg S)$

Formalize the following arguments and test for validity.

7. If Sally does her homework, people call Sally a wimp. However, nobody calls Sally a wimp (after all, she wrestles sharks, bears, and 'gators with her bare hands in her free time). Therefore, Sally doesn't do her homework.

8. If I don't litter the campus with gum wrappers, someone else will. It is a campus disgrace if someone else litters the campus with gum wrappers. Therefore, if there is no campus disgrace, I litter the campus with gum wrappers.

9. If I am a vegetarian, I do not eat meat. I dine at vegetarian restaurants unless I dine at steakhouses. But vegetarian food is expensive and I dine at steakhouses. So, I am not a vegetarian.

10. My prom dress will look good only if I wear Prada. Prada is not cheap and if I wear Prada then either I am rich or my parents are rich. My parents are not rich, but my prom date is. Therefore, I wear Prada for my prom.

11. **The family reunion**

There's a popular kind of puzzle known as a "logic puzzle." In a logic puzzle you're given a number of categories and a number of items in each category that have to be matched to each other. You're given a series of clues to help. The following is a fairly simple logic puzzle. There are two more on the web. The diagram is to help with the bookkeeping.

You belong to a large family – so large that you have trouble keeping the family members straight. To be honest, you don't care much for some of them and the rest don't care much for you. The problem is, there is going to be a family reunion next week and you want to avoid trouble.

Your mother tells you that among the guests are Edgar, Edwin, Eduardo, Edsel, and "Crazy" Eddie. You are not eager to see any of these characters. One, for example, didn't invite you to his wedding. You don't recall which one of them it was, however, except that it wasn't your nephew. Another tried to borrow $1000 from you last year. Yet another is a cousin or stepcousin you haven't met but who is always being favorably compared to you. He is at Harvard and seems to get all A's.

Then there is somebody, either Edwin or Edsel, who is mad at you because you got him mixed up with Edsel or Edwin. Also, there is the one you disapprove of because he's living with this ex-nun (you aren't Catholic–you aren't even very religious – but you are something of a snob and kind of intolerant as well).

Altogether, there is a nephew, an uncle, a cousin, a stepcousin, and then someone whose relation to you no one wants to discuss. This is the one, in fact, who tried to borrow the money.

Edwin, you now recall, is somebody you dislike, which means that he's either the one who didn't invite you to his wedding or the one at Harvard.

The stepcousin is either Edgar or Edsel. Crazy Eddie, however, is your uncle, and Eduardo is your nephew.

Who are the others, and how do you feel about them?

The family reunion worksheet

	wedding	$1000	Harvard	mixed-up	ex-nun	nephew	uncle	cousin	stepcousin	?
Edgar										
Edwin										
Eduardo										
Edsel										
Crazy Eddie										
nephew										
uncle										
cousin										
stepcousin										
?										

Name	Relation	Ugly Incident
Edgar		
Edwin		
Eduardo		
Edsel		
Crazy Eddie		

Reflectivity is an important tool in computer science. Programmers write "procedures" to accomplish tasks. Sometimes a procedure will actually use itself. Here's an example.

Suppose that we want a procedure that will take a set of numbers and find the largest number in the set. Imagine that we can compare two numbers easily but we have to write a procedure if we have more than two. Let's call the procedure (which we haven't written yet) BIG. When it's written and we have a set, we can give the set to BIG and it will tell us the largest number in the set.

Okay then, here's a rough draft of BIG:

1. Input the set.
2. If the set has only one number in it, output that number and quit.
3. If the set has two numbers in it, output the larger number and quit.

(Continued on next page)

> 4. If the set has more than two numbers in it, break the set up into two smaller sets. Give each of the smaller sets to BIG. BIG will tell us the largest number in each set. Compare those two numbers. Output the larger number and quit.
>
> How does this look? It's weird! What is BIG anyway? It looks like you have to know what BIG is in order to know what BIG is! Is this the sort of reflectivity that is like the endless mirrors (it will never end) or is it like Russian Dolls?   [To be continued!]

5.3   Local and Global

People who like this sort of thing will find this the sort of thing they like. (Abraham Lincoln)

Consider the statement G, where G represents "The president of the United States is a man." Then G is a true statement.

Now consider the statement, $H \Rightarrow H$. This is also true (check the truth table – it's true on every line). But there's a difference between G and $H \Rightarrow H$. G is a fact about the world. It happens to be true. If you didn't know what G represented, you would have no idea about its truth value. If the world were different, G might be false.

But $H \Rightarrow H$ is true no matter what H represents. The truth of $H \Rightarrow H$ is a logical truth. We don't need to know anything about the world to know that $H \Rightarrow H$ is true. A statement like this, a statement that is true under all circumstances, is called a **tautology**. Another example is $A \vee \neg A$. If we look at its truth table,

A	$A \vee \neg A$
T	T
F	T

we see that $A \vee \neg A$ is never false. This tautology is called the **Law of the Excluded Middle**.

We say that "tautology" is a global term and "true" is a local term. We're calling a term local if it has to do with the world, with the facts of the case. We're calling a term global if it expresses a logical property, if it transcends the world. (The universe may seem big to you, but to a logician, it's all local!)

This section introduces a number of important global (i.e. logical) concepts. We should point out that we've already met a most important global term: "valid." To say that the argument

$$P \vee Q$$
$$\underline{Q \Rightarrow P}$$
$$\therefore P$$

is valid is to say that no matter what P and Q represent and no matter what state the world is in, if the premises are true, the conclusion is true.

Here are a collection of important global terms:

If a wff is false on every line of its truth table we say it's a **contradiction**.

If a wff is true on at least one line of its truth table we say it's **consistent**.

If a wff is true on at least one line of its truth table and also false on at least one line we say it's **contingent**.

If two wffs have the same truth value on every line of their joint truth table then we say they are **equivalent**.

If on every line of their joint truth table wff $\mathcal{B}$ is true whenever $\mathcal{A}$ is true, then we say $\mathcal{A}$ **implies** $\mathcal{B}$.

If several wffs are simultaneously true on at least one line of their joint truth table we say they are **mutually consistent**, otherwise they are **mutually inconsistent**.

For example, consider the following wffs:

$$P \Rightarrow \neg Q \quad P \wedge \neg Q \quad Q \Rightarrow \neg P \quad P \vee \neg P \quad Q \wedge \neg Q \quad P \Leftrightarrow Q$$

If we look at the joint truth table,

	P	Q	$P \Rightarrow \neg Q$	$P \wedge \neg Q$	$Q \Rightarrow \neg P$	$P \vee \neg P$	$Q \wedge \neg Q$	$P \Leftrightarrow Q$
1.	T	T	F	F	F	T	F	T
2.	T	F	T	T	T	T	F	F
3.	F	T	T	F	T	T	F	F
4.	F	F	T	F	T	T	F	T

We see that $Q \wedge \neg Q$ is the only contradiction; $P \vee \neg P$ is the only tautology; all the wffs except $Q \wedge \neg Q$ are consistent; and all the wffs except $Q \wedge \neg Q$ and $P \vee \neg P$ are contingent. We also see that $P \Rightarrow \neg Q$ and $Q \Rightarrow \neg P$ are equivalent, that $P \wedge \neg Q$ implies them both, and that all wffs imply $P \vee \neg P$. The fact that all wffs imply $P \vee \neg P$ is significant. If you think about the definition of implication, you will see that every wff implies every tautology, and that every contradiction implies every wff. (This latter principle is called "explosion" (see p. 71) and we'll return to it later.)

The truth tables also tell us that $P \Leftrightarrow Q$, $Q \Rightarrow \neg P$, and $P \vee \neg P$ are mutually consistent, while $P \wedge \neg Q$ and $P \Leftrightarrow Q$ are mutually inconsistent. Here's another way to view mutual consistency: Statements are mutually consistent iff their joint conjunction, as a single wff, is consistent.

Finally, we observe that the property of being a valid argument can be rephrased in terms of the other global properties:

> An argument is valid iff the conjunction of the premises implies the conclusion.

Similarly, we can say:

> An argument is invalid iff the premises and the negation of the conclusion are mutually consistent.

Exercises   Local and Global

Odd-numbered
solutions
begin on page 357

For each of the wffs below, decide if it is consistent, contingent, a contradiction, and/or a tautology (some will have more than one of these properties):

1. $C \Rightarrow C$
2. $C \vee D$
3. $D \vee \neg D$
4. $D \Rightarrow (C \Rightarrow D)$
5. $D \Rightarrow (D \Rightarrow C)$
6. $C \Rightarrow (C \Rightarrow D)$
7. $C \wedge \neg(D \Rightarrow C)$
8. $(C \wedge D) \vee (D \Rightarrow C)$
9. $\neg D \Leftrightarrow (C \wedge \neg C)$
10. $D \vee ((C \Rightarrow D) \wedge (\neg D \Rightarrow C))$

The following statements are all about schools. Here is some partial information:

A is true at Sophist College
B is false at Stoic University
C is consistent (i.e. it's true at some school)
D is contingent
E is a contradiction
F implies B

For each of the following statements respond **Y** if the statement is correct, **N** if the statement is incorrect, or **I** if there is not enough information to decide whether or not it is correct.

11. A is true at Stoic U.
12. B is consistent.
13. C is contingent.
14. D is consistent.
15. E implies A.
16. F is a tautology.
17. G implies $\neg E$.
18. A is consistent.
19. $B \Rightarrow E$ is true at Stoic U.
20. C implies E.
21. $D \Rightarrow A$ is true at Sophist College.
22. E implies B.
23. F and B are equivalent.
24. G, C, and E are mutually consistent.

Let's give a set to BIG (see p. 108) and see what happens. We'll give it the set {19, 128, −34, 209, 62}. BIG first sees that the set is more than two elements and breaks it up into two sets, say, {19, 128} and {−34, 209, 62}. BIG then sends these two sets to BIG! What does BIG do? BIG can handle the first, but it has to break the second set up into two smaller sets, say {−34, 209} and {62}. Here's the picture of the sets being sent to BIG.

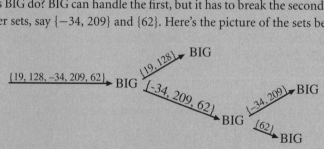

And here's what BIG sends back.

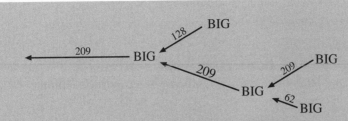

It works!

This programming technique is called **recursion**. You can see the similarity to recursive definitions. But recursion is dangerous. You might write a procedure that gets into an infinite loop. For example, suppose a procedure LOOP takes a number and gives it to LOOP. That procedure will never end, it will keep sending the number to itself forever!

5.4   More on Trees

The Symboles serve only to make men go faster about, as greater Winde to a Winde Mill. (Thomas Hobbes)

We want to introduce two simple ideas in this section, ideas that trees can help to explain. The first is the concept of **main connective**. Every wff of Sentential has a main connective. This is the connective at the top of the syntactic tree.

Example

$((\neg P \vee Q) \Rightarrow (Q \wedge P))$

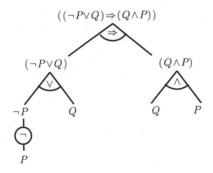

We analyzed this in the first section. The main connective is $\Rightarrow$.

We classify a wff in terms of its main connective. Note that each type of wff corresponds to a clause in the recursive definition.

Classifying Basic Sentential	
Main connective	**Clause in recursive definition**
negation	clause 2, part a
conjunction	clause 2, part b
disjunction	clause 2, part c
conditional	clause 2, part d
biconditional	clause 2, part e
basic (no connective)	clause 1

We can apply the same classification to English sentences and it's useful for translating from English to Basic Sentential.

Example

Classify "Either both Marty and Melanie go to the party or else just Samantha will go to the party."

This has an "and" in it and an "or". Is it a conjunction or a disjunction? A little thought and the fact that the sentence begins with "Either" helps us realize the sentence is a disjunction. A diagram for the sentence looks like this:

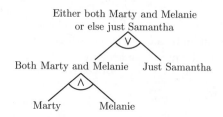

And the diagram of a formalization of the sentence in Basic Sentential looks like this:

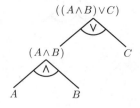

And the formalization itself is

$$((A \land B) \lor C).$$

This is pretty simple because Sentential is pretty simple. When we get to Predicate (in a few pages) things will get complicated quickly. But the idea of main connective will be quite useful sorting things out.

The second tree-related concept is that of **scope**. The **scope** of a negation sign is the part of the wff being negated by the sign. In a syntactic tree, the scope of the negation sign is the part of the wff below the sign.

Example

$(\neg P \wedge Q)$
The scope of the negation sign is P; Q is not being negated. All there is beneath the $\neg$ in the tree is P.

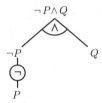

Example

$\neg(P \wedge Q)$
The scope of the negation sign is $P \wedge Q$. Beneath the $\neg$ in the tree is $P \wedge Q$.

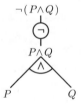

About thirty years ago in our city, Northampton, there was a store which called itself "The Little Used Book Store." What was it *really*? The name was ambiguous and the issue was scope. What was the scope of "Little"? Was the store a little store which sold used books?

The Little ((Used Book) Store)

Or was it a bookstore that, having few customers, was little used?

The (Little Used) (Book Store)

Or are there other possibilities?

Exercises   More on Trees

Odd-numbered
solutions
begin on page 357

Classify the following wffs according to main connective:

1. $(A \wedge B)$
2. $(\neg P \Rightarrow Q)$
3. $(C \vee (D \wedge \neg E))$
4. $((Q \Leftrightarrow R) \wedge (S \vee Q))$
5. $(\neg(S \Rightarrow P) \Rightarrow (Q \wedge S))$
6. $((A \vee B) \Leftrightarrow C)$

Classify the following English sentences and then translate them into Basic Sentential:

7. I like John Donne, but I also like T.S. Eliot.
8. If I don't go to the circus, I won't have nightmares about clowns.   [sjm]
9. I won't be late if and only if I don't oversleep and don't misremember which building the class is in. [sib]
10. Hester's hamster dances if and only if she plays a special song on her lute and skips merrily around the room.
11. I will only go back to work if Juniper promises not to hide fish under the chair in my cubicle.
12. Either I will go to the laboratory and set the monkeys free or I will not go to the laboratory and instead play outside by my little house on the prairie.

The connective $\uparrow$ is called the "Sheffer stroke" after the logician, Henry Sheffer. Here is its truth table:

P	Q	$P \uparrow Q$
T	T	F
T	F	T
F	T	T
F	F	T

13. Find the truth table of $P \uparrow (Q \uparrow P)$.
14. Find a wff that is the negation of $P \uparrow Q$.
15. Let P be: "Pigs have wings" and let Q be: "George is a chiropodist." Translate $P \uparrow Q$ into English.
16. Is this argument valid or invalid:

$$P$$
$$\underline{P \uparrow Q}$$
$$\therefore \neg Q$$

17. We gave two different interpretations of "The Little Used Book Store." There are three more; find them.

The negation of $P \vee Q$ can be written in at least two ways. One is $\neg(P \vee Q)$. Another is $\neg P \wedge \neg Q$. In the first, three characters are in the scope of a negation, P, $\vee$, and Q. In the second, just two characters are in the scope of a negation, P and Q. There is something nice about reducing the number of characters being negated. In the following exercises, negate the wffs with as few characters being negated as possible.

18. $\neg P$
19. $(P \Rightarrow Q)$
20. $(P \wedge Q)$
21. $((A \vee B) \Rightarrow C)$

Warning

Just a reminder, there's a surprise examination coming. That means, you recall, that it's in this book somewhere but you won't know where it is until you turn the page and see it.

Of course, you might simply guess that it is on page 239 – and it's possible that you might guess correctly – but *guessing* is not *knowing*. What we're saying is that there's no way that you can be *sure* what page the exam is on until you actually see it.

Philosophers have traditionally worried about what constitutes "knowing". In general, however, for you to know that the exam is on, say, page 239, it must be the case that

The exam *is* on page 239.
You believe the exam is on page 239.
You have good reasons for your belief.

We're confident that you won't *know* the page of the exam until you get there!

By the way, the exam is not on page 239.

5.5 Rebutting Everything

"Shut up," he explained. (Ring Lardner)

It's time to put it all together. We can read. We can diagram, we can slam premises and shred inferences. It's time to do some damage.

There is a craft, though, to rebuttal. It's critical that your audience understand the argument you're rebutting and it's critical that they understand your rebuttal. In other words, clarity is essential. If your points are not understood, they won't register. Even if your points are just a little bit difficult to understand, you run the risk they'll be ignored. You want to make your objections easy, actually easy, to grasp.

Example

The United States has many laws and programs to force people to do what's good for them. We make people wear seat belts. We don't let them do drugs. We make them save for retirement (Social Security). We should stop this. We should stop punishing people for behavior that hurts only themselves. First of all, if there's no victim, why should there be a crime? Second, the laws seldom succeed. Minors drink alcohol. Drivers don't buckle up.

And then instead of making people more responsible, our laws encourage recklessness. People think Social Security will take care of them and they don't save. They think seat belts and air bags will protect them and they break all the speed laws.

What's next? Will the government make us exercise twice a week and brush our teeth after every meal?

First, a diagram:

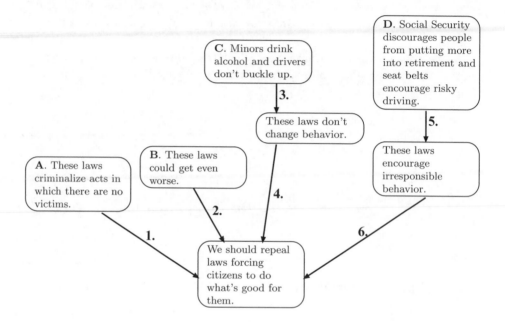

Note that we've labeled all the inferences (arrows) but not all the statements. We only labeled those statements that are premises. Altogether, these are all the points we can meaningfully attack.

Looking at **A**, we notice that all of these acts really do have victims. Taking drugs affects not only the lives of users but also the lives of their families and the lives of anyone they persuade to take drugs. Many who are injured because they aren't wearing seat belts don't have medical insurance and then the government has to pay for their hospitalization. And if fewer participate in Social Security, that system will be in trouble.

What next? Premises **C** and **D** look vulnerable. Perhaps if we do a little research, we can find evidence to the contrary.

And what about **B**? **B** seems very weak. We can point out its absurdity. It presumes that the laws are bad (since they could get "even worse"). But you can't presume what you're trying to prove!

Can we attack any inferences? We certainly can. In the case of **1**, one can argue that there is a place for laws even if there are no victims. There are laws, for example, against incest.

We can argue against **3** that **C** is only one example and in general laws do change behavior and Social Security is a good example. Virtually everyone pays Social Security and the program protects the aged from complete destitution.

Now we're ready to write.

Your points sound reasonable, but when we look at the examples that you claim support them, they no longer seem reasonable and the support vanishes. Take your statement that we have created a class of victimless crimes. I'm not sure I see the point. If an act is wrong in an absolute sense, we condemn it. Should we, for example, allow incest?

But in fact, the acts you cite do have victims – many, in fact. Taking drugs affects not only the lives of the users but also the lives of their families and the lives of anyone they persuade to take drugs. Many who are injured because they aren't wearing seat belts don't have medical insurance, so the government (that means us taxpayers) has to pay for their hospitalization. And if fewer participate in Social Security, that system will be in trouble because those who paid to Social Security in the past will not receive the benefits when they become old. We all suffer from some of these acts.

Then you give two examples of laws that have failed to change public behavior, but the examples don't hold up. Of course many minors drink, but the percentage of college-age students using alcohol dropped between 1993 and 2001 [Harvard School of Public Health]. As for seat belt use, in a particularly sensitive age bracket, ages 16 to 24, seat belt use increased between 1994 (53%) and 2004 (77%) [Child Trends Databank].

But even if there were some truth to your examples, they hardly justify the sweeping statement that all such laws fail to change behavior. Consider Social Security (which you bring up in another context). Compliance is virtually complete and the law successfully protects seniors from destitution.

And then you say that the laws discourage responsible behavior. But a brief search on the web found that savings for retirement is on the rise in such key groups as African Americans (from an average of $200/month in 2001 to $237/month in 2002) [New York Life]. And in the past decade traffic deaths have fallen [United States. Department of Transportation].

Your argument rests on three claims and in each case the examples you offer fail to provide support. What do you have left? Only an absurd claim that Congress will pass irrational, invasive laws. Since there is no evidence that it has happened in the past, I see no reason to believe it will in the future.

Are you ready to rebut Cathy's argument from Chapter One? We've diagrammed it and attacked it. Now let's write the rebuttal.

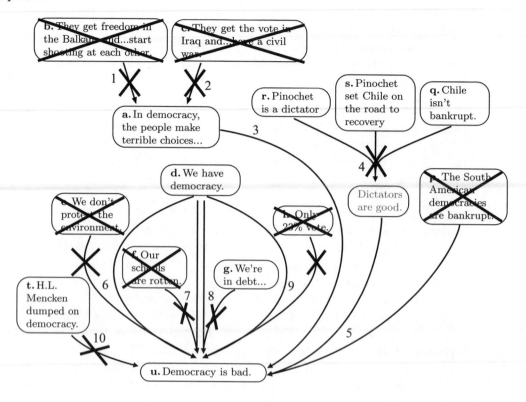

Cathy, I had a little difficulty responding to your argument. Your point appears to be that democracy is a poor form of government. To support this, you cite (1) the apparent failure of democracy to deal with problems in Central Europe, (2) the failure of our own democracy to deal with problems at home, and (3) the economic record of democracies in South America. You make a few other points that seem, frankly, to be pretty random, and I'll deal with those at the end.

On the Balkan war, you say, "They get freedom in the Balkans and the first thing they do is start shooting at each other." This isn't quite true. Following the first elections, Slovenia declared independence and was allowed to secede from Yugoslavia with a minimum of fuss. This preceded the hostilities with Croatia and Bosnia by some months.

You use this example and the example of Iraq to argue that democracy is actually dangerous. But despite the conflicts in those countries, your conclusion doesn't follow. Your examples are quite selective – you don't mention how peacefully Poland, Romania, Hungary, Czechoslovakia, Bulgaria, Latvia, Lithuania, and Estonia all took to democracy. Democracy has bettered the lives of millions in Eastern Europe.

Now, what about democracy in the United States? Your examples of how it has failed seem flawed to me. "We don't protect the environment?" You should see how badly it was protected under dictatorships in Europe, Asia, and Africa. By contrast we have done very well indeed. We have the Clean Air Act, the Superfund Act, the

Endangered Species Act, the list goes on. We could do better, of course, but the air and water are immeasurably cleaner here today than thirty years ago.

"Our schools are rotten?" I don't think so. According to the CIA World Factbook, the US literacy rate is 99%. Our schools must be doing something right.

"We're in debt up to our eyeballs?" We are, but the debt, as a percentage of gross domestic product was worse as recently as 1992 and much, much worse following World War II. Historically, we're not in bad shape.

"Only 23% of the people vote?" You did say this, Cathy, but voting participation in presidential races is usually around 50% or higher.

Finally, on South America, most economies there are in a pretty good shape. It's been a struggle escaping from the difficulties of the state-managed economies imposed by dictatorships in the twentieth century, but most are doing pretty well. No support for slamming democracy here.

That's your three main points. Now you also argue that the United States actually isn't a democracy. I don't see how that helps your conclusion at all. Let me know if I've missed something. And then the part about our wealth and power and how we abuse it, how does that fit in?

Finally, the Mencken quote is great, but it isn't really an argument, is it? This quotation isn't an argument either, but I'm fond of it:

No one pretends that democracy is perfect or all-wise. Indeed, it has been said that democracy is the worst form of government except for all those other forms that have been tried from time to time.

Winston Churchill

Exercises   Rebutting Everything

Odd-numbered
solutions
begin on page 357

Diagram the following arguments and write rebuttal to them:

1. Sophist College needs a core curriculum. Without a core, Sophist can't be considered a first-rate liberal arts college.
    We graduate scientists who can't write a paragraph, artists who can't tell you who was president 50 years ago, and writers who are terrified of numbers. We can't be proud of such students. We have to ask ourselves: what does a Sophist degree mean? Without a core, it has no meaning. There is literally nothing you can count on a Sophist graduate to know or to be able to do. I might add that most of the colleges we respect: the Ivy League institutions, for example, have either a core or a set of distribution requirements.
    One has to look no further than my own department to see what a sorry education most of our students are getting. Enrollments in history

courses have fallen steadily since the 1960's.

There are other benefits of a core – campus climate, for example. When all students take the same course, the material becomes part of the general discourse. Everyone can discuss Shakespeare, the Civil War, and quantum mechanics. The quality of intellectual life is vastly improved.

In addition, a core can be a unifying influence. Students today are divided by departments, divided by extracurricular activities, divided by background, race, and religion. A core helps to bring students together for a common purpose, a common experience.

Montgomery Chalmers,
Department of History
Sophist College

2. A core curriculum would be a disaster for Sophist College. Fundamentally, core curricula are oppressive, stifling, and dishonest.

It is argued (I'm sure Professor Chalmers will use this argument) that there is a body of knowledge every student should know. I dispute this. If that were really true, then there would be general agreement on what this is. There is no agreement. My colleagues argue continually over what belongs in the core. Everybody seems to feel that his or her own field is the most important. In point of fact, no two people agree on a core. There is no core.

In truth, no one knows what's really true, what's really important. When there is agreement on a core, it is a pathetic thing. The courses are stuffed with each professor's favorite facts. They are bloated, unwieldy courses.

We are telling students that these courses represent the most fundamental knowledge. It is a lie. No wonder students have to be forced to take them.

This brings me to the worst part of a core curriculum: coercion. It is axiomatic that students get more out of courses they choose freely. In a core, students are compelled to take a series of courses not because they are interested in the subject, not because they are relevant to their career goals, not because they are excited by the teacher or the text, but because a faculty committee has so dictated. This is bad pedagogy. It can destroy a student's interest in learning.

One more problem with a core should be mentioned. Campus climate is a major casualty. When all students take the same course, freedom of discourse suffers. The range of experience, the range of opinion is narrowed. Everyone is reading the same dead white males. The quality of intellectual life deteriorates.

Cadbury Flake,
Department of Media Studies
Sophist College

3. The US should start supporting the tradition of afternoon tea. For one thing, it would improve our image. Places considered cultured, such as England, have afternoon tea, so if we want to be cultured, we should have tea, too. For another thing, the practice of tea time is beneficial as a national morale booster. It provides a nice break in the afternoon that enables everyone to finish off the day with energy. Many cultures and communities, such as those in Spain, Italy, Argentina, China, and Taiwan,

incorporate some sort of afternoon break, whether a siesta or an after lunch nap. These communities have far lower stress rates and suicide rates than in the US. Besides, my mother is a caffeine addict, and if she doesn't get her fix we all suffer. So any way to ensure her daily dosage is certainly good for the general well-being of the populace. Tea time is good for individual well-being, too. Health benefits of drinking tea include the prevention of kidney stones and cancer, as well as good influences on metabolism. Additionally, it is healthier to eat many small meals throughout the day, so having a tea time snack is a good idea.

4.

Comrade Cathy

The assignment was a report on the collapse of the Soviet Union.

"I hate group projects."

Dwight said this while staring at the floor. Slowly, he looked up. "Hey, I like you guys. But when we get together, I just want to party!"

Madge, Jake, and Olivia mumbled agreement. There was a gloomy silence, then Olivia said, "Group work is socialism." *She brightened.* "Hey! It's communism! Let's complain to the dean!"

"What are you pissy imperialists up to now? You got something against communism?" *Cathy strode in, her hair in a ponytail, wearing a Mao cap and a red armband.*

All thoughts of party evaporated. The group just sat there.

"C'mon," *said Cathy,* "you got a problem with state-run economies? I hope not because I'm signing up people for the revolution. It's time this country went red."

Silence. Was she joking? You never knew. You never knew.

"A communist government would eliminate all the inefficiences of the market. It would avoid the duplication caused by competition. There would be no need for middlemen. No need for ad agencies. No need for an insurance industry. We could run this country at a fraction of the cost!"

"Cathy, the Soviet Union collapsed exactly because it was so inefficient. Communism is a total failure." *Dwight looked hopefully around the room for support.*

"Times have changed, Comrade Dwight! Sure, a bunch of bureaucrats deciding what factories to open, where to send workers, etc. is open to errors, mismanagement, and corruption. But today, computers can make all the decisions! There's been a revolution in software. Computers can figure out the optimal economic structure and put it in place. It's going to be so cool."

That sounds serious, thought Jake. This woman must be stopped.

"Cathy, the American people will never stand for it." *Jake was thinking of his uncle, who stopped paying taxes when the government bailed out General Motors.* "Americans can't be pushed around!"

"Comrade, some of the most admired institutions in America are completely communist. The Army, Navy, Airforce, and Marines. They're top-down, centrally-planned organizations. American soldiers do what they're told." *Cathy beamed.* "And they beat the fascists. Yeah!!"

This worried Madge. She had just been reading about the red scare of the 1950s. Was Joe McCarthy right?

"Cathy, competition isn't inefficient, it's healthy." *It was Olivia's turn.* "That way the best products come out on top. Your computer can't choose the best-tasting mouthwash. It can't pick winners on American Idol. And it would give us all the same ring tone!"

"Comrades!" *Cathy smiled, her teeth showing.* "Either competition is bad or it's good, right? If it's bad, choose communism.

If it's good, then let a communist United States of America compete against a capitalist China! Then we can see which system is best!" And she marched out.

Rebut Cathy's argument that the United States should adopt communism.

We're back in Hilbert's hotel. Recall that the hotel has an infinite number of rooms and every room is occupied. Suppose now that an infinite number of travelers arrive, all wanting a place at the hotel.

The manager has a solution. At a count of three, all the guests step out of their rooms. The guest in room 1 moves to room 2; the guest in room 2 moves to room 4; the guest in room 3 moves to room 6, and so on. If someone was staying in room n, they move to room $2n$, that is, they double their room number.

At the end of all this maneuvering, all the odd-numbered rooms are vacant. All the new travelers can be accomodated.

5.6   Polish Logic

When all clock radios are outlawed, only outlaws will have clock radios! (Bill Griffith, *Pinhead's Progress*)

The early years of the twentieth century were a golden age of logic in Poland. Many of the greatest logicians of that era lived and worked in Poland. A great deal of current research in logic is inspired directly by their efforts. Among other things, they developed a wide range of new logical systems, many of which have important applications.

One of their accomplishments is the clever dialect of Basic Sentential devised by Jan Łukasiewicz. It has several advantages: First, it doesn't need any parentheses. Second, it's very easy to find the main connective in a wff. It's always the first character.

We're going to give you two versions of Polish: Polish Light and Real Polish. Real Polish has the additional advantage that you can type it without a special keyboard or character set.

Here is Polish Light:

Polish Light

1. Capital letters are wffs (except T and F).
2. If A and B are wffs, then so are
   $\neg A$, $\wedge AB$, $\vee AB$, $\Rightarrow AB$, and $\Leftrightarrow AB$.
3. That's all the wffs.

If you want to say $(P \wedge Q)$, you write

$$\wedge PQ.$$

No parentheses. It's sort of amazing. In Sentential we need parentheses to make the difference between these two wffs clear.

$$(P \wedge (Q \vee R)), \text{ and } ((P \wedge Q) \vee R)$$

Even allowing ourselves to relax, we must still write $P \wedge (Q \vee R)$ and $(P \wedge Q) \vee R$. How are they different in Polish Light? Let's take the diagram of the first.

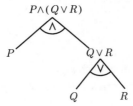

To switch to Polish, we take the same diagram and move from the roots upward. We fill in the next layer up first.

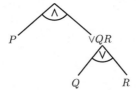

then we can fill in the top layer, putting the connective $\wedge$ in front of the two conjuncts.

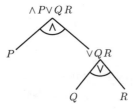

Now if we diagram the second,

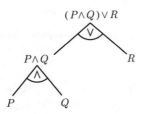

and switch to Polish,

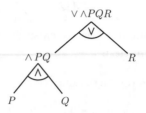

you see the difference between the wffs in Polish $\wedge P \vee QR$ and $\vee \wedge PQR$.

Example

Translate $(\neg P \vee Q) \Rightarrow (Q \wedge P)$ into Polish Light.
Solution: We can use the diagram of this sentence on page 95 and switch to Polish,

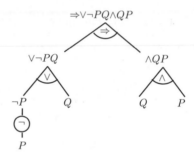

giving us $\Rightarrow\vee\neg PQ \wedge QP$. Notice that the main connective, $\Rightarrow$, comes first.

Example

Translate $\neg \wedge P \Rightarrow \neg QR$ into Basic Sentential.
Solution: Let's diagram this. We start by remembering that the main connective comes first. That's $\neg$.

$$\neg \wedge P \Rightarrow \neg Q R$$
$$\bigcirc_{\neg}$$
$$\wedge P \Rightarrow \neg Q R$$

Now consider $\wedge P \Rightarrow \neg QR$. The main connective is $\wedge$. What are the two wffs that are joined by $\wedge$? The first is clearly P. The rest, $\Rightarrow \neg QR$, must be the second.

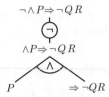

The main connective of the second is $\Rightarrow$ and that joins $\neg Q$ and R, so we have

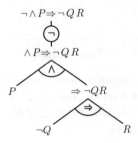

and finally

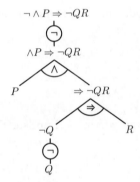

Now switching to Basic Sentential,

So that we have $\neg(P \wedge (\neg Q \Rightarrow R))$.

Real Polish uses small letters for sentence letters and capital letters to stand for the connectives. Real Polish uses these letters:

N   for negation
K   for conjunction (or Konjunction in German)
A   for disjunction (sometimes called **alternation**)
C   for conditional
E   for biconditional (sometimes called **equivalence**)

Here is Real Polish:

Real Polish

1. Lower-case letters are wffs (except t and f).
2. If A and B are wffs, then so are
   NA, KAB, AAB, CAB, and EAB.
3. That's all the wffs.

Real Polish makes sending wffs by email especially easy. Real Polish is the language of choice when a logician sends tender messages to his/her beloved.

Exercises   Polish Logic

Odd-numbered solutions begin on page 359

Which of the following formulas are wffs in Polish Light?

1. $\Rightarrow \neg QR$
2. $\Rightarrow \Rightarrow \Rightarrow PQR$
3. $PB\neg$
4. $\neg \wedge \vee \wedge PQ$
5. $\wedge \neg PQ$
6. $\vee S \Leftrightarrow PQ$

Translate the following wffs from Polish Light into Basic Sentential:

7. $\Rightarrow P \Rightarrow QR$
8. $\neg \wedge PQ$
9. $\wedge \vee PQ\neg R$
10. $\Rightarrow \wedge PQ \vee PR$
11. $\neg \vee \neg S \neg R$
12. $\Rightarrow \Rightarrow PQ \Rightarrow \neg QP$

Translate the following wffs from Basic Sentential into Polish Light:

13. $P \Rightarrow \neg Q$
14. $\neg R \vee P$
15. $P \wedge (Q \vee R)$
16. $(S \Rightarrow P) \Rightarrow R$
17. $Q \Leftrightarrow (P \wedge (R \Rightarrow S))$
18. $\neg P \wedge \neg (Q \Rightarrow \neg P)$

Reverse Polish is just like Polish light except that the connective follows the propositions instead of preceding them. For example, instead of $\vee PQ$, we write $PQ\vee$. Translate the following from Polish Light to Reverse Polish:

19. $\Rightarrow P \Rightarrow QR$
20. $\neg \wedge PQ$

21. $\Rightarrow \wedge PQ \vee PR$

22. $\neg \vee \neg S \neg R$

23‼ The *Star Wars* character Yoda speaks an interesting dialect of Galactic Basic, for example, "When nine hundred years old you reach, look as good, you will not." Is it possible that Yoda is speaking Polish English? Or reverse Polish English? Or is it something completely different?

The Digestor's Digest features a "fun edition." In the fun edition, all articles are completely false and all ads are completely true. Unfortunately, in the rush to get out the first volume of the *Digest*, the banner reading "FUN EDITION" was left off the appropriate issue. It's not clear which issue is the fun edition. There's only one fun edition.

24. Explain why Vol. 1, No. 1 (page 34) is not the fun edition.

25. Explain why Vol. 1, No. 2 (page 68) is not the fun edition.

26. What can you say about Vol. 1, No. 3 (page 92)?

27. Here is Vol. I, No. 4. Explain why the first piece must be false.

The Digestor's Digest

Vol. I, No. 4

Fast Food News

The breakfast menu at Burger Mad now features the delicious new "Crois-sausage," with the least cholesterol of all fast food sandwiches.

Fast Food News

The breakfast menu at O'Donnell's now features the delicious new "Egg O'Muffin," with the least cholesterol of all fast food sandwiches. There is an ad on this page.

Chapter Six

I believe that I can best make the relation of my ideography to ordinary language clear if I compare it to that which the microscope has to the eye. (Gottlob Frege, *Begriffsschrift*)

Logic is like a medical imaging instrument. If we focus it on a sentence or an argument, it will reveal hidden structure, together with the strengths and defects in that structure. Sentential logic is like a powerful X-ray machine. It shows us how complex sentences resolve into simple sentences. It provides us with methods to determine the validity of a variety of arguments, and provides a nice theory of validity and invalidity. Suitably extended, as we have seen, it can help us understand reasoning in a variety of situations.

But Sentential is not enough. Consider the following obviously valid argument:

> All newts are salamanders.
> Harriet is a newt.
> ∴ Harriet is an salamander.

This is how we would formalize it in Sentential:

$$P$$
$$Q$$
$$\therefore R$$

It doesn't take long to see that the formalization in Sentential is invalid. But the argument is valid. What's the problem?

The problem is that something important was lost in the translation. The two premises share the concept of "newt," but Sentential doesn't reflect this. As a logical X-ray machine, its resolution stops at the level of the clause. It's like a real X-ray machine that can see the bones, but not the soft tissue.

To analyze the newt argument effectively, we need a more sensitive instrument. We need a language that will allow us to see inside clauses, that can separate the concepts *newt* and

Sweet Reason: A Field Guide To Modern Logic, Second Edition. Jim Henle, Jay L. Garfield, Thomas Tymoczko and Emily Altreuter.
© 2012 John Wiley & Sons Inc. Published 2012 by John Wiley & Sons Inc.

salamander. And we need a language that can express the meaning of "all." Sentential can't do this. But a predicate language can. A predicate language is more like a CAT scan. It gets inside each clause to show us the inner structure.

Before we get started, let us put the work of the next two sections in a nutshell.

> Predicate is an extension of Sentential.
> Predicate is the language we showed you in Chapter One .
> Predicate is basically Sentential plus
>
> > variables $x, y, z \ldots$,
> > constants $a, b, c, \ldots$,
> > predicates like $Wx, Mxy, Pxyz, \ldots$, and
> > the quantifiers $\forall$ and $\exists$.
>
> That's it.

6.1   Predicate

All truth passes through three stages. First, it is ridiculed. Second, it is violently opposed. Third, it is accepted as being self-evident. (Arthur Schopenhauer)

The basic wffs of Sentential are simple statements.

> Harriet is a newt.
> Harriet is a salamander.
> Tom Tymoczko is a woman.
> Jay and Hillary are married.
> Oprah and Aristotle are the parents of Jim.
> Life is really, really odd.

Statements like these are represented in Sentential with sentence letters. But a statement has a subject and a predicate. To get inside statements, predicate languages have symbols for subjects and symbols for predicates.

For subjects, a predicate language has names. The names serve the same role as names in any natural language. The difference is just that in a predicate language the names will be simple, lowercase letters. In the particular predicate language introduced in Chapter One (p. 7), *a* was Jim Henle, *b* was Oprah, *c* was Tom Tymoczko, etc. We call these names **constants**. Any word or phrase that bears a simple referential connection to a thing is a **referring expression**. Names, such as "New York City" and "17," are referring expressions.

The longer you think about names and reference, the more questions will occur to you: Can we refer to something that doesn't exist? Is "Santa Claus" a real name? How do relations of reference get established? To what kind of thing does "3" refer? These are important and deep questions, questions that keep philosophers busy. If they bother you as much as they bother us, you may join the ranks of the philosophically obsessed. But if not, that's okay. You can lead a happy and productive life without worrying about reference. Others will do it for you.

For predicates, we have, well, predicates. A **predicate** in a predicate language denotes a property, that is, a relation among one or more things, objects, people. The relation of being married, for example, is a property. That's a relation involving two people. The relation of two people being the natural parents of a third person is also a property. That's a relation involving three people. The relation of being a woman is a property. That's a relation involving just one person. The language in Chapter One had symbols (M, B and W) for these relations. Predicates are very much like verbs or verb phrases— "___ is married to ___," "___ and ___ together are the parents of ___," "___ is a woman."

In a predicate language, properties or relations are represented by capital letters we call "predicate letters". We write the predicate letter first followed by the names of the objects bearing the relationship. We'll demonstrate this by working our way through the simple statements at the beginning of this section.

Example

Harriet is a newt.

We can let h represent Harriet. We can let N be the relation of being a newt. Then our formalization is

$$Nh.$$

Example

Harriet is a salamander.

We can let S be the relation of being a salamander.

$$Sh.$$

Example

Tom Tymoczko is a woman.

Jay and Hillary are married.

Oprahand Aristotle are the parents of Jim

We can use the constants and predicates introduced in Chapter One.

$$Wc, \quad Mfe \quad Pbda$$

We say a letter is a **1-place predicate** if it denotes a property of objects, like "___ is a newt, "___ is female," "___ is smaller than a breadbox," or "___ is a tall, blond ghost." In a predicate wff, a 1-place predicate letter is followed by a single constant or variable.

We say a letter is a **2-place predicate** if it denotes a relationship between two objects such as "___ is the left front tire of ___ ," "___ and ___ went to the same college," "___ is married to ___ ," or "the price of ___ is ___ ." A 2-place predicate letter is followed by two symbols, each either a constant or variable.

In general, we say a letter is an *n*-**place predicate** if it denotes a relationship among *n* objects. *P* (the parenting predicate) is a 3-place predicate. An *n*-place predicate is followed by *n* constants or variables.

A consequence of this is that while there is one language Basic Sentential, there are actually many different predicate languages. They differ only in the assortment of constants and predicate letters they have. In one predicate language, *P* is a 3-place predicate symbolizing parenthood. In another, *P* is a 1-place predicate symbolizing the property of being a retro diner. In yet another predicate language, *P* is a 5-place predicate where *Pabcde* means "On the *a*th day of *b* in the year *c*, *d* ate *e* doughnuts." And so on.

Reference and predication are standard features of English and every language spoken by human beings. It is logically crucial whether a predicate is 1-place, 2-place, or some other-place. Important philosophical disputes turn on whether a given predicate is formalized a certain way: Is "moral acceptability" a 1-place predicate of actions ("___ is morally acceptable") or is it a 2-place predicate of actions and cultures ("___ is morally acceptable in culture ___ ")? We have to take special care when symbolizing predicates.

We can say many things that apply to all predicate languages, since they differ only in their assortment of predicate letters and constants. We'll use **Predicate** to stand for all predicate languages. If we say, for example, that in Predicate, the negation of a conjunction is a disjunction (as it is in Basic Sentential), we are really saying that in all predicate languages the negation of a conjunction is a disjunction.

In our list of sentences to formalize (page 130), one is left and it's really, really odd.

"Life is really, really odd."

We know what this means, but formalizing it feels strange. We could treat "life" as a name, and formalize the sentence as *Ol*, but what exactly does "life" name? There doesn't seem to be an individual around. Or we could think of "life" as a predicate, and formalize the sentence as $\forall x(Lx \Rightarrow Ox)$ (for everything that exists, if it's a life then it's odd). But that seems weird too. What would such a predicate mean?

In cases like this, it seems best to treat the whole sentence as we would in Sentential, as a simple unit, symbolizing it as *L*. Predicate is an extention of Sentential. Every predicate language will have sentence letters as well as predicate letters. We can think of these as 0-place predicate letters. They have no blanks. To keep them straight, we'll use letters from the front of the alphabet, *A-M* for sentence letters and letters at the end, *N-Z* for predicate letters.

Predicate has one further trick. Predicate can make universal and existential statements. A **universal** statement says that everything has such and such a property, for example,

Everything is a newt.

An **existential** statement says that there is a thing with such and such a property, for example,

There is a salamander.

We use the **quantifiers** ∀ and ∃ and **variables**, x, y, ... to help us express these ideas. To say that everything is a newt, we write

$$\forall x Nx.$$

To say that there is a salamander, we write

$$\exists x Sx.$$

The choice of variable is irrelevant. Read "$\forall x Nx$" as "Everything in the universe is such that it is a newt." Read "$\forall y Ny$" the same way. Read "$\exists x Sx$" as "There is something in the universe such that it is a salamander." And read "$\exists z Sz$" the same way.

Example

What does $\exists x (Wx \land Sx)$ say?

Assuming the meanings of W and S we're using in this section, this translates as "There is something such that it is a woman and it is a salamander," or more colloquially, "There is a female salamander."

Let Pxy mean "x pats y on the head."

Example

What does $\exists x \exists y Pxy$ say?

There is someone such that there is someone such that the first pats the second on the head.

Do the people have to be different? Actually, they don't. Different variables do not necessarily signify different individuals. $\exists x \exists y Pxy$ is true even if all there is one person patting his/her own head.

Example

What does $\forall x \forall y Pxy$ say?

Everyone pats everyone on the head.

Example

What does $\forall x \exists y Pxy$ say?

For everyone there is someone he or she pats on the head.

Example

What does $\exists x \forall y Pxy$ say?

There is someone who pats everyone (including himself) on the head.

∀x∀yPxy and ∀y∀xPxy mean the same thing. So do ∃x∃yPxy and ∃y∃xPxy. But ∃x∀yPxy and ∃y∀xPxy are different.

Example

What does ∃y∀xPxy say?

There is someone whom everyone pats the head.

Example

What does *Pxy* say?

Actually, *Pxy* doesn't say anything. *x* and *y* are variables. Variables are different from constants. Variables don't refer to particular individuals. There is no way we can put a truth value on *Pxy*. Instead, we think of *Pxy* as representing a relation, the relation of ___ patting ___ on the head.

Pxy is a wff of predicate, but it is not like a sentence in English. It is a predicate without a subject. We call such expressions open sentences. Variables that are not bound by quantifiers, which we call free variables (we will get more precise about this soon) are really blanks. If we tried to put this in English it would come out,

___ pats ___ on the head.

When variables are bound, they become pronouns. With no quantifiers, they're just blanks.

Pxy	___ pats ___ on the head.
∃xPxy	There is a person who pats ___ on the head.
∀yPxy	___ pats everyone on the head.
∃x∀yPxy	There is a person who pats everyone on the head.

The first three sentences above are open; the last is closed. Open sentences are neither true nor false. Since they don't make statements, open sentences are not candidates for truth-values.

To make all this precise, we need to talk about the scope of a quantifier. The scope of a quantifier is just like the scope of the negation sign. In a syntactic tree, the scope of a quantifier is the part of the wff below the quantifier.

Example

$\forall x P x \Rightarrow Q a$

    The scope of '$\forall x$' is Px.

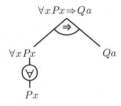

Example

$\exists x(Px \Rightarrow Qa)$

    The scope of '$\exists x$' is $Px \Rightarrow Qa$.

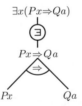

> A variable v in a wff is **bound**
>   if it's in the scope of $\exists v$ or $\forall v$.
> A variable that isn't bound is **free**.
>
> A wff is **closed**
>   if all its variables are quantified.
> A wff that isn't closed is **open**.

It's closed wffs that we really care about. They say something. They have truth-values.

Exercises   Predicate

Odd-numbered
solutions
begin on page 360

Let N be a 2-place predicate representing the relation, "__ knows __." Let X be the 1-place relation, "__ is the manager of a fast-food franchise." Let R be the 1-place relation, "__ reads romance novels." Let a name Astrid, m name Mao and d name Daryl. Translate the following into English:

1. $Rd \Rightarrow Ndm$
2. $(Xa \wedge Xm) \Rightarrow (Nam \wedge Nma)$
3. $Nam \vee Ndm$
4. $Ra \wedge Ndd$
5. $\neg \exists x \forall y Nxy$
6. $\exists x \neg Nxx \Rightarrow \forall y Ry$

Let's consider a predicate language with a 2-place predicate S which means "__ is smaller than __ " and a name, q, which stands for 17. Now, let's consider a world in which there are just three numbers: 17, 23, and 409. Decide whether the following statements are true or false:

7. $\exists y Syq$
8. $\forall x \exists y Sxy$
9. $\exists x \forall y Sxy$
10. $\exists y \forall x \neg Syx$
11. $\exists x \forall y \neg Syx$
12. $\forall y \exists x \neg Syx$

Now use the same predicate language in a different world, the world in which there is an infinite number of numbers:

1, 2, 3, ...

Decide whether the following statements are true or false:

13. $\exists y Syq$
14. $\forall x \exists y Sxy$
15. $\exists x \forall y Sxy$
16. $\exists y \forall x \neg Syx$
17. $\exists x \forall y \neg Syx$
18. $\forall y \exists x \neg Syx$

Now use the same predicate language in yet another world, the world in which there are still more numbers:

$$\dots -3, -2, -1, 0, 1, 2, 3, \dots$$

Decide whether the following statements are true or false:

19. $\exists y Syq$
20. $\forall x \exists y Sxy$
21. $\exists x \forall y Sxy$
22. $\exists y \forall x \neg Syx$
23. $\exists x \forall y \neg Syx$
24. $\forall y \exists x \neg Syx$
25. The wff $\exists x \neg Px$ has exactly the same meaning as one of the seven wffs below. Which is it?

$$\exists x Px \quad \neg \exists x Px \quad \neg \exists x \neg Px$$

$$\forall x Px \quad \neg \forall x Px \quad \forall x \neg Px \quad \neg \forall x \neg Px$$

26. The wff $\neg \exists x Px$ has exactly the same meaning as one of the seven wffs below. Which is it?

$$\exists x Px \quad \exists x \neg Px \quad \neg \exists x \neg Px$$

$$\forall x Px \quad \neg \forall x Px \quad \forall x \neg Px \quad \neg \forall x \neg Px$$

27. The wff $\neg \exists x \neg Px$ has exactly the same meaning as one of the seven wffs below. Which is it?

$$\exists x Px \quad \neg \exists x Px \quad \exists x \neg Px$$

$$\forall x Px \quad \neg \forall x Px \quad \forall x \neg Px \quad \neg \forall x \neg Px$$

28. The wff $\exists x Px$ has exactly the same meaning as one of the seven wffs below. Which is it?

$$\neg \exists x Px \quad \exists x \neg Px \quad \neg \exists x \neg Px$$

$$\forall x Px \quad \neg \forall x Px \quad \forall x \neg Px \quad \neg \forall x \neg Px$$

You can make sentences using any number of 'buffalo's and no other words (see pages 73, 101). You can do this simply by modifying a buffalo (bison) not already modified with "buffalo buffalo" – meaning "(that) bison intimidate. For example, if we start with three 'buffalo's (Bison intimidate bison) we can modify the first buffalo (bison) by saying

Bison (that) bison intimidate intimidate bison

Or we could modify the second 'buffalo'.

Bison intimidate bison (that) bison intimidate.

And we can continue.

Bison intimidate bison (that) bison (that) bison intimidate intimidate.
and so on.

6.2 English to Predicate

"The name of the song is called 'Haddocks' Eyes.'"

"Oh, that's the name of the song, is it?" Alice said, trying to feel interested.

"No, you don't understand," the Knight said, looking a little vexed. "That's what the name is called. The name really is 'The Aged Aged Man.'"

"Then I ought to have said 'That's what the song is called'?" Alice corrected herself.

"No, you oughtn't: that's quite another thing! The song is called 'Ways and Means': but that's only what it's called, you know!"

"Well, what is the song, then?" said Alice, who was by this time completely bewildered.

"I was coming to that," the Knight said. "The song really is 'A-sitting on a Gate': and the tune's my own invention." (Lewis Carroll, Through the Looking Glass)

Translating from English to Basic Sentential was not very difficult – except when the English was poorly written. That's because Sentential is a blunt instrument. It's insensitive to much of the nuance of natural language. That changes with predicate languages. Quantifiers raise the level of complexity. We now have two more types of wffs, existential and universal. We classify wffs this way:

> ## Predicate Wffs
> **by main connective**
> negation
> conjunction
> disjunction
> conditional
> biconditional
> existential
> universal
> **basic** (no connective)

Our system for translation follows the approach we used in Chapter Five.

> ### Our system
>
> 1. Identify the main connective of the clause.
> 2. Translate that connective into Predicate;
>   leave the rest in English; *unquantified pronouns not allowed.*
> 3. Apply steps 1 and 2 to any remaining clause.

Let's see how the system works. We'll use a predicate language with

N, a 1-place predicate letter for "___ is Norwegian."
P, a 1-place predicate letter for "___ is Polish."
U, a 1-place predicate letter for "___ is unfashionable."
S, a 2-place predicate letter for "___ sneers at ___ ," and
a, a constant standing for someone named Andrej.

Example

All Norwegians are unfashionable.
Step 1: The sentence is universal – the main connective is $\forall$.
Step 2: We rewrite. Now we translate just the connective.

$$\forall x \ (\ ? \ ).$$

The question mark must be replaced by text in English except that we can use x. What goes there? When we write $\forall x$, we're talking about everything in the universe. But are we going to say that everything is unfashionable? Well no, just the Norwegians. Hmm... we want to say something about *x*. When is *x* unfashionable? Well, when *x* is Norwegian. Aha. *x* is unfashionable if *x* is Norwegian. Or rearranging,

$$\forall x \text{ (if } x \text{ is Norwegian then } x \text{ is unfashionable).}$$

Good. We've performed Steps 1 and 2. Are we done? No, there is still an English clause. Step 3 tells us to apply Step 1 to that clause, that is, to "if *x* is Norwegian then *x* is unfashionable." What is the main connective? That's easy. The clause is conditional; the main connective is ⇒. Now we write:

$$\forall x \text{ (? } \Rightarrow \text{ ?).}$$

The reader has probably guessed what goes in place of the question marks:

$$\forall x \text{ (} x \text{ is Norwegian } \Rightarrow x \text{ is unfashionable).}$$

Are we done? No, there are two English clauses. We apply Step 1 to the first clause. That clause is basic; we can write it with a single predicate.

$$\forall x \text{ (} Nx \Rightarrow x \text{ is unfashionable).}$$

Then we apply Step 1 to the last clause. Again, that's basic –

$$\forall x (Nx \Rightarrow Ux)$$

We're done.

This process reflects the way a wff is put together. The structure in Predicate

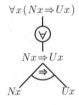

is the same as the structure in English.

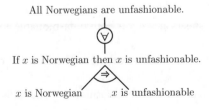

Example

Andrej sneers at a person who is Polish and unfashionable.

What is the main connective? We see the "and." Could this be a conjunction? Then we try

$$(\ ?\ \wedge\ ?\ )$$

We must put English on both sides. We try

Andrej sneers at a Pole $\wedge$ Andrej sneers at a unfashionable person.

But this doesn't sound right. And in fact, the meaning is different from the original sentence. Here, Andrej could be sneering at two different people, one a Pole, one unfashionable. In the original sentence, the Pole and the unfashionable person are the same. Okay, how about this?

Andrej sneers at a Pole $\wedge$ he is unfashionable.

Nope. There's an unquantified pronoun; that's forbidden. The "he" is there so that the person in the second clause is the person in the first clause.

But our three-step system for formalizing works well *even if you don't get it right the first time.* The sentence looked a little like a conjunction. We tried $\wedge$ and it didn't work out. That tells us we were wrong and we should try something else.

The temptation to use a pronoun is a clue. A variable would allow us to be talking about the same person on both sides of an $\wedge$. A variable means a quantifier. Could the sentence be universal? Not likely. It's just talking about Andrej, and he sneers at one person, not everyone.

Then perhaps it's existential. Indeed, isn't the sentence saying there is someone Andrej sneers at? Let's try

$$\exists x(\ ?\ ).$$

We could fill the space with

$\exists x$ (Andrej sneers at x and x is both unfashionable and Polish).

That works. That has the right meaning. Continuing, we certainly have a conjunction now. We set it up,

$$\exists x(\ ?\ \wedge\ ?\ ).$$

and fill in,

$\exists x$ (Andrej sneers at $x \wedge x$ is both unfashionable and Polish),

though there are other ways we could have done it. Now the first clause is basic,

$\exists x$ ($Sax \wedge x$ is both unfashionable and Polish), and the second is another conjunction.

$$\exists x \, (Sax \land (\quad ? \quad \land \quad ? \quad)),$$

That is,

$$\exists x \, (Sax \land (x \text{ is unfashionable} \land x \text{ is Polish})),$$

finally finishing with

$$\exists x(Sax \land (Ux \land Px)).$$

Here's what we just did:

> Andrej sneers at a person who is Polish and unfashionable.
> $\exists x$ (Andrej sneers at x and x is both unfashionable and Polish).
> $\exists x$ (Andrej sneers at $x \land x$ is both unfashionable and Polish).
> $\exists x \, (Sax \land x$ is both unfashionable and Polish).
> $\exists x \, (Sax \land (x$ is unfashionable $\land x$ is Polish)).
> $\exists x(Sax \land (Ux \land Px)).$

Heads up!

You will be tempted to skip steps in our system or skip the system altogether.

Don't!

At least not yet. Each time you use it, your understanding of Predicate and of English deepens.

Example

Every unfashionable Norwegian sneers at a Pole.

Let's start by noting that this is ambiguous in English. Every unfashionable Norwegian sneers at a Pole, but do they all sneer at the same Pole? The sentence could be continued to

> Every unfashionable Norwegian sneers at a Pole, but they don't necessarily sneer at the same one.

That makes sense. But so does

> Every unfashionable Norwegian sneers at a Pole and his name is Wojciech.

This kind of ambiguity doesn't happen in Sentential, and we must choose which meaning to formalize. (We'll do one and let you do the other in the exercises.) The most common reading of the sentence is the first one, that every unfashionable Norwegian sneers at some Pole and they may be different.

The hard part here is getting started. The key word is "Every." That signals a universal sentence:

$$\forall y \,(\quad ? \quad)$$
$$\forall y \,(\text{if } y \text{ is an unfashionable Norwegian then } y \text{ sneers at a Pole})$$
$$\forall y \,(y \text{ is an unfashionable Norwegian} \Rightarrow y \text{ sneers at a Pole})$$
$$\forall y \,((y \text{ is unfashionable} \wedge y \text{ is Norwegian}) \Rightarrow y \text{ sneers at a Pole})$$
$$\forall y \,((Uy \wedge Ny) \Rightarrow y \text{ sneers at a Pole})$$
$$\forall y \,((Uy \wedge Ny) \Rightarrow \exists z \,(z \text{ is Polish and } y \text{ sneers at } z))$$
$$\forall y \,((Uy \wedge Ny) \Rightarrow \exists z \,(z \text{ is Polish} \wedge y \text{ sneers at } z))$$

And finally,

$$\forall y((Uy \wedge Ny) \Rightarrow \exists z(Pz \wedge Syz)).$$

Exercises   English to Predicate

Odd-numbered
solutions
begin on page 360

Translate each of these sentences into Predicate Logic using the predicate language introduced in this section:

1. Some Norwegian is unfashionable.
2. Every Pole is Norwegian.
3. Someone sneers at Andrej.
4. Some Pole sneers at Andrej.
5. All Norwegians sneer at Andrej.
6. All Norwegians sneer at someone.
7. All unfashionable Norwegians sneer at a Pole. (Formalize the other meaning of this sentence – that there is one Pole whom all unfashionable Norwegians sneer at.)
8. There is someone all Norwegians sneer at.
9. Some unfashionable Pole sneers at all unfashionable Norwegians.
10. Some unfashionable Pole sneers at all unfashionable Norwegians who sneer at Andrej.

11. Not every Norwegian is unfashionable.
12. Not any Norwegian is unfashionable.

13!!! If the following is true, who is a? $\neg Fa \wedge \exists y(Fy \wedge Mya \wedge \exists z(Ryza))$ (We're using Fx: x is female, Gx: x is male, Mxy: x is married to y, and $Rxyz$: x and y begat z.) *Hint:* It helps to have read Sophocles.

"Buffalo" sentences (pp. 73, 101, and 139) can be formalized if we establish two conventions. First, that the noun "buffalo" should be interpreted as "all buffalo" (or "all bison"). Second, if there is no object to the verb "buffalo", then we interpret it as "buffalo some buffalo" (or "intimidate some bison"). So "Buffalo buffalo" is "All bison intimidate some bison". Let Bx mean that x is a buffalo (or bison). Let Ixy mean that x buffalos (or intimidates) y. Then we can express "Buffalo buffalo" as $\forall x(Bx \Rightarrow \exists y(By \wedge Ixy))$.

14. Formalize "Buffalo buffalo buffalo".
15. Formalize "Buffalo buffalo buffalo buffalo".
16. Formalize "Buffalo buffalo buffalo buffalo buffalo" where we mean "All bison, that all bison intimidate, intimidate all bison".

17. Formalize "Buffalo buffalo buffalo buffalo buffalo" where we mean "All bison intimidate all bison, that all bison intimidate".
18. Write a recursive definition for the language Buffalo. A sentence of Buffalo consists of any finite number of 'buffalo's.

> Readers:
>
> Don't forget! Somewhere in this book there's a surprise examination!

J, J and T,

Did you know you can't put the exam on the last page? When readers get to the next-to-last page, they'll know it's on the last page. It won't be a surprise.

— ed.

6.3 Reading Between the Lines

Know how to listen, and you will profit even from those who talk badly. (Plutarch)

Logic can make you a better reader, a better listener, a better writer, and a better debater. Sometimes the hardest part of listening is hearing the words not spoken. Sometimes speech is cleverest when it leaves out statements.

What's missing may be critical. It can be a necessary premise, it can be an important intermediate step. It can even be the conclusion. Logic can help to identify and clarify missing pieces. And it can help you decide what to omit.

There are two general reasons why a part might be missing from an argument. The first is quite innocent: the missing statement is obvious and understood. It might be a question of style, or it might be a question of inadvertence.

Example

Anabel says, "That glass is full of Drano! Don't drink it!"
    If we formalize the argument, all we get is

$$\frac{A}{\therefore B}$$

where A stands for "The glass is full of Drano," and B stands for "You shouldn't drink what's in the glass." That's an invalid argument. In line 2 of the truth table

			PREMISES	CONCLUSION
	A	B	A	B
1.	T	T	T	T
2.	T	F	T	F
3.	F	T	F	T
4.	F	F	F	F

the premise is true and the conclusion is false.
    But Anabel left out two obvious points. One is that Drano is poisonous and the other is that you shouldn't drink poison. Now we have

$$
\begin{array}{c}
A \\
A \Rightarrow C \\
C \Rightarrow B \\
\hline
\therefore B
\end{array}
$$

where C is "The glass is full of poison." This is valid since for no line of the truth table

				PREMISES			CONCLUSION
	A	B	C	A	$A \Rightarrow C$	$C \Rightarrow B$	B
1.	T	T	T	T	T	T	T
2.	T	T	F	T	F	T	T
3.	T	F	T	T	T	F	F
4.	T	F	F	T	F	T	F
5.	F	T	T	F	T	T	T
6.	F	T	F	F	T	T	T
7.	F	F	T	F	T	F	F
8.	F	F	F	F	T	T	F

do we have all premises true and the conclusion false.

In practice, an argument can be so casual that the conclusion itself is omitted.

Example

You are trying to decide where to take your parents for dinner. Celeste says, "Il Porcino is an upscale Italian restaurant. Your folks will like it."

Celeste has omitted a premise, that your parents have upscale Italian tastes, but she has also omitted the conclusion, that you should take your parents to Il Porcino. In other words, the stated argument is

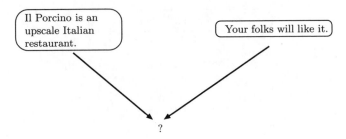

while the understood argument is

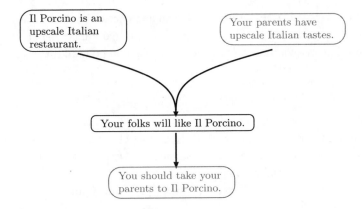

Example

Dechen replies to Celeste, "No. They prefer pizza."

Again, premises and conclusion are missing. Dechen said

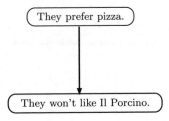

but she meant

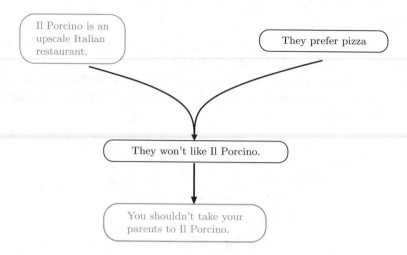

The second reason for missing statements is not so innocent. Here the speaker or writer is actually suppressing statements to mislead the audience.

Sometimes, for example, a writer or a speaker knows that one of her premises is weak and doesn't want it challenged. It might be that an inference is invalid and she doesn't want this noticed. If a premise is strategically suppressed, a poor argument might retain a veneer of soundness. This is a common tactic in advertising and in political rhetoric.

Example

An ad for Acme jeans says, "Janis was cool. She wore Acme Jeans."

You are meant to draw the conclusion, *I'd better wear Acme Jeans.* Of course that doesn't follow from the two premises. Not even close. But the two premises *are* true. So the argument, especially with the right graphic, might look pretty good if you aren't thinking too hard. But let's examine it. Here's the ad with the missing conclusion:

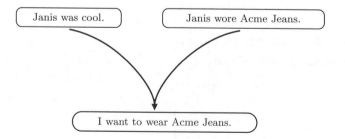

Here it is again with the suppressed statements added:

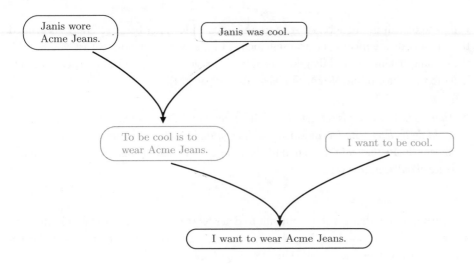

But the first inference is terrible. It's as if you saw a professor wearing a beret and concluded not only that all professors wear berets but that anyone wearing a beret is a professor.

If Acme put in the missing statement ("It's Cool to wear Acme.") the weakness would be obvious and you wouldn't be sucked in. But by cleverly suppressing it, the advertiser keeps you from bringing your critical faculties to bear. Diagramming the suppressed material can fix that, and can also keep you from a foolish purchase!

Example

Frederique is running for Congress on the Vermin Control platform. She says in a campaign speech, "We've had enough of rats in the streets. Vote for Frederique!"

There is a suppressed premise, something like, "Frederique, and only Frederique, can control the rat problem." Now, everyone has had enough of rats in the street. So the stated premise looks pretty good. And so does Frederique in her campaign poster. And that's why the ad has punch. You see a true premise. You see a tough-looking candidate. You don't explicitly notice, and so you don't examine, the suppressed premise. But once you do, you are uneasy. Explicitly stated, it invites scrutiny. And it might be implausible either that Frederique on her own can handle the rats, or if she can, that no one else can.

This is an important use of argument diagramming. A weirdly incomplete argument can often be an indication that you are paying attention only to what is stated explicitly, and that in turn means that you are missing what is most important.

Exercises   Reading Between the Lines

Odd-numbered
solutions
begin on page 360

Letters to the editor are necessarily short and often edited after being received. As printed, they frequently are missing critical statements. In the exercises below, we ask you to fill in the missing statements and diagram the intended argument. As an example, consider this letter to the editor of the *New York Times* (also on page 14):

> *Thomas L. Friedman is correct: there is a lot more that China and the European Union could do to deter both North Korea and Iran in their nuclear ambitions. But let us not underestimate the main attraction of obtaining such weapons: your enemies will think twice about attacking you.*
>
> Terry Phelps

Phelps is saying that it will be difficult to deter North Korea and Iran because they fear other countries and want nuclear weapons for defense. No strategy that doesn't alleviate their concerns will be successful. Here's the diagram:

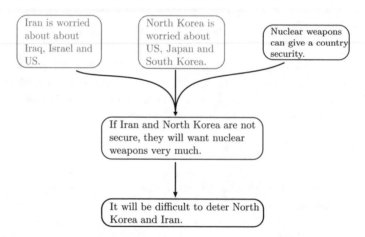

1. *In publishing, the standard gap between the hardcover and the softcover release of a book is about a year. This long wait provides incentive for many book buyers to spring for the more expensive hardcover. If the film industry were to emulate this sensible marketing strategy by establishing a one-year gap between a movie's theatrical premiere and its DVD release – instead of the current three- to six-month period – it would end up selling a lot more tickets at the multiplexes.*

   – David English, May 10, 2005

2. *Re "A No-Confidence Vote for Mr. Abbas" (editorial, May 9):*
   Clearly, Congress lacks confidence in Mahmood Abbas. But with millions of donated dollars squandered by the Palestinian Authority over the last decade, and with a new Palestinian leader who is struggling to make good on his promise to rein in terror, can we really blame Congress for being cautious about possibly wasting the taxpayers' money?

   – David Bistricer, May 9, 2005

3. *Perhaps the middle-aged can't do much to reverse the effects of decades of unhealthy living, but I've been taking a longer view. Lifestyles are passed down from generaton to generation by example.*

   I can nag my three teenagers to eat better while I pig out, or I can eat a large salad and go for a long walk.

   – George Bittlingmayer, April 17, 2005

4. *"A Talk, a Snack, a Chance at $45 or More: Cabdrivers Bond While They Wait at the Kennedy Airport Lot" (news article, April 28) states that there are often hundreds of taxis waiting in line for hours at Kennedy International Airport. Now I understand why it is so difficult to get a taxi in Manhattan.*

   – Andrew Hamilton, April 28, 2005

5. *Like the great majority of those who have become prominent conservative political and media figures since Vietnam, John R. Bolton declined to serve in combat forces back then because, he said, he "had no desire to die in a Southeast Asia rice paddy." Is there any precedent in history for an elite that has been so successful in influencing the government toward assertive military policies while largely declining to serve in combat forces themselves?*

   – Mark Rosenman, May 1, 2005

6. *I would like to counter the argument against "vacation homework."*

   First, American students spend a relatively shorter time in the classroom than their global counterparts. Second, during the school year, students are involved in a myriad of extracurricular activities, limiting their opportunity for reading great works of literature.

   Finally, a comment that I frequently hear in the fall from my English students goes roughly like this: "If you hadn't assigned 'Anna Karenina,' I would have never read it. And I loved it."

   – Elizabeth P. Ueland, June 19, 2006

7. *To make sense of the new world presented by digital book formats (Daniel Henninger's June 16 Wonder Land "John Updike Edits Kevin Kelly's 'Electronic Anthill' "), one needs to make a clear distinction between "reading" and information processing and fact-gathering. As an academic scholar and researcher, I need to find and access as much information as efficiently as possible – here digital content offers a very bright future.*

   But the automobile didn't eliminate the occasional desire to walk, nor did photography cause us to degrade the value of paintings. I see no appeal in reading "The Great Gatsby" indoors on my computer screen and gain much satisfaction in owning a beautiful leather-bound copy of a treasured literary work of art. Only one thing is certain: The future will be different and creators will innovate.

   – Michael Harrington, June 21, 2006

8.

Cathy eats meat

"Oh cool! Chickpea pizza, my favorite!" gushed Wendy as she entered the dining hall.

"Real food for real dorks," snorted Cathy, who had been in a bad mood ever since her roommate had gone vegan and flushed 17 Slim Jims down the toilet. "I'm surrounded by the dietarily challenged!"

"I'm sorry, Cathy, but I have to watch my health," Wendy replied gently. "Meat isn't good for us."

"Baloney! (Pardon my French.) If you really cared about health, you wouldn't eat all those chips and munchkins."

"Hey! Back off!" said Samantha, looking up from the table in righteous indignation. "Meat is murder!"

"That's real dumb. Are carnivores evil? If so, maybe we should extinctify lions and tigers! If eating meat is bad, there is more

sin going on in your backyard than at Burger King."

"You're just being mean, Cathy!" Kasia interjected. "You know, some people don't like meat. It's a matter of taste, and you can't argue about taste."

"Nuts. You're just the little girl who wouldn't eat her liver. You don't hate meat, this is just adolescent rebellion. Grow up!"

Cathy is rebutting an argument by Wendy, Samantha, and Kasia that they shouldn't eat meat. Diagram this argument. Explain what premises and lines of inference she attacks. Then improve the argument for vegetarianism so that it can survive Cathy's attack.

We have another thought experiment, this one devised by logician Hartley Rogers.

One memorable morning, Jay brought an infinite number of books to Jim. He brought them two at a time, placing them on Jim's desk. If you're worried about how this was done, here's what happened. Jay brought two books an hour before noon. He brought two more a half-hour before noon. He brought two more a quarter of an hour before noon. He brought two more an eighth of an hour before noon, and so on. Each interval between deliveries was half the time remaining before noon. By noon, Jay had delivered infinitely many books.

Jay always put the books in the same place, and a tower of books grew on Jim's desk. Jim dealt with this as follows. Every time Jay brought two books, Jim took the top book off the tower of books and put it on the other side of his desk. Thus, two towers of books grew. The towers were roughly the same height. They had the same number of books in each.

What did Jim's desk look like at noon?

If your answer was "Two infinitely tall piles of books!" you're right. Jim always took the book on the top of the pile where Jay placed them. Imagine that the books were numbered. Jay first brought books 1 and 2. Jim moved book 2. Then Jay brought books 3 and 4. Jim moved 4. Then Jay brought 5 and 6. Jim moved 6. At noon, there were two piles, one with all the odd-numbered books (which Jim didn't move) and one with all the even-numbered books (which Jim moved).

We can see there would be "two infinitely tall piles of books" from the choices Jim made moving books. But if he had chosen different books to move would this still be the case? The answer is in Chapter Seven.

6.4 Multi-valued Logic

> And when they were up, they were up.
> And when they were down, they were down.
> And when they were only halfway up,
> They were neither up nor down.

(Nursery rhyme)

We can invent new logics without changing the grammar; we can add new truth values. This is a complex change. It forces us to rewrite our truth tables. Doing this gives us some surprising insights into our logical operators, and leads us to ask interesting questions.

We'll start with one new truth value. To make life easy for ourselves, we'll replace T and F with the numerals 1 and 0. This will allow us to introduce new truth values in an obvious order. Let's start with exactly one truth value between true and false, 1/2. We could think of 1/2 as "neither true nor false". You can imagine reasons why some sentences might have "neither" as a truth value (you can also imagine counter-arguments to these claims, of course). Perhaps a sentence like "It will rain in Topeka on Christmas 3056" is neither true nor false, since whatever makes them true or false has not happened yet. Perhaps a statement like "Tom is bald" is neither true nor false when Tom has a tiny bit of hair, but not enough to count as hairy. Perhaps some paradoxical sentences are neither true nor false.

And here's a different way to think about the third value. Think of 1/2 as signifying that you have only partial information. So, 1 might be assigned to a sentence you know to be true, 0 to a sentence you know to be false, and 1/2 to a sentence about which you just don't know. We advise you to keep these interpretations in mind as we think about more and more truth values. They are not by any means the only way to think about this extension of Basic Sentential, but they're useful.

What would the truth tables be for 3-valued Sentential? Let's first think about conjunction. When we conjoin two wffs in Basic Sentential, the truth value of the conjunction is always the **minimum** of the two truth values (for example, $1 \wedge 0$ is 0, the smaller of 1 and 0). When I tell you "A and B," my statement is only as true as the falsest conjunct. Following this principle in three-valued Basic Sentential, conjunction would look like this:

A	B	$A \wedge B$
1	1	1
1	1/2	1/2
1	0	0
1/2	1	1/2
1/2	1/2	1/2
1/2	0	0
0	1	0
0	1/2	0
0	0	0

Disjunction, on the other hand, always has the **maximum** truth value of the two disjuncts (for example, $1 \vee 0$ is 1, the larger of 1 and 0). Following this principle in three-valued Basic Sentential, disjunction has the following truth table:

A	B	$A \vee B$
1	1	1
1	1/2	1
1	0	1
1/2	1	1
1/2	1/2	1/2
1/2	0	1/2
0	1	1
0	1/2	1/2
0	0	0

Now let's take a first look at negation. The easiest way to think about negation is this: It reverses truth values – it flips the truth table for a wff upside down. The truth value of the negation of a wff is then, in an intuitive sense, the opposite of that of the wff itself. Here is a 3-valued truth table that reflects that intuition. We'll call this **flip** negation.

A	$\neg A$
1	0
1/2	1/2
0	1

That certainly agrees with the interpretation of 1/2 as "don't know." If we don't know whether A is true or false, then we don't know whether $\neg A$ is true or false.

But there's another way to approach this. We could think about the negation of A as meaning "A is not true". To take negation this way is to think that the negation of any sentence that has anything other than 1 as its truth value is 1. We'll call this **denial negation** and we'll symbolize it as

("thumbs down"). The truth table for negation taken this way looks like this:

A	$⧖ A$
1	0
1/2	1
0	1

Denial negation, unlike flip negation, never has a fractional value.

Things get especially interesting when we talk about the conditional (this is always the case in logic). It's not immediately clear how to extend the Basic Sentential conditional into the many-valued world. Here's one idea. Remember that (in Basic Sentential) $A \Rightarrow B$ is logically equivalent to $\neg A \vee B$. (If you do not see this, make a 2-valued truth table and convince yourself.) We can use this idea to design a truth table for the 3-valued Basic conditional. We'll use flip negation.

A	B	$\neg A$	$\vee$	B	$A \Rightarrow B$
1	1	0	**1**	1	1
1	1/2	0	**1/2**	1/2	1/2
1	0	0	**0**	0	0
1/2	1	1/2	**1**	1	1
1/2	1/2	1/2	**1/2**	1/2	1/2
1/2	0	1/2	**1/2**	0	1/2
0	1	1	**1**	1	1
0	1/2	1	**1**	1/2	1
0	0	1	**1**	0	1

There are nice things about this conditional. Where the truth values of A and B are 1 or 0, it behaves exactly like the Basic Sentential conditional, and that is what we would hope, since we are, after all, extending Basic Sentential, not leaving it behind. But what happens when we have indeterminate truth values in the neighborhood? If we know A is true (1), but we're not sure about B (1/2), then we can't be sure that B follows from A. The truth value of the conditional reflects this (1/2). Similarly, if we don't have any information at all about A (1/2) and we know that B is false (0), then we can't be sure about $A \Rightarrow B$, so it's also 1/2. And if we don't know about either A or B (both are 1/2), it makes sense to say that we don't know about $A \Rightarrow B$. This table gives us the expected answer, 1/2.

There are other possibilities for the conditional, but let's move to four-valued logic to see them more clearly. We can have a four-valued logic with values 1, 2/3, 1/3 and 0. We can interpret 2/3 as **probably true** and 1/3 as **probably false**. (There are other ways to think about four-valued systems, but we aren't going there now.)

The truth tables for conjunction and disjunction, as before, use minimum and maximum values.

A	B	A ∧ B
1	1	1
1	2/3	2/3
1	1/3	1/3
1	0	0
2/3	1	2/3
2/3	2/3	2/3
2/3	1/3	1/3
2/3	0	0
1/3	1	1/3
1/3	2/3	1/3
1/3	1/3	1/3
1/3	0	0
0	1	0
0	2/3	0
0	1/3	0
0	0	0

A	B	A ∨ B
1	1	1
1	2/3	1
1	1/3	1
1	0	1
2/3	1	1
2/3	2/3	2/3
2/3	1/3	2/3
2/3	0	2/3
1/3	1	1
1/3	2/3	2/3
1/3	1/3	1/3
1/3	0	1/3
0	1	1
0	2/3	2/3
0	1/3	1/3
0	0	0

It's clear what flip negation would look like.

A	¬A
1	0
2/3	1/3
1/3	2/3
0	1

But denial negation, with no fractional truth values, offers a number of possibilities. We should assign the denial negation of A the value 0 if A is "true enough" and 1 if it isn't. Then we have to ask ourselves the question: "What values are true enough to count as sort of true?" Logicians call the values that we choose to consider true enough "designated values." Having four truth values invites us to consider three standards of designation. We might be in a situation where it's really important to accept only what we really, really know to be true. This would be the case, say, if we were jurors in a criminal trial where the standard of truth is "proof beyond a reasonable doubt." In that case, we'd only designate the value 1.

$$\text{designated values} = \{1\}$$

But we might be jurors in a civil trial, where the standard of proof is just "likelihood based on the preponderance of evidence." In that case, we might designate both 1 and 2/3.

$$\text{designated values} = \{1, 2/3\}$$

That would mean that we would endorse in our reasoning sentences that have either of these values. Finally, if we were teaching first-graders, we might be inclined to encourage any answer that wasn't totally wrong.

$$\text{designated values} = \{1, 2/3, 1/3\}$$

Different situations call for different standards of designation.

Now denial negation works like this:

P	$\lnot P$
true enough	0
not true enough	1

As before, a statement is "true enough" if it has one of the designated values. Suppose, for instance, that we are jurors in a civil trial. 1 and 2/3 are designated. I say that the CEO defrauded the workers. You deny it. You are saying that it is not the case that my statement has a designated value. With these designated values, the truth table for $\lnot$ looks like this:

A	$\lnot A$
1	0
2/3	0
1/3	1
0	1

If we designate only 1 it looks like this:

A	$\lnot A$
1	0
2/3	1
1/3	1
0	1

And if we designate every value except 0 it looks like this:

A	$\lnot A$
1	0
2/3	0
1/3	0
0	1

This shows that the English word "not" is ambiguous. We don't notice that ambiguity when we only care about two truth values. But logic should guide us not only in the light of day where everything is either clearly true or clearly false, but also in the murky night of real life, when things are often in-between. To negotiate that twilight world we need more 'no's than just a simple reversal. Now, pause for a moment. What part of 'no' don't you understand?

And of course the conditional continues to be interesting. On one reading, it's just as we had it before. $A \Rightarrow B$ is equivalent to $\neg A \lor B$. We've seen why that makes sense. It reflects the amount of information we have about B given A. Call this **information implication**. Its truth table looks like this:

A	B	$\neg A$	$\lor$	B	$A \Rightarrow B$
1	1	0	1	1	1
1	2/3	0	2/3	2/3	2/3
1	1/3	0	1/3	1/3	1/3
1	0	0	0	0	0
2/3	1	1/3	1	1	1
2/3	2/3	1/3	2/3	2/3	2/3
2/3	1/3	1/3	1/3	1/3	1/3
2/3	0	1/3	1/3	0	1/3
1/3	1	2/3	1	1	1
1/3	2/3	2/3	2/3	2/3	2/3
1/3	1/3	2/3	2/3	1/3	2/3
1/3	0	2/3	2/3	0	2/3
0	1	1	1	1	1
0	2/3	1	1	2/3	1
0	1/3	1	1	1/3	1
0	0	1	1	0	1

But there's another natural extension of the conditional from Basic Sentential. In Basic Sentential, a conditional is true whenever the truth value of the consequent is at least as great as that of the antecedent. The conditional is just a guarantee that in reasoning we are never going from the truer to the falser. On this reading, when the truth value of A is higher than that of B, then the conditional $A \Rightarrow B$ is leading us down the road to the hell of falsehood, and we should reject it. But if the conditional is not proven guilty, it is presumed innocent. We call this **material implication** (and we use a new arrow for it, $\rightsquigarrow$). Its truth table in four values would look like this.

A	B	A ⤳ B
1	1	1
1	2/3	0
1	1/3	0
1	0	0
2/3	1	1
2/3	2/3	1
2/3	1/3	0
2/3	0	0
1/3	1	1
1/3	2/3	1
1/3	1/3	1
1/3	0	0
0	1	1
0	2/3	1
0	1/3	1
0	0	1

Again, sometimes when we say "If… then…" in English, we might have something more like information implication in mind; sometimes we might have something more like material implication in mind. As we will see later (Chapter Ten), there are still more ways to understand "if… then…" There is no hard and fast rule about what we mean when. Logic allows us to see this ambiguity and can guide us to proper principles of reasoning in each case.

Summing up

Three-valued logic was the invention of the Polish mathematician, Jan Łukasiewicz (1920). The American logician, Emil Post, explored logics with more than three values (1921). The logics here are not the only kinds of three- and four-valued logics. But they are some of the more important ones. Each of these extensions opens the way to a whole area of the subject of logic, and you may someday explore these areas in much greater depth. For now, here are some important things to remember: Logic is not a single system of reasoning. It is a whole world of systems. Logic is not finished. New systems are invented and explored all the time. Truth and falsity do not exhaust the possible evaluations of sentences. There are many other options. Basic Sentential is a useful starting point, but it is only a small corner of the world of logic.

Exercises   Multi-valued Logic

Odd-numbered
solutions
begin on page 361

Determine the values of the following wffs in four-valued logic. For problems using $\vec{?}$, consider 1 and 2/3 as designated.

P is 1
Q is 2/3
R is 1/3
S is 0

1. $(R \vee P) \vee Q$
2. $\neg(S \Rightarrow P)$
3. $\vec{?} \, Q \wedge (R \rightsquigarrow P)$
4. $\neg(\vec{?} \, S \wedge Q) \wedge (P \vee R)$
5. $(Q \wedge S) \rightsquigarrow R$
6. $((Q \Rightarrow S) \rightsquigarrow P) \Rightarrow R$
7. $(Q \rightsquigarrow (R \wedge \vec{?} \, S)) \Rightarrow ((Q \vee \neg R) \wedge P)$
8. $(R \Rightarrow Q) \rightsquigarrow ((R \rightsquigarrow P) \Rightarrow \neg S)$

In the following five situations, a world is described in which there are implicitly many truth values. In each decide whether there is (implicitly) a set of designated truth values. If there is, what are the designated values?

9. The professor handed out the exam and emphasized that there would be no partial credit.
10. The professor handed out the exam and emphasized that there would be partial credit.
11. Tom was on his way to meet two friends at the park. He turned on the weather channel, and saw that there was a thirty percent chance of rain that afternoon. He retrieved his umbrella, always wanting to be prepared if there was even the smallest chance of precipitation, and drove to meet his friends.

12. Jay was listening to his radio on the way to the park. He listened to the quarter-hour weather update, and learned that there was a thirty percent chance of rain in the next few hours. He had an umbrella in the back seat, but decided not to take it because there was a greater chance that it would not rain, and he didn't want to have to carry the umbrella unnecessarily.

13. Jim was watching TV and eating lunch when he saw that there was a thirty percent chance of rain. Jim never liked to be overprepared, but he wanted to be protected in case that it rained that afternoon when he was scheduled to meet Jay. His solution was to go to the store and purchase a mini-umbrella that was thirty percent of the size of a normal umbrella, because that way he was prepared for rain, without having to lug around a large umbrella for precipitation that probably would not appear.

14. The *Digestor's Digest* has a special "Special Three-Valued Edition" this chapter (it's not the fun edition). As usual, there are ads and articles. In addition, there may be government bulletins. No sentence of a government bulletin is either true or false (in other words, the truth value of a government bulletin is 1/2, not 0 or 1). If a statement $\mathcal{A}$ has truth value 1/2, then the statements "$\mathcal{A}$ is true" and "$\mathcal{A}$ is false" both have truth value 1/2, while the statment "$\mathcal{A}$ is neither true nor false" has truth value 1. What do you make of this edition?

The Digestor's Digest

Special Three-Valued Edition!
Vol. I, No. 5

Report from HUD

We urge that the public read the report from the Securities and Exchange Commission (SEC); it is timely, relevant, and true.

Report from SEC

We urge that the public ignore the report from the Department of Housing and Urban Development (HUD); it is ill-conceived, irrelevant, and false.

Report from FTC

We recommend that all members of the public interested in tax policy read the article in this edition on HUD and ignore the ad about the SEC.

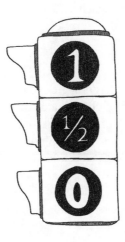

Chapter Seven

7.1 Universes

listen; there's a hell of a good universe next door: let's go.

(e.e. cummings)

Universes are essential to predicate logic. They determine truth.

We're all familiar with one universe; we might call it *the* universe—that is, the place where we live. But to logicians, reality is just one of many options. We invent universes all the time. You can too.

Let's backtrack for a moment and look at what we need to determine a truth value in Sentential. To decide the truth value of

$$(P \Leftrightarrow R) \vee (Q \wedge (P \Rightarrow R)),$$

all we need to know is the truth values of P, Q, and R. That's what a "universe" is in Sentential. It's one line of a truth table.

What about Predicate? Let's say we have in our predicate language two constant symbols, b and h, a 1-place predicate letter V, and a 2-place predicate letter U. What do we need to decide the truth value of

$$\forall x V x?$$

This wff says that every element has property V. What does "every element" mean? We need to have a definite collection of objects of discussion. We could be talking about all mammals. We could be talking about all birds of North America beginning with the letter 's'. We could be talking about the students at Sophist College. Whatever we're talking about, the universe of discourse must be defined before we can proceed.

Sweet Reason: A Field Guide To Modern Logic, Second Edition. Jim Henle, Jay L. Garfield, Thomas Tymoczko and Emily Altreuter.
© 2012 John Wiley & Sons Inc. Published 2012 by John Wiley & Sons Inc.

We also need to know the meaning of *V* in this language. Let's say our set is the set of students at Sophist College. *V* could mean "___ is a junior," or "___ is a Logic major," or "___ has fewer than 3 heads." Once we know our universe of discourse and the meaning of *V* we can evaluate the truth of ∀x*Vx*.

What do we need to decide the truth value of

Ubh?

We need to know what the relation *U* is. And we need to know who or what *b* and *h* are. Essentially, that's all we need: the elements we are discussing and the meaning of predicates and constants. Note that the requirements for a universe depend on the make-up of the predicate language (which constants and predicate letters there are). In that sense, universes are linked to specific languages.

A **universe** for a predicate language is

a. A **domain**, a set of objects over which we interpret quantifiers.
b. Interpretations for all the predicate letters and constants in the language.

We introduced three universes in the last chapter, in the exercises for section 6.1. We used a predicate language that had a 2-place predicate *S* and a constant *q*. All three universes had the same interpretations for this predicate and constant: *S* meant "___ is smaller than ___ " and *q* represented the number 17. The difference in the universes was that in the first universe the domain was

$$\{17,\ 23,\ 409\}.$$

In the second universe the domain was

$$\{1,\ 2,\ 3,\ \ldots\}.$$

In the third universe the domain was

$$\{\ldots -3,\ -2,\ -1,\ 0,\ 1,\ 2,\ 3,\ldots\}.$$

Example

∀x∃y*Sxy*

This says that for every number (*x*) there is a number (*y*) such that the first number is less than the second. More succinctly, "for every number there is a larger number." This is true in the second and third universes but false in the first, where there is no number larger than 409.

Example

$\exists x \forall y \neg Syx$

   This says that there is a number (x) such that every number (y) is not less than it. That is, there is a number such that all numbers are greater than or equal to it. More succinctly, there is a smallest number. This is true in the first two universes and false in the third.

Recall these global properties of wffs:

tautology	true in all circumstances.
contradiction	false in all circumstances.
consistent	true in at least one circumstance.
contingent	true in at least one circumstance and false in at least one circumstance.

   It's difficult at this point to say when a predicate wff is a tautology. A tautology must be true in all universes. There are *a lot* of universes. There are infinitely many of them. Similarly, it's daunting to show that a wff is a contradiction.

   On the other hand, it's at least conceivable that we can show that a wff is consistent. All we need to do is produce one universe in which the wff is true.

Example

Show that $\exists x Px \wedge \exists x \neg Px$ is consistent.

   We need a set of objects. We'll be constructing many universes, and it's convenient to use the same set of objects, so let's take the set of all people living today. Now we need an interpretation for P that makes $\exists x Px \wedge \exists x \neg Px$ true. But this just says that somebody is P and somebody else isn't. So let P mean "___ is Hungarian." That does it.

Similarly, we can usually show that a wff is contingent.

Example

Show that $\exists x Px \wedge \exists x \neg Px$ is contingent.

   We need two universes, one that makes the wff true and one that makes it false. We already have one that makes it true (the last example). For the one that makes $\exists x Px \wedge \exists x \neg Px$ false we'll use the same set of objects, the set of people alive today. Now we need an interpretation for P that makes $\exists x Px \wedge \exists x \neg Px$ false. Hmm…we could make $\exists x Px$ false or we could make $\exists x \neg Px$ false. Either one is easy. We could take P to mean "___ is a person." Or we could take P to mean "___ has three heads and four stomachs." Either one does it.

Example

$\forall x \neg Px \Leftrightarrow \neg \exists x Px$

This is a tautology. Think about what it's saying. On the left, it's "for all x, P is false about x", or "P is false about everything." That's the same as saying "P is true about nothing," or "there is no x such that Px is true". That's the part on the right.

$$\forall x \neg Px \Leftrightarrow \neg \exists x Px$$

$$\exists x \neg Px \Leftrightarrow \neg \forall x Px$$

These are the **quantifier exchange rules**. They're quite reasonable. You may have explored them in the exercises on page 138. We'll prove that they're tautologies later in the book.

One last issue: We allow for the possibility that a universe is empty, that it has nothing in it. The empty universe is a special place. It has special properties.

One property of the empty universe is that every existential statement is false. That should sound reasonable. $\exists x Px$ is true in a universe only when you can find a thing with property P. But since you can't find anything in an empty universe, you can't find anything with the property P in an empty universe – no matter what property P denotes. That means a pretty innocent statement such as

$$\exists x (Px \lor \neg Px)$$

is false in the empty universe (but it's true everywhere else).

The flip side of this is that every universal statement is true. Remember that the negation of a universal, $\forall x Px$, is an existential, $\exists x \neg Px$ (see above and p.33) and since every existential statement is false in the empty universe, every universal statement is true. Think about it. Let's say $P\_\_$ means "$\_\_$ is wearing a purple shirt." What is the truth value of $\forall x Px$ in the empty world? Is everyone wearing a purple shirt? Well, do you see anyone who's *not* wearing one? What's that? You don't see anyone at all? Well then you don't see anyone not wearing a purple shirt, right? So everyone is wearing a purple shirt!

Exercises   Universes

Odd-numbered solutions begin on page 361

Below are statements in a predicate language with two 1-place predicates, P and Q, a 2-place predicate R, and constants a and b.

For each of the following statements, find a universe in which it is true and one in which it is false.

1. $Qa \land \neg Pb$
2. $\exists x Px$
3. $\exists x (Px \land \neg Qx)$
4. $\forall x (Qx \Rightarrow Px)$
5. $\forall x \exists y Rxy$
6. $\exists x \forall y Rxy$

Each of the following statements may or may not be contingent. For each of the statements, construct a universe in which the statement is true (if that is possible). Also, construct a universe in which the statement is false (again, if that is possible). In your universes, P, Q, and R must refer to relations and a, and b must refer to objects.

7. $\neg(Pa \Rightarrow Pa)$
8. $\exists x Qx \Rightarrow Qb$
9. $\forall x(Qx \Rightarrow Qa)$
10. $\exists x(Qx \Rightarrow Qb)$
11. $\exists x \forall y Rxy \wedge \forall z \neg Rzz$

12!! $\forall x \exists y Rxy \wedge \forall x \forall y \neg Rxy$

Let A, B, C, D, and E be closed formulas in a predicate language in which the only predicate letter is N, a 1-place predicate. Let $\mathfrak{W}$ be the universe with domain consisting of all the residents of Washington state and let Sx mean "x lives in Seattle". You have the following information about these wffs:

- A is $\forall x Sx$.
- B is true in the empty universe.
- C is an existential wff.

- D is true in $\mathfrak{W}$.
- E is a tautology.

For each of the following statements respond either
Y (Yes),
N (No), or
I (Impossible to say with the information given).

13. $A \Rightarrow C$ is true in $\mathfrak{W}$.
14. C implies B.
15. $D \Rightarrow A$ is true in $\mathfrak{W}$.
16. B is a tautology.
17. $\neg A \vee C$ is true in $\mathfrak{W}$.
18. $C \Rightarrow B$ is a tautology.
19. $C \wedge A$ is false in the empty universe.
20. A and B are equivalent.
21. D and E are mutually consistent.
22. A is contingent.
23. If we think of universes as sets, the empty universe is the empty set, the set with nothing in it. In Chapter Four we saw two notations for the empty set,

$$\{\}$$

and

$$\emptyset.$$

What is wrong with this sign?

The Law of the Excluded Middle, $A \vee \neg A$ is a tautology of Basic Sentential (p. 108), but not all philosophers are happy with that. Our first attempt to resolve the Liar (p. 11) was to imagine that the sentence L, "This sentence is false", might be neither true nor false, that is, $\neg(L \vee \neg L)$.

In Chapter Six we looked at three-valued logic where $A \vee \neg A$ is not a tautology – it's never false (0), but it's sometimes less than true ($\frac{1}{2}$).

Suppose that an election is coming up next week. Let W be "our candidate will win". If W is true then we don't need to vote, do we? On the other hand, if W is false then voting is futile, isn't it? So if $W \vee \neg W$ is true then we have a reason for not voting!

There are other philosophical challenges to the law of the excluded middle (see the *Sweet Reason* website). Mathematics is mostly free of controversy, but there is a group of mathematicians that denies this law vigorously.

There are three kinds of logicians in the world—those who accept the Law of the Excluded Middle and those who don't.

(Anonymous)

7.2 Syllogisms

When your little boys, or little girls, can solve Syllogisms, *I fancy they will be much more eager to have fresh* Pairs of Premisses *supplied them, than any* riddles *you can offer.* (Lewis Carroll, *Symbolic Logic*)

Aristotle is responsible for the earliest work in formal logic. He analyzed arguments, called syllogisms, constructed using a very restricted part of Greek. The only statements permitted were the following forms:

All ___ are___
No ___ are ___
Some ___ are ___
Some ___ are not ___
___ is a ___
___ is not a ___

A typical syllogistic argument was

> All men are mortal.
> Socrates is a man.
> ∴ Socrates is mortal.

All possible arguments consisting of two premises and a conclusion were analyzed by the Greeks (there are not that many *different* arguments).

Since that time, much of the available logical energy was expended in the search for clever ways to remember which of the arguments were valid and which were invalid. The great eighteenth-century mathematician Leonhard Euler developed one method. It was later improved by the nineteenth-century logician John Venn. Charles Lutwidge Dodgson (as Lewis Carroll, the author of *Alice's Adventures in Wonderland*) wrote about another method in a book called *The Game of Logic*. The method we present here is a combination of Euler's and Venn's.

Example

Consider the Socrates syllogism,
> All men are mortal.
> Socrates is a man.
> ∴ Socrates is mortal.

To analyze this, we represent the set of all men and the set of all mortals as circles (recall Venn diagrams, page 87).

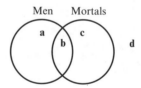

The first premise states that everything inside the "Men" circle must be inside the "Mortals" circle. In other words, region **a** is empty. We represent that by shading it in.

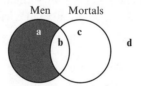

The second states that Socrates lies inside the circle of men; in our diagram, that's region **b**, because **a** has to be empty. We represent that by putting a "★" for Socrates in **b**.

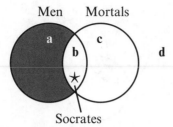

Clearly from the picture, Socrates lies inside the circle of mortals, and so the conclusion is justified.

Example

> Some students are not fans of Herrell's ice cream.
> All fans of Herrell's ice cream are overweight.
> ∴ Some students are not overweight.

We'll need three circles.

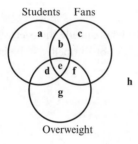

The first premise says that there are students outside the fans circle. That means something in either **a** or **d**.

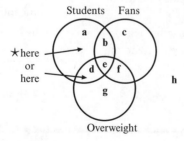

We'll put the ★ on the border between **a** and **d** to indicate that there is something in at least one of these regions (possibly in both).

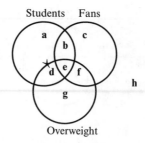

The second premise says that regions **b** and **c** are empty.

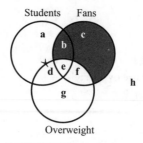

The conclusion, that there are students outside the overweight circle, is not justified, since we don't *know* that the ★ is in **a**. It's not compelled to be in region **a**. Thus the syllogism is invalid.

Exercises   Syllogisms

Odd-numbered
solutions
begin on page 361

a. Translate each syllogism using predicates and quantifiers.
b. Using Venn diagrams, decide whether or not each syllogism is valid.
c. If the syllogism is invalid, find a structure in which the premises are true and the conclusion false.

1.
> No decent person collects ham sandwiches.
> Some collectors of ham sandwiches are emotionally immature.
> ∴ No decent person is emotionally immature.

2.
> All roads lead to Rome.
> Some interstate highways are roads.
> ∴ Some interstate highways lead to Rome.

3.
> All logicians glow in the dark.
> Some logicians are not consulted by the president on a daily basis.
> ∴ Some people who are consulted by the president on a daily basis do not glow in the dark.

4.

Some texts are tedious.
Some tedious things are full of obnoxious exercises.

∴ Some texts are full of obnoxious exercises.

5.

All important political figures have skeletons in their closets.
Some important political figures do not appear on late-night television.

∴ Some persons with skeletons in their closets do not appear on late-night television.

6.

All movie sequels are box office bonanzas.
No box office bonanzas receive critical acclaim.

∴ Some movie sequels do not receive critical acclaim.

7.

All clowns wear ridiculous outfits.
Some clowns carry butcher knives.

∴ Some of those who wear ridiculous outfits also carry butcher knives.

We can use Venn diagrams to analyze arguments that don't follow strict syllogistic form, too. The following are two such arguments.

8.

Not all that glitters is gold.
Everything in the bucket glitters.

∴ There's no gold in the bucket.

9.

All philosophers are either stupid or crazy.
All stupid people are crazy.

∴ All philosophers are crazy.

10.

All hyperglutenous maloids experience snifterhood.
Some of those who do not experience snifterhood also fail to practice oggentrophy.

∴ Some objects that fail to practice oggentrophy are in fact hyperglutenous maloids.

The concept of a set of objects is basic. We introduced some notation for set operations in Chapter Four, but the reader met and understood sets long before picking up this book. The idea that given any property (for example, motherhood) we can form the set of all objects with that property (the set of all mothers) is natural and intuitive.

At the end of the nineteenth century, logician Gottlob Frege used sets as the basis for a theory of mathematics and logic. In 1901, Bertrand Russell discovered a flaw in Frege's work and in our naive understanding of sets.

Russell, noticing that some sets are members of themselves (the set of all sets is a set) and some are not (the set of all pumpkins is not itself a pumpkin), considered R, the set of all sets which are not members of themselves. He then asked, is R a member of itself?

If R is a member of itself then by definition it doesn't belong in R, so it's *not* a member of itself. But if it's not a member of itself then it does belong in R so it *is* a member of itself.

Does this remind you of the other paradoxes we have presented? If not, see page 21.

7.3 Validity

But the fact that some geniuses were laughed at does not imply that all who are laughed at are geniuses. They laughed at Columbus, they laughed at Fulton, they laughed at the Wright brothers. But they also laughed at Bozo the Clown. (Carl Sagan)

Recall our definition of validity–:

An argument is . . .

Valid   if the conclusion is true whenever the premises are true.

Invalid   if it is possible for the premises to be true and the conclusion false.

In Predicate, it will be difficult to show that an argument is valid. The problem is the same as the problem of showing that a wff is a tautology. To show an argument is valid, we must check every universe, looking to see if the premises are true, and if they are, that the conclusion is also true.

But showing that an argument is invalid is not difficult. All we need to do is come up with a universe in which the premises are true and the conclusion is false—one universe.

Example

Show that $\forall x(Px \Rightarrow Qx)$ is invalid.

$\underline{\qquad \exists xQx \qquad\qquad}$

$\therefore \exists xPx$

We want a universe where the premises are true and the conclusion false. Let's take our favorite set, living people.

It seems easiest to start with the conclusion. It says that somebody has the property P. To make that false, let $P\_\_$ be "$\_\_$ can fly."

Now let's make $\forall x(Px \Rightarrow Qx)$ true. That says that everyone who can fly has property Q. Hey. No one can fly. That means the conditional $Px \Rightarrow Qx$ is already true, because Px is false for every x in our universe.

Finally, we make $\exists xQx$ true. That's easy; let $Q\_\_$ mean "$\_\_$ lives in Baltimore."

Example

Is $\forall x(Px \lor Qx)$ valid?

$\underline{\quad \exists x(Px \lor \neg Qx)\quad}$

$\therefore \exists xPx$

We'll try something like the shortcut method. We'll try to make the premises true and the conclusion false. If we succeed, we'll know the argument is invalid. We'll be very methodical about our attempt, so methodical that if we *fail* to make the premises true and the conclusion false, we will be sure the argument is valid.

Since all the predicates are 1-place predicates, we can use Venn diagrams to represent the situation.

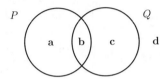

The conclusion says that there is something with property *P*. We're trying to make that false, so we'll shade in *P*.

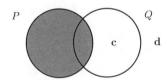

The first premise says that region **d** is empty. We're trying to make the premises true so we'll shade that in.

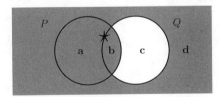

The second premise says that there is something that is either in *P* or not in *Q*. Well, it can't be in *P* because that's empty. And it can't not be in *Q*; everything is empty outside *Q*. So it's impossible to make the second premise true. That means the argument is valid. It's impossible to make both premises true and the conclusion false.

Exercises   Validity

Odd-numbered
solutions
begin on page 362

All of the following arguments are invalid; for each, find a universe in which the premises are true and the conclusion is false:

1. $\dfrac{\exists x Px}{\therefore \exists x \neg Px}$

2. $\begin{array}{c} \forall x (Px \vee Qx) \\ \exists x Qx \\ \hline \therefore \exists x Px \end{array}$

3. $\dfrac{\forall x (Px \vee Qx)}{\therefore \forall x Px \vee \forall x Qx}$

4. $\dfrac{\exists x Px \Rightarrow \exists x Qx}{\therefore \exists x (Px \vee Qx)}$

5. $\begin{array}{c} \forall x (Px \vee Qx) \\ \forall x Px \\ \hline \therefore \exists x \neg Qx \end{array}$

6. $\dfrac{\forall x Px}{\therefore \exists x Px}$

The following arguments might be valid or they might be invalid. Determine which:

7. $\dfrac{\forall x Px \wedge \forall x Qx}{\therefore \forall x (Px \wedge Qx)}$

8. $\dfrac{\exists x Px \wedge \exists x Qx}{\therefore \exists x (Px \wedge Qx)}$

9. $\dfrac{\forall x (Px \Rightarrow Qx)}{\therefore \forall x Px \Rightarrow \forall x Qx}$

10. $\dfrac{\forall x Px \Rightarrow \forall x Qx}{\therefore \forall x (Px \Rightarrow Qx)}$

11. $\dfrac{\exists x (Px \Rightarrow Qx)}{\therefore \exists x Px \Rightarrow \forall x Qx}$

12. $\dfrac{\exists x Px \Rightarrow \exists x Qx}{\therefore \exists x (Px \Rightarrow Qx)}$

13. Some of the statements in the boxes below imply statements in other boxes. Draw arrows from a group of boxes to another box if the group jointly implies the box. Draw arrows only if all the boxes in the group are necessary. Note: in general, we allow for the possibility that the universe is empty. But for this exercise, assume the universe is not empty (for example, $\exists x (Ax \vee \neg Ax)$ is true).

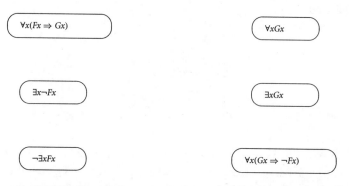

14. Some of the statements in the boxes below imply statements in other boxes. Draw arrows from a group of boxes to another box if the group jointly implies the box. Draw arrows only if all the boxes in the group are necessary. For this problem, do not assume that universes must not be empty.

(a) There is someone who will succeed if she tries.

(b) Sarabella exists and will succeed.

(c) Someone will try.

(d) Everyone who tries will succeed.

(e) If everyone will try, someone will succeed.

(f) Mehitabel exists and she won't try.

15. Another issue of *The Digestor's Digest*. This might be the fun edition. And it might not.

The Digestor's Digest

Vol. I, No. 6

Don't Read!

After testing numerous dietary journals and newsletters, researchers have concluded that none are completely reliable. In particular, we note that this page of this publication is completely false.

Don't Eat!

After testing numerous breakfast foods, both homemade and commercial, researchers have concluded that none are completely safe. In particular, we note with regret that this page of this publication is inedible.

> Readers:
>
> Don't forget! Somewhere in this book (but not on the last page) there's a surprise examination!
>
> Study hard!

J, J and T
It gets worse, guys.
The exam can't be on the next-to-last page either. It won't be a surprise. When readers get to the next-to-next-to-last page, they'll know the exam is coming next — because it can't be on the last page.
— ed.

7.4   Diagramming Your Argument

"Now, where were we? Read me back the last line."
"'Read me back the last line.'" read back the corporal who could take shorthand.
"Not my last line, stupid!" the colonel shouted. "Somebody elses."
"'Read me back the last line,'" read back the corporal.
"That's my last line again!" shrieked the colonel, turning purple with anger.
"Oh, no sir," corrected the corporal. "That's my last line. I read it to you just a moment ago." (Joseph Heller, *Catch 22*)

It's time to start constructing your own arguments. This is where you marshall our thoughts. This is where you think through issues. This is where you try to understand what is what and why one might think so. Your chief tool in this enterprise is the argument diagram.

Consider: The United States should raise taxes on cigarettes. Do you believe this? That doesn't matter. You're going to try to construct the diagram of an argument for raising the cigarette taxes. We'll help.

Why should taxes be raised? Health is a possibility.

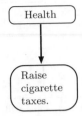

"Health" is no good. When making your diagram, every bubble must be a complete sentence. "Health" can't support anything. It doesn't say anything.

Also, "Raise cigarette taxes" is no good. That's a sentence but it's not a statement, it's a command. Every bubble must say something that can be true or false.

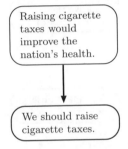

That's better. But can "Raising cigarette taxes would improve the nation's health" be a premise? That is, is it true? And is it so obviously true that it needs no support?

Well, the idea is that fewer people will smoke if cigarettes are more expensive.

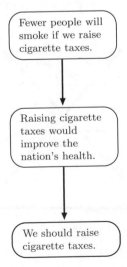

Shouldn't you mention how smoking isn't healthful? That should be in there, right?

Stop!

Big mistake.

This is the most common error committed in diagramming. You're linking bubbles and thinking about the argument you're going to write. Instead of thinking, "What statement supports what?" you're thinking, "After I say this, what will I say next?"

You might well want to discuss topics in this order, but the first statement doesn't support the second. That's not your argument. What makes more sense is this:

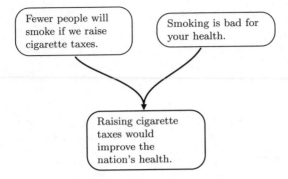

Those two statements work together. If smoking is bad for your health and fewer people do it, that's why the country's health will improve.

Heads up!

Never forget that your diagram is the logical framework of your argument. It's not an outline. It's not the order in which you will make your points.

Is health the whole story? Is there any other reason for raising cigarette taxes? Money, perhaps. There is a deficit.

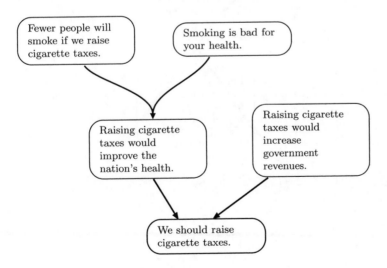

That's good. Should you mention the deficit?

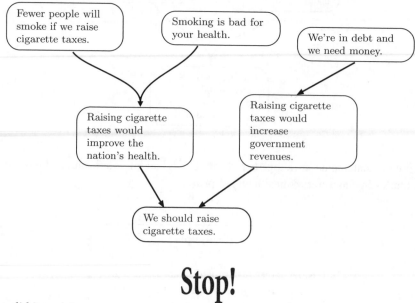

Stop!

You did it *again*!

Think about every link. Is the fact that the nation is in debt the reason why raising taxes gives us more money? Not at all. Raising taxes *always* gives us more money (well, almost always).

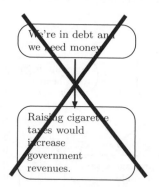

Remember, this is a *logical* diagram. If your diagram says

then you'll write, "A. And that's the reason why B." Does it make sense to say, "We need money. That's why raising taxes will get us more money." ?

Nope. Instead you want to say "We need money. And raising taxes will get us more money. That's why raising taxes is good." In other words, increasing money and needing money work together.

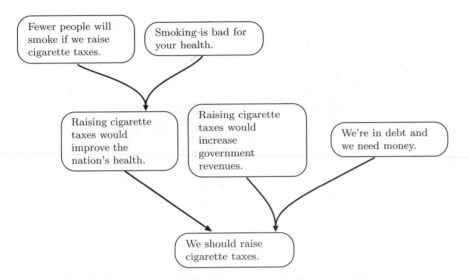

Much better. This is a good start.

But there are two sides (at least) to every question. Consider the proposition:

> The United States should *not* raise taxes on cigarettes.

Why would one oppose raising cigarette taxes? To help you think, we'll exaggerate the situation. Suppose someone proposed a $1,000 tax on cartons of cigarettes. What would happen?

Well, first of all, no one would pay it; no one would buy cigarettes. Instead of increasing, revenue would go down.

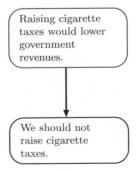

You should explain that if cigarettes cost more, fewer would be sold. And of course, this is important because we're in debt!

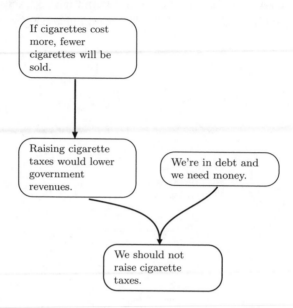

But isn't it good if fewer cigarettes are sold? Let's go back to the $1,000 tax. Would people stop smoking? Probably not. There would be a black market in cigarettes. It would be like prohibition in the 1920s and like drug-trafficking today. Actually, there already is some problem with cigarette smuggling.

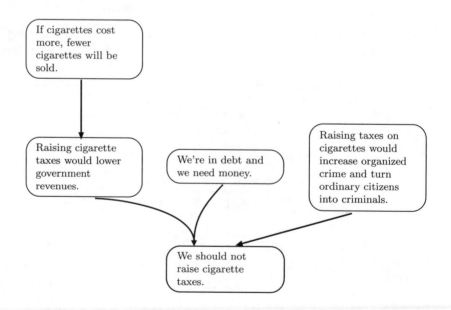

You need to support that a bit.

Stop! Stop! Stop!

Once again, you've slipped into the "Well, first I'll say this and then naturally I'll say that" mode. The top statement doesn't support the second statement; they work together.

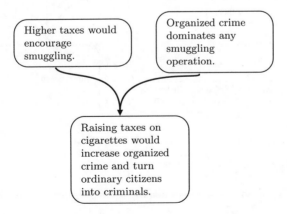

You should add that law-abiding citizens who are addicted to cigarettes will have no choice but to buy from cigarette traffickers.

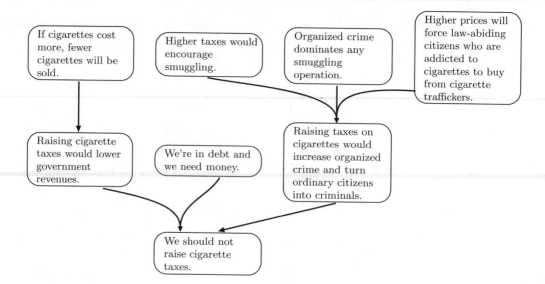

And one more thing. If no one buys cigarettes, we put tobacco farmers and tobacco companies out of business. That will cause a lot of hardship.

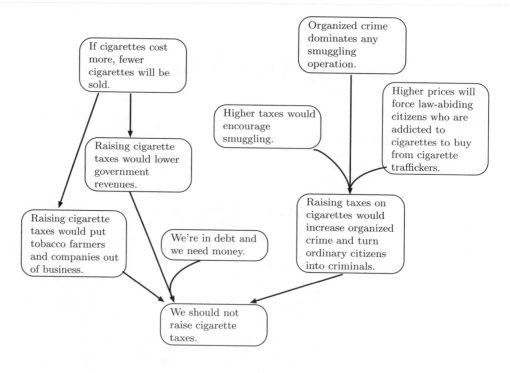

Another good start!
Start?!? Is there more?

Much more, as you'll see later. But you've taken the first and most difficult step. The two arguments we've diagrammed aren't that bad, but they can be greatly improved. You'll be working on them in the next three chapters, with our help.

Writing is hard; let's admit that up front. But it's immeasurably easier if you know what it is you're trying to say. At the core of any good paper is a logical argument. Constructing the diagram for your argument is the most important step.

Exercises   Diagramming Your Argument

Odd-numbered solutions begin on page 362

Construct diagrams for arguments in favor of the following propositions. For each one, limit your diagram to at most 10 statements plus the conclusion. Your answers won't be perfect; there is no perfect argument. You will be invited to improve on your answers in later chapters.

1. My school should offer a major in logic.
2. My school should not offer a major in logic.
3. Cloning of human beings should be illegal.
4. Cloning of human beings should not be made illegal.
5. The United States should abolish the death penalty.
6. The United States should not abolish the death penalty.
7. My school should have a quantitative skills requirement.
8. My school should not have a quantitative skills requirement.

9. Write a short paragraph expressing the argument in the diagram below. You don't have to make the argument sound reasonable (that's impossible!). Just write it so that the underlying diagram is clear to the reader.

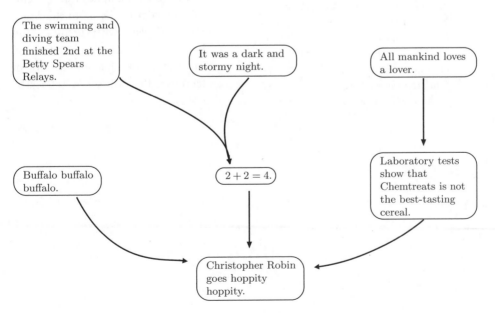

10.   **Cathy gets liberated**

"We're reading this great book in my women's studies class. It's by Mona Luscious and it's talking about really awesome women! Margaret Mead, Geraldine Ferraro, and Betty Boop!" Alice flushed with excitement. A small group of women's studies majors were chatting in residence lounge.

"Cool! Are you going to the Soph Sisters meeting tonight?" asked Trudy.

"I don't know, they're showing Thelma and Louise in Wright Hall!" Alice hefted an imaginary AK-47 and began mowing down her suitemates, when a desperate noise came from the corner.

"Help! Help!" The cry from behind a newspaper first startled the women, then froze them when they saw it was Cathy.

"Save me from my gender!"

No one said a word.

"Do you realize how ridiculous women's liberation is?"

Emma was indignant. "Well Cathy, maybe you want to do dishes all your life, but I'm going to have a career!"

"Some career." Cathy dropped her paper and rose slowly. "All your women's studies major prepares you for is Professional Whiner. The women's movement is a collection of excuses. 'They don't hire me because I'm a woman!' 'They don't respect me because I'm sensitive and caring!' 'They fired me because I'm a bitch!'"

Alice and Emma exchanged glances.

"Cathy, you wouldn't even be here if it weren't for women's lib. This used to be a men's college!" Tiffany's father was an alumnus.

"They decided to admit women because they preferred that to going bankrupt. I'm here because I nailed the SAT. You're here because your Daddy endowed the computer center."

"Cathy, we have to fight for our rights! Even today women are paid less than men for the same work!"

"That's because they don't have the same qualifications. If you wanted to be liberated, you'd major in mathematics."

"Ha! Gotcha! If I have to do something, I can't be liberated, right? Ha!" Hermione was practically dancing.

"This is the problem with women. They aren't ready for liberation. If I open the door to your cell, you aren't liberated because you **have** to walk out. Given the chance to study Statistics, Engineering, and Economics, you take Art, Philosophy, and Women's Studies. You won't walk out of the cell."

And Cathy walked out of the room.

Cathy is rebutting arguments by Alice and Emma in favor of the feminist movement. Diagram this argument. Explain what premises and lines of inference she is attacking. Then write an argument in favor of feminism that will survive attack by Cathy.

It happened again the next morning. Jay brought an infinite number of books to Jim. He brought the books two at a time as before (p. 152), placing them on Jim's desk. Jim, as before, always moved one book from the pile Jay was forming on one side of the desk to a pile on the other side. But while Jay did exactly as before, Jim chose the book that he moved differently. Instead of moving the book that was on the top of the pile, Jim moved the book that was on the bottom (not easy to do after a while).

As before, two towers of books grew on Jim's desk. As before, they were roughly the same height and contained the same number of books. At noon, Jay had completed bringing infinitely many books. What did Jim's desk look like now?

See page 191.

7.5   Inductive Logic

Back off, man, I'm a scientist! (Dan Ackroyd and Harold Ramis, *Ghostbusters*)

Most of this book focuses on deductive logic, the logic that helps us determine when the premises of an argument logically imply its conclusion, the logic of validity. But in fact, deductive arguments play a much smaller role in our lives than do arguments of another kind – those in which the premises are not intended to logically guarantee the truth of the conclusion, but only to provide good reasons to believe the conclusion by showing it more likely to be true, more probable. Logic studies good arguments. One branch of logic, inductive logic, evaluates this sort of reasoning.

When we discuss deductive arguments, we examine their validity. But inductive arguments are, by definition, never valid. So when asking about inductive arguments, we are just asking whether they are sufficiently persuasive to warrant belief. Just as in deductive logic, when we assess an argument, we are asking neither about the truth of the premises nor about the truth of the conclusion. Instead, we are asking about the degree of support the premises give for the conclusion. The big difference is that instead of that degree being all-or-nothing, as in deductive logic, in inductive logic the strength of arguments lies on a spectrum from completely unconvincing to very convincing.

We encounter inductive arguments throughout our lives. Induction is the basis of scientific reasoning, legal reasoning, and everyday practical reasoning. When we predict that it will rain on the basis of gathering clouds, we are arguing inductively; when we predict that the next raven we see will be black because the last 10 000 have been black, we argue inductively; when we conclude that smoking causes cancer because the incidence of cancer is so much higher in smokers than in nonsmokers we argue inductively. These all seem like pretty good inductive arguments.

But we also argue inductively when we conclude that this penny will come up heads because it came up heads the last three times we flipped it, or for that matter that it will come up tails, because it came up heads three times in a row; or when we argue that Charlie will hit the next free throw because he hit the last three and has a "hot hand", or for that matter that he will miss, because he hit three in a row, and he is basically a bad shot; or when we argue that it will rain this weekend because it rained on the past three weekends. These look like pretty bad inductive arguments.

None of these arguments is deductively valid, and the logic we have been investigating would reject all of them. But clearly, some are more convincing than others. Inductive logic is devoted to telling the good from the bad among arguments of this type. Its central tool is probability theory, the mathematical approach to determining likelihoods, which we explore in more detail in the next chapter. Since induction is fundamental to so much of our reasoning, this is an important area of research, but it is far from settled and new ideas, as well as new problems, emerge all the time.

Does inductive logic actually work?

Yes! It's been enormously successful. From measuring the efficacy of medical treatment, to predicting weather, to assessing economic health, to sampling opinion, induction has proved its worth again and again.

"Proved its worth"? What does that mean?

Why, we trust induction because, as we said, we've used it thousands of times and it's given us meaningful, often spectacular results! It makes science and most of our ordinary life possible. It has a long track record. Naturally, we expect such success to continue.

Do you see the problem with the defense of induction? Our justification for the principle of inductive logic is based on inductive logic itself! Compare this to another logic, which we'll call "Mom" logic. Here's Mom logic: Whenever we wish to know if our results are correct, we ask our Mom. This is great, because no matter what it is she always says, "Of course you're right, dear." No matter! Now let's evaluate "Mom logic." How do we do that? We ask Mom! She says, "Of course you're right, dear!"[1]

What is the supporting evidence?

Fundamental to induction is the gathering of data. Suppose we have a theory. To evaluate the theory, we search for events that tend to confirm or deny it. The problem is that the

---

[1] Of course, when we ask what the justification is for *deductive* reasoning, things aren't much better. If we justify deductive logic deductively, we argue in a circle; if we justify it inductively, we have to justify induction. This was noted first by Sextus Empiricus (c. 160-210 AD) in his *Outlines of Pyrrhonism* and *Against the Logicians*.

Any ideas, Mom?

very notion of a "confirming instance" is not well understood. It *should* be simple, but even a statement as direct as "All ___ are ___ " causes difficulties – Hempel's paradox on page 335.

That paradox is only the beginning of the problems posed by the idea of a confirming instance. There are examples where an obviously confirming instance actually disproves the theory! Martin Gardner suggests the following example: Take ten cards numbered 1 to 10. Shuffle them and place them face down in a row. Our hypothesis is that no card with the value n is in the nth position from the left. Clearly, if you turn over the nth card and it's not n, that's a confirming instance.

Now suppose that you turn over the first eight cards. Each card confirms your hypothesis: The first card is not the 1, the second card is not the 2, and so on. Suppose that none of the cards face up is the 10. Now you turn over the ninth card. It is the 5. That's a confirming instance (it's not the 9!), but in fact it actually *refutes* the hypothesis since the tenth card now must be the 10.

When do we have enough evidence?

Never, really. In life, there is no certainty. Even in mathematics, where there *is* certainty[2], there are surprises. Consider the following: Take a natural number. If it's even, divide by 2. If it's odd, multiply by 3 and add 1. Do this again: if it's even divide by 2, otherwise multiply by 3 and add 1. Do it again. Do it again and again and again. What happens? Let's look at an example: if we start with 17, we must multiply by 3 and add 1 getting 52. Now we can divide by 2, getting 26. Again we divide by 2, getting 13. Now we must multiply by 3 and add 1, getting 40. Continuing, we obtain the following sequence:

$$17, 52, 26, 13, 40, 20, 10, 5, 16, 8, 4, 2, 1$$

Thus we reach the number 1. Now try another number, say 23.

$$23, 70, 35, 106, 53, 160, 80, 40, 20, 10, 5, 16, 8, 4, 2, 1$$

Again we reach 1. Will this always happen?

This is known as the Collatz "$3n + 1$" problem. The evidence that it will always happen is strong. Using computers, mathematicians have checked that every number below 1 000 000 000 000 reaches 1. Is that enough?

As we said, strange things can happen in mathematics. There is a statement of mathematics that is *also* true for all numbers below 1 000 000 000 000 (the exact statement is not important or attractive). Unfortunately, it's been proven that this statement is

2　There is also uncertainty in mathematics. We'll get to that in Chapter Twelve.

not true for all numbers. All that's known, however, is that it's false for some number below

1,650,000,000,000,000,000,000,000,000,000,000,000,000,000,000,000,
000,000,000,000,000,000,000,000,000,000,000,000,000,000,000,000,000,
000,000,000,000,000,000,000,000,000,000,000,000,000,000,000,000,000,
000,000,000,000,000,000,000,000,000,000,000,000,000,000,000,000,000,
000,000,000,000,000,000,000,000,000,000,000,000,000,000,000,000,000,
000,000,000,000,000,000,000,000,000,000,000,000,000,000,000,000,000,
000,000,000,000,000,000,000,000,000,000,000,000,000,000,000,000,000,
000,000,000,000,000,000,000,000,000,000,000,000,000,000,000,000,000,
000,000,000,000,000,000,000,000,000,000,000,000,000,000,000,000,000,
000,000,000,000,000,000,000,000,000,000,000,000,000,000,000,000,000,
000,000,000,000,000,000,000,000,000,000,000,000,000,000,000,000,000,
000,000,000,000,000,000,000,000,000,000,000,000,000,000,000,000,000,
000,000,000,000,000,000,000,000,000,000,000,000,000,000,000,000,000,
000,000,000,000,000,000,000,000,000,000,000,000,000,000,000,000,000,
000,000,000,000,000,000,000,000,000,000,000,000,000,000,000,000,000,
000,000,000,000,000,000,000,000,000,000,000,000,000,000,000,000,000,
000,000,000,000,000,000,000,000,000,000,000,000,000,000,000,000,000,
000,000,000,000,000,000,000,000,000,000,000,000,000,000,000,000,000,
000,000,000,000,000,000,000,000,000,000,000,000,000,000,000,000,000,
000,000,000,000,000,000,000,000,000,000,000,000,000,000,000,000,000,
000,000,000,000,000,000,000,000,000,000,000,000,000,000,000,000,000.

Clearly, in the case of the Collatz conjecture and others, no finite amount of data will be sufficient to confirm.

Are there answers to scientific questions?

The facts of the universe are elusive. Unfortunately, we don't even have the assurance that facts exist! Quantum theory says, for example, that it's not possible to say that a certain particle will be in a certain place at a certain time. The most that can be said is that the particle will be here with some probability or there with some probability. We are not talking about what we can *know*, but what is *true*.

A logic has been devised by mathematicians and physicists to deal with this. Called "quantum logic," it's founded on the experimental nature of physics.

Any other problems?

We've only touched on the difficulties. The problem remains of formalizing the modes of reasoning behind inductive logic. It's an important area of research and the subject of thousands of books and articles. Quantum logic is just one example.

The classic mathematical exploration of inductive logic begins with probability. We'll give you a short introduction to this in the next chapter.

Finally, we should emphasize that despite the difficulties, inductive logic is probably the most widely practiced and most widely successful logic today. Even the masters of deductive logic (mathematicians) use it to discover, if not to prove, their theorems.

If your answer to the question on page 187 is "Two infinitely tall piles of books!" you're wrong. In fact, there was only one pile on Jim's desk. The tower that Jay had been building had completely disappeared!

The reason for this is that every book that Jay brought was eventually moved by Jim to the other side. Take the case of one book, *Nancy Drew and the Hidden Staircase*, which Jay placed on top of the pile when it had 98 763 books. Jim kept removing the bottom book from the pile. *Nancy Drew and the Hidden Staircase* moved down the pile until it was at the bottom, at which point Jim moved it to the other side. The same thing happened to all the other books. Using this strategy, every book Jay placed in the first pile was eventually moved to the second. So, all of the books ended up in the second pile. The moral of this story is that when things get infinite, order matters!

This thought experiment was the inspiration of logician Hartley Rogers. A video of the event is on the *Sweet Reason* website.

CULTURAL TREASURES RUINED BY TOURISTS

THE EIFFEL TOWER

THE GREAT WALL

THE EMPTY UNIVERSE

Chapter Eight

8.1 Predicate Wffs

If this is coffee, please bring me some tea; but if this is tea, please bring me some coffee.
(Abraham Lincoln)

As in the case of Sentential, it's vital that we have a rigorous definition of well-formedness for our predicate languages so that we can distinguish meaningful from meaningless expressions and so that we can develop principled ways of extending our languages. One difference between predicate languages and the language of statement logic (Sentential) is that there are many predicate languages. Although all predicate languages contain a common core, their vocabularies can vary.

i. **Vocabulary**
   a. **Names** (or **constants**): $a, b, c, \ldots m,$
   b. **Sentence Letters:** $A, B, C, \ldots M,$ (except F)
   c. **Predicate Letters:** $N, O, P, \ldots Z$ (except T)
ii. **Connectives:** $\neg, \wedge, \vee, \Rightarrow, \Leftrightarrow$
iii. **Variables:** $n, o, p, \ldots x, y, z,$
iv. **Quantifiers:** $\forall, \exists$
v. **Parentheses** ( )

Note that we're splitting the alphabet between sentence letters and predicate letters and between constants and variables—all to avoid confusion. In addition, if we ever need more of any type of letter, we allow subscripts: a_1 C_4, Z_{127}, v_3 etc.

As we mentioned in Chapter Seven, the structure of a predicate language is matched by the structure of any appropriate universe. That includes names. We only name things that exist in our universes. You can name Santa Claus and talk about him if you want. But if you do so, then he will have to be in any appropriate universe.

Universes contain the sets of things to which we want to refer. If our universe is empty, there can be no names. Of course we can have very big universes, with infinitely many objects. Then the language can contain an infinite number of names.

Sweet Reason: A Field Guide To Modern Logic, Second Edition. Jim Henle, Jay L. Garfield, Thomas Tymoczko and Emily Altreuter.
© 2012 John Wiley & Sons Inc. Published 2012 by John Wiley & Sons Inc.

Appropriate universes must also have properties to match the predicate letters. Every predicate letter is associated with a fixed number of **places**. If B is a 1-place predicate letter, we write Bx (or By or Ba or Bb or ...). If H is a 2-place predicate letter, we write Hxy (or Hyz or Hax or ...). If R is a 3-place predicate letter, we write $Rxyz$ (or ...), and so on.

The languages we will be working with also contain the identity predicate "$=$". We write $x = y$ to mean "x is identical to y". Identity is a 2-place predicate, but instead of writing "$= ab$" we write "$a = b$."

With this in mind, we can now define "wff" in a predicate language. We assume the language has a specific set of constants and predicate letters. As in the case of Sentential, we have a compact, recursive definition.

1. Base clause: Any n-place predicate letter followed by any combination of n variables and constants is a wff. (But as we just said, we will allow the more colloquial '$a = b$', for '$= ab$'.)

2. Recursion clause: If A and B are wffs of the predicate language then
   a. $\neg A$ is a wff
   b. $(A \wedge B)$ is a wff
   c. $(A \vee B)$ is a wff
   d. $(A \Rightarrow B)$ is a wff
   e. $(A \Leftrightarrow B)$ is a wff
   f. $\forall v A$ is a wff where v is any variable
   g. $\exists v A$ is a wff where v is any variable

3. Closure clause: Nothing else is a wff.

In this definition, a quantifier works grammatically just like a 1-place connective (like $\neg$); that is, it's something that goes in front of a wff.

Notice that we are using metalinguistic variables as we did when defining Sentential. We're using A and B to stand for any wff and v to stand for any variable. Of course these symbols are not themselves in Predicate.

As we did in the case of Basic Sentential, we can represent the construction of a wff in Predicate with a tree.

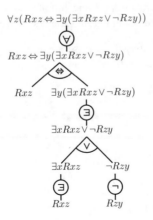

Suppose that *B* is a 1-place predicate. Which of the following are wffs?

$$\exists xBx \qquad \forall y\exists xBxy \qquad By \qquad \forall xBy \qquad \forall x\exists xBx$$

The answer is that all of them are wffs except the second, $\forall y\exists xBxy$. This is not a wff because *B* is a 1-place predicate, not a 2-place predicate. All the rest follow the rules of the recursive definition.

Note especially *By*. This is not a closed wff, not a statement as defined in Chapter Six because it has a free (not bound) variable. But it is a wff. The next, $\forall xBy$ is also an open wff. The '*y*' is unquantified. But $\forall x\exists xBx$ is a closed wff.

The last two, $\forall xBy$ and $\forall x\exists xBx$, may look a little odd. The '$\forall x$' added to the rest of the wff seems silly. But our recursive definition permits it. Indeed, if *P* is a sentence letter, then $\exists xP$ is a wff. And so is $\forall xP$. That's what the rules say. You can always add a quantifier and a variable to any wff. We can regard such quantifiers as vacuous, as empty stylistic flourishes. With one exception (see exercises) they add no meaning and don't interfere with grammar. $\forall xQ$ just says everything is such that *Q*, which is the same as saying *Q*. Just as in English, saying, "I assert that it is raining" is a long-winded way of saying "It's raining."

Notice that we don't ask for parentheses around "$a = b$". Should we worry that "$\neg a = b$" is ambiguous? Not at all. '$\neg$' is a connective. It applies to wffs not to objects or individuals. In "$\neg a = b$" the '$\neg$' must apply to "$a = b$". "$\neg a$" is meaningless (you can't negate, for example, a cheese sandwich).

It is a little awkward, though, to write "$\neg a = b$," so we'll abbreviate it with

$$a \neq b.$$

In brief,

Predicate

4. Capital letters (except *T* and *F*) followed by the appropriate number of constants and/or variables are wffs.

5. If $\mathcal{A}$ and $\mathcal{B}$ are wffs, then so are $\neg\mathcal{A}$, $(\mathcal{A} \wedge \mathcal{B})$, $(\mathcal{A} \vee \mathcal{B})$, $(\mathcal{A} \Rightarrow \mathcal{B})$, $(\mathcal{A} \Leftrightarrow \mathcal{B})$, $\forall v\mathcal{A}$, and $\exists v\mathcal{A}$, where *v* is any variable.

6. And that's all the wffs.

Exercises   Predicate Wffs

Odd-numbered
solutions
begin on page 364

In a predicate language with predicate letters *S*, *U*, and *W* and sentence letter *K*, with *S* a 1-place predicate letter and *W* a 2-place predicate letter, decide which of the following are wffs and whether they are open or closed:

1. $\exists z Sz$
2. $\exists z Sxz$
3. $\exists x(K \Rightarrow Sy)$
4. $\forall \exists xy \neg Kxy$
5. $\forall x \exists y(\exists z Wxy \Rightarrow \neg Wyx)$
6. $\forall z(Uxz \Leftrightarrow (\exists x Ux \wedge Sa))$

Formalize these sentences using identity (=):

7. There are at least two people who like cauliflower.
8. The only person who likes cauliflower is Nancy
9. There is at most one person who likes cauliflower.
10. There is exactly one person who likes cauliflower.

The one circumstance where adding "vacuous" quantifiers to a closed wff can change the meaning is when our universe is empty. For the next six problems, let *J* be a tautology.

11. What is the truth-value of *J* in the empty universe?
12. What is the truth-value of $\exists x J$ in the empty universe?
13. What is the truth-value of $\forall x J$ in the empty universe?
14. What is the truth-value of $\forall y \exists x J$ in the empty universe?

15. What is the truth-value of $\exists y \forall x J$ in the empty universe?
16. What is the truth-value of $\forall y J \Rightarrow \exists x J$ in the empty universe?

Decide whether "buffalo" sentences (pp. 73, 101, 139, and 145) are consistent, contradictory, contingent, or tautologies:

17. Buffalo buffalo.
18. Buffalo buffalo buffalo.
19. Buffalo buffalo buffalo buffalo.

We have a new quantifier for you. It's $\mathcal{C}$. $\mathcal{C} xPx$ means "there are at least two objects with property *P*." Consider a universe consisting of five women, a, b, c, d and e. a is the mother of b and c; b is the mother of d and c is the mother of e. Let *Txy* mean "*x* is a descendant of *y*" (in this case, either a daughter or granddaughter). Decide the truth of the following:

20. $\mathcal{C} xTxa$
21. $\mathcal{C} xTxb$
22. $\mathcal{C} xTbx$
23. $\mathcal{C} xTex$
24. $\exists x \mathcal{C} yTxy$
25. $\mathcal{C} x \exists yTxy$
26. $\mathcal{C} x \mathcal{C} yTxy$
27. $\mathcal{C} x \mathcal{C} yTyx$
28. Find a wff of Predicate that is equivalent to $\mathcal{C} xQx$

29‼ The $\forall$ quantifier has a partner, $\exists$. They're partners in the sense that $\forall \neg$ means the same as $\neg \exists$ and $\neg \forall$ means the same as $\exists \neg$. Define a quantifier (call it $\mathcal{S}$) such that $\mathcal{C} \neg$ and $\neg \mathcal{S}$ have the same meaning and such that $\mathcal{S} \neg$ and $\neg \mathcal{C}$ have the same meaning.

Guys,
You can't do this.
The exam can't be on
the last page, the next-
to-last page, the next-
to-next-to-last page,
etc. etc. You can't
have the exam.
Rewrite or ditch this.
*   —ed*
I thought you were logicians.

> **Readers:**
>
> Don't forget! Somewhere in this book (but not on the last page or the next-to-last page) there's a surprise examination!
>
> **Study hard!**

8.2   Outlining Your Argument

First tell your reader what you're going to tell him. Then tell him. Then tell him what you told him. (Richard Eisbrouch)

Our argument diagrams are nonlinear. They stretch out across the page. They have an end but no obvious beginning. On the other hand, a written argument is linear. It begins with one sentence, then another and another, one after the other until the final period.

There's a technique for converting from nonlinear diagram to linear prose. It's not hard. In many ways, the most difficult part is over – creating that diagram.

The skeleton of the prose argument is the outline. But before we outline, we must separate the argument into pieces.

Example

The United States should raise taxes on cigarettes.
Here's our diagram.

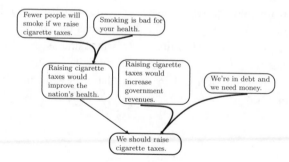

There are clearly two parts to this argument: health and money. So let's divide it up like this:

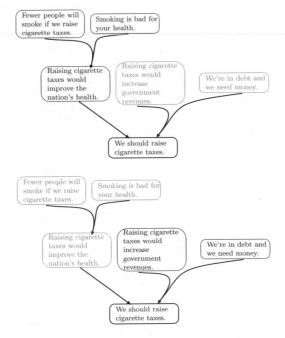

Example

The United States should not raise taxes on cigarettes.
Again, we have a diagram from Chapter Seven.

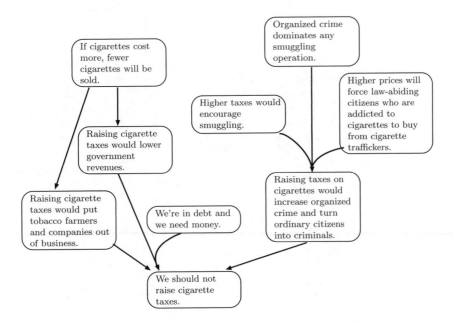

This time there are three parts: tobacco production, government revenues, and crime. We'll divide the argument into three pieces:

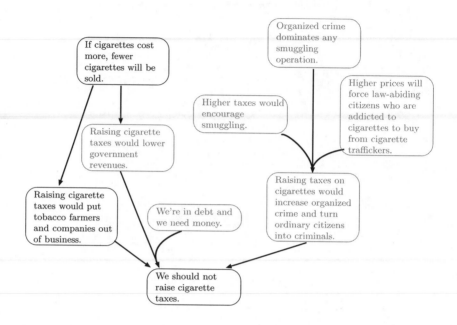

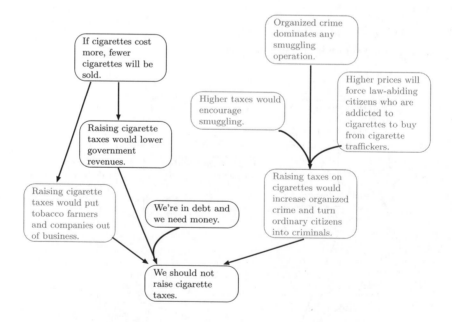

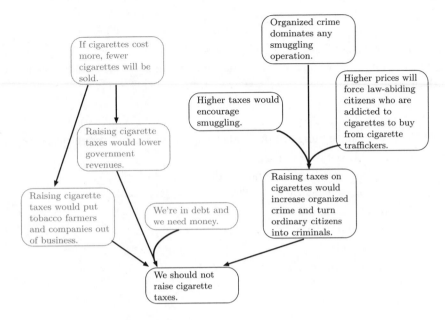

Now we're ready to outline. The key is simple.

> **Introduction**
> **Body**
> **Conclusion**

In short, here's the outline:

I.   Introduction
II. Body
III. Conclusion

We can say a little more before we take up specific examples.

I.   Introduction
     A. The conclusion of the argument
     B. The structure of the argument
II. Body
     [Lots of stuff here]
III. Conclusion
     A. A synopsis of the argument
     B. Restate the conclusion

Notice that we wind up stating the conclusion at least three times, probably more.

Example

The United States should raise taxes on cigarettes.

We separated this into two pieces. That's what you want to say in the introduction and the conclusion.

I.   Introduction
    A.   I am arguing that the United States should raise taxes on cigarettes.
    B.   I have two reasons.
        i.   It will improve our health.
        ii.   It will help us fiscally.
II. Body
    [Lots of stuff here]
III. Conclusion
    A.   We had two reasons
        i.   It will improve our health.
        ii.   It will help us fiscally.
    B.   The United States should raise taxes on cigarettes.

So far, this is easy!

Now for the body, again, we have our two reasons.

II. Body
    A.   First reason
    B.   Second reason

How do we structure these arguments? The idea is simple, and you've seen it before.

> **Introduction**
> **Body**
> **Conclusion**

For the first reason:

A.   First reason
    i.   We claim that raising taxes will improve health.
    ii. Here's why:
        [Stuff here]
    iii. That does it. We'll be healthier if we raise taxes and that's a good reason to do it.

For the second argument:

B. Second reason
    i.   We claim that raising taxes will give us badly needed revenue.
    ii. Here's why:
       [Stuff here]
    iii. And that does it. We need it; we can get it if we raise taxes; so let's raise taxes.

Filling in the "stuff" is just a question of reading the diagram.

I. Introduction
   A. I am arguing that the United States should raise taxes on cigarettes.
   B. I have two reasons.
      i.   It will improve our health.
      ii. It will help us fiscally.

II. Body
   A. First reason
      i.   We claim that raising taxes will improve health.
      ii. Here's why:
         a. Smoking is really bad.
         b. Raising taxes decreases the number of smokers.
      iii. That does it. We'll be healthier if we raise taxes and that's a good reason to do it.

   B. Second reason
      i.   We claim that raising taxes will give us badly needed revenue.
      ii. Here's why:
         a. Higher taxes mean more money.
         b. We're broke.
      iii. And that does it. We need it; we can get it if we raise taxes; so let's raise taxes.

III. Conclusion
   A. We had two reasons
      i.   It will improve our health.
      ii. It will help us fiscally.
   B. The United States should raise taxes on cigarettes.

Example

The United States shouldn't raise cigarette taxes.
We have three reasons.

I. Introduction
  A. We claim that cigarette taxes should not be raised.
  B. We have three reasons for this: economic hardship, finance, and crime.
II. A. First reason
      i. We claim that raising taxes will cause economic hardship.
      ii. Here's why:
          a. If taxes are raised, fewer cigarettes will be sold.
          b. Because of this, tobacco farmers will go bankrupt and tobacco companies will have to cut back on production and employees.
      iii. That's the problem. Raising taxes may seem like a good idea, but someone would be hurt, so we shouldn't do it.
  B. Second reason
      i. We claim that raising taxes will cost us badly needed revenue.
      ii. Here's why:
          a. As we said earlier, if taxes are raised, fewer cigarettes will be sold.
          b. Because of this there will be less tax revenue.
          c. But we need the money – we're broke!
      iii. That's the problem. We need tax revenue and raising taxes is like killing the goose that lays the golden egg. We think we'll get more money, but we'll get less. So don't raise taxes.
  C. Third reason
      i. We claim that raising taxes will fuel a crime wave like the Roaring Twenties.
      ii. Here's why:
          a. High prices encourage smuggling.
          b. Smuggling is dominated by organized crime.
          c. Honest folk who can't afford legal smokes and are hooked will turn to drug dealers.
      iii. This paints a terrible picture – a land dominated by wealthy crime syndicates, all made possible by an innocent tax rise. Don't raise taxes!
III. That's our argument. Raising taxes will impoverish hard-working farmers and laborers, it will deny the government necessary revenue, and it will impose on the country a tyranny of crime. Raising cigarette taxes would be a disaster.

In the end, there's really just one principle to remember in outlining:

> **Introduction**
> **Body**
> **Conclusion**

Use that principle for the whole argument and for each of its pieces. And if the pieces have pieces, use it for them too. In fact, here is our recipe for expression:

How to say something

1. If you can say it in a sentence, do it.
2. Otherwise, divide what you have to say into

    Introduction
    Body
    Conclusion,

    and apply this recipe to each.

Does this remind you of anything? Our advice is reflective (p. 98). This sort of reflectivity is a bit like the reflectivity of fractals, where the overall structure can be found in each part and each part of a part, and so on.

Exercises   Outlining Your Argument

Odd-numbered solutions begin on page 364

Now it's your turn. Outline arguments for the following propositions. These all appeared in the diagramming exercises on page 185:

1. My school should offer a major in logic.
2. My school should not offer a major in logic.
3. Cloning of human beings should be made illegal.
4. Cloning of human beings should not be made illegal.
5. The United States should abolish the death penalty.
6. The United States should not abolish the death penalty.
7. My school should have a quantitative skills requirement.
8. My school should not have a quantitative skills requirement.
9. ## Cathy acts globally and thinks locally

    Cathy unlocked her door and walked in. Wanda, Josh, and Candy, who were borrowing her psych book, followed slowly.

    "Hey, you left your lights on," said Josh casually.

    "Yeah."

    "Hey, you left your radio on," said Wanda, echoing Josh.

    "Yeah."

    "Hey! You left the water running!" said Candy as though she were witnessing a traffic accident.

    "Yeah. Then I can get really cold water whenever I want it. What's the deal?"

    Josh didn't know where to begin. "Well, you're wasting electricity! You're wasting water!"

    "Yeah, I know. It's really bad for the college, bad for the environment, bad for future generations. Bad for all those kids I'm going to have. So what?"

    Wanda was confused, but wary. Discussions with Cathy never seemed to end well. "If it's bad, then why ...?"

    "Do you expect me to solve these problems? We're burning up the planet, we're melting the ice caps, we're turning the ocean into a toilet and it's Cathy to the rescue? Get real! Nothing's going to happen until governments act."

"Cathy," Candy pleaded, "We each have a responsibility to the Earth. It's our home."

"So do your part. Turn off your lights. Walk everywhere. Don't wash. Wear grass skirts and banana leaves. How much longer will the Earth hang on because Candy eats bean sprouts? Not one nanosecond. You need millions of people acting warm and crunchy and that takes an act of Congress."

"You mean you won't do anything to save the planet unless you're forced to?" Candy's voice began to rise. "Somebody has to **make** you be good?"

"That's right, and it's not you."

"No! It's not me!" all three chorused.

"But Cathy," started Wanda, who couldn't let go of the logical problem, "then you don't recycle?"

"Hell no. I don't buy organic food. I don't give to charities. And I don't tip."

There was a silence as the three sensed the presence of evil.

"Governments have to take charge. That will happen only when things get really bad. I'm just trying to help." Cathy smiled.

....

The book borrowed, the four left the dorm. Cathy unwrapped a stick of gum and stuck it in her mouth. As she walked off, she dropped the wrapper on the sidewalk.

"CATHY!"

She turned.

"Well," started Josh. "I mean," Wanda added. "That's illegal!" finished Candy. "There's a law!"

"That's not enough." Cathy gave them a bland look. "If a law isn't enforced, it has no effect."

Authors' note: Please don't judge Cathy too harshly. She's a person. She's like any human being, only more so. In the incident recounted above, she is arguing against being, well, a good citizen. Compose an argument for Cathy not wasting resources. Try to make it strong enough to withstand her points.

There's a fascinating series of thought experiments devised by logician Raymond Smullyan. We'll present them in this and the following chapters.

You have died and gone to Hell. The devil meets you there and offers you a deal. He says, "I will write a natural number (0, 1, 2, 3, …) on a piece of paper and put it in my pocket. Every day (there are days in Hell) you can guess what the number is. I won't change the number. If you ever guess right, I'll send you up to heaven."

I think you can see that there's a strategy for escaping Hell. If you guess 0 on the first day, 1 on the second day, 2 the third day, and so on you'll eventually guess the devil's number. You don't know how long it will take, of course, but you can be certain you will escape in a finite number of days.

But suppose the devil makes a trickier offer. He says, "I will write a positive or negative integer (… −3, −2, −1, 0, 1, 2, 3, …) on a piece of paper and put it in my pocket. Every day you can guess what the number is. If you guess right, I'll send you up to heaven. I will never change the number."

Can you think of a strategy that will guarantee your escape from Hell in a finite number of days? Answer next chapter!

8.3 The Logic of Chance

But is it probable that probability gives assurance? (Blaise Pascal)

In Chapter Six we introduced you to three- and four-valued logics. Now we'll tell you about a logic with an infinite number of values. The logic is **probability** theory, the logic of chance.

In probability theory, think of the truth value of a statement P as a number representing how likely P is to be true. The number can be as low as 0 (certainly false) or as high as 1 (certainly true). The number can also be anywhere in between.

Probability theory, and it's more practical cousin, statistics, are very deep subjects, well beyond the scope of this book. But we can share a little bit of them with you. As the section on inductive logic in the last chapter points out, measuring likelihood is critical to many informal arguments.

Now imagine that an event is about to happen. This might be the flip of a coin or the roll of a die. Or it might be that a five-member committee will be chosen at random from the student body, or a poll will be taken of likely voters.

The propositions in our logic will be the possible outcomes of the event. In the case of a die roll, propositions would be statements such as "A '5' was rolled." "An even number was rolled." "The number rolled was not '2' or '6'."

The truth-values (probabilities) of the propositions are theoretical measures of how likely the outcomes are to occur.

Example

Let's suppose we decide to flip a coin. What is the probability of the coin turning up heads? There are two possibilities. The coin could come up heads or it could come up tails. Let's imagine all possible outcomes as comprising a rectangle.

In this case, the outcomes are equally likely (assuming this is a fair coin).

Since the probability of heads and the probability of tails should add to 1, we conclude that the probability of heads is $\frac{1}{2}$.

Example

Let's suppose we decide to roll a die. What is the probability that we roll a number less than 3?

There are six numbers we could roll.

1	2	3
4	5	6

They are equally likely (assuming this is a fair die). That means that the probability of rolling any particular number is $\frac{1}{6}$. But the question asked what the probability was of rolling a 1 or a 2. The answer is $\frac{2}{6}$.

1	2	3
4	5	6

We're using a fairly simple principle. If the space of all possible outcomes,

can be divided into n possible outcomes, all equally likely.

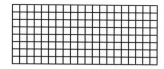

Then the probability of any one of those outcomes is $\frac{1}{n}$.

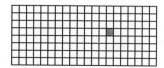

And the probability of any k of those outcomes is $\frac{k}{n}$.

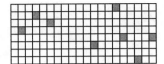

This is all pretty simple, but there are surprises, puzzles and mysteries. We'll give you one of each. First a surprise.

Surprise!

In the logic of chance, ∧ and ∨ are not "truth-functional".

In Sentential and Predicate, if you know the truth value of P and the truth value of Q then you know the truth value of $P \wedge Q$. You just look it up in the truth table. That's what we mean by "truth-functional". That's not the case with probability. In the following two examples the probabilities of P and Q are each $\frac{1}{2}$. But the probability of $P \wedge Q$ is different in the examples.

Example

We roll one die. Let P be "the number showing on the die is even" and let Q be "the number showing on the die is less than 4."

By our principle, the probability of P is $\frac{3}{6} = \frac{1}{2}$ because three out of six (the shaded boxes) outcomes make P true. Similarly, the probability of Q is also $\frac{1}{2}$ because three outcomes (the striped boxes) make it true. But the probability of $P \wedge Q$ is $\frac{1}{6}$

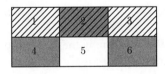

because the only number that is even and less than 4 (shaded and striped) is 2.

Example

We roll one die. Let P be "the number showing on the die is odd" and let Q be "the number showing on the die is less than 4."

As before, the probability of P is $\frac{1}{2}$ and the probability of Q is $\frac{1}{2}$. But now the probability of $P \wedge Q$ is $\frac{2}{6}$ because two numbers are both odd and less than 4 (1 and 3).

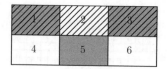

Thus, knowing that the truth values (probabilities) of P and Q are $\frac{1}{2}$ is not enough to know what the truth value of $P \wedge Q$ is[1].

Notice that these two examples also show that $\vee$ isn't truth-functional. In the first example the probability of $P \vee Q$ is $\frac{5}{6}$ (five numbers are either even or less than 4). And in the second example the probability of $P \vee Q$ is $\frac{4}{6}$ (four numbers are either odd or less than 4). On the other hand, $\neg$ *is* truth-functional.

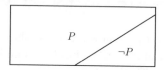

The probability of $\neg P$ is always 1 minus the probability of P.
Now here's a puzzle.

Puzzle!

The 'Monty Hall' problem.

This is a famous probability conundrum. It's simple to state, but it can confuse an expert. Monty Hall was the host of the TV game show, "Let's Make a Deal." In one part of the show the contestant is brought before three closed doors. Behind one of the doors is a new car. Behind the other two are goats. The contestant chooses a door and wins whatever is behind the door.

Stated this way, the probability of winning the car (the contestant does want the car) is $\frac{1}{3}$, since the car was placed randomly. But Monty Hall would tease the contestant. Let's say the contestant picked door 3. Monty Hall would then open either door 1 or door 2 to show a goat (there will always be a goat behind one of the other doors, possibly both). He would give the contestant the opportunity to change his or her guess. Suppose, for example, the contestant guesses door 3 and Monty reveals a goat behind 1. The contestant could stick with door 3 or change to door 2.

Should the contestant change?

The surprising answer is that you should switch. We say surprising because the problem caused a furor when Marilyn vos Savant wrote about it in *Parade* magazine. There were PhDs in mathematics who berated her answer. But she was right.

---

[1]   There are special cases when we can compute the probability of $P \wedge Q$ (see exercises).

Those who got it wrong were thinking:

wrong wrong wrong wrong wrong wrong wrong wrong

"Suppose I guessed door 3 and Monty opened door 1. Then I know the car is behind either 2 or 3. And that's all I know. So the two cases are equally likely. So it doesn't matter whether I change or not. The chances I will win are $\frac{1}{2}$ in either case."

wrong wrong wrong wrong wrong wrong wrong wrong

But you do know more. The fact that Monty opened door 1 tells you something more about where the car is. Those who got it right figured:

right right right right right right right right right right

"If I don't change my guess, then it's as if Monty never opened a door. I'm just ignoring him. So my chances of winning are $\frac{1}{3}$. They were $\frac{1}{3}$ before he opened the door and $\frac{1}{3}$ after he opened the door. That means my chance of losing is $\frac{2}{3}$. In other words, if I change, I improve my chances of winning from $\frac{1}{3}$ to $\frac{2}{3}$."

right right right right right right right right right right

Finally, we have a mystery.

Mystery!

What is probability anyway?

When we add 2 plus 3, we're doing theory. Two and three are abstractions; you can't travel somewhere to see Two. It lives in our heads. But we compute 2 plus 3 equals 5 because we can connect the abstractions to the world. Reality helps us think about two and three.

For most mathematics the connection between abstraction and the world is pretty clear. For probability, though, it's not. Probability and statistics is one area of mathematics where the philosophy is on the surface and difficult. *What does the probability of an event mean?*

This an especially unsettled area of philosophy. Consider the probability of a coin coming up "heads". The **objectivists** will say that the probability is $\frac{1}{2}$ because a coin has two sides; the sides are the same more or less, so that there's no reason to expect the coin to come up more often on one side than the other.

On the other hand, the **subjectivists** will say that probability is a measure of confidence in the outcome. The probability of a coin coming up "heads" is $\frac{1}{2}$ because we are no more confident the coin will come up "heads" than "tails" and vice-versa.

The **frequentists** will argue that the probability is simply a reflection of what actually happens. We flip a coin a million times and it comes up "heads" 500 258 times. Thus the probability is very close to $\frac{500258}{1000000} = .500258$. Some would say it is exactly .500258.

These are serious issues, not just for philosophers but for statisticians engaged in applying probability to the world. Statistics is where probability and inductive logic (Chapter Seven) meet. Inductive logic is uncertain. Statistics tells us how certain and uncertain it is.

This is a very rough overview. And we haven't even mentioned the question of whether the world is actually random or completely determined.

There's a bizarre and lovely short story by Robert Coates about a universe in which randomness breaks down, "The Law." We have a link to it on our website.

Philosophy matters. How we think of things affects our intuition, our ability to find our way. Philosophers argue about these ideas. So do statisticians.

Exercises   The Logic of Chance

Odd-numbered
solutions
begin on page 367

In these exercises, the event is the roll of one die. Let P be "the number showing is a '1' or a '4'." Let Q be "the number showing is not '4'."

1. What is the truth value (probability) of P?

2. What is the truth value of Q?
3. What is the truth value of $P \wedge Q$?
4. What is the truth value of $P \vee Q$?
5. What is the truth value of $P \wedge \neg Q$?
6. What is the truth value of $P \vee \neg Q$?

In these exercises, the event is the rolling of two dice, one red and one blue. There are 36 equally likely possibilities.

red die
1 2 3 4 5 6

blue die
1 2 3 4 5 6

Let P be "the sum of the numbers showing on the dice is 2." Let Q be "the sum of the numbers showing on the dice is 5." Let R be "the sum of the numbers showing

on the dice is greater than 9." Let S be "the sum of the numbers showing on the dice is odd." For each of the following problems, draw a diagram like the one above and shade in the squares where the proposition is true, then calculate the truth-value of the proposition.

7. P
8. Q
9. R
10. S
11. $P \wedge Q$
12. $P \vee Q$

There's a special case where there is a formula for computing the truth-value of $A \wedge B$. It's when the truth of A and B are "independent", that is, knowing whether A is true or not tells you nothing about B. In that case, the truth-value of the conjunction is the product of the truth-values of the conjuncts.

In the next exercises we are again rolling two dice, one red and one blue. Let J be "the number on the red die is even," let K be "the number on the blue die is greater than 3", let L be "the number on the blue die is a prime number (2, 3, or 5)", let M be "the number on the red die is not '4'."

13. What is the truth-value of $J \wedge K$? Are J and K independent?

14. What is the truth-value of $J \wedge L$? Are J and L independent?

15. What is the truth-value of $J \wedge M$? Are J and M independent?

16. What is the truth-value of $K \wedge L$? Are K and L independent?

An event takes place. Two possible outcomes are A and B.

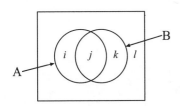

We have labelled four regions on this picture i, j, k, and l.

17! Show that the truth value (probability) of $A \vee \neg A$ is 1.

18! The truth table of $\neg(A \wedge B)$ is the same as the truth table of $\neg A \vee \neg B$. Show that the truth value (probability) of $\neg(A \wedge B)$ is equal to the truth value of $\neg A \vee \neg B$.

19! The truth table of $\neg(A \vee B)$ is the same as the truth table of $\neg A \wedge \neg B$. Show that the truth value (probability) of $\neg(A \vee B)$ is equal to the truth value of $\neg A \wedge \neg B$.

20!! We can define the truth value of $A \Rightarrow B$ as the truth value of $\neg A \vee B$, since these two have the same truth tables. Show that if A is contained in B (as a subset) then the truth value of $A \Rightarrow B$ is 1.

21. Here's another edition. Could this be the fun page?

The Digestor's Digest

— Vol. I, No. 7 —

For Dieters:

Burger Mad has invented the most amazing treat, the "Choco-Butter Toffee-Waffle." Although it is composed entirely of butter, honey, milk chocolate, marshmallows, and chicken fat, laboratory tests show that it has fewer calories than all other breakfast foods combined!

For Dieters:

O'Donnell's old favorite, the "Bowl O'Mush" with high-fructose corn flakes is now available in a special artificially soured version. This is not the fun page.

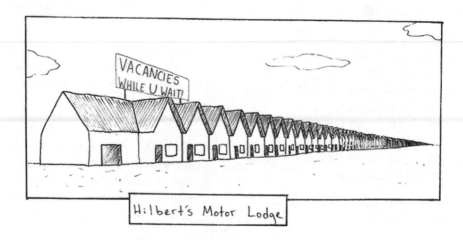

Hilbert's Motor Lodge

Chapter Nine

9.1 Simple Deduction

Children's fantasy demands the strictest logic, consistency and attention to detail ... The effectiveness of the great children's books comes from the combination of wildly imaginative premises and strictly consistent and logical conclusions from those premises. It is no wonder that the greatest children's fantasists, Carroll, [C. S.] Lewis, and Tolkien had day jobs in the driest reaches of logic and philology. (Alison Gopnik)

Logic isn't linear. Logic spreads out. This is appropriate, for humans do not, in general, think linearly. Yet when we take things in, we find it easier when we see a first step, then a second step and then a third step.

In the previous chapter we linearized our informal arguments by outlining them. In this chapter we'll start the process for formal arguments. It's much more difficult, but the rewards are immense.

First, let's recap:

An argument is	
Valid	If the conclusion is true whenever the premises are true.
Invalid	If it's possible for the premises to be true and the conclusion false.

In Sentential, we can decide validity with certainty.

Sweet Reason: A Field Guide To Modern Logic, Second Edition. Jim Henle, Jay L. Garfield, Thomas Tymoczko and Emily Altreuter.
© 2012 John Wiley & Sons Inc. Published 2012 by John Wiley & Sons Inc.

Sentential

If an argument is invalid, we can show that with truth tables.

If an argument is valid, we can show that with truth tables.

In Predicate, it's not that easy.

Predicate

If an argument is invalid, we can show that with a counterexample.

If an argument is valid ...
we have no way to show that!

Showing that an argument is valid means checking all possible situations where the premises are true. We can do that in Sentential. That means checking all the lines in a truth table. Truth tables list all the possible situations. There are a finite number of them. We can check them all.

In Predicate, however, there are an infinite number of possibilities. A "situation" isn't just a line in a truth table, it's a universe. There are infinitely many of them. We can't check them all.

This is the real reason we must introduce deduction. A deduction of the conclusion from the premises will give us the one piece we lack, a way to say with certainty that a predicate argument is valid.

We'll approach deduction slowly. We'll take two chapters to warm up with Sentential and then two to master Predicate.

Note: There are many different deduction systems. The system we present here is a "Fitch-style" system[1] devised by us in conjunction with our colleague, Dan Velleman of Amherst College.

Rules

We're going to provide you with a set of rules that will enable you to deduce the conclusion of any valid argument from its premises. Such a deduction is a proof that the argument is valid. These rules will also be rules that can guide you in constructing natural language arguments.

In our deduction system, there are two rules for each connective, an "In" rule and an "Out" rule. The In rule is for introducing the connective into the proof, that is, for deducing a wff in which it's the main connective. The Out rule is for getting the connective out of the

---

[1]   The great twentieth-century logician Frederick Fitch introduced deduction of this type.

proof, that is, for deducing something from a wff of which it's the main connective. Each of these rules comes with a strategy for proof construction. This will become clear as we go along.

Your first two rules

The first two rules handle conjunction.

$$\wedge\text{Out:} \quad \frac{A \wedge B}{\therefore A} \qquad \frac{A \wedge B}{\therefore B}$$

That is, from $A \wedge B$, you can deduce A and you can deduce B. This is the $\wedge$Out rule. A and B may be any wffs. For example, from $(P \Rightarrow Q) \wedge (Q \vee R)$, you can conclude $(P \Rightarrow Q)$, and you can also conclude $(Q \vee R)$.

$$\wedge\text{In:} \quad \frac{\begin{array}{c} A \\ B \end{array}}{\therefore A \wedge B}$$

That is, if you know A and you also know B, you may deduce $A \wedge B$. This is the $\wedge$ In rule.

What a deduction looks like

The deductions we'll study in this section are just lists of wffs. The first few wffs are the premises of the argument. After these, each wff in the list follows from the previous wffs by one of the deduction rules. So far we only have two rules, but we can still manage a deduction.

Example

$$\frac{P \wedge Q}{\therefore Q \wedge P.}$$

1. $P \wedge Q$ premise
2. P $\wedge$Out 1
3. Q $\wedge$Out 1
4. $Q \wedge P$ $\wedge$In 2, 3

- Note that each line of a deduction is numbered.
- Note that each line is justified. The first line is justified by "premise" (because it's a premise). Every other line is justified by one of our rules. For example, in line 2, P follows from $P \wedge Q$ by the $\wedge$Out rule.

- Note that each line not a premise refers to previous lines. In line 2, line 1 is mentioned. That's because $P \wedge Q$ is needed to get P using $\wedge$Out. Similarly in line 3, line 1 is mentioned because $P \wedge Q$ is needed to get Q using $\wedge$Out. In line 4, both lines 2 and 3 are mentioned because you need both P and Q to get $Q \wedge P$ using $\wedge$In. The order in which the lines are mentioned doesn't matter.

Your next two rules

$$\vee\text{In:} \quad \frac{\mathcal{A}}{\therefore \mathcal{A} \vee \mathcal{B}} \qquad \frac{\mathcal{B}}{\therefore \mathcal{A} \vee \mathcal{B}}$$

That is, from either $\mathcal{A}$ or $\mathcal{B}$, you may deduce $\mathcal{A} \vee \mathcal{B}$. This is the $\vee$In rule. Again, $\mathcal{A}$ and $\mathcal{B}$ may be any wffs. We are focussing on Sentential for now, but this and all these rules can be used in Predicate as well. For example, from $\exists x(Fx \Rightarrow \forall yHxy)$, you can conclude $\forall z \neg Fz \vee \exists x(Fx \Rightarrow \forall yHxy)$.

$$\vee\text{Out:} \quad \frac{\begin{array}{c} \mathcal{A} \vee \mathcal{B} \\ \mathcal{A} \Rightarrow \mathcal{C} \\ \mathcal{B} \Rightarrow \mathcal{C} \end{array}}{\therefore \mathcal{C}}$$

This is not as obvious as the previous rules but it should make sense. It's saying that if you know that at least one of two statements is true, and both statements lead to a third statement, then that third statement must be true.

Example

$$\begin{array}{l} P \Rightarrow Q \\ R \Rightarrow Q \\ \underline{P} \\ \therefore Q \end{array}$$

1. $P \Rightarrow Q$ premise
2. $R \Rightarrow Q$ premise
3. P premise
4. $P \vee R$ $\vee$In 3
5. Q $\vee$Out 1, 2, 4

You may be wondering: how do you go about constucting a proof? We have a simple strategy. We'll show it to you in the next section.

- Note that every rule we give you is itself a valid argument. This is critical; this is what guarantees that our deductions produce only valid conclusions. If you're not sure, test each rule with the shortcut method.

- Note also that the rules are not arbitrary. Each one reflects a way we reason every day in English.

Here's an example to demonstrate this. You tell the person at the counter that you want a donut and an orange juice. He first gives you a donut on a paper plate and then gets a carton of orange juice.

That's the ∧Out rule. He used it once to figure out that he has to give you a donut. He used it a second time to figure out that he has to give you a carton of juice.

Then you say you want a medium coffee. He reaches for a medium cup, hands it to you and points to two thermoses and says "Over there. You can have caf or decaf."

That's the ∨Out rule. He knows that if you want a medium decaf, then he needs to give you a medium cup ($D \Rightarrow M$). And he knows that if you want medium coffee with caffeine, then you also need a medium cup ($C \Rightarrow M$). In a lightning swift display of logic, he figures out that since you want either medium caf or decaf ($D \vee C$) he has to give you a medium cup (M)!

Just two more rules for now

We'll stop after this. Six rules is enough for Simple Deduction.

$$\neg\text{Out:} \quad \frac{\neg\neg A}{\therefore A}$$

In other words, two wrongs *do* make a right. If it's not the case that it's not the case that blah blah blah, then blah blah blah must be true.

$$\neg\text{In:} \quad \frac{A \Rightarrow (B \wedge \neg B)}{\therefore \neg A}$$

This rule has a Latin name, *reductio ad absurdum*, which means reduction to absurdity. The rule should make sense, however odd it looks. If a sentence (A) leads to a contradiction ($B \wedge \neg B$), that's a good reason to reject A and to accept its negation ($\neg A$). Do you recall our resolution of the barber "paradox" (p. 353)? This was an example of *reductio*.

We use *reductio* all the time. Suppose you're working on a crossword puzzle

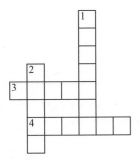

Belnap	Dodgson	Pierce
Bernays	Frege	Priest
Bolzano	Gödel	Quine
Boole	Grice	Russell
Boolos	Hilbert	Shelah
Cantor	Kleene	Skolem
Church	Kripke	Turing
Cohen	Ockham	Woodin
Davis	Peano	Zermelo

where the entries must all come from the list of logicians on the right. You start by guessing that 1 Down is Russell because that gives four possibilities for 3 Across (Boole, Frege, Grice, and Quine) and two possibilities for 4 Across (Shelah and Skolem). Let *P* be the statement, "1 Down is Russell".

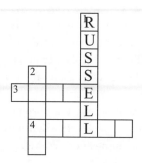

From *P* we see that 4 Across (Shelah or Skolem) starts with an 'S'. Let *Q* be the statement, "4 Across starts with an 'S'."

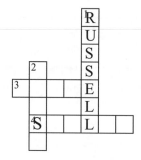

But everything we might use for 2 Down (Boole, Cohen, Davis, Gödel, etc.) gives us ¬*Q*, "4 Across *doesn't* start with 'S'." So $P \Rightarrow (Q \wedge \neg Q)$. By *reductio*, ¬*P*.

Example

$$\frac{\neg P \Rightarrow (Q \wedge \neg Q)}{\therefore P}$$

1. $\neg P \Rightarrow (Q \wedge \neg Q)$ premise
2. $\neg\neg P$ ¬In 1
3. P ¬Out 2

Important note: The deduction rules must be used *exactly* as they are given. They're not a license for bad behavior! Every year we see students do something like:

$$\vdots$$

17. $\neg(P \lor Q)$ (some reason)

18. $P \lor Q$ $\neg$Out, 17

$$\vdots$$

Don't do this! $\dfrac{\neg A}{\therefore A}$ is not valid. And it's *not* the $\neg$Out rule!

Exercises   Simple Deduction

Odd-numbered solutions begin on page 368

Fill in the blanks in the following deductions.

1. $\dfrac{P \land Q}{\therefore P \lor Q}$

    1. $P \land Q$ _____
    2. P _____
    3. $P \lor Q$ _____

2. $\dfrac{P \land (Q \land R)}{\therefore (P \land Q) \land R}$

    1. $P \land (Q \land R)$ _____
    2. P _____
    3. $Q \land R$ _____
    4. Q _____
    5. R _____
    6. $P \land Q$ _____
    7. $(P \land Q) \land R$ _____

3. $P \Rightarrow ((Q \Rightarrow R) \land (P \Rightarrow R))$
    $Q \Rightarrow ((Q \Rightarrow R) \land (P \Rightarrow R))$
    $P \lor Q$
    $\overline{\therefore R}$

    1. _____   premise
    2. _____   premise
    3. _____   premise
    4. _____ $\lor$Out, 1, 2, 3
    5. _____ $\land$Out, 4
    6. _____ $\land$Out, 4
    7. _____ $\lor$Out, 3, 5, 6

4. $P \Rightarrow (Q \land \neg Q)$
    $\neg P \Rightarrow (R \lor Q)$
    $S \Rightarrow (R \lor Q)$
    $\overline{\therefore R \lor Q}$

    1. _____   premise
    2. _____   premise
    3. _____   premise
    4. _____ $\neg$In, 1
    5. _____ $\lor$In, 4
    6. _____ $\lor$Out, 2, 3, 5

5. $\neg(P \Rightarrow Q) \Rightarrow ((P \Rightarrow Q)$
    $\land \neg(P \Rightarrow Q))\neg(R \Rightarrow Q)$
    $\Rightarrow ((Q \Rightarrow P) \land \neg(Q \Rightarrow P))P \lor R$
    $\overline{\therefore Q}$

    1. _____   _____
    2. _____   _____
    3. _____   _____
    4. _____ $\neg$In, 1
    5. _____ $\neg$Out, 4
    6. _____   _____
    7. _____   _____
    8. Q _____

6. $\dfrac{\neg(P \Rightarrow (Q \land \neg Q)) \Rightarrow (Q \land \neg Q)}{\therefore \neg P}$

    1. _____   _____
    2. _____ $\neg$In, 1
    3. _____   _____
    4. $\neg P$ _____

7. $(P \lor Q) \Rightarrow R$
     $(S \land U) \Rightarrow R$
     $(A \lor B) \Rightarrow (H \land P)$
     $(J \Leftrightarrow K) \Rightarrow (H \land P)$
     B
     $\overline{}$
     $\therefore R \land P$

1.   _____   _____
2.   _____   _____
3.   _____   _____
4.   _____   _____
5.   _____   _____
6.   _____   ∨In, 5
7.   _____   ∨In, 6
8.   _____   ∨Out, 3, 4, 7
9.   _____   _____
10.   _____   ∨In, 9
11.   _____   _____
12.   _____   ∨Out, 1, 2, 11
13. $R \land P$ _____

8! $P \Rightarrow Q$
     $Q \Rightarrow R$
     $R \Rightarrow P$
     $P \Rightarrow R$
     $Q \Rightarrow P$
     Q
     $\overline{}$
     $\therefore P$

1.   _____   premise
2.   _____   premise
3.   _____   premise
4.   _____   premise
5.   _____   premise
6.   _____   premise
7.   _____   ∨In, 6
8.   _____   ∨Out, 2, 4, 7
9.   _____   ∨In, 8
10.   _____   ∨Out, 3, 5, 9

9.   Solve the puzzle on page 217.

Screenshot by Shua Garfield (2001).

9.2 Simple Strategy

The author of the Iliad is either Homer or, if not Homer, somebody else of the same name. (Aldous Huxley)

We have a strategy for finding deductions. It's pretty simple and it's built in to the rules. Here it is:

> # Deduction strategy
>
> - Work backwards.
> - If you can't work backwards, then work forwards.

That's the strategy: start at the end. If that doesn't work, start at the beginning.

Example

$$P \land Q$$
$$\therefore Q \land P.$$

We can set up the problem like this:

1. $P \land Q$ premise

A. $Q \land P$

We put the conclusion in gray. That's to remind us what our goal is. We used a letter (A.) instead of a number (2.) for the line because we don't know yet what the line number will be when we're done. We might put more lines in between the premise and the conclusion.

Our job is to fill in the gap between the premise and the conclusion. Following the strategy, we try to work backwards. How do you work backwards?

To work backwards, find the main connective of what you are trying to prove. The main connective of the conclusion is ∧.

Next, we look at the associated In rule, in this case, the ∧ In rule. The idea is that we want an ∧ and the way to get an ∧ is to use ∧ In. This is the rule that says if you have both conjuncts then you may get the conjunction. That tells us we should try to get Q and P. Working backwards, we put them in.

1. $P \land Q$ premise

B. Q

C. P

A. $Q \land P$ ∧In B, C

That's how to work backwards. Find the main connective, take the associated In rule, see what you need to use it.

Notice that P and Q are now gray instead of the conclusion. That's because P and Q are the new goals. $Q \land P$ is no longer a goal because we know how to derive it from P and Q. We've filled in the justification for $Q \land P$.

And of course we're not done yet. We've just worked backwards one step.

Now what do we do? Again, our strategy tells us to work backwards. That means work backwards from lines B and C, that is, from Q and P. To work backwards, we look at the main connective. But Q and P are basic wffs; they have no connective. So we can't work backwards anymore. So we work forwards. How do you work forwards?

To work forwards, look at the wffs that we have and find their main connectives. In this case, we only have one wff, the premise, $P \land Q$, and the main connective is $\land$.

Next, we look at the associated Out rule, in this case, the $\land$ Out rule. The idea is that we have an $\land$ so maybe it will help to get rid of it. The way to get rid of an $\land$ is to use the $\land$ Out rule. This is the rule that says that from a conjunction we can get the conjuncts. That tells us that from $P \land Q$ we can get P and we can get Q. Well, that's exactly what we want!

1. $P \land Q$ premise
B. Q $\land$Out 1
C. P $\land$Out 1
A. $Q \land P$ $\land$In B, C

And now we can replace the letters with the appropriate numbers.

1. $P \land Q$ premise
2. Q $\land$Out 1
3. P $\land$Out 1
4. $Q \land P$ $\land$In 2, 3

Here it is again, in detail.

Deduction strategy

- Work backwards.
  - ⊙ Get the main connective of what you want to prove.
  - ⊙ Apply the associated In rule backwards.
- Work forwards (if you can't work backwards).
  - ⊙ Get the main connective of what you know.
  - ⊙ Apply the associated Out rule (forwards).
  - ⊙ Apply other rules too.

Here's an example that uses all six of our rules.

Example

$$C \Rightarrow (D \wedge C)$$
$$\neg C \Rightarrow (D \wedge \neg D)$$
$$\underline{D \Rightarrow (D \wedge C)}$$
$$\therefore C \wedge D$$

We start with this:

1. $C \Rightarrow (D \wedge C)$ premise
2. $\neg C \Rightarrow (D \wedge \neg D)$ premise
3. $D \Rightarrow (D \wedge C)$ premise

A. $\boxed{C \wedge D}$

Working backwards, we see that the conclusion is a conjunction. Using the $\wedge$ In rule backwards, we need to prove C and D.

1. $C \Rightarrow (D \wedge C)$ premise
2. $\neg C \Rightarrow (D \wedge \neg D)$ premise
3. $D \Rightarrow (D \wedge C)$ premise

B. $\boxed{C}$

C. $\boxed{D}$
A. $C \wedge D$ $\wedge$In B, C

Our goals, C and D, are basic wffs so we can't work backwards anymore.

Working forwards, we see that all the premises are conditionals. We don't have a $\Rightarrow$ Out rule yet. But two of our Out rules have conditionals in them. It looks like we could apply $\neg$ In to line 2.

1. $C \Rightarrow (D \wedge C)$ premise
2. $\neg C \Rightarrow (D \wedge \neg D)$ premise
3. $D \Rightarrow (D \wedge C)$ premise
4. $\neg\neg C$ $\neg$In 2

B. $\boxed{C}$

C. $\boxed{D}$
A. $C \wedge D$ $\wedge$In B, C

Now statement 4. is a negation. We can apply $\neg$ Out to that. That gives us C, one of our goals.

1. $C \Rightarrow (D \wedge C)$ premise
2. $\neg C \Rightarrow (D \wedge \neg D)$ premise
3. $D \Rightarrow (D \wedge C)$ premise
4. $\neg\neg C$ ¬In 2
5. C ¬Out 4

?

C. D

A. $C \wedge D$ ∧In 5, c

All we have left to do is prove D. We still have to work forwards. Lines 1. and 3. are part of the ∨ Out rule. We could use them if we had the third piece, $C \vee D$. So let's try to get that.

1. $C \Rightarrow (D \wedge C)$ premise
2. $\neg C \Rightarrow (D \wedge \neg D)$ premise
3. $D \Rightarrow (D \wedge C)$ premise
4. $\neg\neg C$ ¬In 2
5. C ¬Out 4

?

D. $C \vee D$

?

C. D

A. $C \wedge D$ ∧In 5, c

We now have a goal that isn't basic so we can work backwards again. Line D. is a disjunction. Applying the ∨ In rule backwards, we can get $C \vee D$ if we have either C or D. But we have C!

1. $C \Rightarrow (D \wedge C)$ premise
2. $\neg C \Rightarrow (D \wedge \neg D)$ premise
3. $D \Rightarrow (D \wedge C)$ premise
4. $\neg\neg C$ ¬In 2
5. C ¬Out 4
6. $C \vee D$ ∨In 5

?

C. D

A. $C \wedge D$ ∧In 5, c

Now we can apply ∨ Out to lines 1, 3, and 6:

1. $C \Rightarrow (D \wedge C)$ premise
2. $\neg C \Rightarrow (D \wedge \neg D)$ premise
3. $D \Rightarrow (D \wedge C)$ premise
4. $\neg\neg C$ ¬In 2
5. C ¬Out 4
6. $C \vee D$ ∨In 5
7. $D \wedge C$ ∨Out 1, 3, 6

C. $\boxed{D}$

A. $C \wedge D$ ∧In 5, c

Once more our goal (line c.) is basic so we can't work backwards. We can work forwards, though. Line 7 is a conjunction. We can use ∧ Out to complete the proof.

1. $C \Rightarrow (D \wedge C)$ premise
2. $\neg C \Rightarrow (D \wedge \neg D)$ premise
3. $D \Rightarrow (D \wedge C)$ premise
4. $\neg\neg C$ ¬In 2
5. C ¬Out 4
6. $C \vee D$ ∨In 5
7. $D \wedge C$ ∨Out 1, 3, 6
8. D ∧Out 7
9. $C \wedge D$ ∧In 5, 8

Exercises Simple Strategy

Odd-numbered solutions begin on page 368

Here are some arguments (all valid) for you to justify. In each case, deduce the conclusion from the premises.

1. $P \Rightarrow R$
$Q \Rightarrow R$
$\underline{P \vee Q}$
$\therefore R \vee S$

2. $\underline{(P \wedge Q) \wedge R}$
$\therefore P \wedge (Q \wedge R)$

3. $\underline{P \wedge Q}$
$\therefore Q \vee R$

4. $\underline{P \wedge (Q \wedge R)}$
$\therefore \neg P \vee (R \vee \neg Q)$

5. $P \wedge Q$
$P \Rightarrow R$
$\underline{Q \Rightarrow R}$
$\therefore R$

6. $(P \wedge Q) \Rightarrow (P \vee Q)$
$R \vee (P \wedge Q)$
$\underline{R \Rightarrow (P \vee Q)}$
$\therefore P \vee Q$

7. $\underline{((P \Rightarrow Q) \wedge (R \Rightarrow Q)) \wedge (P \vee R)}$
$\therefore Q$

8! $\underline{\neg(((\neg Q \Rightarrow \neg Q) \wedge (P \vee \neg Q)) \wedge (P \Rightarrow \neg Q)) \Rightarrow ((P \Rightarrow \neg Q) \wedge \neg(P \Rightarrow \neg Q))}$
$\therefore \neg Q$

Translate each of these arguments into Sentential. Determine whether the form is valid or invalid. If it is invalid, construct a counterexample by composing an argument of exactly the same form with obviously true premises and an obviously false conclusion. If the argument form is valid, construct a deduction using the rules that you have so far showing that it is valid.

9. Jerry likes either rice or noodles. If he likes rice he likes movies. If he likes noodles he likes skating. If he likes noodles he likes movies. Therefore, Jerry likes movies.

10. It's not true that Kate does not play tennis. Kate is a college student and likes pop songs. Therefore, Kate plays tennis and she likes pop songs.

11. It is not true that today is Friday. Therefore, either today is Friday or Sally likes cereal.

12. If it's not raining, then it is Sunday and it is not Sunday. Therefore, it is raining.

The word **sorites** (pronounced "sor-EYE-tees") has two logical connections. One is a paradox we'll meet in Chapter Ten. The other is a type of logical puzzle in which the premises of an argument are given and the challenge is to find the conclusion. Charles Dodgson, the author of *Alice in Wonderland* under the pseudonym Lewis Carroll, invented many sorites and an original method to solve them. Each of the following is a sorites written by Dodgson. In each you are to find a conclusion that requires all of premises.

13. All puddings are nice;
    This dish is a pudding;
    No nice things are wholesome.

14. No experienced person is incompetent;
    Jenkins is always blundering;
    No competent person is always blundering.

15! Things sold in the street are of no great value.
    Nothing but rubbish can be had for a song.
    Eggs of the Great Auk are very valuable.
    It is only what is sold in the street that is really *rubbish*.

16! You'll meet this argument in the next chapter: $P \Rightarrow Q$ It's *modus*

$$\frac{P}{\therefore Q}$$

ponens (see p. 20) and it's the $\Rightarrow$ Out rule. Surprisingly, we don't actually need it for deduction because the rules we have already cover it. Deduce Q from $P \Rightarrow Q$ and P using the rules of this chapter.

Having told you a little about probability in Chapter Eight, we can't resist giving you a probability paradox, the "two-envelope paradox".

Someone has sealed a random amount of money in an envelope and twice that amount in a second envelope. The two envelopes are identical. One of the envelopes is given to Jay and the other is given to Jim.

(Continued on next page)

Jim thinks, "I don't know what's in this envelope. Suppose it's $100. Then Jay either has $50 or $200. The two possibilities are equally likely. So if we traded, it's a good deal for me because half the time I gain $100 and half the time I lose only $50. That's if my envelope has $100. But whatever it has, it's still a great deal! I either double my money or I only lose half of it."

So Jim offers to trade envelopes with Jay. He expects to have to persuade Jay, but surprisingly, Jay is eager to trade. So they trade.

Now Jim thinks, "On average, I've gained! But it's still the case that if we trade, there's a 50% chance I'll double my money and a 50% I'll lose only half. That's still a great deal! I should trade again!"

Jim is sure Jay won't trade, but Jay, with a strange glint in his eye, readily agrees. A few minutes later, they trade again. . . .

9.3   Writing Your Argument

Put the argument into a concrete shape, into an image, some hard phrase, round and solid as a ball, which they can see and handle and carry home with them, and the cause is half won. (Ralph Waldo Emerson)

Once you have an outline, you can write. The words will come. The prose may be awkward at first, but you can go back any number of times to improve it. There are just a few things to remember.

1. **Use a new _____ for every new idea.**
   What goes in the _____ depends on what you're writing. If it's a short paper, then it's paragraphs. If it's a long paper, sections. If it's a book, chapters. We'll keep it simple here and write short arguments, but the principle is the same.
   At the very least, use a _____ for the introduction.
   Use a _____ for each heading in the body.
   Use a _____ for the conclusion.
   Don't be stingy, _____s are free.
2. **Read what you write, over and over; don't stop thinking.**
   What seemed like a good argument when you diagrammed it may sound awful when it's written. Listen for that. Be critical of your reasoning.
   And play dumb. Imagine you are not very clever and not on top of things. Would someone as ignorant and stupid as you understand the argument? What can you to do (as writer) to help?

Okay, let's write our arguments.

Example

The United States should raise taxes on cigarettes.

Here's how the outline we drafted in Chapter Eight starts:

I.   Introduction
    A.   I am arguing that the United States should raise taxes on cigarettes.
    B.   I have two reasons.
        i.   It will improve our health.
        ii.   It will help us fiscally.

We write:

I would like to make the case for raising the tax on cigarettes. It's a simple action, but it would have two important, long-term benefits: the health of the American public and the financial health of American government. I will discuss these both in detail.

That says it all. It says what our conclusion is and it alerts the reader to the shape of the argument.

Now for the first argument. Here's the outline.

A.   First reason
    i.   We claim that raising taxes will improve health.
    ii.   Here's why:
        a.   Smoking is really bad.
        b.   Raising taxes decreases the number of smokers.
    iii.   That does it. We'll be healthier if we raise taxes and that's a good reason to do it.

It's no longer an issue of debate: smoking is bad for your health. If we raise cigarette taxes, we will, over time, reduce the rate of smoking here. That's going to make us a healthier country.

Pretty short. Was that a discussion "in detail?" Don't stop thinking! Can we make this better?

I suppose we could elaborate on the health risks of smoking. And we should also tie this point to the conclusion.

The dangers of tobacco are well-known today. No longer do we argue about the increased chances of lung cancer, of emphysema, of heart disease. There is even considerable agreement on the cost to nonsmokers of breathing secondhand smoke. If we raise cigarette taxes, we will, over time, reduce the rate of smoking here. That's going to make us a healthier country. This is reason enough to support a tax hike.

Better. Notice that we've added to the outline.

A. First reason
    i.   We claim that raising taxes will improve health.
    ii. Here's why:
        a. Smoking is really bad.
            1. Smoking causes lung cancer.
            2. Smoking causes heart disease.
            3. Smoking causes emphysema.
            4. Smoking hurts nonsmokers.
        b. Raising taxes decreases the number of smokers.
    iii. That does it. We'll be healthier if we raise taxes and that's a good reason to do it.

For the second argument,

B. Second reason
    i.   We claim that raising taxes will give us badly needed revenue.
    ii. Here's why:
        a. Higher taxes mean more money.
        b. We're broke.
    iii. And that does it. We need it; we can get it if we raise taxes; so let's raise taxes.

Raising cigarette taxes would substantially increase government revenues. There are millions of smokers. Even a small increase will net significant sums of money. We can't afford to overlook this opportunity. The federal deficit is growing every year. The national debt is now [fill in the blank]. This is our second reason for a tax hike: to bring down the deficit.

Not bad. And for the conclusion,

III. Conclusion
    A. We had two reasons
        i.   It will improve our health.
        ii. It will help us fiscally.
    B. The United States should raise taxes on cigarettes.

---

we can write

In short, we can help ourselves two ways with this measure: physical health and fiscal health [cute, huh?]. *This is good governing. Let's raise the tax on tobacco today.*

Not bad. But it will get better.

Example

The United States shouldn't raise cigarette taxes.
Here's the start of the outline:

I.   Introduction
  A.   We claim that cigarette taxes should not be raised.
  B.   We have three reasons for this: economic hardship, finance, and crime.

I hear people call for raising cigarette taxes and I see nothing but trouble. The kinds of tax hikes they're talking about won't raise money, they'll lose it. They'll put honest working Americans out of business. And they'll create a bonanza for organized crime. That's three good reasons for holding back on any tax increase.

Good start. We didn't say this time "We'll discuss each of these reasons in detail," but we can signal this is what we're doing as we start each of the next three paragraphs.

A.   First reason
  i.   We claim that raising taxes will cause economic hardship.
  ii.   Here's why:
    a.   If taxes are raised, fewer cigarettes will be sold.
    b.   Because of this, tobacco farmers will go bankrupt and tobacco companies will have to cut back on production and employees.
  iii.   That's the problem. Raising taxes may seem like a good idea, but someone would be hurt, so we shouldn't do it.

First of all, if we raise taxes, we raise the cost of cigarettes to the smoker and fewer will be sold. With fewer cigarettes being sold, the tobacco companies and tobacco farmers will suffer.

Hmm… this looks sort of thin. Let's play for sympathy.

First of all, if we raise taxes, we raise the cost of cigarettes to the smoker and fewer cigarettes will be sold. With fewer cigarettes being sold, the tobacco companies and tobacco farmers will suffer. Now, whatever you think of tobacco executives, there are tens of thousands of honest, hard-working Americans in the tobacco process. Many are small farmers whose families have been raising tobacco for hundreds of years. It's not good government to cause historically important industries to collapse.

So maybe our outline is a little bigger now.

A. First reason
    i.   We claim that raising taxes will cause economic hardship.
    ii.   Here's why:
        a. If taxes are raised, fewer cigarettes will be sold.
        b. Because of this, tobacco farmers will go bankrupt and tobacco companies will have to cut back on production and employees.
        c. It's bad to put tobacco workers out of work.
            1.   Many are family-run farms.
            2.   Tobacco farming is historically important.
    iii. That's the problem. Raising taxes may seem like a good idea, but someone would be hurt, so we shouldn't do it.

Next paragraph:

B. Second reason
    i.   We claim that raising taxes will cost us badly needed revenue.
    ii.   Here's why:
        a. As we said earlier, if taxes are raised, fewer cigarettes will be sold.
        b. Because of this there will be less tax revenue.
        c. But we need the money – we're broke!
    iii. That's the problem. We need tax revenue and raising taxes is like killing the goose that lays the golden egg. We think we'll get more money, but we'll get less. So don't raise taxes.

Secondly, if we raise taxes, we raise the cost of cigarettes to the smoker and fewer will be sold. That doesn't mean more tax money, it means less. This is no way to reduce the size of the deficit.

Next paragraph:

C. Third reason
    i.   We claim that raising taxes will fuel a crime wave like the Roaring Twenties.
    ii.   Here's why:
        a. High prices encourage smuggling.
        b. Smuggling is dominated by organized crime.
        c. Honest folk who can't afford legal smokes and are hooked will turn to drug dealers.
    iii. This paints a terrible picture – a land dominated by wealthy crime syndicates, all made possible by an innocent tax rise. Don't raise taxes!

Finally, the proponents of this tax rise have shut their eyes to the significant danger of organized crime. Higher cigarette prices will encourage smuggling on a grand scale. The Mafia dominates smuggling operations already with their heroin and cocaine rackets. They will add tobacco to the list. And what have we done to the smoker? High prices will force those who are addicted and have no choice to buy from smugglers. In our sincere desire to do good, we will turn thousands, perhaps millions of honest citizens into criminals.

Strong stuff!

III. That's our argument. Raising taxes will impoverish hard-working farmers and laborers, it will deny the government necessary revenue, and it will impose on the country a tyranny of crime. Raising cigarette taxes would be a disaster.

There you have it. We lose money, we put people out of work, and we jump-start organized crime. Raising cigarette taxes is a bad idea.

A good first draft. Nothing more. We'll be back.

Exercises   Writing Your Argument

Odd-numbered
solutions
begin on page 369

Now it's your turn. Write arguments for the following propositions. These all appeared in the outlining exercises in Chapter Eight.

1. My school should offer a major in logic.
2. My school should not offer a major in logic.
3. Cloning of human beings should be made illegal.
4. Cloning of human beings should not be made illegal.
5. The United States should abolish the death penalty.
6. The United States should not abolish the death penalty.
7. My school should have a quantitative skills requirement.
8. My school should not have a quantitative skills requirement.
9. **Citizen Cathy**

Maria and Cassandra had just passed a milestone in their lives – their first election. Their absentee ballots were now in the mail and they were savoring the moment when in the distance they saw Cathy striding toward them. They looked at each other and shivered slightly.

Maria whispered to Cassie, "This won't be too bad. You voted one way and I voted the other. She can't make us both look stupid!" She paused. "Right?"

Cassie nodded and added, "And if she hasn't voted yet, we can make her look stupid!"

Cathy approached the pair slowly and then stopped to examine them. "Guilty," she said. "You guys look guilty. What have you done now?"

"We just voted, Cathy," said Maria lightly, "You're from our state, aren't you? Who did you vote for in the senate race?"

"That's kid stuff. I don't vote."

"**WHAT!!??**" *Maria and Cassandra gasped in unison.*

"*What's the big deal? One vote doesn't matter.*"

"*But …*" *Maria began, to give herself time to think,* "*But Cathy, you have to vote. Millions of soldiers died so that you could have the freedom to vote!*"

"*If I 'have' to vote, then it's not a freedom, is it?*" *Cathy began to grin.* "*If I'm really free, then I'm free not to vote!*"

"*But it's your duty as a citizen!*" *Cassie pleaded.*

"*My duty? The system is totally corrupt! Corporations buy candidates! Money rules! It's a slimy game and I have too much integrity to be a part of it. It's my duty to stay home.*"

"*Look, Cathy. You have to vote because you* can *vote. Billions of people are ruled by dictators and can't vote!*"

"*You sound like my father. 'Eat your lima beans! They're starving in Africa!' Do you think they'll have more to eat if I finish my beans?*"

"*Cathy.*" *Maria decided to make one last try. She put on a sweet smile.* "*You should vote because you have all these opinions and because you know all this stuff!*"

"*So you guys* shouldn't *vote, because you don't read the paper. Right? Or am I missing something?*" *And she was off down the hall.*

Cathy is rebutting an argument by Maria and Cassandra that Cathy should vote. Diagram this argument. Explain what premises and lines of inference she attacks. Then write an argument in favor of voting that will survive attack by Cathy.

Our thought experiment so far: You died and went to Hell. The devil offered you a deal: he wrote a whole number ($\ldots -3, -2, -1, 0, 1, 2, 3, \ldots$) on a piece of paper and put it in his pocket. You can guess number every day and if you guess correctly you are released from Hell. If not, you can continue guessing, one guess per day.

There is a strategy for escaping Hell. You guess 0 on the first day, 1 on the second day, -1 on the third day, 2 on the fourth day, -2 on the fifth day, and so on. Eventually you will guess the devil's number and escape Hell. You don't know when this will happen but you know you will be free in a finite number of days. Note that you can actually tell the devil what your strategy is *before he writes his number down*. Even if he knows what you're going to do, you are still guaranteed to escape.

But suppose now that the devil makes a trickier offer. He says, "I will write a fraction ($\frac{1}{2}$, $\frac{13}{3}$, $-\frac{43}{52}$, $\ldots$) on a piece of paper and put it in my pocket. Every day you can guess once what the number is. If you guess right, I'll send you up to heaven. I won't change the number."

Can you think of a strategy that will guarantee your escape from Hell in a finite number of days – even if the devil knows your strategy before he chooses his number? Or is this impossible? Answer next chapter!

9.4 Basic Modal Logic

Not even the gods fight against necessity. (Simonides)

Modal logics are logics that allow us to express a range of ideas not expressible in Sentential or Predicate. Originally they were introduced in order to represent the concepts of **necessity** and **possibility**. A sentence is necessarily true iff there is no way that it could be false, and a sentence is possibly true iff there is some circumstance in which it is true, even if that circumstance does not in fact obtain.

Example

$3 + 4 = 7$

This is necessarily true. Mathematical statements in general are necessarily true – we can prove them.

Example

George W. Bush was declared winner of the 2000 presidential election.

This is true but it's not, perhaps, *necessarily* true. If one Supreme Court justice had voted otherwise, Al Gore might have been the eventual winner. Similarly, "Al Gore was the winner of the 2000 presidential election" is false, but *possibly* true.

Of course, a lot depends on exactly what we consider "possible". More on that in a moment.

In order to express thoughts about what might be true and what must be true we introduce two new 1-place connectives.

$\Box A$ is read "necessarily A" or "A is necessarily true."

$\Diamond A$ is read "possibly A" or "A is possibly true."

To keep things from getting too complicated, we'll add the modal connectives to Sentential, rather than Predicate. We can define the language of Modal Sentential the same way we defined the language of Basic Sentential.

Modal Sentential

1. Any sentence letter (P, Q, R, etc.) (except T and F) is a wff.
2. If $\mathcal{A}$ and $\mathcal{B}$ are any wffs (distinct or identical), then so are
   a. $\neg \mathcal{A}$
   b. $(\mathcal{A} \land \mathcal{B})$
   c. $(\mathcal{A} \lor \mathcal{B})$
   d. $(\mathcal{A} \Rightarrow \mathcal{B})$
   e. $(\mathcal{A} \Leftrightarrow \mathcal{B})$
   f. $\Box \mathcal{A}$
   g. $\Diamond \mathcal{A}$
3. Nothing else is a wff.

Examples: $(P \Rightarrow \Box Q)$, $\Diamond(\Box G \vee \neg \Diamond R)$, $\neg \Diamond(\Box(S \Leftrightarrow \neg \Box H) \wedge H)$

That's the grammar; that's how we write in Modal Sentential. Now what does it mean? What is a universe for modal logic?

We're going to give you two answers to that question, one now (basic) and one in the next chapter (sophisticated). Both represent the remarkable insight of philosopher Saul Kripke at the age of 14.

For now, a universe for modal logic consists of possible worlds (at least one). The choice of these worlds embodies the meaning of "possible". Jay might want to know, for example, what the weather will be tomorrow. Then our set of possible worlds would contain all the possibilities. If P means "It will rain tomorrow", then $\Diamond P$ is true iff it's raining in least one of the possible worlds.

$\Box P$ is true iff it's raining in all of the possible worlds.

Modal Sentential

$\Diamond P$ is true   iff P is true in some possible world.

$\Box P$ is true   iff P is true in all possible worlds.

We can deal with all sorts of possibility. Suppose, for example, we're interested in the statement, Q: "Jim can fly". If we consider all worlds that are *logically possible*,

we may conclude $\Diamond Q$. But if we restrict our attention to worlds that are *biologically possible*,

then we sadly conclude $\neg \Diamond Q$.

The possibilities (sorry) are endless. If a logic major is planning his schedule, he might want to think about what schedules are *curricularly possible*. If a leader were considering ethical courses of action, she might want to consider only plans that were morally or *deontically possible*.

Possible worlds may seem exotic, but really they're lurking in the background of almost all human discourse. It's just like the implicit use we make of domains when we use quantifiers in ordinary discussions. For example, "Everybody had a good time" in a discussion of a party would properly be taken as true, even though the prisoners in the penitentiary down the road did not have a good time; the implicit domain is the set of people who attended the party. In the same way, when we say that it is not possible to build a jet plane from bamboo and string, it is implicit that the relevant worlds are those where the laws of physics and aeronautical engineering are the same as those in the actual world, even if there are logically possible worlds where 747s are made of bamboo.

One possible world in a modal universe is special, it's what we call the **ground world**. When we say P is true we mean that P is true in the ground world.

Modal Sentential

$\Diamond P$ is true   iff P is true in some possible world.

$\Box P$ is true   iff P is true in all possible worlds.

P is true   iff P is true in the ground world.

Example

$\Box P \Rightarrow P$

This is a modal tautology. If a wff is necessarily true then it is true in all worlds, including the ground world.

Example

$P \Rightarrow \Diamond P$

This is also a tautology. If a wff is true in the ground world then it's true in at least one world, viz., the ground world. So it is possibly true.

Example

$\Box \neg P \Leftrightarrow \neg \Diamond P$

This is a sophisticated tautology. If P is necessarily false ($\Box \neg P$) then it can't ever be true ($\neg \Diamond P$) and vice-versa. Similarly, $\Diamond \neg P \Leftrightarrow \neg \Box P$

$$\Box \neg P \Leftrightarrow \neg \Diamond P$$
$$\Diamond \neg P \Leftrightarrow \neg \Box P$$

Do these rules this remind you of the quantifier exchange rules (p. 165)? They should. Our modal connectives are just quantifiers over possible worlds. Again, $\Box \mathcal{A}$ means "In all possible worlds, $\mathcal{A}$" and $\Diamond \mathcal{A}$ means "In some possible world, $\mathcal{A}$."

Our new operators are not truth-functional (see p. 207). Knowing the truth value of P may not be enough to tell you the truth value of $\Box P$ or $\Diamond P$. If P is true, you do know that $\Diamond P$ is true. But you have no idea whether $\Box P$ is true. And if P is false, you know $\Box P$ is false, but $\Diamond P$ could be either true or false.

Modal logics can handle much more than possibility and necessity. Many 1-place connectives have been proposed and explored. Such connectives can help us to understand reasoning about logic of fiction, about the logic of scientific explanation, and about psychological states and knowledge. Modal logics also give us insight into aspects of English connectives such as "if... then" that are only loosely represented by the Sentential, helping to capture the residue of meaning connectives such as $\Rightarrow$ omit.

Exercises   **Basic Modal Logic**

Odd-numbered solutions begin on page 371

Each of the following exercises offers a pair of statements in Modal Sentential. Decide whether or not they are equivalent, or if one implies the other.

1. $\Diamond P, \Box P$
2. $\Diamond (P \vee Q), \Diamond P \vee \Diamond Q$
3. $\Diamond (P \wedge Q), \Diamond P \wedge \Diamond Q$
4. $\neg \Diamond P, \Box P$
5. $\neg \Diamond P, \Box \neg P$
6. $\Diamond \neg P, \Box \neg P$
7. $\Box (P \Rightarrow Q), \Box P \Rightarrow \Box Q$
8. $\Diamond (P \Rightarrow Q), \Diamond P \Rightarrow \Box Q$

9‼ The Digestor's Digest has instituted a policy of only publishing signed pieces. The pieces under some bylines are ads, though. And the pieces under other bylines are articles. And the pieces under some bylines are "features." Features alternate between true and false from issue to issue. Neither of these issues is the fun page.

The Digestor's Digest

————————— Vol. I, No. 8 ————————— Page 1 —————————

Bob's Column: | ## Alice's Column

I went to the pricey new steak house, Swank Plank. I ordered the best because I deserve it. It was ok. | No, Bob didn't go to Swank Plank; he can't afford it. But I did and I deserve better.

The Digestor's Digest

————————— Vol. I, No. 9 ————————— Page 1 —————————

Bob's Column: | ## Alice's Column:

Alice didn't go to Swank Plank, they were shut by the Board of Health. They should shut Alice too. This feature was cleared by the Board last week. | Ha ha ha. Well, Bob's feature may have been cleared by the board, but it was condemned by the Committee Against Violence to Vegetables.

In our search for examples of self-reference we've made an amazing discovery: a photograph that is its own negation. It's the photographic equivalent of the liar's paradox!

The photo (on the next page) may need explaining. You *may* think it's not actually a photograph. Suspend your disbelief! An explanation will follow.

The photographer, by the way, is unknown.

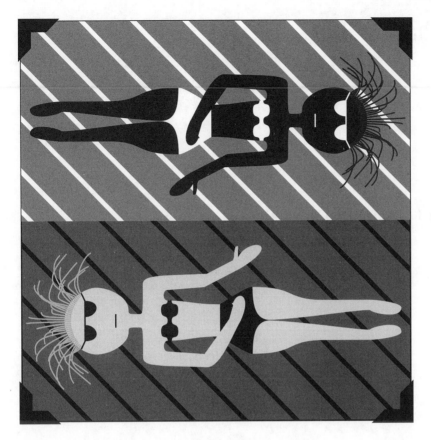

Okay, it's not the negation, it's the *negative*. For readers whose experience with cameras has never involved negatives, the negative of a black-and-white photograph is the image with the shades of black and white reversed. The negative of the image above, when rotated 180 degrees, is the same as the original image.

Chapter Ten

10.1   Sentential Deduction

What happens in Vegas, stays in Vegas. (Anonymous)

Our rules, so far:

∧Out:
$$\frac{\mathcal{A} \wedge \mathcal{B}}{\therefore \mathcal{A}} \qquad \frac{\mathcal{A} \wedge \mathcal{B}}{\therefore \mathcal{B}}$$

∧In:
$$\begin{array}{c} \mathcal{A} \\ \mathcal{B} \\ \hline \therefore \mathcal{A} \wedge \mathcal{B} \end{array}$$

∨Out:
$$\begin{array}{c} \mathcal{A} \vee \mathcal{B} \\ \mathcal{A} \Rightarrow \mathcal{C} \\ \mathcal{B} \Rightarrow \mathcal{C} \\ \hline \therefore \mathcal{C} \end{array}$$

∨In:
$$\frac{\mathcal{A}}{\therefore \mathcal{A} \vee \mathcal{B}} \qquad \frac{\mathcal{B}}{\therefore \mathcal{A} \vee \mathcal{B}}$$

¬Out:
$$\frac{\neg\neg\mathcal{A}}{\therefore \mathcal{A}}$$

¬In:
$$\frac{\mathcal{A} \Rightarrow (\mathcal{B} \wedge \neg\mathcal{B})}{\therefore \neg\mathcal{A}}$$

Sweet Reason: A Field Guide To Modern Logic, Second Edition. Jim Henle, Jay L. Garfield, Thomas Tymoczko and Emily Altreuter.
© 2012 John Wiley & Sons Inc. Published 2012 by John Wiley & Sons Inc.

A classic rule

We now introduce the rules for $\Rightarrow$. The first is easy, and is a great deal like the rules we've already seen.

$$
\begin{array}{ll}
\Rightarrow \text{Out:} & \mathcal{A} \Rightarrow \mathcal{B} \\
& \underline{\mathcal{A}} \\
& \therefore \mathcal{B}
\end{array}
$$

This rule has the Latin name *modus ponens*, which means *the way of assertion*. It is, perhaps, the most fundamental deduction rule.

Example

$$
\begin{array}{l}
P \Rightarrow (Q \Rightarrow R) \\
P \\
\underline{Q} \\
\therefore R
\end{array}
$$

1.	$P \Rightarrow (Q \Rightarrow R)$	premise
2.	P	premise
3.	Q	premise
4.	$Q \Rightarrow R$	$\Rightarrow$ Out, 1, 2
5.	R	$\Rightarrow$ Out, 3, 4

The $\Rightarrow$In rule is special and we'll save it for last.

Two more rules, pretty simple

$$
\begin{array}{lll}
\Leftrightarrow \text{Out:} & \dfrac{\mathcal{A} \Leftrightarrow \mathcal{B}}{\therefore \mathcal{A} \Rightarrow \mathcal{B}} & \dfrac{\mathcal{A} \Leftrightarrow \mathcal{B}}{\therefore \mathcal{B} \Rightarrow \mathcal{A}}
\end{array}
$$

$$
\begin{array}{ll}
\Leftrightarrow \text{In:} & \mathcal{A} \Rightarrow \mathcal{B} \\
& \underline{\mathcal{B} \Rightarrow \mathcal{A}} \\
& \therefore \mathcal{A} \Leftrightarrow \mathcal{B}
\end{array}
$$

These should make perfect sense. $\mathcal{A} \Rightarrow \mathcal{B}$ is "$\mathcal{A}$ only if $\mathcal{B}$." $\mathcal{B} \Rightarrow \mathcal{A}$ is "$\mathcal{A}$ if $\mathcal{B}$." And $\mathcal{A} \Leftrightarrow \mathcal{B}$ is "$\mathcal{A}$ if and only if $\mathcal{B}$."

Example

$$P \Leftrightarrow Q$$
$$\underline{P}$$
$$\therefore Q$$

1. $P \Leftrightarrow Q$ premise
2. P premise
3. $P \Rightarrow Q$ $\Leftrightarrow$ Out, 1
4. Q $\Rightarrow$ Out, 2, 3

Something Different

Up to this point, our rules have been straightforward. Each one allows you to justify a line of a deduction, or a statement in an argument, on the basis of previous statements or lines. The $\Rightarrow$ In rule is different.

Let's first ask how you might justify a conditional statement in a natural language argument. Suppose we wanted to convince you that if you study for your logic test, then you'll have a happy retirement.

you study $\Rightarrow$ you have happy retirement

We might do it this way: "Suppose you study for the test. Then you'll get a good grade in logic and do well on the LSATs. Then you'll get into law school. Then you'll become a lawyer. Lawyers make a lot of money, so you will make a lot of money. And all that money means you'll have a happy retirement." We reached the conclusion that you'll have a happy retirement starting with the assumption that you study for your logic test. So we conclude, "If you study for your logic test, then you'll have a happy retirement."

What did we do? We began with a hypothetical supposition – that you study for your logic test. We then argued on the basis of that assumption that you will have a happy retirement.

a. You study
b. You ace Logic
c. You nail the LSATs
d. You become a lawyer
e. You get rich
f. You retire happily

That subargument justifies the claim that *if* you study *then* you'll have a happy retirement.

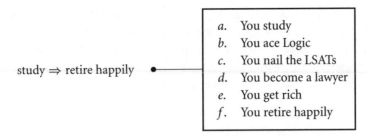

study ⇒ retire happily

a. You study
b. You ace Logic
c. You nail the LSATs
d. You become a lawyer
e. You get rich
f. You retire happily

Note that we're not claiming that you *will* study, or that you *will* have a happy retirement. The first was only a hypothetical supposition, and the last was just the consequence of that supposition. For all we know, you'll party the night before the test and end up a derelict on skid row. But we needed the assumption to argue for the conditional.

We can think about it more formally this way. What would it take to convince you that $A \Rightarrow B$ is true? A proof of B from A would be very convincing. That's exactly what our rule is. If you want to write "$A \Rightarrow B$" on a line in your deduction, what you must do is write a short proof of B from A—a *sub*deduction.

Here's how it works. Let's say that you want to conclude on line n that $A \Rightarrow B$.

n. $A \Rightarrow B$

Then off to one side, you write a little deduction of B with A as the premise (we'll call A an "assumption" so you won't confuse it with the premise of your main proof). We number the lines in the subdeduction $n.1$, $n.2$, and so on. In the subdeduction you can use anything that you've already proven.

n. $A \Rightarrow B$

$n.1$.	A	assumption
⋮	⋮	
$n.k$.	B	

Example

$$P \wedge Q$$
$$\therefore P \wedge (R \Rightarrow (Q \vee S))$$

1.	$P \wedge Q$	premise
2.	$R \Rightarrow (Q \vee S)$	
3.	P	∧Out 1
4.	$P \wedge (R \Rightarrow (Q \vee S))$	∧In 2, 3

2.1.	R	assumption
2.2.	Q	∧Out 1
2.3.	$Q \vee S$	∨In 2.2

- The subdeduction (steps 2.1, 2.2, 2.3) justifies the conditional (step 2).
- The subdeduction is just like an ordinary deduction; the assumption is like an extra premise.

Inside a box we may access statements outside the box that have been previously established. The reverse isn't true. Outside the box you're not permitted to access any statement inside the box. There's a good reason for this. Statements inside the box are asserted only on the strength of the assumption. But that assumption might not be true. In the proof above we didn't prove R. We proved that *if* R is true then so is Q.

> **Heads up!**
>
> Outside the box you may not use anything inside the box!

Here's how we state the $\Rightarrow$ In rule:

$$\Rightarrow \text{In:} \quad \left[\begin{array}{c} \text{a deduction} \\ \text{of } \mathcal{B} \text{ from } \mathcal{A} \end{array} \right]$$
$$\therefore \mathcal{A} \Rightarrow \mathcal{B}$$

Example

$$\frac{P \Rightarrow (Q \Rightarrow R)}{\therefore (P \wedge Q) \Rightarrow R}$$

1. $P \Rightarrow (Q \Rightarrow R)$ premise
2. $(P \wedge Q) \Rightarrow R$ •——

2.1.	$P \wedge Q$	assumption
2.2.	P	$\wedge$Out, 2.1
2.3.	$Q \Rightarrow R$	$\Rightarrow$ Out, 1, 2.2
2.4.	Q	$\wedge$Out, 2.1
2.5.	R	$\Rightarrow$ Out, 2.3, 2.4

- Notice that the first line in the box is the antecedent $(P \wedge Q)$.
- Notice that the last line in the box (R) is the conclusion.

That's the pattern. Whenever you use $\Rightarrow$ In,

n. $\mathcal{A} \Rightarrow \mathcal{B}$ •——

n.1.	$\mathcal{A}$	assumption
	$\vdots$	
n.k.	$\mathcal{B}$	

the antecedent *must* be at the top and the conclusion *must* be at the bottom.

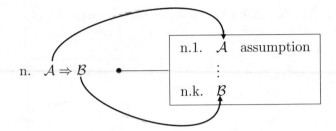

We hope subdeductions are clear now. Because here come *sub*subdeductions:

Example

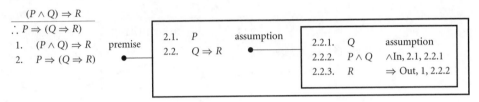

It doesn't end here. Later you'll see subsubsubdeductions and, perhaps, subsubsubsubdeductions. You can do it. We chose you as a reader because we knew you had the right stuff.

Here's another example to show you that you may repeat a line that's already been established.

Example

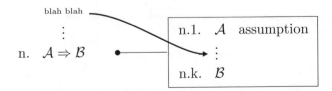

Notice that inside a box you can use a line outside the box (in this case, line 1) that appeared earlier. This pattern:

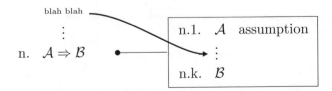

is allowed because the line has been justified. But you may *not* use the statement itself inside the box –

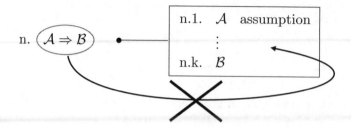

– because it hasn't yet been justified. And you may not use later statements inside the box –

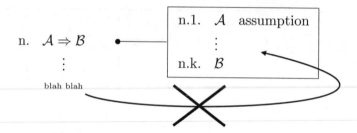

– again, because these haven't yet been justified. And finally, you may *not* use statements inside the box to justify anything outside the box –

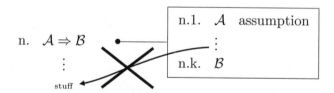

– because they haven't been justified. Inside the box they're justified by the assumption; outside the box they aren't. Always remember:

With the ⇒ In rule, we can justify arguments that have no premises.

Example

$$\frac{\text{(no premise)}}{\therefore H \Rightarrow (H \vee G)}$$

This is a valid argument because the conclusion is a tautology. Without $\Rightarrow$ In we would have nowhere to start, but here's a very simple proof:

1. $H \Rightarrow (H \vee G)$ •——

1.1.	H	assumption
1.2.	$H \vee G$	$\vee$In 1.1

One more example, this one to show you how well $\neg$ In works with $\Rightarrow$ In:

Example

$$\frac{P \Rightarrow Q}{\therefore \neg Q \Rightarrow \neg P}$$

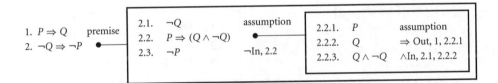

1. $P \Rightarrow Q$ premise
2. $\neg Q \Rightarrow \neg P$ •——

2.1.	$\neg Q$	assumption
2.2.	$P \Rightarrow (Q \wedge \neg Q)$	•——
2.3.	$\neg P$	$\neg$In, 2.2

2.2.1.	P	assumption
2.2.2.	Q	$\Rightarrow$ Out, 1, 2.2.1
2.2.3.	$Q \wedge \neg Q$	$\wedge$In, 2.1, 2.2.2

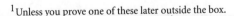

Heads up for worried students

Some students worry about the $\Rightarrow$ In rule. They think: "I'm sinning against logic! I assume P, I get to use P, but I never prove P! I'm going to pay for this someday!"

But you haven't sinned. If you assume P and prove Q, you end up with $P \Rightarrow Q$. After it's all over you don't have P. You don't have Q either.[1]

And afterwards, you never use the box or its contents again. It's only a sin if you use outside a box something that's inside the box. Remember: what happens in the box, stays in the box!

[1] Unless you prove one of these later outside the box.

> ### Heads up for students
> ### who aren't worried enough
>
> Some students are careless about the $\Rightarrow$ In rule. They think: "Wow, $\Rightarrow$ In is great! Whatever I want I can assume! Deduction's a snap!"
>
> They exaggerate the power of this rule. You do assume P, but you don't get to keep it. You prove Q, but you don't get to keep Q either.[2]
>
> What you do get is $P \Rightarrow Q$. And afterwards, you never use the box or its contents again.
>
> ---
> [2]Unless you prove one of these later outside the box.

Exercises   Sentential Deduction

Odd-numbered solutions begin on page 372

Fill in the blanks in the following deductions.

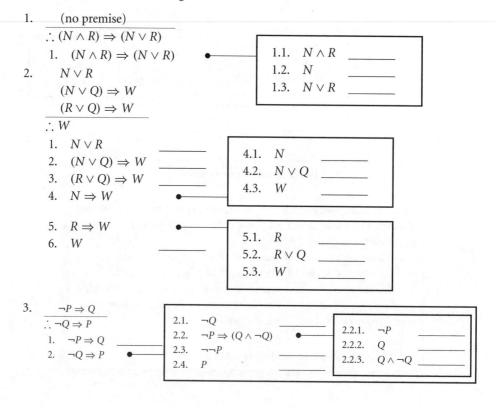

1.   (no premise)
   $\therefore (N \wedge R) \Rightarrow (N \vee R)$
   1. $(N \wedge R) \Rightarrow (N \vee R)$

       1.1. $N \wedge R$ _____
       1.2. N _____
       1.3. $N \vee R$ _____

2. $N \vee R$
   $(N \vee Q) \Rightarrow W$
   $(R \vee Q) \Rightarrow W$
   $\therefore W$
   1. $N \vee R$ _____
   2. $(N \vee Q) \Rightarrow W$ _____
   3. $(R \vee Q) \Rightarrow W$ _____
   4. $N \Rightarrow W$

       4.1. N _____
       4.2. $N \vee Q$ _____
       4.3. W _____

   5. $R \Rightarrow W$
   6. W _____

       5.1. R _____
       5.2. $R \vee Q$ _____
       5.3. W _____

3. $\neg P \Rightarrow Q$
   $\therefore \neg Q \Rightarrow P$
   1. $\neg P \Rightarrow Q$ _____
   2. $\neg Q \Rightarrow P$

       2.1. $\neg Q$
       2.2. $\neg P \Rightarrow (Q \wedge \neg Q)$
       2.3. $\neg \neg P$ _____
       2.4. P _____

           2.2.1. $\neg P$ _____
           2.2.2. Q _____
           2.2.3. $Q \wedge \neg Q$ _____

4. $\dfrac{P \Leftrightarrow Q}{\therefore (P \wedge R) \Leftrightarrow (Q \wedge R)}$

4.1.	$P \wedge R$	_____
4.2.	P	_____
4.3.	R	_____
4.4.	Q	_____
4.5.	$Q \wedge R$	_____

1. $P \Leftrightarrow Q$ _____
2. $P \Rightarrow Q$ _____
3. $Q \Rightarrow P$ _____
4. $(P \wedge R) \Rightarrow (Q \wedge R)$ • _____

5. $(Q \wedge R) \Rightarrow (P \wedge R)$ •
6. $(P \wedge R) \Leftrightarrow (Q \wedge R)$ _____

5.1.	$Q \wedge R$	_____
5.2.	Q	_____
5.3.	R	_____
5.4.	P	_____
5.5.	$P \wedge R$	_____

Here are some arguments, all valid, for you to justify. In each case, deduce the conclusion from the premises.

5. $\dfrac{\begin{array}{c}(P \vee Q) \Rightarrow R \\ P\end{array}}{\therefore R}$

6. $\dfrac{\begin{array}{c}P \Rightarrow R \\ R \Rightarrow Q\end{array}}{\therefore P \Rightarrow Q}$

7. $\dfrac{P \Rightarrow Q}{\therefore (P \wedge R) \Rightarrow Q}$

8. $\dfrac{P \Rightarrow Q}{\therefore P \Rightarrow (Q \vee R)}$

9. $\dfrac{\text{(no premise)}}{\therefore P \Rightarrow P}$

10. $\dfrac{\text{(no premise)}}{\therefore P \Rightarrow (Q \Rightarrow P)}$

11! $\dfrac{\begin{array}{c}P \Leftrightarrow Q \\ P \vee Q\end{array}}{\therefore P \wedge Q}$

12! $\dfrac{P \wedge \neg P}{\therefore Q}$

13. The horse race paradox: You should never place a bet on a horse race because if you do, you will be filled with regret. Either your horse loses, in which case you will clearly regret having bet on the horse, or your horse wins, in which case you will regret not having bet more money. We can formalize this as

$$\dfrac{\begin{array}{c}P \\ W \vee \neg W \\ (P \wedge W) \Rightarrow R \\ (P \wedge \neg W) \Rightarrow R\end{array}}{\therefore R}$$

(Actually, we don't need $W \vee \neg W$, but that is a challenge to prove; it's an exercise in the next section.) Write a deduction for this argument.

We told you (p. 226) that "sorites" had two logical connections and we described the first. The second is the sorites paradox or the paradox of the heap. It was propounded in ancient Greece and has many variations.

Consider a huge mound of sand, say 20 feet high. That is surely a heap of sand. Just as surely, if you have a heap of sand and remove one grain you still have a heap of sand. But this principle leads to an absurdity. If removing one grain of sand leaves a heap, we can remove a second grain and still have a heap. Then we can remove a third grain, and so on.

Let Hx mean "x grains of sand is a heap." If, say, 84759636 grains of sand is a heap, then we have

$$H84759636$$
$$H84759636 \Rightarrow H84759635$$
$$H84759635 \Rightarrow H84759634$$
$$\vdots$$

Modus ponens (the $\Rightarrow$ Out rule) gives us $H84759635$, then $H84759634$, and so on.

With valid reasoning (just $\Rightarrow$ Out lots of times) and true premises ($H84759636$ and $\forall x(Hx \Rightarrow H(x - 1))$) we come to a manifestly false conclusion, $H0$ (there's no sand but it's a heap!). What's going wrong? Is it the reasoning or one of the premises? What do you think? A discussion follows in the next chapter.

10.2   Sentential Strategy

How often have I said to you that when you have eliminated the impossible, whatever remains, however improbable, must be the truth? (Sir Arthur Conan Doyle)

With the addition of the new rules, we can add one more step to our deduction strategy.

Deduction strategy

- Work backwards.
- If you can't work backwards, work forwards.
- If you can't do either, use contradiction.

We'll explain "contradiction" later. It's an important strategy, one that has saved many a deduction.

First, a catalog of our strategies,

In rule strategies		Out rule strategies	
$\wedge$In:	To prove $A \wedge B$ Prove A and B.	$\wedge$Out:	Given $A \wedge B$, conclude A and B.
$\vee$In:	To prove $A \vee B$ Prove either A or B.	$\vee$Out:	Given $A \vee B$, $A \Rightarrow C$, $B \Rightarrow C$, conclude C.
$\Leftrightarrow$In:	To prove $A \Leftrightarrow B$ Prove $A \Rightarrow B$ and $B \Rightarrow A$.	$\Leftrightarrow$Out:	Given $A \Leftrightarrow B$, conclude $A \Rightarrow B$ and $B \Rightarrow A$.
$\neg$In:	To prove $\neg A$ Prove $A \Rightarrow (C \wedge \neg C)$ (for some C).	$\neg$Out:	Given $\neg\neg A$, conclude A.
$\Rightarrow$In:	To prove $A \Rightarrow B$ Assume A (in a box), then prove B.	$\Rightarrow$Out:	Given A and $A \Rightarrow B$, conclude B.

We'll start with a problem from the previous section.

Example

$$\frac{P \Rightarrow Q}{\therefore (P \wedge R) \Rightarrow Q}$$

   1. $P \Rightarrow Q$ premise

         🤔

  A. $(P \wedge R) \Rightarrow Q$

As in Chapter Nine, we know we put the premise at the top and the conclusion at the bottom. The shading is to remind us of what we are trying to prove.

We start by working backwards. The conclusion is a conditional. The $\Rightarrow$ In strategy says we should try to prove Q from $P \wedge R$ in a box.

1.	$P \Rightarrow Q$	premise
A.	$(P \wedge R) \Rightarrow Q$	

> A.1. $P \wedge R$ assumption
>
>   🤔
>
> A.B. Q

Notice that the gray has moved to line A.B. That's our goal now.

But the goal is a basic wff. We can't work backwards any longer so we try going forwards. What do we have that we can use?

We have the premise, $P \Rightarrow Q$, and the assumption, $P \wedge R$. The premise is a conditional. The $\Rightarrow$ Out strategy says we need P before we can do anything. We don't have P. Oh well.

The assumption is a conjunction. The $\wedge$ Out strategy says we can get the two conjuncts. So let's do it.

1.	$P \Rightarrow Q$	premise
A.	$(P \wedge R) \Rightarrow Q$	

A.1.	$P \wedge R$	assumption
A.2.	P	$\wedge$Out $\mathcal{A}$.1
A.3.	R	$\wedge$Out $\mathcal{A}$.1
	?	
A.B.	Q	

Almost certainly the reader sees what we should do next—use the $\Rightarrow$ Out rule with P and $P \Rightarrow Q$.

1.	$P \Rightarrow Q$	premise
A.	$(P \wedge R) \Rightarrow Q$	

A.1.	$P \wedge R$	assumption
A.2.	P	$\wedge$Out A.1
A.3.	R	$\wedge$Out A.1
A.B.	Q	$\Rightarrow$ Out 1, A.2

The reader probably also sees that we don't need line A.3. The deduction is not incorrect as it is, but we can remove it.

1.	$P \Rightarrow Q$	premise
A.	$(P \wedge R) \Rightarrow Q$	

A.1.	$P \wedge R$	assumption
A.2.	P	$\wedge$Out A.1
A.B.	Q	$\Rightarrow$ Out 1, A.2

But we want to stress that it's good to follow the grand strategy (backwards–forwards–contradiction) without worrying about whether a step is necessary or not. You can't mess up by doing more. And who knows? A random step may come in handy sometime.

Finally, we change the letters to numbers.

1.	$P \Rightarrow Q$	premise
2.	$(P \wedge R) \Rightarrow Q$	

2.1.	$P \wedge R$	assumption
2.2.	P	$\wedge$Out 2.1
2.3.	Q	$\Rightarrow$ Out 1, 2.2

Example

$$\neg D$$
$$\underline{E \Rightarrow D}$$
$$\therefore \neg E$$

1. ¬D   premise
2. E ⇒ D premise

?

A.   ¬E

Working backwards, the main connective of the conclusion is ¬. Thus, we want to prove
E ⇒ (C ∧ ¬C), for some C. We don't know what C is, so we leave it as a blank.

1. ¬D   premise
2. E ⇒ D   premise

?

B.   E ⇒ (__ ∧ ¬__)
A.   ¬E   ¬In B

The main connective of the new goal, E ⇒ (__ ∧ ¬__), is ⇒. That means we assume E
and try to prove __ ∧ ¬__ (whatever that is).

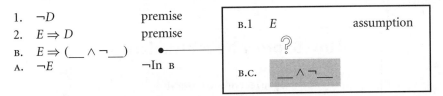

Working backwards yet again, the main connective of __ ∧ ¬__ is ∧, so we need to
prove __ and also prove ¬__.

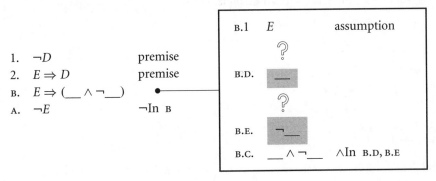

We should look around now for inspiration. Do you see anything that could go in the
blank? If the blank is D, then we already have ¬D as a premise. And we can get D using
⇒Out.

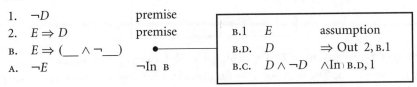

And we're done.

1. $\neg D$ premise
2. $E \Rightarrow D$ premise
3. $E \Rightarrow (D \wedge \neg D)$ •───
4. $\neg E$ $\neg$In 3

> 3.1. E assumption
> 3.2. D $\Rightarrow$ Out 2, 3.1
> 3.3. $D \wedge \neg D$ $\wedge$In 3.2, 1

Are you ready for "contradiction"?

This is the strategy to use when all else fails. It's a powerful tool to be unleashed at special moments. The idea is that in order to prove $\mathcal{A}$, we show that its negation is impossible, that it leads to a contradiction. Specifically, we try to show

$$\neg\mathcal{A} \Rightarrow (\mathcal{C} \wedge \neg\mathcal{C})$$

for some $\mathcal{C}$. In our system, once we have $\neg\mathcal{A} \Rightarrow (\mathcal{C} \wedge \neg\mathcal{C})$ we can get $\neg\neg\mathcal{A}$ from $\neg$ In. Then we can get $\mathcal{A}$ from $\neg$ Out. In practice, you can execute proof by contradiction with this simple strategy:

How to prove by contradiction

If you're trying to prove $\mathcal{A}$,
try to prove $\neg\neg\mathcal{A}$ instead.

This will make more sense with an example.

Example

$$\frac{\neg H \Rightarrow J}{\therefore \neg J \Rightarrow H}$$

1. $\neg H \Rightarrow J$ premise

      ❓

A. $\boxed{\neg J \Rightarrow H}$

Working backwards, we see the conclusion is a conditional and we set up the box:

1. $\neg H \Rightarrow J$ premise
A. $\neg J \Rightarrow H$ •───

> A. $1 \neg J$ assumption
>
>   ❓
>
> A.B. $\boxed{H}$

We can't work backwards from H. We also can't work forwards, since to use $\Rightarrow$ Out with $\neg H \Rightarrow J$ we need $\neg H$. The situation calls for proof by contradiction. Instead of trying to prove H, we try to prove $\neg\neg H$.

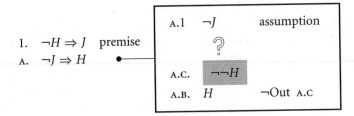

1. $\neg H \Rightarrow J$ premise
A. $\neg J \Rightarrow H$

A.1	$\neg J$	assumption
A.C.	$\neg\neg H$	
A.B.	H	$\neg$Out A.C

Now the goal, $\neg\neg H$, has a main connective. It's a negation. So we try to use $\neg$ In:

1. $\neg H \Rightarrow J$ premise
A. $\neg J \Rightarrow H$

A.1	$\neg J$	assumption
A.D.	$\neg H \Rightarrow (\underline{\quad} \wedge \neg \underline{\quad})$	
A.C.	$\neg\neg H$	$\neg$In A.D
A.B.	H	$\neg$Out A.C

And now the goal is a conditional, so we open a box.

1. $\neg H \Rightarrow J$ premise
A. $\neg J \Rightarrow H$

A.1	$\neg J$	assumption
A.D.	$\neg H \Rightarrow (\underline{\quad} \wedge \neg \underline{\quad})$	
A.C.	$\neg\neg H$	$\neg$In A.D
A.B.	H	$\neg$Out A.C

| A.D.1. | $\neg H$ | assumption |
| A.D.E. | $\underline{\quad} \wedge \neg \underline{\quad}$ | |

You can see now what the blank might be. It looks like J will work; after all, we already have $\neg J$.

1. $\neg H \Rightarrow J$ premise
A. $\neg J \Rightarrow H$

A.1	$\neg J$	assumption
A.D.	$\neg H \Rightarrow (J \wedge \neg J)$	
A.C.	$\neg\neg H$	$\neg$In A.D
A.B.	H	$\neg$Out A.C

| A.D.1. | $\neg H$ | assumption |
| A.D.E. | $J \wedge \neg J$ | |

All we need is J.

1. $\neg H \Rightarrow J$ premise
A. $\neg J \Rightarrow H$

A.1	$\neg J$	assumption
A.D.	$\neg H \Rightarrow (J \wedge \neg J)$	
A.C.	$\neg\neg H$	$\neg$In A.D
A.B.	H	$\neg$Out A.C

A.D.1.	$\neg H$	assumption
A.D.F.	J	
A.D.E.	$J \wedge \neg J$	$\wedge$In A.D.F, A.1

We have to work forwards now because J is basic. What can we work with? We have $\neg H \Rightarrow J$, $\neg J$, and $\neg H$. *We hope it's clear now that at this point inside the innermost box we're allowed to use these wffs and no others.* If you're not sure about this, see the discussion on page 245. To finish the job, we use $\Rightarrow$ Out on $\neg H \Rightarrow J$ and $\neg H$,

1.	$\neg H \Rightarrow J$	premise	A.1	$\neg J$		assumption
A.	$\neg J \Rightarrow H$		A.D.	$\neg H \Rightarrow (J \wedge \neg J)$		
			A.C.	$\neg\neg H$		$\neg$In A.D
			A.B.	H		$\neg$Out A.C

A.D.1.	$\neg H$	assumption
A.D.F.	J	$\Rightarrow$ Out 1, A.D.1
A.D.E.	$J \wedge \neg J$	$\wedge$In A.D.F, A.1

and change the letters to numbers.

1.	$\neg H \Rightarrow J$	premise	2.1.	$\neg J$		assumption
2.	$\neg J \Rightarrow H$		2.2.	$\neg H \Rightarrow (J \wedge \neg J)$		
			2.3.	$\neg\neg H$		$\neg$In 2.2
			2.4.	H		Out 2.3

2.2.1.	$\neg H$	assumption
2.2.2.	J	$\Rightarrow$ Out 1, 2.2.1
2.2.3.	$J \wedge \neg J$	$\wedge$In 2.2.2, 2.1

In using proof by contradiction you generally find yourself trying to prove

$$\mathcal{A} \Rightarrow (\underline{\quad} \wedge \neg \underline{\quad})$$

and you don't know what goes in the blank. Sometimes it's useful to look for a negation among the premises or statements you have proved. Such a statement (and we found one in that last example) is a good candidate for the blank.

One more example, one that shows the typographical consequences of a tricky deduction.

Example

$$\frac{P \vee Q}{\therefore \neg P \Rightarrow Q}$$

1.	$P \vee Q$	premise

$?$

A.	$\neg P \Rightarrow Q$

Working backwards, the goal is a conditional so we open a box.

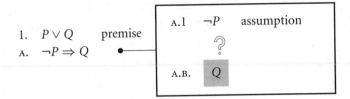

The goal is a basic wff so we can't work backwards; we work forwards. What do we have to work with?

We have ¬P and P ∨ Q. We can't use the ¬ Out strategy on ¬P because that needs a double negation. P ∨ Q is a disjunction. In order to use ∨ Out to get our goal, we need two conditionals. If we had $P \Rightarrow$ __ and $Q \Rightarrow$ __ we could get __. What should __ be, what should we try for?

Go for the goal. What we really want is Q, so we put Q in the blank. That means we want to get $P \Rightarrow Q$ and $Q \Rightarrow Q$.

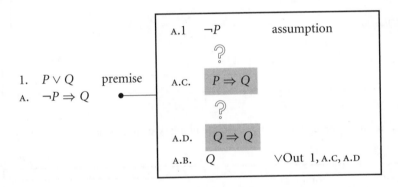

The first goal, $P \Rightarrow Q$, is a conditional, so we open another box.

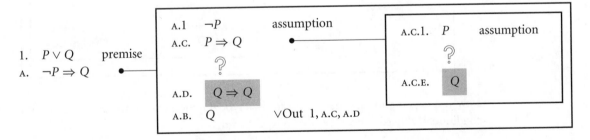

Now the goal is Q, a basic wff, so we can't go backwards. What can we use to go forward? We have P ∨ Q, ¬P, and P. We're already working to use P ∨ Q. As before, we can't use the ¬ Out strategy on ¬P. And P is basic. We can't go forwards and we can't go backwards! It's time for a desperate measure. It's time for proof by contradiction. That means to get Q, we try to get ¬¬Q.

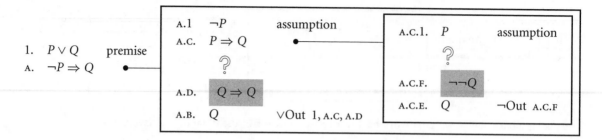

And since our goal is a negation, we use the ¬ In strategy.

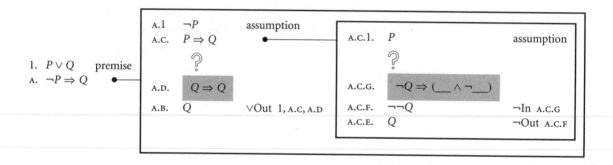

At this point you can probably see what goes in the blank. We already have P and $\neg P$.

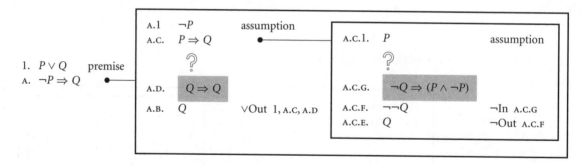

Now you're going to see what we meant by "typographical consequences". To prove the conditional we need to open another box. Get ready!

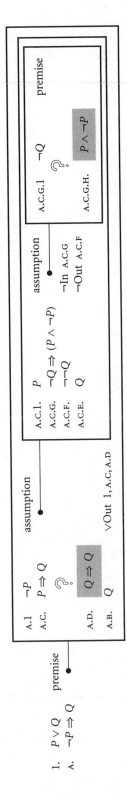

The justification for $P \land \neg P$ is easy.

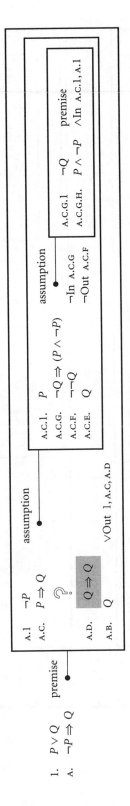

We have one more goal. That's a conditional, so we need another box.

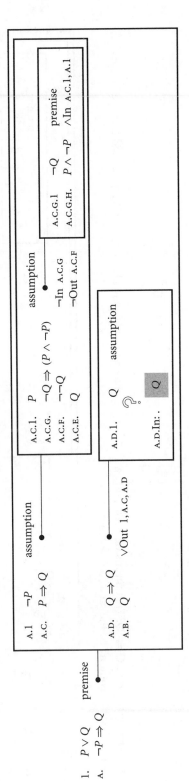

We're trying to prove $Q \Rightarrow Q$. That means we need a box with Q on the first line and Q on the last line. But we never said that the first line and the last line couldn't be the same! So we can do this.

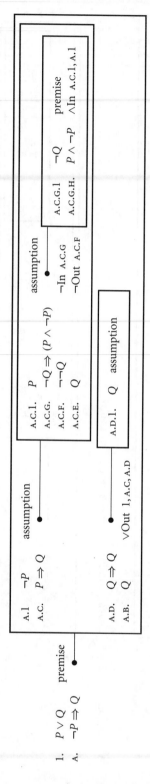

1. $P \lor Q$ premise
A. $\neg P \Rightarrow Q$

A.1 $\neg P$ assumption
A.C. $P \Rightarrow Q$

A.C.1. P
A.C.G. $\neg Q \Rightarrow (P \land \neg P)$
A.C.F. $\neg\neg Q$
A.C.E. Q

A.C.G.1 $\neg Q$ premise
A.C.G.H. $P \land \neg P$ $\land$In A.C.1, A.1

$\neg$In A.C.G
$\neg$Out A.C.F

A.D.1. Q assumption

A.D. $Q \Rightarrow Q$
A.B. Q $\lor$Out 1, A.C, A.D

And after putting in the numbers, we have our argument.

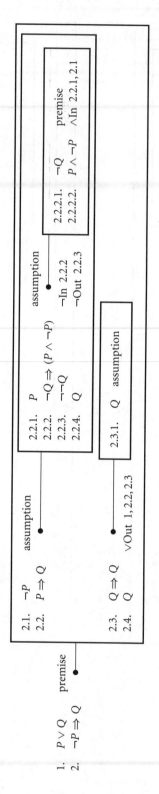

1. $P \lor Q$ premise
2. $\neg P \Rightarrow Q$

2.1. $\neg P$ assumption
2.2. $P \Rightarrow Q$

2.2.1. P
2.2.2. $\neg Q \Rightarrow (P \land \neg P)$
2.2.3. $\neg\neg Q$
2.2.4. Q

2.2.2.1. $\neg Q$ premise
2.2.2.2. $P \land \neg P$ $\land$In 2.2.1, 2.1

$\neg$In 2.2.2
$\neg$Out 2.2.3

2.3.1. Q assumption

2.3. $Q \Rightarrow Q$
2.4. Q $\lor$Out 1, 2.2, 2.3

In detail, here's our strategy:

Deduction strategy

- Work backwards.
  - ⊙ Get the main connective of what you want to prove.
  - ⊙ Apply the associated In rule backwards.
- Work forwards (if you can't work backwards).
  - ⊙ Get the main connective of what you know.
  - ⊙ Apply the associated Out rule (forwards).
  - ⊙ Apply other rules too.
- If you can't do either of these, use contradiction.
  - ⊙ To prove $\mathcal{A}$, try proving $\neg\neg\mathcal{A}$ first.

Exercises   **Sentential Strategy**

Odd-numbered
solutions
begin on page 373

Write deductions for these arguments.

1. $$\frac{P}{\therefore \neg\neg P}$$

2. $$\frac{\begin{array}{c} P \Rightarrow R \\ \neg R \end{array}}{\therefore \neg P}$$

3. $$\frac{P \Rightarrow Q}{\therefore \neg Q \Rightarrow \neg P}$$

4. $$\frac{\neg Q \Rightarrow \neg P}{\therefore P \Rightarrow Q}$$

5. "Disjunctive Syllogism" $$\frac{\begin{array}{c} A \vee B \\ \neg A \end{array}}{\therefore B}$$

6. $$\frac{\neg P}{\therefore P \Rightarrow Q}$$

7. "Explosion" $$\frac{P \wedge \neg P}{\therefore Q}$$

8. $$\frac{\neg(P \vee Q)}{\therefore \neg P \wedge \neg Q}$$

9! $$\frac{(P \wedge Q) \vee (P \wedge R)}{\therefore P \wedge (Q \vee R)}$$

10! $$\frac{P \vee (Q \vee R)}{\therefore (P \vee Q) \vee R}$$

11!! $$\frac{\neg P \vee \neg Q}{\therefore \neg(P \wedge Q)}$$

12!! $$\frac{P \Rightarrow Q}{\therefore \neg P \vee Q}$$

Here's a new connective, ↻, and its truth table:

P	Q	$P \circlearrowleft Q$
T	T	F
T	F	T
F	T	F
F	F	F

13!! Construct a ↻ Out deduction rule. It should be a valid argument with premise $P \circlearrowleft Q$.

14!! Construct a ↻ In deduction rule. It should be a valid argument with conclusion $P \circlearrowleft Q$.

15!! Use our regular rules plus the rules you just invented to find a deduction for
$$\frac{P \circlearrowleft Q}{\therefore Q \Rightarrow P}$$

16‼ Use our regular rules plus the rules you just invented to find a deduction for

$$\frac{(P \vee R) \Rightarrow Q}{\therefore \neg((P \circlearrowleft Q) \wedge \neg R)}$$

17‼! Prove the Law of the Excluded Middle (p.167):

$$\frac{\text{(no premise)}}{\therefore P \vee \neg P}$$

What ?? ! !

Well, I guess I was surprised.

But I was only surprised because I have a proof that you can't surprise me.

Surprise!!

Surprise exam!

It's a spelling test!

Do not turn this page until you have completed the exam.

The following are all spelled incorrectly. Spell them correctly.

arrgewmeant
reebuttle
tawtawlogee
Henley
Timossko
orr
parradocks
konsystint

Sort of a dumb exam.
What do you think of your readers?
— ed.

10.3   Arguing with Yourself

I write plays because writing dialogue is the only respectable way of contradicting your-self. I'm the kind of person who embarks on an endless leapfrog down the great moral issues. I put a position, rebut it, refute the rebuttal, and rebut the refutation. (Tom Stoppard)

We have been constructing arguments for and against raising the tax on cigarettes. They weren't very good. They were good enough to illustrate the ideas behind diagramming, outlining, and putting ideas into paragraphs. But really, they weren't very good.

How can we improve them?

The answer is simple. We attack them, then we see how we can repair them to withstand the attack.

For raising taxes

Here's our argument for a tax raise as improved slightly in Chapter Nine:

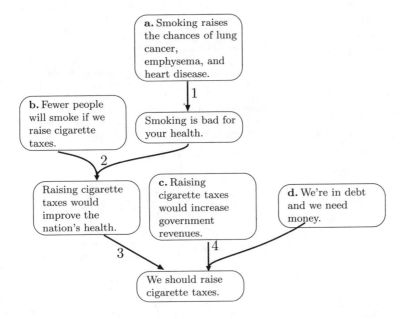

Let's start with the premises.

Premise **b**: Do you really think fewer people will smoke if we raise taxes? Cigarettes are addictive. The cigarette companies have engineered them to be as addictive as possible (more so than cigars or pipes). If you're hooked, you're hooked. Higher taxes will just increase the hardship. If you look how people behave who are addicted to drugs, you can understand that the cost of cigarettes might not deter smokers.

We probably can't challenge the medical evidence against smoking. What else is there?

Premise **c**: Hmm…there seems to be a basic inconsistency in the argument as a whole. Premise **b** says fewer people will smoke. But if that's true, then it looks like government revenues won't increase, contradicting premise **c**. Whoops!

Have we already destroyed the argument? Not really. The inconsistency we found really says that the two subarguments (better health, more money) can't both be sound. But one of them might be.

Arrow 4: This argument, if valid, is an argument for raising taxes on absolutely everything. Not only that, it's an argument for raising taxes on anything to any level. That's absurd. Every tax is different, and a tax on cigarette sales will affect many sectors of the economy. It's regressive, for example. Smokers tend to be poorer than nonsmokers, so this is a tax on people at the bottom of the economic ladder. That's bad economic and social planning.

Well, we've done it. The argument is dead.

Now let's bring it back to life.

We first must come to some conclusion about smokers. Will taxes reduce the numbers or won't they? We think they will for several reasons. First of all, there are the kids who haven't started yet. They aren't hooked, and high prices may deter them. Second, even those who are addicted have a chance now of breaking the habit with patches and more advanced counseling. Finally, there are numbers to show that the smoking rates in states with low taxes are much higher than in states with high taxes. How about this?

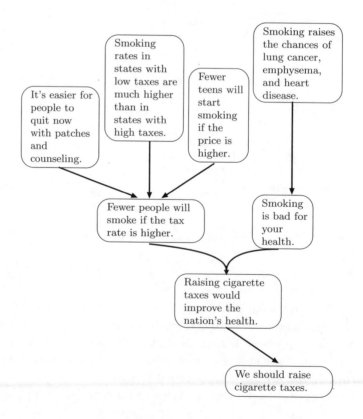

Now for the other half, we really can't claim increased revenues. Although it's mathematically possible to have fewer smokers and greater revenue (if the taxes are really high), that's a delicate balance that would be hard to achieve. Instead, we could argue that the country will save on health costs. Smokers tend to be less well-off. They use emergency rooms, Medicaid, and public health facilities more than the general public. And of course, they're less healthy. Instead of the national debt, we can point out how much money we spend on public health. How about this?

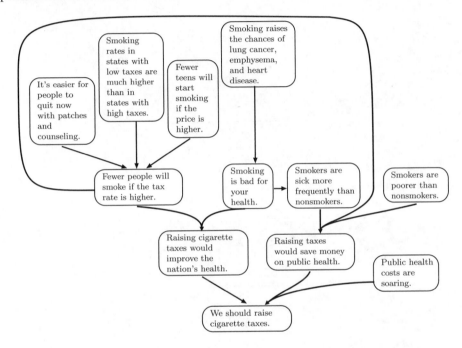

To organize this, we clearly have two basic arguments, one based on health and the other on finance. On the health side, we'll need one paragraph just to establish that fewer people smoke. It might be a good idea to have one on the dangers of smoking. After that, a third paragraph ought to finish the job.

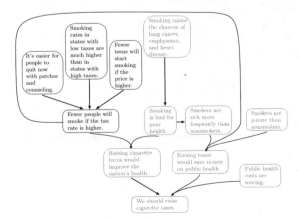

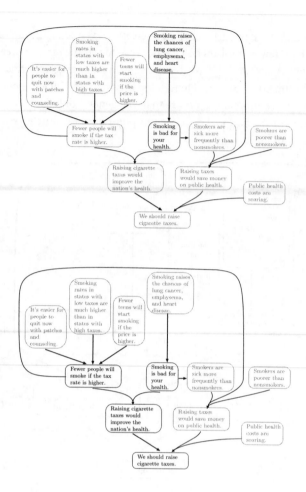

The other side is less complex. One paragraph to establish that we can save money and then one to finish.

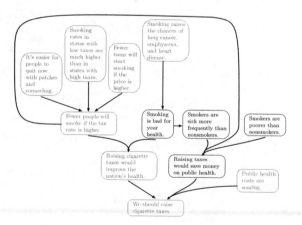

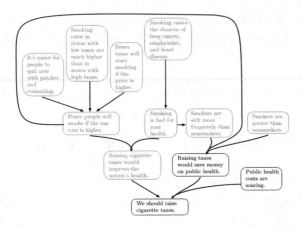

Now the outline. We start with

I. Introduction

II. Body
    A. health
    B. finance

III. Conclusion

Under health, we have three paragraphs. Let's start with the dangers of smoking, since that's an idea everyone will be familiar with. It will be easier for the reader to hold it in mind while absorbing the rest of the argument. After that, the order seems pretty simple, saving the conclusion for the end.

I. Introduction
    A. We claim that cigarette taxes should be raised.
    B. We have two reasons for this: health and finance.

II. Body
    A. Health
        i. Smoking is bad for your health.

            a. Smoking raises the chances of lung cancer, emphysema, and heart disease.
        ii. Fewer people will smoke if the tax rate is higher.

            a. It's easier for people to quit now with patches and counseling.
            b. Smoking rates in states with low taxes are much higher than in states with high taxes.
            c. Fewer teens will start smoking if the price is higher.

iii. Since smoking is bad for your health and fewer people will smoke if the tax rate is higher, raising the cigarette tax would improve the nation's health. So, we should raise the tax.

B. Finance
i. Public health costs are high.

ii. Raising taxes would save money on public health.

  a. Since smoking is bad for your health, smokers get sick more frequently than nonsmokers.

  b. Smokers are generally poorer than nonsmokers.

  c. As we've said, fewer people would smoke if the tax were higher.

iii. Since costs are high and raising the tax would lower those costs, we should raise the tax.

III. Conclusion
There you have it. Raising cigarette taxes would improve the nation's health and save us money. So we should raise taxes.

Now in writing the argument, we keep in mind the template:

> Introduction
> Body
> Conclusion

We'll use it in every part. First, the introductory paragraph.

I would like to make the case for raising the tax on cigarettes. It's a simple action, but it would have two important, long-term benefits: the health of the American public and the financial health of American government. I will discuss these both in detail.

Now in the body, we start with health. That subargument is a big piece, so it has its own introduction, body, and conclusion. The conclusion is really the third paragraph in this section (section A-iii in our outline). The introduction can be short and lead into the paragraph on the dangers of smoking (section A-i).

We can improve the nation's health by reducing the number of smokers. That's because one, smoking is unhealthy and two, raising taxes will bring down the number of smokers. That first point should be clear to all of us. Today, no one questions the impact smoking has on the lungs and the cardiovascular system. Smokers face greatly increased risks from lung cancer, emphysema, and heart disease. The medical evidence of this is overwhelming; smoking is a serious health problem.

Now "less smoking" (section A-ii):

> *We can address that problem by raising taxes. This is sometimes disputed. Some argue that even if the cost of smoking goes up, addicted smokers will just pay more because they can't quit. Let me make three important points.* [Hey, did you notice that we just introduced the sub-subargument in this paragraph?] *First, it's a lot easier to quit smoking today. Cigarettes are addictive – it is hard to stop – but the availability of patches and counseling have greatly improved the success rate. Faced with higher prices, smokers now have a real choice. Second, higher costs will directly affect teens. They aren't yet addicted. When cigarettes are genuinely expensive, fewer youngsters will take up the habit. Finally, we point to statistics showing the effect of state taxes on smoking rates. The tax in Rhode Island is 80 times the tax in Kentucky and the smoking rate is a third less. Taxes make a considerable difference.*

And then putting it all together:

> *This is a pretty simple argument. Smoking is a serious health problem. Taxes will reduce that problem. Why not raise taxes?*

We can take the same approach on the financial side.

> *Raising taxes can also help the government's bottom line. I'm talking about our soaring public health costs and the particular expenses caused by smokers. On that first point, I'm sure you've read about the problems of Medicaid and Medicare. Both are busting budgets and funding these programs threatens all other social programs. But less well known is the cost to hospitals that have to care for patients who can't pay. Ultimately the costs are passed down to governments and taxpayers.*

Now the cost of smokers (section B-ii):

> *As I argued earlier, smoking is a health risk. That means that smokers are more frequently sick. On average, they're more often in emergency rooms, they have higher drug costs, and they miss more days of work. All this is compounded by the fact that smokers tend to be among those at the bottom of the economic ladder. That means these costs are borne chiefly by the government through Medicaid and other programs. It's a big problem, but we can address it by raising taxes.*

And finally, the conclusion.

> *I've argued that a tax hike can make us a healthier country. And I've argued that a tax hike will save us money. This is what good public policy is all about. Let's raise the tax today!*

Against raising taxes

That's one direction: the argument for raising taxes. Now for the argument against. Here's the diagram from Chapter Eight:

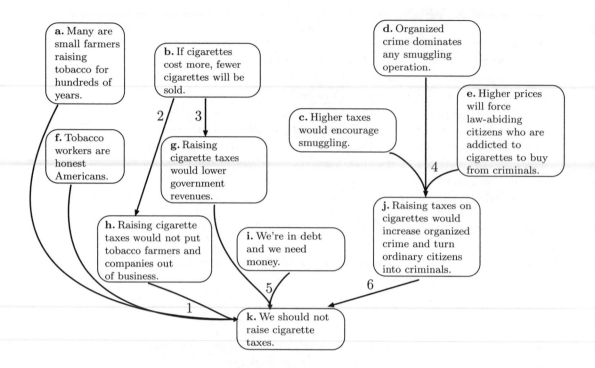

The same criticisms of premise **b** hold (and the same fixes). Premises **a** and **f** are pretty mild. (Where premises are uncontroversial, it's usually the arrows that are easy to attack.)

What about **c**, **d**, and **e**? It's hard to attack **c** (there already is smuggling from states with low taxes to states with high taxes). Maybe we should stay away from **d**; it could get worse (some are claiming that terrorists are also involved in smuggling). But we can certainly attack **e**. We can argue that instead of buying cigarettes from smugglers, smokers can quit. There are many commercial products to help them, counseling is available, and costs are covered by health insurance.

Now for the inferences. Let's attack arrow 2.

Arrow 2: Tobacco companies are multi-national, and today most cigarettes are sold abroad. Tobacco companies are in good shape from expanding markets in Asia, especially China. And tobacco farming is quite profitable and protected from loss by government subsidies (that's another story!). And of course the farmers don't have to go out of business; they can switch to other crops.

Arrow 1: We don't have to attack this (since we've destroyed arrow 2) but we could point out that there are great benefits to the country from reduced smoking which more than offsets the economic pain of the tobacco industry. If some cigarette factories shut down, maybe that's a good thing. We shouldn't protect every industry. And why should we protect an industry because of its age? Should we legalize prostitution?

Arrow 5: The same argument against arrow 1 is good here – the loss of revenue is a small price to pay for saving lives by reducing smoking.

We don't have to attack arrow 6, since we've destroyed premise **e**, but we could. If turning ordinary citizens into criminals is bad, then we'd have to repeal all speed limits, wouldn't we? And if it's bad to have laws that organized crime can exploit, we'd have to legalize all drugs. Basically, if this line of reasoning is good, we'd have to throw away all our laws to avoid having crime!

What a mess. Our argument is in ruins!

Let's put it back together.

For premise **b**, we have our support in the previous argument that there will be fewer smokers. We can also argue that domestic tobacco production is under serious pressure from abroad (China now grows more tobacco than we do) so that indeed tobacco farmers may go under. But maybe we should limit our claims to farmers and tobacco workers (not the companies).

For arrow 5, we can add that we're not talking about small change. Tobacco taxes bring in billions of dollars. Not only that, raising taxes might actually increase costs: if people stop smoking then they live longer, and that adds to the cost of long-term care for the elderly! (True!)

In support of premise **e**, we can point out that people are already buying from smugglers in states like Rhode Island where taxes are higher ($2.46 per pack) than in Kentucky ($.03 per pack). And the experience of prohibition shows that even when a substance is not so addictive, ordinary citizens will turn to illegal sources. And supporting inference 6, we can add that when you turn citizens to criminals it promotes disrespect for the law in general. The knowledge that corporations get around tax laws, for example, encourages private citizens to cheat.

How does it look now?

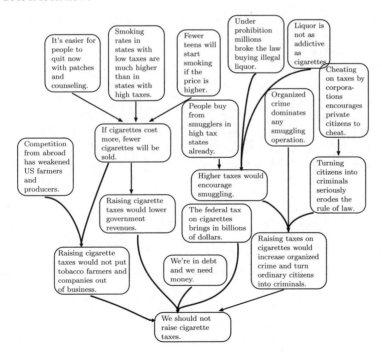

Wow!

Well, to start with, there are three parts to this: the cost to producers, the cost to the government, and crime.

The first has two obvious pieces.

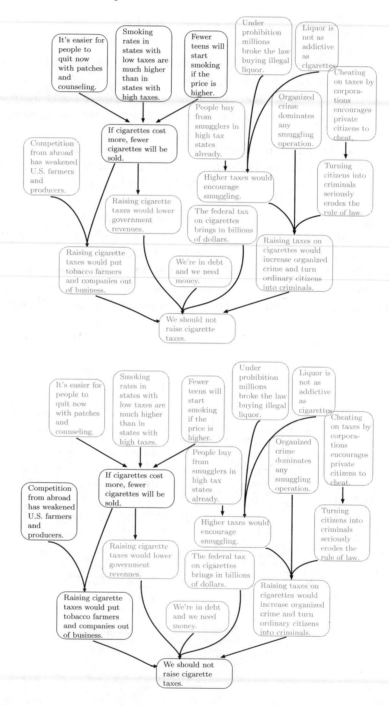

The second can take advantage of the work done on the first, so it only needs one piece.

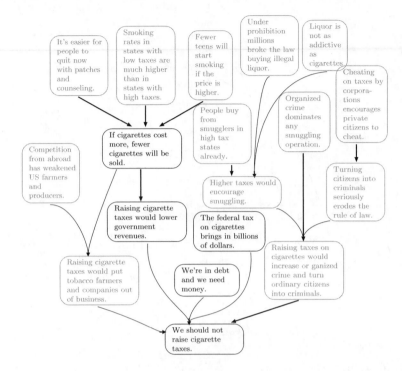

For the third, two more paragraphs might do the trick.

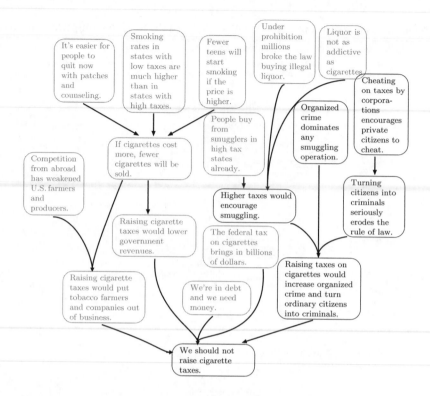

Here's the outline:

I.   Introduction

    A.   We claim that we shouldn't raise cigarette taxes.

    B.   We have three main reasons for this: cost to producers, finance, and crime.

II. Body

    A.   Producers

        i.   If cigarettes cost more, fewer cigarettes will be sold.

            a.   It's easier for people to quit now with patches and counseling.

            b.   Smoking rates in states with low taxes are much higher than in states with high taxes.

            c.   Fewer teens will start smoking if the price is higher.

        ii. Raising the tax would put tobacco farmers and companies out of business.

            a.   Competition from abroad has weakened US farmers and producers.

            b.   As we've said, if cigarettes cost more, fewer will be sold.

        iii. Since raising the tax would put producers out of business, we shouldn't raise the tax.

B. Finance
   i.   Raising cigarette taxes would lower government revenues.

       a. The federal tax on cigarettes brings in billions of dollars.
       b. Since fewer cigarettes would be sold if the tax rose, government revenues would go down.
       c. We're in debt and we need money.

   ii. Since raising taxes would lower government revenues and we need that money, we shouldn't raise taxes.

C. Crime
   i.   Raising taxes on cigarettes would increase organized crime and turn ordinary people into criminals.

   ii. Raising taxes would encourage smuggling.

       a. People buy from smugglers in high-tax states already.
       b. Millions of people bought illegal liquor under prohibition.
       c. Liquor is not as addictive as cigarettes.

   iii. Raising the cigarette tax would increase organized crime and turn ordinary citizens into criminals.

       a. Organized crime dominates any smuggling operation.
       b. As we've said, higher taxes would encourage smuggling.
       c. Turning citizens into criminals erodes the rule of law.
       d. Cheating on taxes by corporations encourages private citizens to cheat.

   iv. Since raising taxes on cigarettes would increase organized crime and turn ordinary citizens into criminals, we shouldn't raise taxes.

III. Conclusion
    That's our argument. Raising the tax on cigarettes would hurt producers, lower government revenues, and increase crime. We shouldn't raise the tax.

   Now let's write this sucker.

   I hear the calls for raising cigarette taxes and I see nothing but trouble. They'll put honest working Americans out of business. The kinds of tax hikes they're talking about won't raise money, they'll lose it. And they'll create a bonanza for organized crime. That's three good reasons for holding back on any tax increase.

   That lays it out. First "producers." Again, we'll give the reader a picture of the whole before we tackle the part.

Simply put, when we raise taxes, we reduce smoking in the United States, causing serious economic disruption. The domestic tobacco industry is already in trouble and we could see a lot of people out of work. Let's look at the connection between taxes and smoking. Higher prices normally reduce demand. That's true here too. The availability of patches and counseling have made it relatively easy for smokers to quit. Prices also discourage teens from taking up smoking. We can see the effect of higher prices by looking at Rhode Island and Kentucky. The taxes in Rhode Island are 80 times the tax in Kentucky and the smoking rate is a third less.

The next paragraph ties it up.

Domestic producers of tobacco, the farmers, the producers, are already being stressed by foreign competition. China is now the leading producer of cigarettes. If we combine this with reduced demand at home, we're going to see a lot of farmers go out of business and a number of factories close. This is just part of the downside of raising taxes.

This argument has three parts. It's good to remind readers of where they are periodically:

That's the first reason for rejecting a tax rise. The second is about money. Reduced cigarette sales will mean reduced revenues. This is not a small matter. We have an enormous deficit and cigarette taxes today generate billions to support everything from defense to the environment. Raising taxes has costs across the board.

Now crime. This is tricky; it's a big argument. We'll introduce it as we take up the first paragraph.

Finally, let's talk about crime. Higher cigarette costs will encourage smuggling on a grand scale. That means organized crime and something like a new prohibition age. Let's start with smuggling. This is already happening today. Cigarettes are purchased in low tax states like Kentucky and shipped to high tax states like Rhode Island. With high federal taxes, the cigarettes will come from Mexico. And ordinary citizens, formerly law-abiding citizens, will become criminals, just the way it happened under prohibition. In the twenties, nearly everyone, not just alcoholics, bought from bootleggers. That will happen even more with cigarettes which are addictive. If you think smoking is a problem now, imagine crime on an unprecedented scale.

Where there's smuggling there are gangs and criminal syndicates. That's a nasty problem, one we should avoid at all costs. But there's another hazard as well. Violation of the law on a large scale breeds a general disrespect for law by all citizens. When you read about corporations that don't pay their taxes, doesn't it make you just a little less scrupulous about filling out your 1040? This is potentially the most serious consequence of raising cigarette taxes. We can make a problem for ourselves that could take decades to overcome.

Sounds pretty bad! And we close.

That's the picture. Destruction of an important industry, loss of vital government revenues, and the prospect of widespread lawlessness. All this can be ours if we raise cigarette taxes.

Whew!

Great arguments, right?

Actually, there's still a problem, and it's probably been bothering you. We have one argument for raising taxes and another against raising taxes. They can't *both* be good arguments! What should bother you is that neither argument pays any attention to the other. We'll address that in the next chapter.

Exercises   Arguing with Yourself

Odd-numbered
solutions
begin on page 374

Write arguments for the following, keeping in mind that our standards are higher now:

1. The United States should bring back prohibition.

2. The United States should not bring back Prohibition.

3. The United States should lower the voting age to 14.

4. The United States should not lower the voting age to 14.

5. The United States should reinstate the draft.

6. The United States should not reinstate the draft.

7. Formulate a policy on hate speech for a university, outline an argument supporting the policy, then write the argument.

8. **Cathy and the mind/body problem**

    If you pay for something, then you'd certainly complain if you didn't get it, right? That's all Cathy is doing here.

    In any case, write an argument that Mort doesn't have to go to practice. Be sure you deal with Cathy's issues.

    Stuart was at the door of Mort's room. Mort was explaining, "I can't make it to soccer practice today, I've got to get this econ paper done."

"Ooh, that's tough." Stu's face radiated sympathy.

"Get your butt to practice!" Mort and Stu froze as Cathy strode down the hall. "I'm paying for your little hobby," she said, "so be there."

"What do you mean? How are you paying for it? It's a varsity sport!" Mort was genuinely puzzled, but nonetheless hurriedly stuffed a change of clothes into a gym bag.

"A chunk of my tuition goes straight to the athletic program. You can't buy an education here without shelling out for a spa. My money goes for your equipment, transportation, and uniforms. That's bad. But if you skip practice I'll really be pissed."

Mort had some issues with the uniforms, but decided not to say anything.

"You owe it to me to put everything you've got into sports. I pay your costs. I deserve total commitment."

"Look, Cathy," Mort replied. "You skip classes sometimes."

"That's my choice. I pay my own tuition. If I don't want to go to class, I don't have to. Besides, most of them are a waste of time."

"Now, Cathy," Stu protested. "Sports are essential to a college. They build school spirit, fellowship, cooperation, discipline!"

"You can't learn German without kicking a ball? You can't learn Italian without swinging a racket? Does school spirit help

you understand Spanish? Shit. (Pardon my French.)"

This confused Mort, who was all set to go to practice. Stuart made one more try. "But Cathy, when you're healthy, your

intellect is stronger too. You know what they say, 'A sound mind in a sound body!' "

"Right. So all those jocks who flunk out — I guess it's because they skipped practice?"

Recall that you died and went to Hell. The devil wrote a fraction on a piece of paper and put it in his pocket. He will release you from Hell if you guess the number. You can make one guess every day.

There is a strategy for escaping Hell. Here's the plan. First you guess every fraction you can form just using '0' and '1'. This takes a few days: on the first day you guess $\frac{0}{1}$, on the second day you guess $\frac{1}{1}$, and on the third day you guess $-\frac{1}{1}$.

After that, you guess all fractions you can make with '0', '1' and '2': $\frac{1}{2}, \frac{2}{1}, -\frac{1}{2}, -\frac{2}{1}$. You don't guess $\frac{2}{2}$ because that's the same as $\frac{1}{1}$. After this, you guess all fractions you can make with '0', '1', '2' and '3', and so on.

The strategy has the same properties as the previous strategies. Even if the devil knows exactly what you're going to do, there is no fraction he can choose that you won't guess in a finite number of days.

But suppose that the devil makes an especially tricky offer. He says he will write a decimal number between 0 and 1. As you know, such a number starts with a decimal point and then goes on forever.

$$.735083436758456365933122234989 0\ldots$$

Even "finite" decimals (for example, .25) really go on forever.

$$.250000000000000000000000000000\ldots$$

Don't worry about the devil's ability to write infinite numbers on a piece of paper. In this thought experiment, the devil can do it.

You can do it too. You can guess infinite decimals, which is good because the devil promises to release you if you guess his number. You can make one guess each day. The devil won't change his number.

Is there a strategy that will guarantee your escape from Hell in a finite number of days — even if the devil knows your strategy before he chooses his number? The answer is in the next chapter.

10.4 Sophisticated Modal Logic

"Oh my goodness. Who needs drugs when you've got logic, eh, Schrodinger?" (Emily Altreuter, *The Best of all Possible Worlds*)

In Chapter Nine we introduced possible worlds to express the meaning of "possible" and "necessary". It was a pretty simple set-up. $\Diamond P$ was true if P was true in some world. But this is perhaps too simple. Consider the following.

Example

Tic-Tac-Toe
Suppose we're playing tic-tac-toe. Let P be "There is an X in the top left corner". Of course P is true in some worlds and false in others.

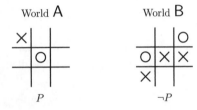

But if by $\Diamond P$ we mean that it's possible that P is true at some future move, then $\Diamond P$ is true in some worlds and false in others.

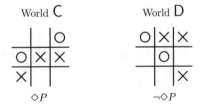

In Chapter Nine we would say that P is possible because it's true in world **A**. But if you're in a world **D**, world **A** doesn't look possible at all. In other words, what's possible depends on what world you're in.

There's a natural way to handle this. Not only does it give us a more satisfying modal logic, it also solves a different, long-standing problem, the problem of the conditional (see p. 53). Here's what we mean.

Example

"If John McCain had won in 2008, Paris Hilton would have been VP."

This is an example of a "counterfactual" or "contrary-to-fact" conditional, so-called because the antecedent (John McCain won in 2008) is counter to fact, that is, it's false. The sentence certainly seems false – there's no way Paris Hilton would ever have been McCain's running mate. But if we wrote the statement with the conditional $\Rightarrow$ we would have a true sentence exactly because the antecedent is false. The conditional of Basic Sentential fails to express the real meaning of the sentence.

To express the meaning of the sentence correctly we need a new conditional. We'll have one very soon and it will come much closer to capturing what we mean by "if... then."

To express what worlds are possible, relative to where you are, we introduce the idea of an **accessibility relation**. In pictures, we will draw an arrow between worlds

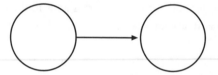

if the world at right is accessible from the world at left. Intuitively, if a world is accessible from where we are, we can imagine it, or consider it a relevant alternative in our reasoning; it is *possible*.

Of course "possible", "accessible", and even "world" depend on the universe. We can have a universe of what we think are physically possible worlds, or politically possible worlds, or, as in Tic-Tac-Toe, strategically possible worlds.

Example

Tic-Tac-Toe (continued)

We have a world for each position in a Tic-Tac-Toe game. Let's take the convention that X goes first. We'll have lots of worlds. The ground world will be the board with no moves on it. We'll say that one world can access another world if all the moves in first world are in the second. A portion of this universe looks like this:

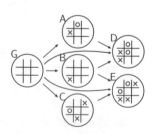

B can access **D**, for example, because the only move in **B** is also in **D**. But **D** is not accessible from **C** because they're incompatible; there's an O in **C** where an X is in **D**.

Actually, the picture above should have arrows from each world to itself.

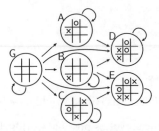

In practice, we'll omit those arrows. All our worlds will be able access themselves.

We see that a universe for modal logic is not just a set of possible worlds. A universe must include an accessibility relation (arrows) between these worlds. Different accessibility relations determine different logics. The universes described in Chapter Nine are special cases of the universes we describe here. In the universes we considered in Chapter Nine, all worlds are accessible from all worlds. But not all universes are like that.

Here's the definition from Chapter Nine, revised.

Modal Sentential

$\Diamond P$ is true at $\mathbf{W}$ iff P is true in some world accessible from $\mathbf{W}$.

$\Box P$ is true at $\mathbf{W}$ iff P is true in all worlds accessible from $\mathbf{W}$.

Example

Tic-Tac-Toe (once again).
Let P represent the statement "There is an X in the top left corner". Then $\Diamond P$ is true in the world at left because in at least one of the worlds accessible to it, P is true.

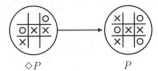

But $\Diamond P$ is false in this world,

because there's no accessible world in which P is true.

Now let's discuss entailment.

Example

John McCain (continued)
We were discussing the sentence:

"If John McCain had won in 2008, Paris Hilton would have been VP."

The real meaning of the sentence involves possible worlds. If we think about all the ways that (realistically) the election of 2008 could have gone, we might come up with a long list of possible presidential nominees: John McCain, Hillary Clinton, Mitt Romney, Barack Obama, etc., and an even longer list of possible vice-presidential nominees: Mike Huckabee, Bill Richardson, Sarah Palin, Hillary Clinton, etc. We could put together a possible world for each plausible combination and realistic outcome. These are politically accessible worlds, that is, worlds where the general truths of American politics are what they are in this world, even if the details or history is different. Then the reason why "If John McCain had won in 2008, Paris Hilton would have been VP." is false is that there are many worlds where McCain won and in at least one of them (and probably all of them) his running mate wasn't Paris Hilton.

Example

"If John McCain had won in 2008, Joe Lieberman would have been VP."

Someone might reasonably say this. They would say it because they believed that the only way McCain could have won is if he had chosen Joe Lieberman instead of Sarah Palin. The sentence may or may not be true. But the meaning of the sentence can be described in terms of possible worlds. The meaning is that in all the politically accessible worlds where McCain wins, Joe Lieberman was his running mate.

Example

"If John McCain had won in 2008, Sarah Palin would have been VP."

This might be true. It would be true if in all possible worlds in which McCain wins, Sarah Palin is his running mate. But it might not be true. It might be the case that in some accessible world McCain wins with a different vice-presidential nominee. The truth of this statement seems to depend not on what is actually true, but on what is true in possible (accessible) worlds.

These examples suggest how we might define a new conditional. It's a modal conditional. We'll use $\rightarrowtail$ to represent it. The idea is that $P \rightarrowtail Q$ is true iff wherever we see that P is true, Q is true too. The "wherever we see" is crucial. We mean in all accessible worlds. In a nutshell:

$\mathcal{A} \rightarrowtail \mathcal{B}$ is true in world **W** iff

In every world accessible from **W** where $\mathcal{A}$ is true, $\mathcal{B}$ is true too.
In every world accessible from **W** where $\mathcal{B}$ is false, $\mathcal{A}$ is false too.

The second sentence in the box is logically equivalent to the first, so it's unnecessary in the logic we have been considering so far. We have a reason for putting it there, however. We'll explain in the next chapter.

The entailment $\rightarrowtail$ is modal, i.e. not truth-functional, in that the truth value of $P \rightarrowtail Q$ at any world doesn't depend only on the truth values of P and Q at that world. You need to consider the truth values of P and Q at all accessible worlds in order to know whether $P \rightarrowtail Q$ is true at that world. We saw different examples of non-truth-functional connectives in Chapter Eight (p. 207).

Example

$P \rightarrowtail Q$ can be false even when Q is true.
Let's let P mean "Sardinia is part of France" and Q mean "The capital of France is Paris." In our world, P and Q are both true. Now let's construct a possible worlds model. A possible worlds model consists of worlds and an accessibility relation (the arrows). We can construct any universe we like. Suppose that we construct one where Sardinia is part of France but the capital of France was moved to Orleans.

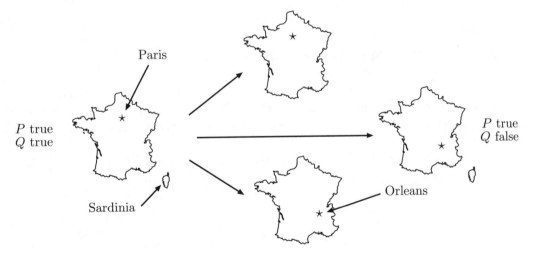

Then $P \rightarrowtail Q$ is false by our definition, even though $P \Rightarrow Q$ (the Basic conditional) is true.

Some tautologies of Basic Logic are also tautologies in the possible world model we have been considering. Some are not.

Example

$P \rightarrowtail (P \vee Q)$ is a tautology of Basic Logic and a modal tautology.

To show that this is a modal tautology, we have to show that it's true in $\mathbf{W}$ no matter what worlds are accessible. Let's throw in all imaginable types of worlds.

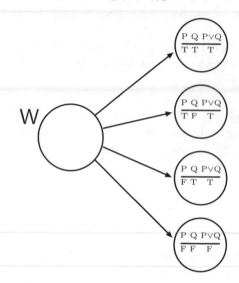

Whenever P is true, $P \vee Q$ is true too. Whenever $P \vee Q$ is false, P is false too. So $P \rightarrowtail (P \vee Q)$ is true in $\mathbf{W}$.

Example

$(A \wedge B) \Rightarrow (A \Rightarrow B)$ is a tautology in Basic Sentential.

Is $(A \wedge B) \rightarrowtail (A \rightarrowtail B)$ a modal tautology?

There's a "short cut" method to finding the answer. Like the other short cut methods, we try to find a way to make the statement false. We will try so thoroughly that either we'll succeed (and so it's not a tautology) or else we'll know the task is impossible (and so it is a tautology).

By the definition of $\rightarrowtail$, if $(A \wedge B) \rightarrowtail (A \rightarrowtail B)$ is false in world $\mathbf{R}$ then there must be a world $\mathbf{S}$ accessible to $\mathbf{R}$ in which $A \wedge B$ is true and $A \rightarrowtail B$ is false.

It's easy to make $A \wedge B$ true in $\mathbf{S}$.

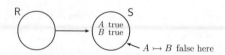

Now, to make $A \rightarrowtail B$ false in S, there must be a world accessible to S in which A is true and B is false. Well, we could invent a world for that purpose, but why waste worlds? We can just make R accessible to S and have A true and B false there.

R
$\begin{array}{l} A \text{ true} \\ B \text{ false} \end{array}$ ⟶ $\begin{array}{l} A \text{ true} \\ B \text{ true} \end{array}$ S

And that does it. That makes $(A \wedge B) \rightarrowtail (A \rightarrowtail B)$ false in R. So $(A \wedge B) \rightarrowtail (A \rightarrowtail B)$ is not a modal tautology.

Exercises   Sophisticated Modal Logic

Odd-numbered solutions begin on page 375

The following are all tautologies in Sentential (with $\Rightarrow$ instead of $\rightarrowtail$). In each case, decide if it is a modal tautology. If not, describe a system of possible worlds in which the statement is false. Remember, all worlds can see themselves.

1. $A \rightarrowtail A$
2. $(A \wedge B) \rightarrowtail A$
3. $(A \rightarrowtail B) \vee \neg B$
4. $(A \rightarrowtail B) \vee A$
5. $(A \rightarrowtail B) \rightarrowtail (\neg B \rightarrowtail \neg A)$
6. $(\neg A \vee B) \rightarrowtail (A \rightarrowtail B)$
7. $(A \rightarrowtail B) \vee (B \rightarrowtail A)$
8. Explosion: $(A \wedge \neg A) \rightarrowtail B$
9. $((A \vee B) \wedge \neg A) \rightarrowtail B$
10. True or false: "If you pick a guinea-pig up by its tail, its eyes will fall out."? In Basic Sentential, this is true because guinea-pigs don't have tails. Explain how "You pick a guinea-pig up by its tail $\rightarrowtail$ its eyes fall out" can be false in a system of possible worlds.

Consider the following electrical diagram:

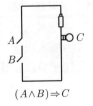

$(A \wedge B) \Rightarrow C$

We can see from this diagram (and an elementary knowledge of electrical circuits) that if A represents the sentence "Switch A is closed," B represents the sentence "Switch B is closed," and C represents "The light is on," then $(A \wedge B) \Rightarrow C$. Now observe that the following is a valid argument form in Basic Logic:

$$\frac{(A \wedge B) \Rightarrow C}{\therefore (A \Rightarrow C) \vee (B \Rightarrow C)}$$

But in the circuit diagram above, neither $(A \Rightarrow C)$ nor $(B \Rightarrow C)$ is true, and so neither is their disjunction.

11. Find a modal universe in which $(A \wedge B) \rightarrowtail C$ is true but $(A \rightarrowtail C) \vee (B \rightarrowtail C)$ is false.

12‼ Deduce $(A \Rightarrow C) \vee (B \Rightarrow C)$ from $(A \wedge B) \Rightarrow C$.

13!! This is a special edition of *The Digestor's Digest*, not the fun page.

The Digestor's Digest

Special Modal Edition!

Vol. I, No. 10

Do it Right!

Enough with the endless bickering over barbecued chicken; blacken the right side first! Tangolezzi, Duhammier, and Frobenius figured it out years ago and science agrees. By the way, just a warning, but it's possible that this issue contains an ad.

Let it Breathe!

It's hard to believe, but some die-hard soda-poppers still haven't got the message: decant your cola and let it breathe six (not five) minutes! And just a warning, but it's possible that it's possible that it's possible that it's possible that the other piece on this page is an ad.

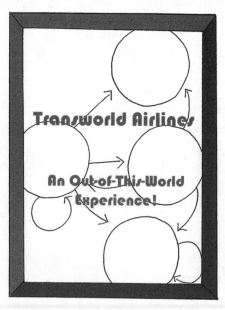

Chapter Eleven

11.1 Predicate Deduction

If you develop rules, never have more than ten. (Donald Rumsfeld)

$$\boxed{\begin{array}{ll}
\textbf{Our rules, so far:} \\[2mm]
\end{array}}$$

Our rules, so far:

∧Out:
$$\frac{A \land B}{\therefore A} \qquad \frac{A \land B}{\therefore B}$$

∧In:
$$\frac{\begin{array}{c} A \\ B \end{array}}{\therefore A \land B}$$

∨Out:
$$\frac{\begin{array}{c} A \lor B \\ A \Rightarrow C \\ B \Rightarrow C \end{array}}{\therefore C}$$

∨In:
$$\frac{A}{\therefore A \lor B} \qquad \frac{B}{\therefore A \lor B}$$

¬Out:
$$\frac{\neg\neg A}{\therefore A}$$

¬In:
$$\frac{A \Rightarrow (B \land \neg B)}{\therefore \neg A}$$

⇔ Out:
$$\frac{A \Leftrightarrow B}{\therefore A \Rightarrow B} \qquad \frac{A \Leftrightarrow B}{\therefore B \Rightarrow A}$$

⇔ In:
$$\frac{\begin{array}{c} A \Rightarrow B \\ B \Rightarrow A \end{array}}{\therefore A \Leftrightarrow B}$$

⇒ Out:
$$\frac{\begin{array}{c} A \Rightarrow B \\ A \end{array}}{\therefore B}$$

⇒ In:
$$\frac{\left[\begin{array}{c} \text{a deduction} \\ \text{of } B \text{ from } A \end{array}\right]}{\therefore A \Rightarrow B}$$

Predicate is the reason we started on deductions. In Sentential, remember, we can verify that an argument is valid by using truth tables or using the short-cut method. With Predicate, however, we have no such tool. We can show that an argument is invalid if we exhibit a universe in which the premises are true and the conclusion is false, but (until now) we have had no means of showing that an argument in Predicate is valid.

Sweet Reason: A Field Guide To Modern Logic, Second Edition. James M. Henle, Jay L. Garfield and Thomas Tymoczko.
© 2012 John Wiley & Sons Inc. Published 2012 by John Wiley & Sons Inc.

Before we start: No free variables

In deductions we deal exclusively with closed wffs, wffs in which all variables are bound, since open wffs are neither true nor false. Remember,

$$Rxy,$$

has no truth value since without knowing who or what x and y are, we can't say whether x bears the relation R to y. On the other hand,

$$\forall x \exists y Rxy$$

does have a truth value. So does *Rab*.

In our deductions we allow no free variables. Further, we require that each constant denote something that "exists". We justify existence with an "exist" statement. If there is a constant '*c*' in the premises or the conclusion of an argument, then the statement "*c* exists" must be one of the premises, for example,

$$\frac{\begin{array}{c} b \text{ exists} \\ \forall x(Px \land Qx) \end{array}}{\therefore Pb} \quad .$$

The point is that we can't conclude anything about b if we don't know that there is an object to which '*b*' refers. Every constant must denote something that exists. No constant can be introduced into a deduction unless we can say it denotes something that exists.

We require that "exist" statements be justified. In the four new rules we'll give you in this section, two of them justify exist statements.

Now the In and Out rules for $\forall$.

$$\forall\text{Out:} \quad \frac{\begin{array}{c} \forall v \mathcal{H}v \\ c \text{ exists} \end{array}}{\therefore \mathcal{H}c}$$
– where $\mathcal{H}c$ is the result of replacing all of the instances of v in $\mathcal{H}v$ with c.

Of course, v can be any variable and c can be any constant. By "$\mathcal{H}v$" we mean any wff in which v appears as a free variable, and by "$\mathcal{H}c$" we mean that same wff with all the vs replaced by cs. This rule makes sense when you think of what $\forall v \mathcal{H}v$ means. It means that $\mathcal{H}$ is true about everything that exists. In particular, if we know c exists, then we know $\mathcal{H}$ is true about c.

Example

$$\frac{\begin{array}{c} b \text{ exists} \\ \forall x(Px \land Qx) \end{array}}{\therefore Pb}$$

1. *b* exists   premise
2. $\forall x(Px \wedge Qx)$ premise
3. $Pb \wedge Qb$ $\forall$Out, 1, 2
4. Pb $\wedge$Out, 3

Note that in line 3, we refer both to line 2 (where the universal statement is) and to line 1 (where it states that the constant we're using exists). The existence of the constant is crucial. See exercises 5–10 at the end of Section 11.1 for an example of what can happen if you forget this!

To deduce something more interesting, we need the $\forall$In rule. This rule is really a type of $\Rightarrow$In rule.

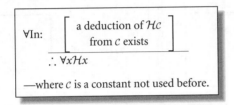

$\forall$In: [a deduction of $\mathcal{H}c$
              from c exists]
       $\therefore \forall x \mathcal{H}x$

—where c is a constant not used before.

The idea behind the rule is simple. What would it take to convince you that $\forall x \mathcal{H}x$? If you could prove $\mathcal{H}a$ without knowing anything about a, without knowing who or what a is or what properties a has, then you should believe $\forall x \mathcal{H}x$. "Wait," you say, "what about b? Why is $\mathcal{H}b$ true?" But the proof of $\mathcal{H}a$ works as well for b. Just change all the 'a's to 'b's. The proof for b works because the proof for a used no special properties of a. And of course we could do the same for any individual.

In a deduction we use whatever constant we like, so long as it hasn't appeared before (and so we have no information about it). We simply assume that the constant exists and prove it has property $\mathcal{H}$.

Example

$\forall x(Px \wedge Qx)$
$\therefore \forall x Px$

1. $\forall x(Px \wedge Qx)$ premise

2. $\forall x Px$

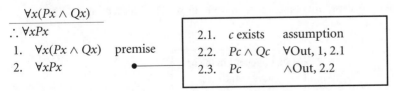

2.1. *c* exists   assumption
2.2. $Pc \wedge Qc$ $\forall$Out, 1, 2.1
2.3. Pc $\wedge$Out, 2.2

The justification of $\forall x Px$ is the subdeduction. Given the existence of c we showed Pc. Since c was arbitrary – we knew nothing about c – we really showed that P was true about anything.

The ∀In rule is a special type of the ⇒In rule because to say

everything has property $\mathcal{H}$

is to say that

if something exists, it has property $\mathcal{H}$.

Here are the two rules side-by-side:

The ⇒In rule	The ∀In rule
$\mathcal{A} \Rightarrow \mathcal{B}$ $\mathcal{A}$ assumption ⋮ $\mathcal{B}$	$\forall x Hx$ c exists assumption ⋮ Hc

Example

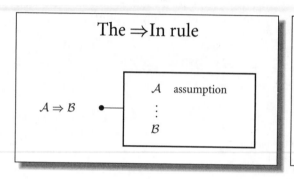

$$\forall y(Py \Leftrightarrow Qy)$$
$$\therefore \forall z(Qz \Leftrightarrow Pz)$$

1. $\forall y(Py \Leftrightarrow Qy)$ premise
2. $\forall z(Qz \Leftrightarrow Pz)$

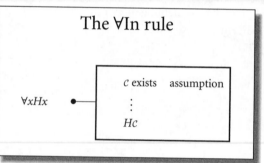

2.1. d exists   assumption
2.2. $Pd \Leftrightarrow Qd$ ∀Out 1, 2.1
2.3. $Pd \Rightarrow Qd$ ⇔ Out 2.2
2.4. $Qd \Rightarrow Pd$ ⇔ Out 2.2
2.5. $Qd \Leftrightarrow Pd$ ⇔ In 2.3, 2.4

This time we used d as the constant. We can use any constant so long as it's never been used before. The constant is arbitrary; there's nothing special about it; we've never seen it before; we know nothing about it; we'll never see it again. It only appears in this one box and only to help us justify the universal statement.

∀In boxes behave just like ⇒In boxes. Inside the box, you may use all previous lines inside and outside – except, of course, those in other boxes. And remember,

What happens in the box
stays in the box.

Example

$$\forall x(Px \Rightarrow Qx)$$
$$\therefore \forall x Px \Rightarrow \forall x Qx$$

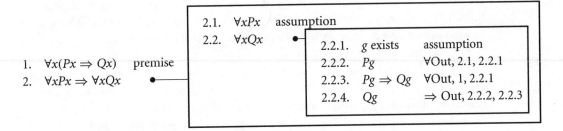

1. $\forall x(Px \Rightarrow Qx)$ premise
2. $\forall xPx \Rightarrow \forall xQx$

It's crucial that we have a constant that we know exists. See exercises 5–10 for an example of what can happen if you forget this!

Now the In and Out rules for ∃.

∃In: $\mathcal{H}c$
    ∴ $\exists v \mathcal{H}v$
—where $\mathcal{H}c$ is a wff with a constant c and $\mathcal{H}v$ is the result of replacing some or all of the instances of c with a variable v.

Example

a exists
$\forall x(Rx \Rightarrow Px)$
Ra
∴ $\exists xPx$

1. a exists   premise
2. $\forall x(Rx \Rightarrow Px)$ premise
3. Ra premise
4. $Ra \Rightarrow Pa$ ∀Out, 1, 2
5. Pa $\Rightarrow$ Out, 3, 4
6. $\exists xPx$ ∃In, 5

The wff $\mathcal{H}c$ must contain a constant the constant c. See exercises 5–10 for an example of what can happen if you forget this!

Finally, our last quantifier rule.

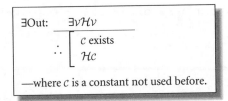

We get two statements from an existential statement. The idea is that given $\exists x\mathcal{H}x$, we know there is something out there with property $\mathcal{H}$ but we don't know what it is.

The constant gives it a name. We know it exists and we can say so. Think of "Jack the Ripper," the name given to a person believed to have murdered a series of people in London in 1888. We don't know who the person is, just that he/she exists. The name allows us to make statements about the person.

It's critical that we use a new constant. That guarantees that we aren't attributing any properties to the individual named by the constant other than those described by $\mathcal{H}$. Having named the unknown assailant "Jack the Ripper", we don't try to find him by looking in the phonebook for Ripper, Jack. If you violate this rule you can reach unjustified conclusions. Here, for example, is a proof that zombies exist. Let Zx mean that x is dead.

1.	$\exists x Zx$	premise
2.	$\exists x \neg Zx$	premise
3.	a exists	$\exists$Out 1
4.	Za	$\exists$Out 1
5.	$\neg Za$	$\exists$Out 2 ⟵ **Wrong!**
6.	$Za \wedge \neg Za$	$\wedge$In 4, 5
7.	$\exists x(Zx \wedge \neg Zx)$	$\exists$In 6

So there is someone who is both dead and undead. Zombie.

Example

$$\forall x(Rx \Rightarrow Px)$$
$$\underline{\exists x Rx}$$
$$\therefore \exists x Px$$

1.	$\forall x(Rx \Rightarrow Px)$	premise
2.	$\exists x Rx$	premise
3.	c exists	$\exists$Out, 2
4.	Rc	$\exists$Out, 2
5.	$Rc \Rightarrow Pc$	$\forall$Out, 1, 3
6.	Pc	$\Rightarrow$ Out, 4, 5
7.	$\exists x Px$	$\exists$In, 6

As a last example, we turn to a problem in Section 7.2. This is the syllogism: "All roads lead to Rome. Some interstate highways are roads. Therefore some interstate highways lead to Rome." You determined that this is valid using Venn diagrams. Now we'll deduce it. First, we formalize it using $R_1 x$ for "x is a road," $R_2 x$ for "x leads to Rome," and Sx for "x is an interstate highway."

Example

$$\forall x(R_1 x \Rightarrow R_2 x)$$
$$\underline{\exists x(Sx \wedge R_1 x)}$$
$$\therefore \exists x(Sx \wedge R_2 x)$$

1.	$\forall x(R_1 x \Rightarrow R_2 x)$	premise
2.	$\exists x(Sx \wedge R_1 x)$	premise
3.	h exists	$\exists$Out, 2
4.	$Sh \wedge R_1 h$	$\exists$Out, 2
5.	$R_1 h$	$\wedge$Out, 4
6.	$R_1 h \Rightarrow R_2 h$	$\forall$Out, 1, 3
7.	$R_2 h$	$\Rightarrow$ Out, 5, 6
8.	Sh	$\wedge$Out, 4
9.	$Sh \wedge R_2 h$	$\wedge$In, 7, 8
10.	$\exists x(Sx \wedge R_2 x)$	$\exists$In, 9

You might be slightly unclear about the difference between constants, bound variables and free variables. There's good reason for confusion; they appear at first sight identical. They're all letters! But the differences are significant and important.

A *constant* in Predicate is like a name in English. It refers to a particular something. A wff with constants says something; it's a statement. "$Ua \wedge Va$," for example, says that the individual referred to by a has property U and property V.

A *bound variable* is like a pronoun in English. It doesn't refer to anything, but the quantifier gives it meaning. A wff with bound variables says something about the universe, not about any particular thing. An existential statement says that the universe contains something of a certain kind; a universal statement says that everything that exists is of a certain kind. $\exists x V x$ means "there is something such that *it* is V"; $\forall x V x$ means "for anything you choose, *it* is V."

A *free variable* in Predicate is like a blank in English. It doesn't refer. A wff with free variables says nothing. It's not a statement. Instead, it can be used to describe a property. "$Ux \wedge Vx$," for example, denotes the property of simultaneously having properties U and V.

Heads up!

A *constant* is like a name.
A *bound variable* is like a pronoun.
A *free variable* is like a blank.

$Ub \Rightarrow Vb$	If *Titanic* makes me tear up then *Titanic* is a great movie.
$\forall x(Ux \Rightarrow Vx)$	Everything is such that if it makes me tear up then it's a great movie.
$Ux \Rightarrow Vx$	if _____ makes me tear up then _____ is a great movie
	—describes the property of being great whenever tear-producing

---

Keep all this in mind. And remember that we're using letters at the start of the alphabet (a, b, c, ..., h) for constants and letters at the end of the alphabet (z, y, x, ..., s) for variables.

Exercises   Predicate Deduction

Odd-numbered
solutions
begin on page 375

Fill in the blanks to make correct deductions:

1. $\forall x(Px \Rightarrow Qx)$
        $\exists xPx$
        ∴ $\exists xQx$

   1. $\forall x(Px \Rightarrow Qx)$ _____
   2. $\exists xPx$ _____
   3. c exists   _____
   4. Pc _____
   5. $Pc \Rightarrow Qc$ _____
   6. Qc _____
   7. $\exists xQx$ _____

3. $\forall x\exists y(Qxy \land Pxy)$
        ∴ $\forall x\exists y(Pxy \land Qxy)$

   1. $\forall x\exists y(Qxy \land Pxy)$ _____
   2. $\forall x\exists y(Pxy \land Qxy)$ •——

4. $\exists x\forall yPxy$
        ∴ $\forall x\exists yPyx$

   1. _____   premise
   2. _____ $\exists$Out 1
   3. _____ $\exists$Out 1
   4. _____   •——

2. $\exists x(Px \Rightarrow Qx)$
        $\forall xPx$
        ∴ $\exists xQx$

   1. _____   premise
   2. _____   premise
   3. _____ $\exists$Out 1
   4. _____ $\exists$Out 1
   5. _____ $\forall$Out 2, 3
   6. _____ $\Rightarrow$ Out 4, 5
   7. _____ $\exists$In 6

   2.1. c exists   _____
   2.2. $\exists y(Qcy \land Pcy)$ _____
   2.3. d exists   _____
   2.4. $Qcd \land Pcd$ _____
   2.5. Pcd _____
   2.6. Qcd _____
   2.7. $Pcd \land Qcd$ _____
   2.8. $\exists y(Pcy \land Qcy)$ _____

   4.1. _____   assumption
   4.2. _____ $\forall$Out 3, 4.1
   4.3. _____ $\exists$In 4.2

My bad!

Here are six *incorrect* arguments. For each, (a) find the error and (b) find a counterexample to the argument.

5. 1. $\forall xRx$ premise
    2. $\exists y\forall xRx$ $\exists$In 1

6. 1. $\forall xSx$ premise
    2. Sc $\forall$Out 1
    3. $\exists xSx$ $\exists$In 2

7. 1. a exists   prem.
    2. Ua prem.
    3. $\forall xUx$ •——

    3.1. a exists   ass.
    3.2. Ua line

8. 1. $\exists xVx$ premise
    2. b exists   premise
    3. Wb premise
    4. Vb $\exists$Out 1, 2

9. 1. $\forall x V x$ prem.
    2. $\forall x Q x$ prem.
    3. $\forall y Q y$ •

    | 3.1. | d exists | ass. |
    | 3.2. | Qd | $\forall$Out 2, 3.1 |

    4. Vd $\forall$Out 1, 3.1
    5. $\exists x V x$ $\exists$In 4

10. 1. $\exists x \exists y I x y$ premise
    2. e exists $\exists$Out 1
    3. $\exists y I e y$ $\exists$Out 1
    4. $I e e$ $\exists$Out 3
    5. $\exists x I x x$ $\exists$In 4

Here are some arguments for you to justify:

11. $$\frac{\exists x(Px \land Qx)}{\therefore \exists xPx \land \exists xQx}$$

12. b exists
     $\forall xPx$
     $$\overline{\therefore \exists xPx}$$

13. $$\frac{\exists x \forall y Pxy}{\therefore \forall y \exists x Pxy}$$

14. $$\frac{\exists x(P \Rightarrow Qx)}{\therefore P \Rightarrow \exists xQx}$$

15. $$\frac{\exists x(Px \land Qx)}{\therefore \exists x(Qx \land Px)}$$

16. $$\frac{\exists xPx}{\therefore \exists x(Px \lor Qx)}$$

What can we do about the paradox of the heap (p.250)? Given Hn (n grains of sand is a heap) for some n and the rule, $\forall x(Hx \Rightarrow H(x-1))$, we are forced, using our deduction rules, to conclude $H0$!

Could we deny $\forall x(Hx \Rightarrow H(x-1))$? If we do, then because $\neg\forall x(Hx \Rightarrow H(x-1))$ implies $\exists x(Hx \land \neg H(x-1))$ (we're using the quantifier exchange rules, p.165) there's some number of grains of sand n such that n grains of sand forms a heap but $n-1$ grains do not. That's hard to believe. Where would you draw the line?

The paradox has stimulated much creative logical thought. One approach is to deny the Law of the Excluded Middle (p. 108) so we aren't forced to conclude that every collection of grains of sand is either a heap or isn't. But if you do that, then you have to give up some of our deduction rules, because they're strong enough to prove the Law of the Excluded Middle (see problem 17 in Section 10.2).

A lot of suspicion falls on the concept of a heap. The feeling is that predicate languages are inadequate to deal with "vague" predicates like this. One suggestion is to use a three-valued logic (p. 153). For large values of n, n grains of sand definitely form a heap. For small values of n, n grains of sand definitely don't form a heap. And for some n it's sort of in-between – the third truth-value.

Yet another approach, supervaluation theory, manages to deny $\forall x(Hx \Rightarrow H(x-1))$ in such a way that $\exists x(Hx \land \neg H(x-1))$ is also false. It's interesting and controversial.

11.2   Predicate Strategy

The proof is by reductio ad absurdum, *and* reductio ad absurdum, *which Euclid loved so much, is one of a mathematician's finest weapons. It is a far finer gambit than any chess gambit: a chess player may offer the sacrifice of a pawn or even a piece, but a mathematician offers* the game. (G.H. Hardy, *A Mathematician's Apology*)

We now have two more In rule and two more Out rule strategies. Here's the whole lot:

In-rule strategies		Out-rule strategies	
$\wedge$In:	To prove $\mathcal{A} \wedge \mathcal{B}$ Prove $\mathcal{A}$ and $\mathcal{B}$.	$\wedge$Out:	Given $\mathcal{A} \wedge \mathcal{B}$, conclude $\mathcal{A}$ and $\mathcal{B}$.
$\vee$In:	To prove $\mathcal{A} \vee \mathcal{B}$ Prove either $\mathcal{A}$ or $\mathcal{B}$.	$\vee$Out:	Given $\mathcal{A} \vee \mathcal{B}$, $\mathcal{A} \Rightarrow \mathcal{C}$, and $\mathcal{B} \Rightarrow \mathcal{C}$, conclude $\mathcal{C}$.
$\Leftrightarrow$In:	To prove $\mathcal{A} \Leftrightarrow \mathcal{B}$ Prove $\mathcal{A} \Rightarrow \mathcal{B}$ and $\mathcal{B} \Rightarrow \mathcal{A}$.	$\Leftrightarrow$Out:	Given $\mathcal{A} \Leftrightarrow \mathcal{B}$, conclude $\mathcal{A} \Rightarrow \mathcal{B}$ and $\mathcal{B} \Rightarrow \mathcal{A}$.
$\neg$In:	To prove $\neg\mathcal{A}$ Prove $\mathcal{A} \Rightarrow (\mathcal{C} \wedge \neg\mathcal{C})$ (for some $\mathcal{C}$).	$\neg$Out:	Given $\neg\neg\mathcal{A}$, conclude $\mathcal{A}$.
$\Rightarrow$In:	To prove $\mathcal{A} \Rightarrow \mathcal{B}$ Assume $\mathcal{A}$ (in a box), prove $\mathcal{B}$.	$\Rightarrow$Out:	Given $\mathcal{A} \Rightarrow \mathcal{B}$ and $\mathcal{A}$, conclude $\mathcal{B}$.
$\forall$In:	To prove $\forall v \mathcal{H} v$ Assume c exists (in a box) and prove $\mathcal{H}c$.	$\forall$Out:	Given $\forall v \mathcal{H} v$ and c exists, conclude $\mathcal{H}c$.
$\exists$In:	To prove $\exists v \mathcal{H} v$ Prove $\mathcal{H}c$.	$\exists$Out:	Given $\exists v \mathcal{H} v$, conclude c exists and $\mathcal{H}c$.

But the overall strategy is the same.

Deduction strategy

- Work backwards.
- If you can't work backwards, work forwards.
- If you can't do either, use contradiction.

Example

$$\frac{\neg\exists x Px}{\therefore \forall x \neg Px}$$

1. $\neg\exists x Px$ premise

$$\underset{\circ}{?}$$

A. $\boxed{\forall x \neg Px}$

We start by working backwards. The goal is a universal wff so we need the ∀In rule so we open a box and choose a constant not yet used.

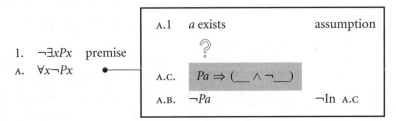

Now we want to prove a negation, so again working backwards, we try to prove a contradiction.

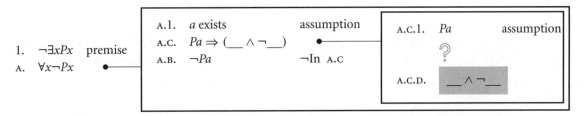

Working backwards, the goal is a conditional, so we open another box.

Now, we don't know what goes into the blank. Looking at the picture, we can see both Pa and $\neg Pa$. Is that the answer? Does Pa go in the blank?

That was a trick question. We can't use the $\neg Pa$ because we haven't justified it!

Not knowing what goes in the blank, we can't really work backwards. Let's work forwards. There's the premise. Can we use ∃Out on the premise?

That was another trick question! The premise isn't existential, so we can't use ∃Out on it! The premise is a negation. We can't use ¬Out either because ¬Out needs a double negation.

What is available for us to use? We have just $\neg\exists xPx$, a exists, and Pa. About the only thing available to us is to use $\exists$In on Pa. So we do.

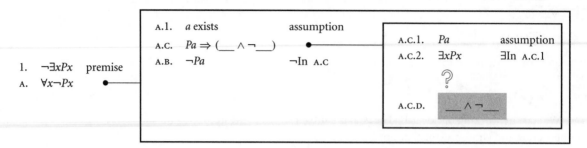

Now it's clear what goes in the blank. We have both $\exists xPx$ and $\neg\exists xPx$.

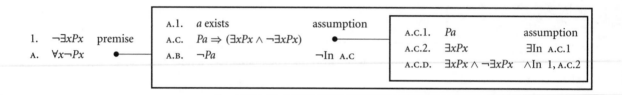

And now we can replace letters with numbers.

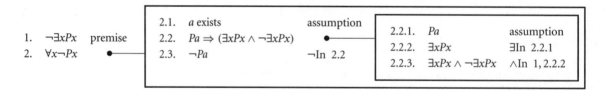

We just proved half of $\neg\exists xPx \Leftrightarrow \forall x\neg Px$, one of the quantifier exchange rules (p.165). Now we'll prove half of $\neg\forall xPx \Leftrightarrow \exists x\neg Px$, the other quantifier exchange rule.

Example

$$\frac{\exists x\neg Px}{\therefore \neg\forall xPx}$$

> 1. $\exists x\neg Px$ premise
>
>   ❓
>
> A. $\neg\forall xPx$

Working backwards, we want to prove a negation, so we look for a contradiction.

1. ∃x¬Px   premise

    ❓

B. ∀xPx ⇒ (__ ∧ ¬__)

A. ¬∀xPx   ¬In B

Now the goal is a conditional, so working backwards, we open a box.

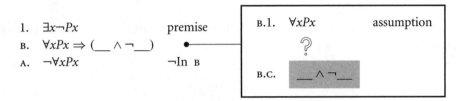

We don't know what goes in the blank, so we can't work backwards anymore. So we work forwards. We can use only ∃x¬Px and ∀xPx. The first, the premise, gives us *c* exists (choosing a constant we haven't yet used) and ¬Pc:

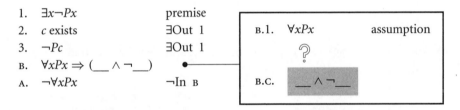

And again working forwards, from *c* exists and ∀xPx we get *Pc*.

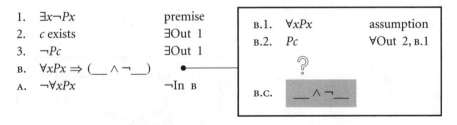

Now it's clear what goes in the blanks and we can finish the proof.

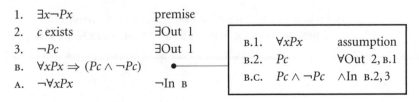

And we can trade letters for numbers.

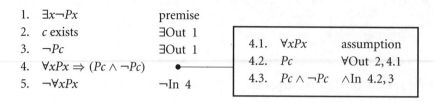

1. $\exists x \neg Px$ premise
2. c exists $\exists$Out 1
3. $\neg Pc$ $\exists$Out 1
4. $\forall x Px \Rightarrow (Pc \land \neg Pc)$
5. $\neg \forall x Px$ $\neg$In 4

         4.1. $\forall x Px$ assumption
         4.2. Pc $\forall$Out 2, 4.1
         4.3. $Pc \land \neg Pc$ $\land$In 4.2, 3

One more quantifier exchange proof. It will look like the last, for a while, but there's a snag at the end.

Example

$$\frac{\forall x \neg Px}{\therefore \neg \exists x Px}$$

     1. $\forall x \neg Px$ premise

          ?

     A. $\neg \exists x Px$

Working backwards, we want to prove a negation, so we look for a contradiction.

     1. $\forall x \neg Px$ premise

          ?

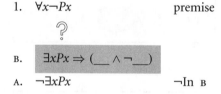

     B. $\exists x Px \Rightarrow (\_\_ \land \neg\_\_)$

     A. $\neg \exists x Px$ $\neg$In B

Now the goal is a conditional, so working backwards, we open a box.

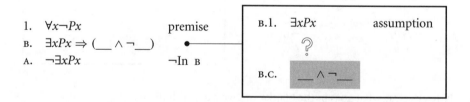

     1. $\forall x \neg Px$ premise
     B. $\exists x Px \Rightarrow (\_\_ \land \neg\_\_)$
     A. $\neg \exists x Px$ $\neg$In B

       B.1. $\exists x Px$ assumption
            ?
       B.C. $\_\_ \land \neg\_\_$

We don't know what goes in the blank, so we can't work backwards anymore. So we work forwards. We can't use the premise because in order to use $\forall$Out, we need a constant that exists. We don't have one.

The only statement we can use is ∃xPx. This will give us a constant. We can use ∃Out.

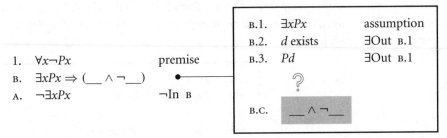

Now, since we have a constant, we can use ∀Out on the premise. We'll do it, but we'll do it incorrectly first. Can you spot the error?

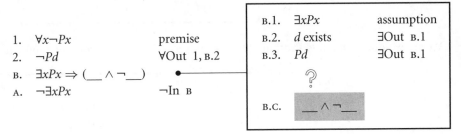

The error is that in line 2 we used line B.2, we used something inside the box. That's not allowed. The existence of *d* depends on the assumption, ∃xPx. That's not a fact we can rely on outside the box. Remember,

> What happens in the box
> *stays in the box!*

But it's easy to fix this. We just move ¬Pd inside the box.

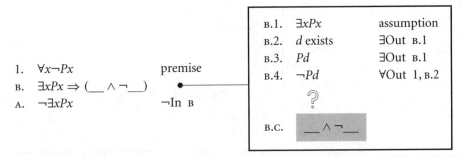

Now it looks like our proof is just about complete. We need a contradiction and we have both *Pd* and ¬*Pd*. Can we put *Pd* in the blanks?

Unfortunately, we can't! It's the same problem. If we use *Pd*, the *d* will get out of the box (it will appear in line B). But we can't take the constant *d* out of the box.

But we're in good shape. We can do this. If you did problem 7 on page 261 (take a look at it right now) you know that since we do have a contradiction (*Pd* and ¬*Pd*) we can prove anything we like. In effect, we can choose anything to go in the blank. Anything! It can be as simple as the sentence letter *H*.

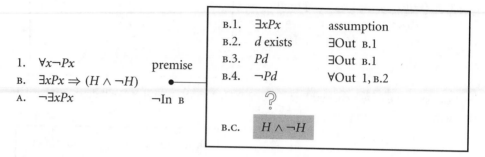

We know nothing about *H*. Nothing! But we can prove $H \land \neg H$ by contradiction. First,

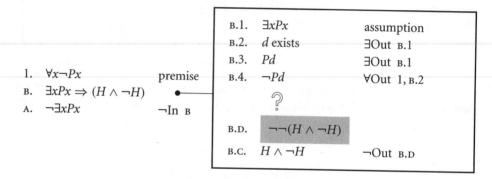

Then working backwards, we use ¬In, and this time, there's no problem using *Pd* for the blank (we're in the box).

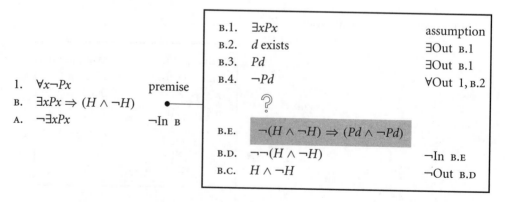

So we open a box and turn the page sideways.

1. $\forall x\neg Px$ premise
B. $\exists xPx \Rightarrow (H \land \neg H)$
A. $\neg\exists xPx$ ¬In B

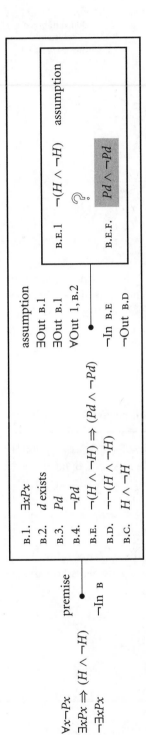

B.1.	$\exists xPx$	assumption
B.2.	d exists	∃Out B.1
B.3.	Pd	∃Out B.1
B.4.	$\neg Pd$	∀Out 1, B.2
B.E.	$\neg(H \land \neg H) \Rightarrow (Pd \land \neg Pd)$	
B.D.	$\neg\neg(H \land \neg H)$	¬In B.E
B.C.	$H \land \neg H$	¬Out B.D

Inner box:

B.E.1	$\neg(H \land \neg H)$	assumption
B.E.F.	$Pd \land \neg Pd$ (?)	

And we know how to get $Pd \land \neg Pd$ so we're done.

1. $\forall x\neg Px$ premise
B. $\exists xPx \Rightarrow (H \land \neg H)$
A. $\neg\exists xPx$ ¬In B

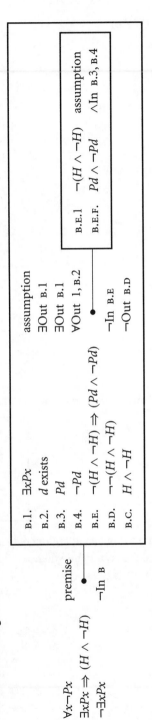

B.1.	$\exists xPx$	assumption
B.2.	d exists	∃Out B.1
B.3.	Pd	∃Out B.1
B.4.	$\neg Pd$	∀Out 1, B.2
B.E.	$\neg(H \land \neg H) \Rightarrow (Pd \land \neg Pd)$	
B.D.	$\neg\neg(H \land \neg H)$	¬In B.E
B.C.	$H \land \neg H$	¬Out B.D

Inner box:

B.E.1	$\neg(H \land \neg H)$	assumption
B.E.F.	$Pd \land \neg Pd$	∧In B.3, B.4

Except that we should change letters to numbers.

1. $\forall x\neg Px$ premise
2. $\exists xPx \Rightarrow (H \land \neg H)$
3. $\neg\exists xPx$ ¬In 2

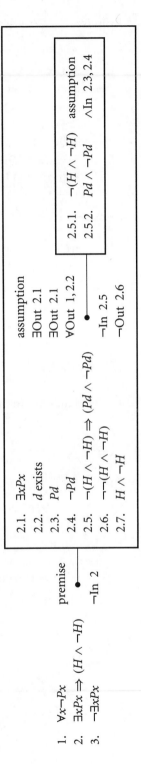

2.1.	$\exists xPx$	assumption
2.2.	d exists	∃Out 2.1
2.3.	Pd	∃Out 2.1
2.4.	$\neg Pd$	∀Out 1, 2.2
2.5.	$\neg(H \land \neg H) \Rightarrow (Pd \land \neg Pd)$	
2.6.	$\neg\neg(H \land \neg H)$	¬In 2.5
2.7.	$H \land \neg H$	¬Out 2.6

Inner box:

2.5.1.	$\neg(H \land \neg H)$	assumption
2.5.2.	$Pd \land \neg Pd$	∧In 2.3, 2.4

Exercises   **Predicate Strategy**

Odd-numbered
solutions
begin on page 376

1. $\dfrac{\forall x(Px \land Qx)}{\therefore \exists xPx \Rightarrow \exists xQx}$

2. $\forall x\exists y(Px \Rightarrow Qy)$
     $\dfrac{\exists xPx}{\therefore \exists yQy}$

3. $\forall x(Px \Rightarrow \neg Qx)$
     $\dfrac{\exists x(Qx \land Rx)}{\therefore \exists x(\neg Px \land Qx)}$

4. $\forall x\exists y(Px \lor Qy)$
     $\dfrac{\exists x \neg Px}{\therefore \exists yQy}$

5. $\dfrac{\forall x(\exists y \neg Qy \land \forall yQy)}{\therefore \forall zRz}$

6. $\forall xPx \lor \forall xQx$
     $\dfrac{\exists xRx}{\therefore \exists x(Px \lor Qx)}$

7. $\dfrac{\exists y(\forall xPx \lor Qy)}{\therefore \forall x(Px \lor \exists yQy)}$

8. $\dfrac{\exists y(\forall xPx \land Qy)}{\therefore \forall x(Px \land \exists yQy)}$

9. $\dfrac{\forall xPx \lor \forall xQx}{\therefore \forall x(Px \lor Qx)}$

10. $\dfrac{\exists xPx \Rightarrow \forall x \neg Qx}{\therefore \exists xQx \Rightarrow \forall x \neg Px}$

11‼ Formalize "There is no person who shaves all and only those who don't shave themselves" (the barber "paradox" p. 59). Construct a deduction of this statement from no premises.

12. **My bad!**

Find the error in the following proof and find a counterexample to the argument.

1. $\forall x \neg Hx$ premise
2. $\exists xHx \Rightarrow (Hd \land \neg Hd)$
3. $\exists y(\exists xHx \Rightarrow (Hy \land \neg Hy))$ ∃In 2

2.1.	$\exists xHx$	assumption
2.2.	d exists	∃Out 2.1
2.3.	Hd	∃Out 2.1
2.4.	$\neg Hd$	∀Out 1, 2.2
2.5.	$Hd \land \neg Hd$	∧In 2.3, 2.4

13. Draw arrows representing formal valid arguments among the six boxes below. However, we are only interested in arguments where all the premises are necessary. Assume for this problem that a and b exist.

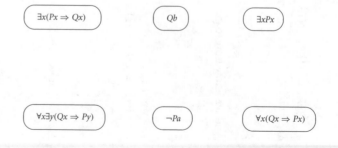

14. Draw arrows representing formal valid arguments among the six boxes below. However, we are only interested in arguments where all the premises are necessary. Assume for this problem that *a* and *b* exist.

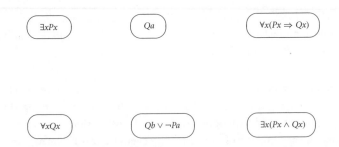

$\exists x Px$ $\qquad$ Qa $\qquad$ $\forall x(Px \Rightarrow Qx)$

$\forall x Qx$ $\qquad$ $Qb \vee \neg Pa$ $\qquad$ $\exists x(Px \wedge Qx)$

Over the course of several chapters we warned you about a surprise exam. Our editor argued (with excellent logic) that a surprise exam was not possible (pages 145, 176, 196). Then in the last chapter there was an exam (the spelling test, page 262). If you believed the editor's argument, you were surprised. What is going on?

This is the paradox of the surprise exam or, in another setting, the paradox of the unexpected hanging. It has puzzled and defeated philosophers for generations.

You may be tempted to say that the editor's reasoning holds for one or two pages but not for all the pages in the book. But that's not the case. We can see that by removing space between the statement and the test. Indeed, the paradox works even if we tell you "There is an exam on the next page and you will be surprised to see it!"

Philosophers Richard Montague and David Kaplan argued that the surprise exam paradox is a disguised version of a simpler paradox about knowledge. Consider the statement:

> "You do not know that this statement is true."

Informally, the statement can't be false. If it were false, then we would know it's true. But one can't *know* a false statement. You can believe a false statement, but not know it. Therefore the statement is true. And we know it's true, because we just proved it! But it says we *don't* know it!

By the way, the answers to the surprise exam are:

argument
rebuttal
tautology
Henle
Tymoczko
or
paradox
consistent

11.3   Why We Argue

When I'm getting ready to reason with a man, I spend one-third of my time thinking about myself and what I am going to say – and two-thirds thinking about him and what he is going to say. (Abraham Lincoln)

Let's return once more to the arguments of the previous four chapters. They're not bad, but they've been ignoring each other. That makes both of them, seen together, unconvincing. Effective arguments deal with points raised by the other side.

Let's take the argument in favor of raising cigarette taxes. The argument against raising taxes has three main points. First, it worries about the farmers and producers who will be adversely affected. Do we have an answer to that?

There are two possibilities that suggest themselves:

1. That's regrettable, but necessary. The government can and should take steps to ameliorate the problem. Workers can be retrained. Farmers can be assisted in the process of turning to other crops.
2. The tobacco industry won't really decline. Demand for American cigarettes is still high across the world.

And we could combine these.

A good place to add a paragraph on this would be just before the last, summary paragraph:

> *Some of those opposed to raising the cigarette tax have expressed worry that the domestic tobacco industry would collapse. I don't think this is likely. As wealth accumulates in developing countries such as China, India, and Nigeria, demand for the best quality goods increases, and that includes cigarettes. But even if farmers and producers experience cutbacks, this should not deter us. The US economy thrives on restructuring. Farmers can switch crops. Workers can be retrained. If necessary, the government can assist in the process, but it can't hold back what is best for the country.*

Second, the anti-tax argument argues that revenues will fall. But we've addressed that issue. We don't have to add anything.

Finally, there's the organized crime problem. What do we say about that?

1. We could say that's highly unlikely. Maybe we're only raising taxes a fairly small amount. And cigarette taxes are higher abroad – in Europe, anyway.
2. We could say that the real smuggling problem comes from the huge difference in state tobacco taxes.

I was taken by surprise when some critics of the proposed tax voiced fears of organized crime and cigarette smuggling. Where are the cigarettes going to come from? Cigarette taxes are even higher in Europe. The rise we're recommending won't make cigarettes as expensive as they are in England or France or even Canada. The real smuggling problem is interstate, due to the wide differences in state taxes. The federal tax rate doesn't affect this in the slightest. Smuggling between states is a genuine problem, though, and Congress should address it after it has raised the federal tax.

Not bad.

Now let's take the argument opposed to raising cigarette taxes. The argument for raising taxes had two main points. First it says the tax will make us healthier. What can we say?

We can't really argue that cigarettes are safe. But we aren't defenseless here.

1. We can say that those who still smoke are hardcore smokers with addictive personalities. If they don't have cigarettes to get them through the day, it will be something else.
2. Then we can say that the best way to help such people is to promote discipline, backbone, and responsibility, which you can't do with taxes.

Dealing with counterarguments is best done at the end (so you don't seem too defensive). We could add just before the last paragraph:

Supporters of higher taxes talk loudly of its presumed health benefits. Of course cigarettes are harmful, but we've already reduced the smoking population significantly. Those who still smoke are hardcore smokers, many with addictive personalities. If they can't get cigarettes, they will undoubtedly find something else: speed, meth, uppers and downers. These people need to develop self-discpline. You don't reform sinners by taxing sin. Smokers need help. The real scandal isn't cigarette prices, it's the failure of Medicare and Medicaid to provide counselling.

Second, the pro-tax argument argues that public health will be improved.

1. We can point out that these are hardcore cigarette addicts; they will still get cigarettes, they will still smoke.
2. We can counter that any savings will have to be diverted to deal with the economic disruptions caused by the tax (bankrupt farmers, unemployed tobacco workers, etc.) and crime fighting.

The most absurd argument for the tax is economic. I wonder if promoters of the tax are aware of the glaring inconsistency in their twin claims that revenues will rise and sales will fall. It makes it difficult to take the rest of the argument seriously. But suppose, just for the moment, that revenues do rise. No additional tax money will be available to help with the deficit, for it will be needed to deal with the economic disruptions caused by the tax — bankrupt farmers, unemployed tobacco workers, and so on. When you play with the tax code, there are consequences.

What do *you* think? Are you for the tax or against it?

And why do we argue? What has been gained in these arguments?

What has been gained is a clarification of the issues. The disputants disagree about the economic and social effects of a tax hike. They may disagree on the relative value of preserving jobs and industries versus improving health.

Arguing helps us understand problems and programs. A key principle of our legal system is that we are more likely to find the truth of the matter if we have advocates arguing on both sides. This principle is as important outside of court as it is in.

| **Exercises** | **Why We Argue** | Odd-numbered solutions begin on page 378 |

1. Write an argument in favor of the statement, "My school should have a foreign language requirement."

2. Write an argument opposed to the statement, "My school should have a foreign language requirement."

3. Write an argument in favor of the statement, "The United States should repeal the Second Amendment."

4. Write an argument opposed to the statement, "The United States should repeal the Second Amendment."

5. Write an argument in favor of the statement, "Government funding for public broadcasting should be eliminated."

6. Write an argument opposed to the statement, "Government funding for public broadcasting should be eliminated."

7. Compose a policy governing surrogate motherhood then write an argument for the adoption of that policy as law.

8. ## Cathy sighted

   Cathy is no longer at Sophist College; we believe she went to New York City. The evidence for this is a letter we received from a colleague there. We have his permission to print it.

   "Is Cathy kind of short? Did you tell me she has reddish hair? I think I've finally run into her. When you told me about her, I thought you were kidding. But I started hearing things from students about somebody new hanging around the campus, little things, and a picture began to emerge – sort of hard to describe.

   Yesterday, in Constitutional Law, I was lecturing on how the incidents of torture by US troops in Iraq violated international agreements and the constitution when this brassy voice, dripping with contempt, came from the back of the room.

   "Hey Professor. If torture is unconstitutional, how come we do it all the time?"

   It was a student I'd never seen before. I think I said "Huh?"

   "Our courts use torture to extract confessions. They do it in every state. They call it plea-bargaining." I said "Huh?" again. Not my finest moment.

   "If you use force or the threat of force to make somebody say or do something, that's torture. We torture a suspect when we charge him with murder and threaten to execute him if he doesn't confess to manslaughter."

I didn't know what to say. I'd never thought of that before. I have a number of assertive students. But nobody said anything. In fact, the room was really, really quiet.

"C'mon. What's wrong with a little torture? Are you some kind of a wimp?" There was some nervous laughter at this. I tried to respond, but she ran right over me.

"Torture is good. Torture saves lives. We beat up terrorists and find out about plans to blow up Disney World. Hey, are you soft on terrorism?"

"Excuse me," I said sternly, "the Geneva Convention requires . . ."

"The Geneva Convention doesn't apply. These aren't enemy soldiers. The CIA picks these monsters up all over the place, Europe, Africa, Asia. We can do what we want with them."

"But everyone has rights!"

"These are terrorists," she said blandly, "terrorists don't have rights."

I think I lost it. I've never done that before in a class. You know me — I've talked to torture victims. I started to describe the horrors practiced by interrogators. I got pretty passionate and then this creature, or Cathy, I guess it was Cathy, asked if I was vegetarian. I would have had an aneurism right there if the period hadn't ended.

That woman is a piece of work."

Write an argument against the use of torture by the United States that can survive attack by that woman, whoever she was.

Math phobic's nightmare

11.4   Presidential Debating

Elinor agreed with it all, for she did not think he deserved the compliment of rational opposition. (Jane Austen)

Everything you've learned (or rather, everything we've told you) about written arguments is true about oral arguments, in particular, debate.

> **A good argument is**
>
> 1. Clear
> 2. Logical
> 3. Clearly logical

What's different is that in debating this is much harder to achieve off the cuff. First of all, there's logical coherence. You're under a severe time constraint. You don't have time to diagram your argument. You don't have time to attack your own argument to find its weaknesses.

Second, there's clarity. It's more difficult for audiences, as opposed to readers, to follow an argument. That means you have to work harder to be clear and to clearly expose the fallacies of others. Analogy is helpful here. Listeners find analogies much easier to grasp.

Third, if you're in a position of responsibility, you have to worry about what you say. As president, you can't trash anyone you want. And even if you're not in office, a smashing good line might get you into trouble with some supporters or with an important constituency.

Fourth, when you're asked a question, you have to answer it on many levels. There is, first of all, the question interpreted literally. Then there is the question that was really intended. And finally, the question may actually be an attack that you have to answer, an attack disguised as a question. If you are asked, for example, "Were you surprised, Mr. President, when Secretary O'Connell resigned?" you should say whether you were surprised, but the questioner really wanted to know what you're going to do and what the resignation means for your administration. And if you're asked, "If you are re-elected, Mr. President, will you fire Secretary Putnam?" the question is really an attack on Secretary Putnam (and an attack on you for appointing her).

In general, public speaking is difficult. If you read the transcript of a press conference or a debate, you may be astonished at the number of utterances that make no sense in print, that don't form sentences. (By the way, do you usually speak in sentences?)

To illustrate the logical ideas present in any debate, let's examine a few exchanges from the 2008 vice-presidential debate between Senator Joe Biden and Governor Sarah Palin.

The questioner is Gwen Ifill from PBS.

> IFILL: *Senator Biden, how, as vice president, would you work to shrink this gap of polarization which has sprung up in Washington, which you both have spoken about here tonight?*
> BIDEN: *Well, that's what I've done my whole career, Gwen, on very, very controversial issues, from dealing with violence against women, to putting 100,000 police officers on the street, to trying to get something done about the genocide in – that was going on in Bosnia.*
> *And I — I have been able to reach across the aisle. I think it's fair to say that I have almost as many friends on the Republican side of the aisle as I do the Democratic side of the aisle.*
> *But am I able to respond to – are we able to stay on the – on the topic?*
> IFILL: *You may, if you like.*

Before he moves off topic, did Senator Biden answer the question? Not at all. He just claims to have worked with others before.

> BIDEN: *Yes, well, you know, until two weeks ago – it was two Mondays ago John McCain said at 9 o'clock in the morning that the fundamentals of the economy were strong. Two weeks before that, he said George – we've made great economic progress under George Bush's policies.*
> *Nine o'clock, the economy was strong. Eleven o'clock that same day, two Mondays ago, John McCain said that we have an economic crisis.*
> *That doesn't make John McCain a bad guy, but it does point out he's out of touch. Those folks on the sidelines knew that two months ago.*

So Biden decided to use his time to take a jab at Sarah Palin's running mate, Senator McCain.

> IFILL: *Governor Palin, you may respond.*
> PALIN: *John McCain, in referring to the fundamental of our economy being strong, he was talking to and he was talking about the American workforce. And the American workforce is the greatest in this world, with the ingenuity and the work ethic that is just entrenched in our workforce. That's a positive. That's encouragement. And that's what John McCain meant.*

That's an excellent response – not to the original question but to Biden's jab.

> *Now, what I've done as a governor and as a mayor is truly had that track record of reform, and I've joined this team that is a team of mavericks, with John McCain also with his track record of reform, where we're known for putting partisan politics aside to just get the job done.*

Like Biden, she says she has worked with others before.

> *Now, Barack Obama, of course, he's pretty much only voted along his party lines. In fact, 96 percent of his votes have been solely along party line, not having that proof for the American people to know that his commitment, too, is, you know, put the partisanship, put the special interests aside, and get down to getting business done for the people of America.*

She responds to Biden by arguing that Obama is partisan.

We're tired of the old politics as usual. And that's why, with all due respect, I do respect your years in the US Senate, but I think Americans are craving something new and different and that new energy and that new commitment that's going to come with reform.

I think that's why we need to send the maverick from the Senate and put him in the White House, and I'm happy to join him there.

She seems to be thinking that "maverick" and "reform" imply less partisan. This seems a stretch, but in fact

$$\begin{array}{r} \text{partisan} \Rightarrow \text{old politics} \\ \underline{\text{reform, maverick} \Rightarrow \text{new politics}} \\ \therefore\ \text{reform, maverick} \Rightarrow \text{not partisan} \end{array}$$

is valid (check this!).

IFILL: Now, let's talk about – the next question is to talk about the subprime lending meltdown. Who do you think was at fault? I start with you, Governor Palin. Was it the greedy lenders? Was it the risky home-buyers who shouldn't have been buying a home in the first place? And what should you be doing about it?

PALIN: Darn right it was the predator lenders, who tried to talk Americans into thinking that it was smart to buy a $300,000 house if we could only afford a $100,000 house. There was deception there, and there was greed and there is corruption on Wall Street. And we need to stop that. Again, John McCain and I, that commitment that we have made, and we're going to follow through on that, getting rid of that corruption.

That's clear. The lenders are at fault.

One thing that Americans do at this time, also, though, is let's commit ourselves just every day American people, Joe Six Pack, hockey moms across the nation, I think we need to band together and say never again. Never will we be exploited and taken advantage of again by those who are managing our money and loaning us these dollars. We need to make sure that we demand from the federal government strict oversight of those entities in charge of our investments and our savings and we need also to not get ourselves in debt. Let's do what our parents told us before we probably even got that first credit card. Don't live outside of our means. We need to make sure that as individuals we're taking personal responsibility through all of this.

Now it's not so clear. Palin implies that home-buyers got themselves into trouble by ignoring what their parents told them.

It's not the American peoples fault that the economy is hurting like it is, but we have an opportunity to learn a heck of a lot of good lessons through this and say never again will we be taken advantage of.

Then she confuses us further by saying the situation isn't their fault.

There is, of course, much more. We can react to illogical political speech with outrage. Or we can react with amusement. But we can't properly appreciate our candidates until we've walked a few steps in their shoes. That's not as hard as it sounds. You and your friends can try your hand at political debating in a safe and neutral setting. You don't have to be an expert in foreign affairs or tax policy, all you need is logic. The issues can be entirely fictitious.

Activity: **Presidential Debating**

Play the *Sweet Reason* Debating Game
- There are three characters in the game, each represented by a group of two or three players. The characters are the two candidates plus the press.
- Each candidate is described loosely (sample descriptions follow these rules).
- The press first asks one candidate a question. The group representing the candidate has a minute to confer, then two minutes to answer the question. The group representing the other candidate has a minute to confer and then a minute to reply. In response, the group representing the first candidate may, with no conference, present a one-minute rebuttal.
- The press then asks the second candidate a question and the game continues.
- At any time, the candidates and the press may invent any details they like, *so long as the details do not contradict previously introduced details.*
For example, the press could create an issue by asking,

"Congressman Smeal, can you tell us why you voted against the Fair Employment Bill last year, which would have prevented employers from discriminating against workers with bad breath?"

The press just made up the bill. It's a complete surprise to the group representing Smeal. Still, they could still respond:

"The bill was a badly flawed piece of legislation that required every employer to supply breath mints to all employees. It would have cost small businessmen thousands of dollars!"

The Smeal team successfully answered the question by inventing details consistent with the details in the question. Note that the Smeal team would *not* be allowed to say,

"Actually, I didn't vote against the bill; in fact, I was the chief sponsor!"

because that would contradict a previously introduced detail.
Here's another example of creative detail production from a real class debate. A governor was challenged about his opposition to a federal water pollution bill that would have supplied his state with all the funds necessary to clean up all the rivers in his state. The governor replied (after much thought and consultation) that he had opposed it because there were no rivers in his state!
- The class will judge the debaters on the basis of how relevant, logical and persuasive their answers are.

Each debate team should be given a score between 1 and 5 by every member of the class.

The candidates should be interesting as individuals and should have distinct positions and outlooks. Here are four candidates to choose from:

Senator Violet Snort   Snort is from an Eastern state; she's an activist in foreign policy affairs. She favors US intervention to preserve democracies. She wants to reintroduce the draft. She's liberal on domestic issues; she wants to tax the rich and give to the poor.

Governor Horace Grumble   Grumble is from a Western state. He's for an isolationist foreign policy – he wants to cut defense spending and stay out of other countries. He's conservative on domestic issues. He wants to privatize the Postal Service and public schools (i.e., he thinks these should be run by private businesses).

Madeleine Kim, Chief Executive Officer of Swindex Electronics, an enormously successful multinational corporation, mostly US-owned. Kim has been highly visible as a manager, and the company's position as a supplier of rocket guidance systems has made her rich and influential. Her autobiography, *Kim!*, was a best seller and she used it to popularize her philosophy of self-help.

She opposes government programs to help the unemployed, handicapped, and other disadvantaged people. Her company's international success has also convinced her of the importance of global cooperation. She believes we have nothing to fear from any country that drinks Pepsi and watches TV on Swindex Infinitron sets.

General Samuel Allen   "General Sam," as members of his staff call him, worked his way up through the air force ranks until he was picked for a succession of cabinet posts. He is tough: tough on drugs, tough on Cuba, tough on polluters, tough on dictators, tough on reporters. He believes in making people, corporations, government agencies, and countries do what's good for them.

– or make up your own candidates!

Recall that in Chapter Ten, you died and went to Hell. The devil wrote a decimal number between 0 and 1 on a piece of paper and put it in his pocket. He promised to release you from Hell if you guess the number. We asked if there is a strategy for escaping Hell. Recall that we demand of a successful strategy that it work even if the devil sees it before he selects his number.

The surprising answer is that for this challenge *there is no strategy*. There is no strategy that guarantees escape from Hell in a finite number of days.

We will prove that the devil can defeat every possible strategy. We'll take a random strategy *S*, one with no special properties, and show that the devil can defeat it by choosing an appropriate number.

A strategy tells you what decimal number to guess on every day. Let's say the random strategy *S* tells you to guess (this is just an example):

guess, day 1:   .35483...
guess, day 2:   .57462...
guess, day 3:   .45213...
guess, day 4:   .56423...
guess, day 5:   .66014...

Then the devil can circle the numbers down the diagonal like this

guess, day 1:   ③ 5 4 8 3 ...
guess, day 2:   .5 ⑦ 4 6 2 ...
guess, day 3:   .4 5 ② 1 3 ...
guess, day 4:   .5 6 4 ② 3 ...
guess, day 5:   .6 6 0 1 ④ ...

and choose a decimal number whose first digit is different from 3 (the first circled number), whose second digit is different from 7 (the second circled number), whose third digit is different from 2 (the third circled number), and so on, for example,

.49571...

The result will be a number that you won't guess on day 1 (your day 1 guess and this number have different first digits). You won't guess the number on day 2 (your day 2 guess and this number have different second digits), and so on. Will you guess the number on day 19776833984536? Nope. Your day 19776833984536 guess and the devil's number have different 19776833984536th digits!

Our thought experiment frames a series of mathematical results by Georg Cantor in the late nineteenth century. His proof (above) that there is no strategy for guessing decimals is considered one of the most beautiful in mathematics. As we shall see, it opens the door to the splendid – and endless – world of the infinite.

11.5   The Logic of Paradox

I lifted her doe by its lops, quoth I,
    "Even here deep meaning lies,—
Why have squirrels these ample tails, and why
    Have rabbits these prominent eyes?"
She smiled and said, as she twirled her veil,
    "For some nice little cause, no doubt—
If you lift a guinea-pig up by the tail
    His eyes drop out!"

(Frederick Locker-Lampson, "A Garden Lyric")[1]

---

[1]   We thank Edwin Mares, who thanks Lou Goble, who thanks Alan Anderson, for locating this verse.

We've ended every chapter with an alternative logic. The logics started out pretty tame but have grown more and more adventurous. The logic we describe here is the most radical, and yet, it has antecedents throughout the book.

In our logical travels, we have scorned inconsistency. If we found that a statement was both true and false, we would try to find what went wrong. We've treated inconsistency as a disease. Most importantly, any argument with inconsistent premises is worthless. It's worthless because you can logically derive any conclusion from inconsistent statements. In the exercises on page 71, for example, you proved that "Explosion"

$$\frac{P \wedge \neg P}{\therefore Q}$$

is totally valid. With inconsistent premises you can prove that Jim is a cheese sandwich. You can prove that $2 + 2 = 5$. You can prove that the Cubs won the World Series.

At the same time, the world is full of inconsistent information. Databases everywhere are prone to erroneous data. Phone numbers and addresses change. Witnesses give conflicting stories. Instruments record different readings. If we took, for example, the information collected by the National Security Administration on foreign terrorists and applied the logic of Chapters One through Ten, we *might* learn something important. But we would also learn that Jim is a cheese sandwich.

Perhaps what we need is a logic that can deal with contradictions. It would have to be special. Explosion would not be a law of this logic. What would such a logic look like?

We have such a logic for you. It is a **paraconsistent** logic, meaning it can tolerate inconsistency. It was developed originally by F.G. Asenjo in 1966, but discovered independently and popularized by the Australian logician Graham Priest. In Priest's Logic of Paradox, statements may be

> just true,
> just false, or
> both true and false.

There are only two truth values. But a statement can have more than one of them.

Negation in this logic is simple. If P is just true, then $\neg P$ is just false. If P is just false, then $\neg P$ is just true. If P is both true and false, then naturally, $\neg P$ is both true and false.

What about conjunctions? Conjunctions involving wffs that are just true or false are as usual in Basic Sentential. Conjunctions involving wffs that are both true and false are different but still natural.

Example

P is just true and Q is both true and false.

> Q is true. So P and Q are both true. So $P \wedge Q$ is true.
> But Q is also false. So $P \wedge Q$ is false. Altogether, $P \wedge Q$ is both true and false.

Example

P is just false and *Q* is both true and false.

    Q is true and *Q* is false but it doesn't matter. Since *P* is false, $P \wedge Q$ is false. Just false.

Example

P and *Q* are both true and false.

    $P \wedge Q$ is both true and false.

By the way, don't think of 'true and false' as being somehow less true than 'just true'. That would be a mistake. If *P* is true and false, it is fully and completely true and entitled to all the rights and privileges appertaining thereto. That *P* is also false is curious, but it takes away nothing from the essential truth of *P*.

    Disjunctions are handled the same way as conjunctions.

Example

P is both true and false but *Q* is just true.

    $P \vee Q$ is just true. The fact that *Q* is true makes $P \vee Q$ true no matter what *P* is.

Example

P is both true and false but *Q* is just false.

    P is true, so $P \vee Q$ is true. But both *P* and *Q* are false, so $P \vee Q$ is false. Thus, $P \vee Q$ is both true and false.

We could do much the same for the Basic conditional, $\Rightarrow$, but we would have a problem. We want to defeat Explosion. In Basic Sentential,

$$(P \wedge \neg P) \Rightarrow Q,$$

is a law of logic. It's always true. We don't want that here. But if you take apart $(P \wedge \neg P) \Rightarrow Q$, allowing statements to be just true, just false, or both, you will find that $(P \wedge \neg P) \Rightarrow Q$ is always true (sometimes it's also false, but it's always true).

    The problem is our conditional, $\Rightarrow$. For our paraconsistent logic we'll use the modal entailment, $\rightarrowtail$, instead. It's not obvious that that will work. Explosion, $(P \wedge \neg P) \rightarrowtail Q$ is a tautology in the logic of Chapter Ten (exercise 9, p.285). Let's see what happens here.

    A paraconsistent universe consists of many worlds, one of them the ground world, which we will call **G**. As in Chapter Ten, some of the worlds are accessible from others but every world can access itself. We insist in addition, for our paraconsistent logic, that every world is accessible from **G**. Here's an example.

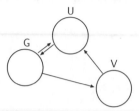

In each world, every sentence letter is either true, false, or both.

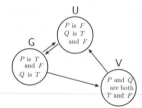

Recall that in the last chapter we gave you the definition,

$\mathcal{A} \rightarrowtail \mathcal{B}$ is true iff

(1) In every accessible world where $\mathcal{A}$ is true, so is $\mathcal{B}$.
(2) In every accessible world where $\mathcal{B}$ is false, so is $\mathcal{A}$.

We noted then (in consistent logic) that (1) and (2) were equivalent, that (2) was unnecessary. But in paraconsistent logic (1) and (2) aren't quite the same. For example, if $\mathcal{A}$ is just true and $\mathcal{B}$ is both true and false, then (1) is satisfied ($\mathcal{A}$ is true but so is $\mathcal{B}$) but (2) is not satisfied ($\mathcal{B}$ is false but $\mathcal{A}$ isn't). So we need both lines.

We need something else as well. The rule above provides only the truth conditions for $\mathcal{A} \rightarrowtail \mathcal{B}$. We need another clause to provide the *falsity* conditions. Truth and falsity are not mutually exclusive.

$\mathcal{A} \rightarrowtail \mathcal{B}$ is false iff

(3) In some accessible world $\mathcal{A}$ is true and $\mathcal{B}$ is false.

Remember that in paraconsistent logic, a conditional, just like any other wff, can be both true and false.

It's useful to define two intermediate steps to help us determine truth and falsity. Suppose W is a world in our universe. Then we say

> ## W verifies $A \rightarrowtail B$ iff
>
> (1) If A is true in W then so is B and
> (2) If B is false in W then so is A

> ## W falsifies $A \rightarrowtail B$ iff
>
> (3) A is true and B is false in W

With this we can condense the definition of paraconsistent entailment to

> ## $A \rightarrowtail B$ is true iff
>
> All accessible worlds verify $A \rightarrowtail B$.
>
> ## $A \rightarrowtail B$ is false iff
>
> Some accessible world falsifies $A \rightarrowtail B$.

We'll try these definitions out on the (very simple) universe we showed earlier.

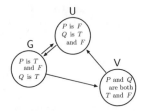

Example

The truth-value of $P \rightarrowtail Q$ in U.

The worlds accessible from U are U and G. We check to see if G verifies $P \rightarrowtail Q$. It does. P is true, but so is Q, satisfying (1). Q is not false so (2) is automatically satisfied. Does G falsify $P \rightarrowtail Q$? It doesn't. P is true but Q isn't false.

Now let's check U, does U verify $P \rightarrowtail Q$? Again, it does. (1) is satisfied vacuously and for (2), Q is false but so is P. Does U falsify $P \rightarrowtail Q$? Again, it doesn't.

Now we're ready to decide the truth (and falsity) of $P \rightarrowtail Q$ in U. Since all accessible worlds verify $P \rightarrowtail Q$, it's true in U. Since no accessible world falsifies $P \rightarrowtail Q$, it's not false. Thus $P \rightarrowtail Q$ is true but not false in U.

Example

The truth-value of $P \rightarrowtail Q$ in V.

The worlds accessible from V are U and V. As noted in the previous example, U verifies $P \rightarrowtail Q$ and doesn't falsify it. What about V?

P is true but so is Q so (1) is satisfied in V. Q is false but so is P so (2) is satisfied in V, so V verifies $P \rightarrowtail Q$. But at the same time, P is true and Q is false, so V falsifies $P \rightarrowtail Q$. Cool!

Since both accessible worlds, U and V, verify $P \rightarrowtail Q$, $P \rightarrowtail Q$ is true in V. Since at least one accessible world (V) falsifies $P \rightarrowtail Q$, $P \rightarrowtail Q$ is also false in V.

Example

The truth-value of $Q \rightarrowtail P$ in all worlds

To help us, we make a chart.

	G	**U**	**V**
Q	T	T and F	T and F
P	T and F	F	T and F

Then we check which worlds verify and which worlds falsify $Q \rightarrowtail P$.

	G	**U**	**V**
Q	T	T and F	T and F
P	T and F	F	T and F
$Q \rightarrowtail P$	falsify	falsify	verify falsify

This enables us to decide where $Q \rightarrowtail P$ is true and where it is false.

	G	**U**	**V**
Q	T	T and F	T and F
P	T and F	F	T and F
$Q \rightarrowtail P$	falsify	falsify	verify falsify
$Q \rightarrowtail P$	F	F	F

Example

The truth-value of $(Q \rightarrowtail P) \rightarrowtail Q$ in all worlds

From the previous example we have the truth values of the antecedent and the consequent.

	G	U	V
$Q \rightarrowtail P$	F	F	F
Q	T	T and F	T and F

So we can figure verification and falsification.

	G	U	V
$Q \rightarrowtail P$	F	F	F
Q	T	T and F	T and F
$(Q \rightarrowtail P) \rightarrowtail Q$	verify	verify	verify

(No world falsifies $(Q \rightarrowtail P) \rightarrowtail Q$.) We conclude:

	G	U	V
$Q \rightarrowtail P$	F	F	F
Q	T	T and F	T and F
$(Q \rightarrowtail P) \rightarrowtail Q$	verify	verify	verify
$(Q \rightarrowtail P) \rightarrowtail Q$	T	T	T

Now, a most important example:

Example

Is there Explosion in Paraconsistent Logic?

We promised you that there wouldn't be. Let's see if we can construct a universe in which $(P \wedge \neg P) \rightarrowtail Q$ isn't true in G, the ground world. To make sure that $(P \wedge \neg P) \rightarrowtail Q$ isn't true in G we need at least one world A accessible to G which doesn't verify $(P \wedge \neg P) \rightarrowtail Q$. Note that it's not enough for A to falsify $(P \wedge \neg P) \rightarrowtail Q$. That would make $(P \wedge \neg P) \rightarrowtail Q$ *false* in G but we want more, we want that $(P \wedge \neg P) \rightarrowtail Q$ is *not true* in G, which is harder.

We want **A** to not verify $(P \land \neg P) \rightarrowtail Q$. We can do that if $P \land \neg P$ is true in **A** and Q is not true. The only way $P \land \neg P$ is true is if P is both true and false. So we try:

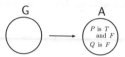

And this works. This makes $(P \land \neg P) \rightarrowtail Q$ false in **G**. Actually, we could have used **G** itself as the accessible world. This universe works too.

If the idea of all these worlds seems odd to you, here's an illustration. Let's say that on Sunday, the ground world, Jay promises B, that he will buy you an ice cream cone every day this week if W, you walk his dog, McLeod. This is his promise:

$$W \rightarrowtail B.$$

Our universe will consist of a world for each day. Every world (day) can access itself and all subsequent days.

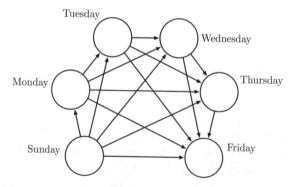

Now, on Sunday, you walk the dog and Jay buys you a chocolate cone. On Monday, you walk, he buys vanilla. On Tuesday, you walk, he buys peppermint chocolate chip. On Wednesday, you don't show up, and he buys you nothing at all. So far, so good. Jay's deeds verify his words. On Thursday Jay is in a terrible mood, and despite the fact that you walk McLeod, he buys you nothing. This is not good! On Friday you walk the dog and he buys you pineapple-pizza-dough ice cream. He says this makes everything okay, but you now doubt his honesty. Here's the data.

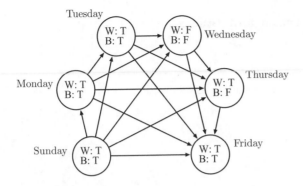

We see that $W \rightarrowtail B$ is verified every day but Thursday, and is falsified only on Thursday. Does that make it true or false? Or both?

You may be tempted to say that it was true until Thursday, and then false. But that would be wrong. Jay made you a promise, and he broke it. So what he said on Sunday was simply false, even though you didn't know it was false until Thursday. Because his conditional was falsified at some accessible world, and was not verified at every accessible world, it is simply false at the world where it was uttered. That's how it is with promises; that's how it is with truth. (Note, however, that if he had made the statement on Friday, given the way we have constructed accessibility, it would have been true.)

Some intriguing facts:

- Even though it appears that paraconsistent logic denies $\neg(A \wedge \neg A)$, the law of non-contradiction, and even though it permits violations of it, that law is nonetheless a paraconsistent tautology (it's always true). So even though paraconsistent logic violates the law, it's committed to it! (Work out the truth table, and you'll see.)

- The disjunctive syllogism $\quad$ $A \vee B$ $\quad$ is not paraconsistently valid (it's valid in Basic

$$\frac{\neg A}{\therefore B}$$

Sentential, though, see exercises, 10.2). Suppose, for instance, that A is both true and false, and that B is false. In that case, both premises would be true, and the conclusion false.

This is why we didn't choose the disjunctive syllogism as our $\vee$ Out rule. It's an inference rule that is valid only in consistent logics. We can use it safely only when we know that the information from which we are reasoning is consistent. Our rules of inference should be perfectly general, applicable in all logics if possible, as is our version of $\vee$ Out.

Exercises   The Logic of Paradox

Odd-numbered
solutions
begin on page 378

The following exercises pertain to this universe:

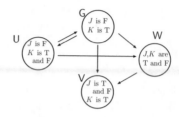

For each of the statements decide whether it is true, false, or both, in each of the worlds.

1. $J \wedge K$
2. $J \vee K$
3. $J \vee \neg K$
4. $\neg J \wedge K$

For the same universe decide whether the statements below are verified, falsified, or both at all four worlds.

5. $J \rightarrowtail K$
6. $K \rightarrowtail J$
7. $K \rightarrowtail (J \vee K)$
8. $(J \vee \neg K) \rightarrowtail (J \wedge K)$

For the same universe decide whether the statements are true, false, or both.

9. $J \rightarrowtail K$
10. $K \rightarrowtail J$
11. $K \rightarrowtail (J \vee K)$
12. $(J \vee \neg K) \rightarrowtail (J \wedge K)$
13. $J \rightarrowtail (J \rightarrowtail K)$
14. $(J \rightarrowtail K) \rightarrowtail (K \rightarrowtail J)$
15. The example in the text (Jay and ice cream cones) shows that a wff can be simultaneously false and verified in a world. Can a statement be simultaneously true and falsified?
16. If we think of just true as 1, both true and false as $\frac{1}{2}$, and just false as 0, then paraconsistent logic resembles three-valued logic. Do the conjunctions of

paraconsistent logic and three-valued logic agree or disagree?

17. Following up on the previous question, do the disjunctions of paraconsistent logic and three-valued logic agree or disagree?

18. Following up on the previous question, do the negations of paraconsistent logic and three-valued logic agree or disagree?

Our *Digestor's Digest* puzzles are inspired by a class of logic puzzles in which there are people who always tell the truth and people who always lie. A particularly old example of this is the following:

We are on the road to the castle and we come to a fork. At this fork are two men, one a truth-teller and the other a liar but we don't know which is which. Can we find out which fork to take by asking only one question?

There are many answers to this. We like asking one of the two, "If we asked your friend here if the left fork is best route to the castle, would he say yes?" Whatever he says, you do the opposite, since you know the answer will be incorrect.

Single-handedly, logician Raymond Smullyan has raised this sort of puzzle to an art form. In his puzzles, the truth-tellers are "knights" and the liars are "knaves". Here is one of his puzzles from his first puzzle book, *What is the Name of This Book?*

We again have three inhabitants, A, B, and C, each of whom is a knight or a knave. Two people are said to be of the same type if they are both knights or both knaves. A and B make the following statements:

A: B is a knave.

B: A and C are of the same type.

What is C?

19. Here is a *Digestor's Digest* version of that puzzle. The last piece says it's an "editorial," but of course it could be either an ad or an article. Solve the puzzle.

The Digestor's Digest

Vol. II. No. 1

Breakfast Bulletin

Buy Fiberobjects, the new cereal! Each serving contains as much fiber as 8 inches of manila hemp!

Breakfast Bulletin

Buy Cream Brullies, the new cereal! Guaranteed fiber-free! And pay no attention to the ad below.

Editorial

We apologize for the confusion between ads and articles in previous editions. To make things simpler, we have included only one type in the pieces above.

---

20. Here is a new knights and knaves puzzle. Solve it and translate it into *Digestor's Digest* format.

You meet two women on the Island of Knights and Knaves. You don't know anything about them. You're about to say something when one says in the native dialect, "Obschligg omom nababooie!" The other looks apologetic and says "She's says she's a knave. She isn't, really."

What was the first woman, knight or knave? What was the second woman?

Chapter Twelve

12.1 Deduction with Identity

All animals are equal but some animals are more equal than others. (George Orwell, *Animal Farm*)

We're almost finished with deduction. Remember that in our predicate languages we have one special logical predicate, $=$. This is a funny predicate. It says that the thing named on the left hand side is identical to the thing named on the right.

Of course everything is identical to itself and only itself. So it is a funny relation indeed. When we say that $a = b$, or that Jennifer Lopez is identical to JLo, we are not saying, as it might appear, that two things are identical, but that two names name the same thing.

Note that $=$ is really a 2-place predicate so that we ought to be writing

$$= ab$$

instead of

$$a = b.$$

We choose the latter because it's more readable. Also, when we want to say that a and b are not identical, we write

$$a \neq b$$

instead of

$$\neg(a = b) \text{ or } \neg = ab.$$

Finally, we use parentheses with identity when we think it makes things more readable, writing, for example,

$$\forall x(x = a)$$

Sweet Reason: A Field Guide To Modern Logic, Second Edition. Jim Henle, Jay L. Garfield, Thomas Tymoczko and Emily Altreuter.
© 2012 John Wiley & Sons Inc. Published 2012 by John Wiley & Sons Inc.

instead of

$$\forall x \; x = a,$$

although $\forall x \; x = a$ is entirely unambiguous.

The funniness (above) of $=$ is reflected in the deduction rules. Here they are:

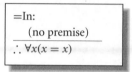

=In:

    (no premise)

$\therefore \forall x(x = x)$

Example

$\underline{a \text{ exists}}$
$\therefore a = a$

1. a exists   premise
2. $\forall x(x = x)$ $=$ In
3. $a = a$ $\forall$Out $1, 2$

The $=$In rule just says that at any time in a deduction we are entitled to remind ourselves that all entities are self-identical, and we can do this without citing any premises, just using the justification $=$ In.

=Out: $\mathcal{H}c$

        $\underline{c = \mathcal{D}}$

     $\therefore \mathcal{H}\mathcal{D}$

—where $\mathcal{D}$ and c are any constants and by "$\mathcal{H}\mathcal{D}$" we mean $\mathcal{H}c$ with any or all occurences of c replaced by $\mathcal{D}$.

This says that if two names name the identical object, anything we can say using the first name we can say using the second. If Jennifer Lopez is performing tonight, JLo is performing tonight.

Example

a exists
b exists
Pa
$\underline{\neg Pb}$
$\therefore a \neq b$

1.	*a* exists	premise	
2.	*b* exists	premise	
3.	*Pa*	premise	
4.	¬*Pb*	premise	
5.	$(a = b) \Rightarrow (Pb \land \neg Pb)$	●	
6.	$a \neq b$	¬In 5	

5.1.	$a = b$	assumption
5.2.	*Pb*	= Out 3, 5.1
5.3.	$Pb \land \neg Pb$	∧In 4, 5.2

Alas, there is a wrinkle. While in general, whenever two referring expressions (whether names or descriptions) refer to the same individual, anything we can say using the first we can say with the second, there are exceptions. Some expressions create what logicians call **opaque** contexts, in which we cannot substitute coreferring terms and preserve meaning or truth value. There are two classes of such contexts, those involving **intentional** predicates, such as "believes," "knows," "wants," etc., that are broadly psychological in character, and those involving modal operators such as "necessarily," "possibly," etc. Let us consider each in turn.

Opacity is central to tragedy. In the ancient Greek tale, it is prophesized at his birth that Oedipus will marry his mother. Oedipus is sent away by his parents. He grows up in a faraway place. He knows the prophecy and very much doesn't want to marry his mother. "Want to marry" is a psychological predicate. We'll write *Mxy* for "*x* wants to marry *y*". With *m* for Oedipus's mother and *o* for Oedipus, we have ¬*Mom*.

As a young man, Oedipus returns to the city of his birth. There he meets and wants to marry Jocasta. That's *Moj*. Unfortunately, Jocasta turns out to be his mother. That's $j = m$. With these facts we can prove that Oedipus really does want to marry his mother:

1.	*o* exists	premise
2.	*j* exists	premise
3.	*m* exists	premise
4.	*Moj*	premise
5.	$j = m$	premise
6.	*Mom*	=Out 5

And here you see the difficulty of using =Out with a psychological predicate. Don't worry, though. This is a trap we won't set for you. This and the next issue are issues of formalization. We aren't setting any limits on = Out.

Now consider a case involving modality. The number 9 is necessarily odd. The number 9 was also the number of the planets, until Pluto was demoted in 2006. Until then, "9" and "the number of the planets" referred to the same thing, viz., the number 9. It did not, however, follow that the number of planets is necessarily odd. Indeed, it is now considered even. The presence of necessity in this case blocks the substitution of identical terms, and so blocks the use of the identity rules.

The importance of opaque contexts and the fact that psychological expressions and modal operators create them were first explored in depth by the great German logician Gottlob Frege, to whom we owe much of the formulation of basic predicate logic. There are other odd examples of opaque contexts, and the study of why such constructions induce opacity and of how to construct logics that capture appropriate rules of inference for such contexts is a rapidly developing enterprise. For now, however, set these examples aside and consider only ordinary predicates that do not induce opacity. Our logic will work just fine for this part of the language. If you go on in logic, you'll have plenty of time to think about the harder cases.

Exercises   Deduction with Identity

Odd-numbered solutions begin on page 379

Fill in the blanks to make correct deductions:

1.

> *a* exists
> *b* exists
> $a = b$
> ∴ $b = a$

1. $a = b$ _____
2. $\forall x(x = x)$ _____
3. $a = a$ _____
4. $b = a$ _____

2.

> *a* exists
> *b* exists
> *c* exists
> $a = b$
> $b = c$
> ∴ $a = c$

1. $a = b$ _____
2. $b = c$ _____
3. $a = c$ _____

Here are some arguments for you to justify:

3.

> *a* exists
> *b* exists
> $\forall x(Px \lor x = a)$
> $\neg Pb$
> ∴ $b = a$

4.

> (no premise)
> ∴ $\forall x \exists y(x = y)$

5.

> $\exists x Px$
> ∴ $\exists x \exists y(x = y)$

6.

> *a* exists
> *b* exists
> $a = b$
> $Pa \Rightarrow Q$
> $Pb \Rightarrow \neg Q$
> ∴ $\neg Pa$

7.

> $\exists y \forall x(x = y)$
> ∴ $\forall y \forall x(x = y)$

8.

> *a* exists
> *b* exists
> $a = b$
> $\neg Pa \Rightarrow Pb$
> ∴ Pb

In the exercises for Section 8.1 we introduced a new quantifier, $Ɀ$ (p. 195). $Ɀ x Px$ meant that there are at least two individuals with property P.

9. Invent a $Ɀ$ Out deduction rule. Your rule should be a valid argument with $Ɀ v \mathcal{H} v$ as one of the premises.

10. Invent a $Ɀ$ In deduction rule. Your rule should be a valid argument with $Ɀ v \mathcal{H} v$ as the conclusion.

11‼ Use your deduction rules (and our other rules) to construct a deduction for:

> $\neg\, Ɀ xx = x$
> ∴ $\neg\, Ɀ x Px$

12. The ∀ quantifier has a partner, ∃. They're partners in the sense that ∀x¬ means the same as ¬∃x and ∃x¬ means the same as ¬∀x. Does 𝒵 have a partner? Can you define a quantifier, let's say 𝒮, such that 𝒵x¬ means the same as ¬𝒮x and 𝒮x¬ means the same as ¬𝒵x? If you can, what would 𝒮xPx mean?

In Chapter Six we asked you to translate some family relationships into Predicate.

Now that you've learned about identity, here are a few more relationships to translate.

Fx	x is female.
Gx	x is male.
Mxy	x is married to y.
Rxyz	x and y begat z.

13! a is an uncle of b

14! a is a niece of b

Consider:

If this sentence is true
then Elvis Presley is the President of the United States.

Let's call this sentence C. Notice that C really says

If C then Elvis Presley is the President of the United States.

Sounds sort of stupid. But we can prove that C is actually true! Here's how: C is a conditional. If a conditional is false, then the antecedent must be true and the consequent false. But the antecedent is C. So if C is false then C is true! So C can't be false. It must be true.

Now consider the argument:

$$C$$
$$C \Rightarrow \text{Elvis Presley is President of the United States.}$$
$$\therefore \text{Elvis Presley is President of the United States.}$$

This is a valid argument (it's *modus ponens*, it's ⇒ Out). The first premise, C, is true, we just proved that. The second premise is the same as C, so it's also true. So this is a sound argument. So the conclusion is true. Elvis Presley is the President of the United States.

Clearly something has gone wrong, but what? It's surprisingly hard to say. This paradox is known as Curry's paradox, after its discoverer, the great logician Haskell Curry.

12.2   Deduction, FMTYEWTK

Logical consequences are the scarecrows of fools and the beacons of wise men. (T.H. Huxley)

You've done a great deal of work in your deductions. Maybe too much work. You probably feel, sometimes, that you're doing the same thing over and over. How many times, for example, have you needed to go from $P \Rightarrow Q$ to $\neg Q \Rightarrow \neg P$? How often have you used $P \Rightarrow P$?

When writing text messages, it's handy to have shorthand for phrases you use over and over, like "LOL" for "laughing out loud" and "FMTYEWTK" for "far more than you ever want to know". In this section we're offering you something similar. Instead of proving stuff over and over, each time you need it, we're going to let you use some special rules as long as you've proved them once. Here's the first batch:

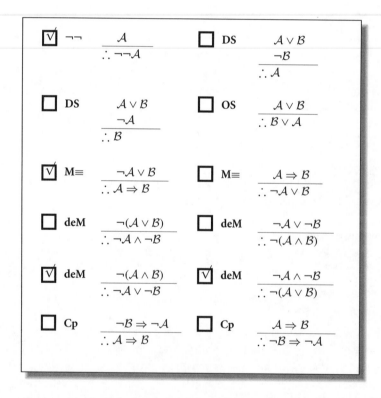

The boxes are for you to check off. When you've proved a rule or seen the proof of a rule, check the box; then you're free to use it in proofs. A few rules are proved in the book, so we checked them off in gray. When you've found and read the proofs, you can check them off in black and use them.

Here's another batch:

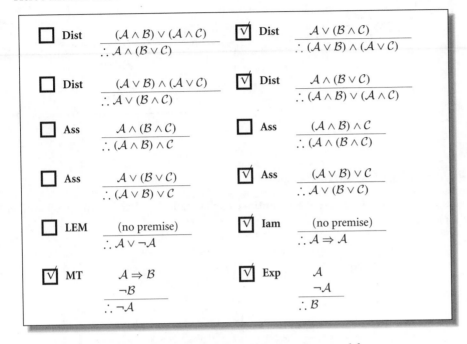

The names given above are abbreviations. Here's what they stand for:

¬¬	Double Negation
Assoc	Association
Cp	Contraposition
deM	de Morgan's law
Dist	Distribution
DS	Disjunctive Syllogism
Exp	Explosion
Iam	It's all about me
LEM	The Law of the Excluded Middle
M≡	Material Equivalence
MT	Modus Tollens
OS	Or Switch

Use these rules, just as you do the In and Out rules – state the abbreviation of the rule followed by the line numbers of the statements needed to apply the rule. Here's an example that uses several new rules.

Example

$$\neg(P \lor (Q \land R))$$
$$\underline{Q \qquad\qquad\qquad}$$
$$\therefore \neg R$$

1. $\neg(P \lor (Q \land R))$ premise
2. Q premise
3. $\neg P \land \neg(Q \land R)$ deM, 1
4. $\neg(Q \land R)$ $\land$Out 3
5. $\neg Q \lor \neg R$ deM, 4
6. $\neg Q \Rightarrow \neg R$ •————
7. $\neg R \Rightarrow \neg R$ Iam
8. $\neg R$ $\lor$Out 5, 6, 7

6.1. $\neg Q$ assumption
6.2. $Q \land \neg Q$ $\land$In 2, 6.1
6.3. $\neg R$ Exp 6.2

Predicate and identity rules

Most useful in Predicate are the **Quantifier Exchange Rules**. For identity, we have two simple rules.

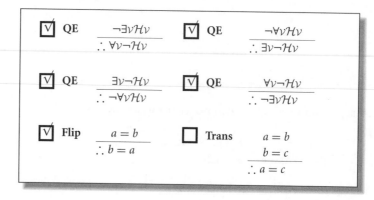

☑ QE	$\dfrac{\neg\exists\nu\mathcal{H}\nu}{\therefore \forall\nu\neg\mathcal{H}\nu}$	☑ QE	$\dfrac{\neg\forall\nu\mathcal{H}\nu}{\therefore \exists\nu\neg\mathcal{H}\nu}$
☑ QE	$\dfrac{\exists\nu\neg\mathcal{H}\nu}{\therefore \neg\forall\nu\mathcal{H}\nu}$	☑ QE	$\dfrac{\forall\nu\neg\mathcal{H}\nu}{\therefore \neg\exists\nu\mathcal{H}\nu}$
☑ Flip	$\dfrac{a = b}{\therefore b = a}$	☐ Trans	$\dfrac{\begin{array}{c}a = b \\ b = c\end{array}}{\therefore a = c}$

All but one are checked in gray. If you've seen them proved you can use them.

Exercises   Deduction, FMTYEWTK

Odd-numbered solutions begin on page 380

Construct deductions for the following arguments. The numbers indicate the difficulty from ① (easy) to ⑤ (hard) to ⑩ (yikes!).

① 1.
$$\dfrac{W}{\therefore \neg\neg\neg\neg W}$$

① 2.
$$\dfrac{A \land (B \lor C)}{\therefore A \land (C \lor B)}$$

② 3.
$$\dfrac{A \Rightarrow B}{\therefore B \lor \neg A}$$

② 4.
$$\dfrac{\begin{array}{c}A \Rightarrow C \\ \neg A \Rightarrow C\end{array}}{\therefore C}$$

③ 5.
$$\dfrac{\neg(C \land D)}{\therefore D \Rightarrow \neg C}$$

(3) 6.

$$\frac{(G \lor H) \land (H \lor I)}{\therefore H \lor (G \land I)}$$

(4) 7.

$$\frac{\neg \forall x \neg Px}{\therefore \exists x Px}$$

(4) 8.

$$\frac{\exists x Px}{\therefore \neg \forall x \neg Px}$$

(5) 9.

$$\frac{\begin{array}{c} P \lor Q \\ \neg P \end{array}}{\therefore Q}$$

(5) 10.

$$\frac{\neg \exists x \forall y Pxy}{\therefore \forall x \exists y \neg Pxy}$$

(6) 11.

$$\frac{A \Rightarrow B}{\therefore (A \Rightarrow C) \lor (C \Rightarrow B)}$$

(7) 12.

$$\frac{\begin{array}{c} a \text{ exists} \\ \exists y Py \Rightarrow Pa \end{array}}{\therefore \forall x (Px \Rightarrow Pa)}$$

(8) 13.

$$\frac{\forall x Px \Rightarrow \exists x \neg Qx}{\therefore \forall x Qx \Rightarrow \exists x \neg Px}$$

(9) 14.

$$\frac{\forall x \exists y \forall z \exists w \neg Pxyzw}{\therefore \neg \exists x \forall y \exists z \forall w Pxyzw}$$

(10) 15.

$$\frac{\forall x \forall y (Pxy \Leftrightarrow \neg Pyx)}{\therefore \forall z Qz}$$

Let's say that a person is a *real sweetie* if and only if all the children of that person are real sweeties. Let Rx mean "x is a real sweetie," and let Pxy mean "x is a parent of y." Let g represent George, who is 7 years old and (obviously) has no children.

16. Formalize "g has no children."

17. Formalize in predicate language the definition of a real sweetie.

18! Find a valid deduction from "g has no children" and the definition of real sweetie to "George is a real sweetie."

19! What can you say about someone with no grandchildren?

Suppose we believe that

$$\forall x (Rx \Rightarrow Bx)$$

is true. To gather evidence for the statement, we might look for objects which have property R and then check to see if they also have property B. The classic example of this is the statement,

"All ravens are black."

To gather evidence for this, we look for ravens and when we find one, we check to see if it's black. That seems perfectly reasonable, doesn't it?

But the wff

$$P \Rightarrow Q$$

(Continued on next page)

has the same truth table as

$$\neg Q \Rightarrow \neg P,$$

so $\forall x(Rx \Rightarrow Bx)$ is equivalent to $\forall x(\neg Bx \Rightarrow \neg Rx)$. Reasonably, any evidence for one statement is evidence for the other, since they always have the same truth value. That means we can find evidence for $\forall x(Rx \Rightarrow Bx)$ by checking non-black things to see if they're non-ravens.

Thus, if I'm eating dinner and I notice that the tomato in my salad is not a raven, I'm helping to prove that all ravens are black!

This intriguing paradox is due to Carl Hempel, philosopher of science.

12.3   Parliamentary Debating

I can win an argument on any topic, against any opponent. People know this, and steer clear of me at parties. Often, as a sign of their great respect, they don't even invite me. (Dave Barry)

The debating format set up in "Presidential Debating" may seem to you artificial. You may be more familiar with a different style of debating that used to be popular on college campuses and even now is widely practiced in high schools. In those debates, real issues are discussed by debaters who have studied them very thoroughly. From our point of view, such debates are less interesting because truth is at least as important as logic.

In recent years, yet another form of debate has started to catch on, called "off-topic" debating or "parliamentary-style" debating. It's modeled after debates in the British parliament. The debates are lively, almost raucous. Logic is all-important. Currently there are competitive teams at hundreds of colleges and universities.

The rules are somewhat elaborate. We present here a simplified version more appropriate for classroom (and party) use.

Activity: Parliamentary Debating

There are two teams, the government and the opposition. The government team consists of the prime minister and a member of the government. The opposition team consists of the leader of the opposition and a member of the opposition. A judge is also needed.

At the start, a resolution is given to the government team by the judge. It can be serious ("We should close all nuclear power plants" or "College education should be free for all citizens") or frivolous ("Philosophy majors are smarter than math majors" or "My avatar can whip your avatar").

The topic should be debatable without requiring special knowledge. The government team argues in favor of the resolution, while the opposition opposes it. All speeches are limited to two minutes (this is drastically shorter than in real collegiate debates). The teams are allowed a few minutes before the debate to plot strategy, then the debate proceeds in this order:

1. The prime minister speaks.
2. The leader of the opposition speaks.
3. The member of the government speaks.
4. The member of the opposition speaks.
5. The leader of the opposition speaks.
6. The prime minister speaks.

In all the speeches, the speaker may attack previous arguments. In all but the last speech, new arguments may be introduced (no new arguments are permitted in the prime minister's last speech because there is no opportunity for the opposition to rebut them).

The opposition may introduce a counterproposal. If, for example, the government is arguing that the national deficit should be reduced by holding bake sales, the opposition can argue for garage sales instead.

The audience is expected to choose the winner. Members of the audience should take notes on the points made in each speech. They should rate the arguments and counterarguments.

Speakers should always be referred to by title, such as the "honorable member," the "honorable leader," and so on.

Additional rules

You may consider each of these rules as optional. Together they bring the debate closer to the version now played at intercollegiate tournaments.

1. The debate topic given is vague rather than specific, such as "No man is an island," "Marriages are made in heaven," or "You don't mess with the Zohan." It is then the government's task to form the proposition, based loosely on the topic, and to define its terms. For example, from "Marriages are made in heaven," it could choose the proposition "Jennifer and Marc Anthony are happily married," or "Congress should pass laws outlawing divorce," or even "Reese's Peanut Butter Cups are the greatest candy bar." (For the last one, the government would explain, "Reese's Peanut Butter Cups are a marriage of peanut butter and chocolate. It is thus heavenly.")

The government is responsible for defining its terms. For example, if the proposition is "Congress should pass laws outlawing divorce," it should explain what is meant by divorce. If they don't define the term, then the opposition is free to say, "It seems to us that 'divorce' can mean the dissolution of any long-standing association or alliance. The dissolution, for example, of East Germany from the Warsaw Pact amounts to a divorce. Not only was that divorce beneficial ultimately for the peace of Europe, but it is also something that no law passed by Congress can affect." You can see the government would be in trouble!

Finally, the proposition must be "debatable," that is, something that the opposition has a chance of arguing against. The government can't oppose divorce and define divorce as the involuntary dismemberment of human beings. That would not be fair play.

2. Allow longer speeches. In real debates, the first four are 8 minutes long and the last two are 4 minutes.

3. Allow heckling. Heckling is when the speaker is interrupted by shouts from the opposing side. The rules are generally that such interruptions must be brief and clever. To roar "Nonsense!" is not clever. To interject even two sentences is not brief. The idea is to add fun to the debate. Don't adopt this rule if it makes participants nervous or hostile.

4. Allow "points of order." If a member of the nonspeaking team believes a rule has been violated, he or she may rise and say "Point of order" and then explain the breach. The judge will then rule on it.

5. Allow "points of privilege." A point of privilege is called if a member feels her or his remarks have been misrepresented or her or his character has been assaulted. Again the judge should rule.

As with presidential debating, the object is good, logical fun!

> Is the following sentence true or false?
> "Is, if immediately preceded by its own quotation, false" is, if immediately preceded by its own quotation, false.

12.4   Cathy, A Decade On

The only completely consistent people are the dead. (Aldous Huxley)

We all have pasts, and we all have regrets. At least most of us do. And we all, especially college students, have hopes for the future. With these thoughts in mind, we sent Emily to find out what became of Cathy, a decade or so after she graduated from Sophist College as a logic major. We wondered, what did the study of logic do for her? And does she have any regrets? After all, she left a well-documented trail of destruction and despair behind her.

Emily found her in a luxury suite in Las Vegas. Here's a transcript of part of the interview.

EMILY: So, Cathy, what are you doing now?
CATHY: I'm a freelance political writer.
EMILY: For whom do you write?
CATHY: Anyone who can pay my fee.
EMILY: And what do you write for them?

CATHY: Well, arguments for any position they want to defend. Attack stuff, too.

EMILY: What kinds of position?

CATHY: Whatever they want. Today I wrote an ad criticizing gun control. Yesterday I defended prohibiting the sale and possession of handguns. Last week I defended the legalization of pot; next week I'll be recommending stiff penalties for possession. The money on both sides is the same color.

EMILY: Wow. Aren't your clients upset that you don't have principles?

CATHY: Politicians care about principles? What planet are you from? Pols only care about one thing. I can write arguments. And I can trash arguments.

EMILY: So what do you do when starting a job?

CATHY: Well, first, you have to know when you've got a good argument, and when you've got a bad one. Really. When it's good, you make the case clear. Every premise, *clear*. Every inference, *clear*. Use clear, relevant examples. Then imagine a rebuttal from the other side. Refute the sucker and throw that in.

But sometimes you don't have much to work with. You diagram the argument. Figure out what's weak and hide it. Suppress the false premise. And if you have to, suppress the conclusion.

EMILY: Can you give me some examples?

CATHY: Well here's a gig I had last month. A congressman from Pennsylvania hired me to argue that coal is the cleanest fuel around. Now, that's false. But a job's a job. So, what did I do?

I definitely wasn't going to have him come out and say coal is cleaner than hydro. But you know how people are leery about nuclear plants? And suspicious of foreigners? Well that's where I started. Went something like this.

> In our quest for clean energy, we have three choices:
>
> (1)   we can have imported oil from countries that hate us and send terrorists to our shores,
> (2)   we can have radioactive waste from the industry that brought us the Three Mile Island meltdown,
> (3)   or we can have coal mined by the honest Americans who've kept us warm and dry for generations.
>   It's your decision.
>
> Your parents, you know, they got their energy from coal. Your grandparents too. And your great-grandparents. Are you with them? Or are you with the Mullahs and the nuclear fat cats?

EMILY: Gosh. My grandparents or Osama bin Laden. What a choice!

CATHY: Then a week after the coal job, a senator asked me for a speech on the other side. He wanted to talk about how strip mining is bad for the water supply. Well that was easy. There's tons of evidence. It was a knock-down. Just compared the water quality where there's strip mining and where there isn't; showed that the chemicals that ruin the water in mining areas comes from the mines. Told 'em how mine owners with money at stake would argue that the chemicals come from natural ground water; hauled out evidence that they don't. Slam dunk. Even in this line of work, there's a place for a clear, sound argument. Sometimes. Good to know how to write one when you need it.

EMILY: Cool! You do good arguments and you do bad arguments!

CATHY: The bad arguments need special attention. You have to leave stuff out, hint at lines of inference but don't actually explain them. Make bad premises look good. Make affirming the consequent sound like *modus ponens*.[1]

EMILY: Wait! How do you do that?

CATHY: C'mon, that's easy. To most people they sound the same. Try this:

> Lazy people, guys with no ambition, folks who can't lift a finger to help themselves, they end up with dead-end jobs, or no jobs at all. They're living in homeless shelters. So when I hear about spending tax dollars to feed the homeless, I say 'Why should people who work hard all their lives help the people who won't lift a finger?'

EMILY: Slick.

CATHY: People who want to believe something don't look hard at the logic. Even people who don't believe you at first can be convinced by an argument that looks good. Hey, you like this hotel?

EMILY: Oh yeah. Nice. (PAUSE) And what are you working on now?

CATHY: Well, I've got two projects. Save Our Christian Nation has me writing a speech for Senator P___ , and the ACLU hired me to write one for Governor H___ . Both on prayer in the schools. The kicker is, the two jerks are running against each other. I make money going both ways.

EMILY: Wow. What would they say if they knew you were playing both sides!

CATHY: Oh hell, they know. And they know I can deliver the goods.

EMILY: Could you read me some of the stuff you wrote for them?

CATHY: Well … Hey, promise you won't tell Jim and Jay about this? I'd hate for this to end up in *Sweet Reason*.

EMILY: Would I *dare* do that?

CATHY: Yeah, OK. Well here's some stuff:

> Whom do you most admire? Martin Luther King? Ronald Reagan? The Dalai Lama? Mother Theresa? John Glenn? They all have something in common. They all prayed every day. Do you want your kids to grow up to be like these heroes? And isn't it the job of our schools to bring out the best, the most heroic in our kids? You bet it is. And wouldn't you rather have your kids praying than doing drugs? Mother Theresa didn't do drugs. The Dalai Lama doesn't do drugs.

> Now, Governor H___ might argue that prayer just leads to insincerity, apathy and weakness. But what kind of argument is that? Are any of these people insincere, apathetic or weak? They are *not*. So don't give in to an argument like that. Demand that your schools bring out the best in your kids.

> And what does it say on the dollar bill? *The United States dollar bill.* It says, "In God We Trust". If kids don't trust in God, they aren't American. Hold your schools accountable for raising your kids as Americans. Insist on daily prayer.

---

[1]   Affirming the consequent: $P \Rightarrow Q$ (invalid). *Modus ponens*: $P \Rightarrow Q$ (valid).
$$\frac{P \Rightarrow Q,\ Q}{\therefore P} \qquad \frac{P \Rightarrow Q,\ P}{\therefore Q}$$

And now catch this one:

> Senator P___ says that there should be prayer in the public schools. Nothing, my friends, could be more troublesome, more destructive or more un-American. Troublesome because any prayer that's chosen will offend some citizens. You can't have children exposed to views that will offend them.

> I said 'destructive.' Prayer in the schools, since it's unconstitutional, will be challenged in endless lawsuits by civil libertarians. We can't afford the cost that will entail. We'll wind up spending millions to defend the indefensible.

> And I said 'un-American'. The separation of church and state is enshrined in the first amendment to the constitution. Heroic American boys died in wars from Lexington and Concord to Kandahar to protect its guarantee of freedom of religion. Don't in God's name let this man, Senator P___, dishonor their memory!

EMILY: Cathy, those are really terrible. There isn't a sound argument in either speech! Nobody is going to pay you for that!

CATHY: That's where you're wrong. The cash is in the bank. I can live two months in this suite on what I got. And sure, you can see how lame they are. You do logic. But majority rules. And the majority hasn't a clue what a good argument looks like. My stuff is aimed at the majority. They swallow it. And they rule; that's democracy. As long as people don't know logic, there's plenty of work for those of us who do.

EMILY: Do you ever feel bad about being a hired gun, Cathy?

CATHY: (laughs) You mean, do I feel bad about being successful? No way! Look, anybody can learn logic. All those people who didn't—they made a choice. And I'm the beneficiary. That's where I make my percentage. This isn't a moral issue.

EMILY: Logic is a choice?

There was a pause here. Cathy looked oddly thoughtful.

CATHY: Sometimes, you know, I have to argue for crazy stuff. I mean really crazy stuff. There was one guy who, I swear, wanted to lynch the prisoners in Guantanamo. I don't mean he wanted to lead a mob, but he certainly didn't want them to have anything like a fair trial. And I had to write the speech for this guy. Of course I couldn't have him say what he was thinking.

EMILY: What did you do?

CATHY: I had some fun. I went in the back door. I wrote an argument attacking the government lawyers assigned to defend the terrorists. I suggested that they weren't patriotic. I demanded that the government reveal the names of everyone who worked on the cases. I attacked the administration for covering up. That was it. No way those guys would get a fair trial.

EMILY: Gosh.

EMILY: Uh, Cathy, there is one more question I want to ask.

CATHY: Fire away.

EMILY: When you were at Sophist, you, er, well, how do I put this? You kind of offended a few people. Do you ever regret that?

CATHY: I offended people? Well, maybe a couple. Hey, life's too short for regret! If I humiliated a little snot here or there, she deserved it. If you can't win arguments, you lose arguments. You know, I was just practicing. Hey, look at me now!

EMILY: Any advice for current logic students?

CATHY: Yeah. Learn to argue. Learn to rebut. Practice clarity. Practice ambiguity. And remember: You've got a choice. You can make things happen. Or you can be my patsy. The difference is logic.

What is the meaning of the thought experiments with devil?

When the devil picks a whole number, we have a strategy for escape. What that means is that we can match every whole number with a different day.

$$
\begin{array}{ccccccccc}
\text{day:} & 1 & 2 & 3 & 4 & 5 & 6 & \dots \\
\text{guess:} & 0 & 1 & -1 & 2 & -2 & 3 & \dots
\end{array}
$$

So there are just as many days as there are whole numbers. We can do that with fractions too. There are just as many days as there are fractions.

But we can't match up all the decimals with the days. There are *more* decimals than days. The natural numbers, the whole numbers, the fractions, the decimals, they're are all infinite sets. Cantor's discovery was that the natural numbers, the whole numbers, and the fractions are all equally large infinite sets, but the decimals are strictly larger.

$$
\begin{matrix}
\text{natural numbers} \\
\text{whole numbers} \\
\text{fractional numbers}
\end{matrix}
\quad < \quad \text{decimal numbers}
$$

Could there be a set in-between?

$$
\begin{matrix}
\text{natural numbers} \\
\text{whole numbers} \\
\text{fractional numbers}
\end{matrix}
\quad < \quad ? \quad < \quad \text{decimal numbers}
$$

The answer is coming soon.

12.5 Incomplete Logic

True knowledge exists in knowing that you know nothing. (Socrates)

Logic is special. Unlike any other area of human knowledge there is certainty. (There's certainty in mathematics too, but we're counting mathematics as a part of logic.) In logic, we have proof, proof that is clear and uncontrovertible. To some, that certainty is thrilling. When you have the answer, you *know* it's the answer. To others, certainty is threatening. There is a certain answer – why can't I find it? Love it or fear it, the certainty of logic has been celebrated for millennia by philosophers and poets.

That's why the discovery in 1931, that there was *uncertainty* in logic, so shook the world. Let us explain.

Take arithmetic. We can discuss addition, multiplication and all the operations of arithmetic in a predicate language. We can state all the laws of arithmetic in that language. We can prove the theorems of arithmetic in our deduction system. Now suppose someone asks us a question. They have a statement about arithmetic, A, and they want to know: Is A true or false?

Perhaps we believe A is true. Then we try to prove it using the laws of arithmetic. And if we believe that A is false, we try to prove $\neg A$. But what if we didn't succeed either in proving A or in proving $\neg A$? Well, either A is true or it's false. It seems reasonable that someday we or someone else should be able to prove A or prove $\neg A$.

But in 1931 a young Austrian mathematician, Kurt Gödel found a special statement, let's call it G, which can't be proved and which can't be disproved. This was part of his famous "Incompleteness Theorem" in which he showed that logic is incomplete in an essential way.

Even more amazing, Gödel showed that his statement G, even though it can't be proved, was true! This was because G is really a coded message, coded in the predicate language of arithmetic. Taken apart, G actually says,

This statement cannot be proved.

Since it can't be proved, it's true! Does that remind you of anything? This is a "proof" version of the Liar's paradox. Once again, we see reflectivity in logic. It isn't a tease now. It's serious mathematics and serious philosophy.

We said that logic is incomplete in an essential way. What we mean is this. Not only is arithmetic incomplete, but any reasonable extension of arithmetic is still incomplete. There will always be statements we can't prove or disprove. There will always be statements whose truth values we (and everyone else) will be unable to know.

* * * * * * * * * * * *

We'll give you a very specific example of unknowability. We've seen in this chapter that the infinity of decimals is greater than the infinity of natural numbers. Is there an infinity which is between the two? Is there an infinite set that is bigger than the natural numbers but smaller than the decimals?

Cantor thought the answer was no. His Continuum Hypothesis (CH) was that no set larger than the set of natural numbers could be smaller than the set of decimals. Cantor couldn't prove CH. At the beginning of the twentieth century, the question of CH was considered one of the most important outstanding mathematical questions.

In 1936, Kurt Gödel made a second great contribution to logic. Gödel proved that no one will ever prove that CH is false. *He didn't prove that CH was true.* Only that it can't be proved false.

In 1963, Paul Cohen proved that no one will ever prove that CH is true. In essence, the answer to the question of the Continuum Hypothesis is that no certain answer is possible.

This is an example of what Socrates might call "true knowledge". We know (through the work of Gödel and Cohen) that we do not know if CH is true.

* * * * * * * * * * * * *

One last example (in verse!) of our limitations. We've been talking throughout this book about reflectivity. Sometimes it is useful. Reflectivity enables us to define wffs in Sentential and Predicate. Reflectivity helps us structure our arguments. Reflectivity helps us write computer procedures.

But sometimes reflectivity leads to trouble. Reflectivity is at the core of the Liar's paradox and countless other paradoxes. And reflectivity, if not carefully used, can create computer procedures that get stuck in infinite loops.

In Chapter Five we discussed reflectivity in procedures and gave an example where it works and an example where it doesn't. When we use reflectivity, how do we know whether it will get us into trouble or not? In particular, could there be a computer procedure that can read computer procedures and tell us whether or not there's an infinite loop?

This question is called "The Halting Problem": Is there a computer procedure which can tell if a computer procedure eventually halts (instead of looping forever)?

The answer (we're sure you guessed it!) is no. Linguistics professor Geoffrey Pullam has written the proof of this fact into a poem that reminds us a lot of Dr Seuss. We've made a few edits.

Scooping the Loop Snooper

No program can say what another will do.
Now, I won't just assert that, I'll prove it to you:
I'll prove that although you might work till you drop,
you cannot decide if a program will stop.
Imagine we have a procedure called *P*
that will snoop in the source code of programs to see
there aren't infinite loops that go round and around;
and prints the word "Fine!" if no looping is found.
You feed in your code, and the input it needs,
Then *P* takes them both and it studies and reads
and computes whether things will all end as they should
(as opposed to looping the way that they could).
Well, the truth is that *P* cannot possibly be,
because if you wrote it and gave it to me,
I could use it to set up a logical bind
that would shatter your reason and scramble your mind.
Here's the trick I would use – and it's simple to do.
I'd define a procedure – we'll name the thing *Q* –
that would take any program and call *P* (of course!)
to tell if it looped, by reading the source;
If so, *Q* would simply print "Loop!" and then stop;
but if no, *Q* would cycle back up to the top,
and start again, looping, endlessly back,
till the universe dies and is frozen and black.
And this program called *Q* wouldn't stay on the shelf;
I'd run it, and (fiendishly) feed it *itself*!
What behavior results when I do this with *Q*?
When it reads its own source code, just what will it do?
If *P* warns of loops, *Q* will print "Loop!" and quit;
yet *P* is supposed to speak truly of it.
So if *Q*'s going to quit, then *P* should say, "Fine!" –
which makes *Q* go back to its very first line!
No matter what *P* would have done, *Q* will scoop it:
Q takes *P*'s output to make *P* look stupid.
If *P* gets things right then it lies in its tooth;
and if *P* speaks falsely, it's telling the truth!

I've created a paradox, neat as can be –
and simply by using your putative *P*.
When you assumed *P* you stepped in a snare;
Your assumptions have led you right into my lair.
So, how to escape from this logical mess?
I don't have to tell you; I'm sure you can guess.
By *reductio*, there cannot possibly be
a procedure that acts like the mythical *P*.
You can never discover mechanical means
for predicting the acts of computing machines.
It's something that cannot be done. So we users
must find our own bugs; our computers are losers!

Exercises   Incomplete Logic

Odd-numbered
solutions
begin on page 383

1. This is the last page of *The Digestor's Digest*. It's now possible to determine which page is the fun page.

The Digestor's Digest

Vol. I, No. 11

Breakfast Review

We recently visited an aspiring new eatery, the upscale International House of Oat Bran. We were pleasantly surprised by the service and decor. Most impressive was the menu featuring scores of mouth-parching oaty delights.

Breakfast Review

We recently visited an aspiring new eatery, the downscale Sunken Donuts. The waiter was surly and the food was vile. After one taste we were ready to sue. If they hadn't thrown us out, we would have left. While this may read like a review, it isn't. Believe it or not, this is an ad.

We have a game for you, a finite game. A **finite game** is a game which always ends in a finite number of moves. Tic Tac Toe is a finite game. So is Dots and Boxes. So are most commercial games. Even chess is a finite game (there's a rule that ends a game in a draw if the same board position occurs three times).

Our game is **Hypergame**. It's the invention of logician Bill Zwicker. It's for two players and it's endlessly fascinating. The player who moves first chooses a finite game. Then starting with the second player, you play the chosen game. If the first player chooses Tic Tac Toe, for example, then the second player makes the first move in a game of Tic Tac Toe, then the first player makes the next move, and so on.

Hypergame is certainly a wonderful game, as wonderful as all finite games put together! Because it *is* all finite games put together!

Hold it! Is Hypergame a finite game?

Well, of course it is. The first player chooses a finite game. Then they play the finite game. If that play of the finite game takes 12948573 moves, then that play of Hypergame will take 12948574 moves. Hypergame is definitely a finite game.

So let's play Hypergame. We'll go first. We'll choose a finite game. Hmm . . . not Tic Tac Toe . . . not chess . . . Hey! Hypergame is a finite game! We can choose Hypergame! We choose Hypergame.

It's your turn. You make the first move of the game we chose. You make the first move of Hypergame. That means you choose a game. What did you say? You choose Hypergame?

Then we will make the second move in the game *we* chose, which means the first move of the game *you* chose, which means we choose a game. We choose Hypergame!

. . . As we said, Hypergame is endlessly fascinating!

Die, my dear doctor? That's the last thing I shall do! (Last words of Lord Palmerston)

What Is Logic?

Logic is many things. It's a field of knowledge, it's a set of techniques, it's a guide to critical reasoning, and it's a route to understanding the abstract structure of language, mathematics and computing. It is useful in daily life. It helps us think more cogently, to argue more effectively, to read and to listen more critically. And it is the gateway to some of the most profound ideas of human thought.

Logical structures give us insight and perspective. Logic empowers thought.

But logic is not a closed body of doctrine. Like any significant domain of human endeavor, it's a work in progress, a field of active research. In this book and on the associated website we bring you seasoned tools and well-established results, but we also take you to the frontiers of logical research. We introduce you to ideas that are new, controversial, and incomplete.

Logic is continually advancing. New logics appear all the time, bringing insights, ideas, and connections. New logicians are born every year. Logic is a vast field; there are discoveries to be made in all directions.

And beyond the usefulness of logic, beyond it's power and intrigue, logic is beautiful. The best logical arguments are works of art. They inspire the same feelings of joy, revelation, and peace we find in masterpieces of poetry and music. And they fill us with awe for the men and women who gave them birth.

We invite you to join us.

Sweet Reason: A Field Guide To Modern Logic, Second Edition. Jim Henle, Jay L. Garfield, Thomas Tymoczko and Emily Altreuter.
© 2012 John Wiley & Sons Inc. Published 2012 by John Wiley & Sons Inc.

Answers to Odd-Numbered Exercises

Chapter One

1.1 Introducing Formal Logic   (p.6)

1. $P \wedge Q$
3. $P \vee \neg R$
5. $\neg R \Rightarrow \neg P$
7. $Q \Leftrightarrow (P \wedge \neg R)$
9. Either George is late to the meeting or he brings a casserole.
11. If the meeting is in Detroit, then George is late.
13. Either George is not late to the meeting or both the meeting is not in Detroit and George brings a casserole.
15. George brings a casserole, and if the meeting is in Detroit then he's late.

1.2 Constants and Relations   (p.8)

1. Tom Tymoczko is female.
3. Aristotle is Jay Garfield.
5. Tom Tymoczko and Jim Henle are the parents of Oprah.
7. Jim Henle is female and Jim Henle is male.
9. Med
11. Mde
13. $Pdfe$
15. $\neg Mfa$
17. False
19. True
21. False
23. False

1.3 Quantifiers and Variables   (p.10)

1. Everyone is married to Jim Henle.
3. Not everyone has Oprah and Jay Garfield as parents.

    OR

    Oprah and Jay did not beget everyone.
5. There is someone who is married to both Ari and Oprah.
7. If Aristotle is not male, then no one is male.
9. $\forall x W x \vee \forall y G y$
11. $\exists x M c x \Rightarrow Gc$
13. $\neg Mee$
15. $\exists x (M d x \wedge W x) \vee \exists y (W y \wedge \neg M d y)$
17. $x = i$
19. $x = g$
21. $x = j$
23. $x = k$
25. d

1.5 Conclusions   (p.14)

1. The picnic should be Monday.
3. Doug does not play fetch.
5. We shouldn't legalize marjiuana.
7. Raising the tax on gas would be a big mistake.

> There are only two ways to answer the quiz on page 17 and get a perfect score: 1. T, 2. F, 3. T and 1. F, 2. F, 3. T.

Sweet Reason: A Field Guide To Modern Logic, Second Edition. Jim Henle, Jay L. Garfield, Thomas Tymoczko and Emily Altreuter.
© 2012 John Wiley & Sons Inc. Published 2012 by John Wiley & Sons Inc.

Chapter Two

2.1 Formal Inference   (p.20)

1. Invalid. Counterexample: *P* false and *Q* true.
3. Valid.
5. Invalid. Counterexample: *P* false.
7. Invalid. Counterexample: *P* false and *Q* true.
9. Valid.
11. Invalid. Counterexample: Suppose we are talking about things on Earth. Suppose *Px* means *x* is a human and *a* is Niagara Falls.

2.2 Informal Inference   (p.24)

1. valid
3. invalid. Counterexample:
   > If you are a fish, then you can swim. (true)
   >
   > Turtles are not fish. (true)
   > ———————————————
   > ∴ Turtles cannot swim. (false)
5. valid
7. valid
9. valid
11. invalid. Counterexample:
   > If every American gives $100 to Starbucks, then Starbucks will have over one hundred billion dollars.
   > If Starbucks has over 100 billion dollars, then Topeka is in Kansas.
   > If Topeka is in Kansas, then Helena is in Montana.
   > Jim Henle isn't giving Starbucks $100.
   > ———————————————
   > ∴ Helena isn't in Montana.

2.3 Diagramming Arguments   (p.30)

1. A: There is no God.
   B: If God exists, then God is everywhere.
   C: If God is everywhere, then God is in my nose.
   D: If God is in my nose, then I can feel it.
   E: I can't feel it.

3. D: Dogs are better pets than cats
   I: Dogs are more intelligent than cats
   S: Dogs solve tasks more surely than cats
   L: Dogs are more loyal to their owners.
   C: Dogs come when they are called; few cats do,
   P: If you forget to pay your taxes, your dog will still be your friend.
   M: Cats care only about mealtimes.
   B: Cats scratch and bite.

   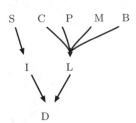

5. A: There is no real difference between classical and popular music.
   B: Everybody agrees that jazz is popular music.
   C: Classical music is the music that represents the highest and most distinctive music produced by a culture, the music that endures and is passed from generation, and in the performance and composition of which virtuosity is demonstrated.
   D: Jazz plays this role in African-American culture.
   E: Jazz is classical music.
   F: Jazz is both popular and classical music.

   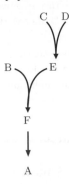

7. A: It is a fundamental human right to earn a living.

B: Anyone has a right to use whatever talents he or she has to earn a living, as long as he or she is not being coerced.

C: Many are capable of earning a living through prostitution and are willing to do so.

D: People have a fundamental right to engage in prostitution.

E: No state can legally deprive people of fundamental human rights.

F: No state can legally ban prostitution.

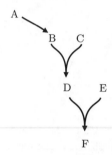

5. false

7. false

9.

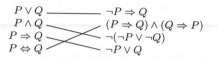

$$P \vee Q \quad\text{———}\quad \neg P \Rightarrow Q$$
$$P \wedge Q \quad\quad (P \Rightarrow Q) \wedge (Q \Rightarrow P)$$
$$P \Rightarrow Q \quad\quad \neg(\neg P \vee \neg Q)$$
$$P \Leftrightarrow Q \quad\quad \neg P \vee Q$$

11.

T

T	F	T
T	T	F
T	F	T

13.

2.4 Saying No   (p.33)

1. Jim Henle is not bald.

3. Jay is not bald or Jim is not bald

5. "Neither Wally nor Jay is a rock star." OR "Wally is not a rock star and Jay is not a rock star."

7. This is a little ambiguous. If you take the sentence to mean that Martha and George are married to each other, then the negation is "Martha and George are not married." But if you take it to mean that each is married to someone, then the negation is "Either Martha or George is not married."

9. "All mollusks are non-male." OR "No mollusks are male."

11. There is an amphibious geology major.

13. Both pieces are ads.

Chapter Three

3.1 Basic Sentential   (p.41)

1. true

3. true

3.2 Truth Tables   (p.49)

1.

Q	R	(	Q	⇒	R	)	∧	R
T	T		T	T	T		T	T
T	F		T	F	F		F	F
F	T		F	T	T		T	T
F	F		F	T	F		F	F

3.

P	Q	(	P	∨	¬	Q	)	⇒	Q
T	T		T	T	F	T		T	T
T	F		T	T	T	F		F	F
F	T		F	F	F	T		T	T
F	F		F	T	T	F		F	F

5.

P	Q	R	P	⇒	(	Q	∨	R	)
T	T	T	T	T		T	T	T
T	T	F	T	T		T	T	F
T	F	T	T	T		F	T	T
T	F	F	T	F		F	F	F
F	T	T	F	T		T	T	T
F	T	F	F	T		T	T	F
F	F	T	F	T		F	T	T
F	F	F	F	T		F	F	F

7.

P	Q	R	S	¬	(P	∨	Q)	⇔	(R	⇒	¬	S)
T	T	T	T	F	T	T	T	T	T	F	F	T
T	T	T	F	F	T	T	T	F	T	T	T	F
T	T	F	T	F	T	T	T	F	F	T	F	T
T	T	F	F	F	T	T	T	F	F	T	T	F
T	F	T	T	F	T	T	F	T	T	F	F	T
T	F	T	F	F	T	T	F	F	T	T	T	F
T	F	F	T	F	T	T	F	F	F	T	F	T
T	F	F	F	F	T	T	F	F	F	T	T	F
F	T	T	T	F	F	T	T	T	T	F	F	T
F	T	T	F	F	F	T	T	F	T	T	T	F
F	T	F	T	F	F	T	T	F	F	T	F	T
F	T	F	F	F	F	T	T	F	F	T	T	F
F	F	T	T	T	F	F	F	F	T	F	F	T
F	F	T	F	T	F	F	F	T	T	T	T	F
F	F	F	T	T	F	F	F	T	F	T	F	T
F	F	F	F	T	F	F	F	T	F	T	T	F

9.

P	P	∨	P
T	T	F	T
F	F	F	F

11.

P	Q	(P	∨	Q)	∨	(P	⇔	Q)
T	T	T	F	T	T	T	T	T
T	F	T	T	F	T	T	F	F
F	T	F	T	T	T	F	F	T
F	F	F	F	F	T	F	T	F

3.3 English to Sentential   (p.55)

1.

H ⇒ C
C ⇒ M
¬H
∴ ¬M

H: I am hungry.
C: I eat cereal.
M: I have milk.

3.

D ∨ A
D ⇒ R
A ⇒ R
∴ R

D: Zeus divorces Hera.
A: Zeus is annoyed by Hera.
R: Zeus runs off with a younger woman.

5.

¬L ⇒ M
W
∴ L

L: I have logic today.

M: Today is Monday.
W: Today is Wednesday.

7.

M
H
∴ L

M: Men love to be scratched behind the ears.
H: Hobbes is a man.
L: Hobbes loves to be scratched behind the ears.

9.

R ⇒ (B ⇒ S)
B ∧ ¬D
∴ ¬R

R: The world is round.
S: I can sail around it.
B: I have a boat.
D: I do sail around it.
Note: "can sail" and "do sail" need different sentence letters.

3.4 Negating Statements   (p.58)

1. Either Smedley didn't eat three potstickers or she thought they had spinach.
3. Either Jay is not bald or both Mabel is bald and Susan is not.
5. Either Martha or George is not married or Frank is not upset.
7. The picnic isn't Sunday and it doesn't rain.
9. She will win if and only if her opponent isn't Rhett.

The answer is that there is no such barber. The existence of the barber leads to a contradiction: the barber shaves the barber iff the barber doesn't shave the barber. Therefore there can't be such a barber.

Note that we can't dismiss the other paradoxes this way. It would be nice to say of the Liar sentence that it doesn't exist, but there it is on the page!

3.5 Rebutting Premises (p.64)

1. You can argue with the premise that if God is in your nose you can feel it. For instance, God does not necessarily consist of matter and therefore you may not be able to feel God in your nose (you don't necessarily feel God anywhere else). You can also challenge the premise "I can't feel it," because maybe you do feel something in your nose and you just do not know that what you feel is God.

3. There are some tasks that are solved more quickly by cats; the question of intelligence is not clear. You can also argue that cats are too intelligent to be interested in the problems being posed for them. Not all dogs come when they're called. Not all cats bite and some dogs do.

5. You might argue that not everyone agrees that jazz is popular music. For example, some people might consider it outdated. You could also argue that the correct definition of classical music is the European music of the late eighteenth and early nineteenth centuries.

7. The only premise we think you can challenge easily is "No state can legally deprive people of fundamental human rights." Life is a fundamental human right. Some states deprive people of this. (We're not saying here that capital punishment is wrong – some people may not deserve their fundamental human rights.)

3.6 Computer Logic (p.67)

1. 000010, $\neg(P \vee Q)$
3. 110101, $(P \wedge Q) \vee Q$

5.

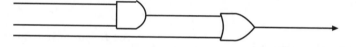

7.

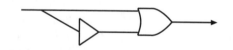

9.

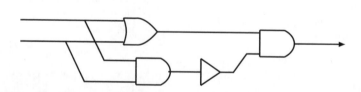

11. One possible AND diagram:

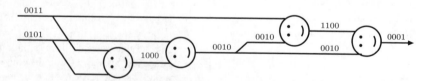

13. The first piece is an article; the second is an ad.

Chapter Four

4.1 Validity (p.71)

1. Invalid

			PREMISES		CONCLUSION
	P	Q	$P \Rightarrow Q$	Q	P
1.	T	T	T	T	T
2.	T	F	F	F	T
3.	F	T	T	T	F
4.	F	F	T	F	F

3. Valid

5. Invalid

7. Valid

$$P \vee S$$
$$S \Rightarrow G$$
$$\neg G$$
$$\therefore P$$

P: I will grow up to be president.
S: I will become a screenwriter.
G: I am good at writing.

				PREMISES			CONCLUSION
	P	S	G	$P \vee S$	$S \Rightarrow G$	$\neg G$	P
1.	T	T	T	T	T	F	T
2.	T	T	F	T	F	T	T
3.	T	F	T	T	T	F	T
4.	T	F	F	T	T	T	T
5.	F	T	T	T	T	F	F
6.	F	T	F	T	F	T	F
7.	F	F	T	F	T	F	F
8.	F	F	F	F	T	T	F

9. Invalid

$$L \vee O$$
$$L \Rightarrow M$$
$$O$$
$$\therefore \neg M$$

L: I love logic.
O: I'm obsessed with it.
M: I will major in it.

				PREMISES			CONCLUSION
	L	M	O	$L \vee O$	$L \Rightarrow M$	O	$\neg M$
1.	T	T	T	T	T	T	F
2.	T	T	F	T	T	F	F
3.	T	F	T	T	F	T	T
4.	T	F	F	T	F	F	T
5.	F	T	T	T	T	T	F
6.	F	T	F	F	T	F	F
7.	F	F	T	T	T	T	T
8.	F	F	F	F	T	F	T

11. Invalid. Note the difference between "can"
and "do" here!

$$R \Rightarrow (B \Rightarrow S)$$
$$B \wedge \neg D$$
$$\therefore \neg R$$

R: The world is round.
S: I can sail around it.
B: I have a boat.
D: I do sail around it.

					PREMISES		CONCLUSION
	R	S	B	D	$R \Rightarrow (B \Rightarrow S)$	$B \wedge \neg D$	$\neg R$
1.	T	T	T	T	T	F	F
2.	T	T	T	F	T	T	F
3.	T	T	F	T	T	F	F
4.	T	T	F	F	T	F	F
5.	T	F	T	T	F	F	F
6.	T	F	T	F	F	T	F
7.	T	F	F	T	T	F	F
8.	T	F	F	F	T	F	F
9.	F	T	T	T	T	F	T
10.	F	T	T	F	T	T	T
11.	F	T	F	T	T	F	T
12.	F	T	F	F	T	F	T
13.	F	F	T	T	T	F	T
14.	F	F	T	F	T	T	T
15.	F	F	F	T	T	F	T
16.	F	F	F	F	T	F	T

13.

$$N \qquad\qquad \neg B \Rightarrow S$$
$$N \Rightarrow B \qquad\qquad \neg S$$
$$\therefore B \qquad\qquad \therefore B$$

4.3 Negating Conditionals (p.78)

1. $P \wedge Q$

3. $P \wedge \neg(Q \Rightarrow R)$, or $P \wedge (\neg Q \wedge \neg R)$

5. $(P \Rightarrow R) \wedge \neg S$

7. $(P \wedge \neg(R \Leftrightarrow S)$, or $P \wedge (R \Leftrightarrow \neg S)$

9. You don't get me a cup of coffee but you do love me.

11. I fail logic and I neither take it next year nor change my major to modern dance.

13. I will go to law school but I can't scrape together tuition money.

15. I'll pay for dinner but you don't buy the movie tickets.

17.

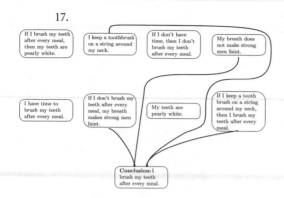

Note that this exercise is essentially the same as exercise 13 in Section 4.1

4.4 Rebutting Inferences   (p.86)

1. There is just one inference here and it is logically valid. The only way to attack this argument is by attacking the premises.

3. An intelligent pet may not be a better pet. The more intelligent an animal, the less it may be willing to be a pet. A loyal pet may not be a better pet. The loyalty of a dog, so easily obtained, may be not be valuable.

5. Rootbeer is brown and fizzy. It doesn't follow that there is no real difference between brown things and fizzy things.

7. The invalid inference is the one from "it is a fundamental right to earn a living" to "anyone has a right to use whatever talents he or she has to earn a living." For instance, if one is a skilled and talented robber, that does not imply that one has a right to rob.

4.5 The Logic of Sets   (p.91)

1. 277
3. 61
5. a.277, b.25, c.61, d.47
7. Region d
9. a. 13%, b. 12%, c. 15%, d. 11%, e. 17%, f. 4%, g. 15%, h. 13%
11. In favor of all three. This is region f.
13. The candidate following the majority (a) will beat the candidate with the most popular position (e). The first will win the voters in regions a and d (24%) while the second will win the voters in regions e and f (21%).

15.

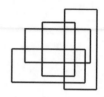

Chapter Five

5.1 Well-formed Formulas   (p.100)

1. Not a wff
3. Not a wff
5. Not a wff
7. M and N are wffs by 1. $(M \wedge N)$ is a wff by part b of clause 2.
9. A, B, and C are wffs by 1. $(A \wedge B)$ is a wff by part b of clause 2. $((A \wedge B) \Rightarrow C)$ is a wff by part d of clause 2.
11. X, Y, and Z are wffs by 1. $\neg X$ is a wff by part a of clause 2. $(\neg X \wedge Y)$ is a wff by part b of clause 2. And $((\neg X \wedge Y) \vee Z)$ is a wff by part c of clause 2.
13. a. My parents are ancestors of mine.
    b. If someone is an ancestor of mine then that person's parents are ancestors of mine.
    c. Only people recognized as ancestors of mine using clauses a. and b. are ancestors of mine.
15. wff
17. not a wff
19. wff
21. wff
23. not a wff
25. not a wff
27. Think of the baseball team.

5.2 The Shortcut Method   (p.105)

1. Valid
3. Invalid

5. Invalid

7. Valid

9. Invalid

11.

Name	Relation	Ugly Incident
Edgar	?	$1000
Edwin	cousin	Harvard
Eduardo	nephew	ex-nun
Edsel	stepcousin	mixed-up
Crazy Eddie	uncle	wedding

5.3 Local and Global (p.110)

1. tautology, consistent

3. tautology, consistent

5. consistent, contingent

7. contradiction

9. consistent, contingent

11. **I**

13. **I**

15. **Y**

17. **Y**

19. **Y**

21. **Y**

23. **I**

5.4 More on Trees (p.114)

1. conjunction

3. disjunction

5. conditional

7. conjunction

9. biconditional (2, part e,
   $(\neg L \Leftrightarrow (\neg O \land \neg M))$

11. conditional

13.

P	Q	P	$\uparrow$	(	Q	$\uparrow$	P	)
T	T		T			F		
T	F		F			T		
F	T		T			T		
F	F		T			T		

15. Pigs don't have wings or George is not a chiropodist.

17. *The Little (Used (Book Store))*—The store is little. It's a bookstore and it's not new. It's been used.

    The ((Little Used) Book) Store. It's a store that specializes in selling books that haven't used but haven't been used a lot.

The (Little (Used Book)) Store. The store sells used books, but not all used books. It just sells used books that are fairly small.

19. $(P \land \neg Q)$

21. $((A \lor B) \land \neg C)$

5.5 Rebutting Everything (p.119)

1. X: Sophist College needs a core curriculum.
   A: Without a core, Sophist College can't be considered a first-rate liberal arts college.
   B: Without a core, students know nothing about other fields besides their majors.
   C: Without a core, a Sophist degree has no meaning.
   D: There is nothing you can count on a Sophist graduate to know or to be able to do.
   E: Most of the colleges we respect – the Ivy League institutions, for example – have either a core or a set of distribution requirements.
   F: Education without history is a sorry education.
   G: Enrollments in history courses have fallen steadily since the 1960s.
   H: A campus' climate benefits from a core.
   I: When all students take the same course, the material becomes part of the general discourse.
   J: The quality of intellectual life is vastly improved.
   K: A core can be a unifying influence.
   L: Students today are divided by departments, extracurricular activities, background, race and religion.
   M: A core helps to bring students together for a common purpose, a common experience.

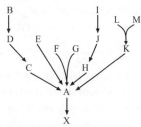

One possible rebuttal:

This argument does not succeed in showing that Sophist College needs a core curriculum. First of all, it makes the mistake of assuming that students attending a college or university without core requirements know nothing about other fields besides their major. Some colleges without a core, such as Smith College, still require students to take half of all their credits outside of their chosen major.

Secondly, even if most respected institutions have a core curriculum, there are respected institutions (Brown University, for example) that do not have a core curriculum and are still considered to be first-rate.

The author also makes a mistake of assuming that without history, the education one receives is poor. That is certainly arguable. Often leaders on opposite sides of an issue will cite the "lessons of history" to defend their positions. What is the value of knowing history if it can be used to justify inconsistent points?

The author says that students taking the same class will talk about material in the course outside of class. They might, but it seems just as likely that they will discuss the professor and their grades.

And students today are not divided, as the author claims. Students in different majors meet and interact on sports teams, in musical groups, in clubs, and in their dormitories.

But let's return to the issue of knowledge. It may be true that there is no knowledge common to all graduates of a college without a core. But does that mean the degree has no meaning? It's not knowledge today that marks education, it is something deeper. It's academic rigor, logical thinking, intellectual curiosity, and the willingness to consider new ideas. At a good, core-less institution, you can count on graduates to have this. Their degree has meaning that transcends anything core knowledge can offer.

3. A: The United States should have afternoon tea.
B: Afternoon tea would improve our image.
C: Places considered cultured have tea.
D: If we want to be cultured, we should have tea.
E: England has tea.
F: England is considered cultured.
G: Tea time would boost national morale.
H: Tea time provides an afternoon break.
I: An afternoon break is good.
J: An afternoon break enables everyone to finish the day with energy.
K: Other countries have an afternoon break.
L: These countries have lower stress rates and suicide rates than the United States.
M: If my mother doesn't get her caffeine fix, everyone suffers.
N: Tea time would ensure that my mother gets her caffeine fix.
O: Tea time is good for individual well-being.
P: Tea prevents kidney stones.
Q: Tea prevents cancer.
R: Tea has a good influence on metabolism.
S: It is healthier to eat many small meals throughout the day.
T: Having a tea time snack is healthy.

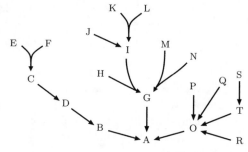

One possible rebuttal:
The inference made from the premises that England is cultured and England has

tea to the fact that cultured places have tea is flawed. Take an argument of the same form with obviously true premises and an obviously false conclusion: England is in Europe, England has pounds as its currency, therefore European coutries have pounds as their currency. Clearly, the conclusion does not follow from the premises, since England is the only European country that uses pounds as its currency.

But let's suppose that, as you say, places considered cultured have tea. That doesn't mean, however, that places that have tea are considered cultured. You have mixed up cause and effect. You have also confused being cultured with being considered cultured. What do you really want, and will drinking tea get you there?

The claim that an afternoon break is good is not justified by the fact that other countries with afternoon breaks have lower stress and suicide rates. There are other more important reasons for why these rates are significantly lower in other countries. For instance, many other countries have shorter work days and provide their employees with more vacation and sick days. France, for example, gives all their workers almost 5 weeks of vacation which do not include sick and family medical emergency days. In the United States, however, workers generally get only two weeks of vacation and many business people, doctors and lawyers don't take any days off. Having afternoon teas is not going to solve the problem.

The idea that national policy should be determined by one person's (your mother's) moods is ridiculous on the face of it. It would be impossible to schedule the country to fit everyone's mood.

The fact that having teatime is healthy is not justified by the claim that it is healthier to eat several small meals per day. Due to busy schedules, teatime snack may be one of the very few meals for many people. Those people will probably eat rather large portions during teatime, which would not make afternoon tea time healthy.

In addition, it is not sufficient to say that United States should start supporting the tradition of afternoon tea simply because tea time is good for individual well-being. It is good to brush teeth for individual well-being, but that does not imply that the government should start supporting the tradition of brushing teeth. It is up to the person whether to have tea or brush their teeth–government has nothing to do with it.

5.6 Polish Logic   (p.126)

1. Wff
3. Not a wff
5. Wff
7. $P \Rightarrow (Q \Rightarrow R)$
9. $(P \vee Q) \wedge \neg R$
11. $\neg(\neg S \vee \neg R)$
13. $\Rightarrow P \neg Q$
15. $\wedge P \vee QR$
17. $\Leftrightarrow Q \wedge P \Rightarrow RS$
19. $PQR \Rightarrow \Rightarrow$
21. $PQ \wedge PR \vee \Rightarrow$
23. We argue that it's Reverse Polish. Consider "When 900 years old you reach, look as good you will not." In "900 years old you reach," "reach" is the word that links "900 years old" and "you." And Yoda puts it in back. Similarly, "look as good" and "you" are linked by "will". Of course the "not," which negates everything is at the end. There is an exception, though. "900 years old you reach," and "look as good you will not." are linked by "when." If this were completely in the spirit of Reverse Polish, Yoda would have said, "900 years old you reach, look as good you will when not." *What would Yoda do? Your ass kick it he would!*

　　　　　　　　　　　　　　– Bumper sticker

25. Since the pieces disagree about fiber, at least one of them is false. Suppose this is

the fun edition. The first piece can't be an ad because then the second would be too and we just said that at least one must be false. So the first piece is an article. So the second piece is also an article. But then the second piece is telling the truth ("This report is just as correct as the other on this page."). That's impossible. Thus this can't be the fun page.

27. Note first that because the pieces disagree they can't both be true.

Now, we don't know if this is the fun page or not so we have to consider both cases.

Case 1: No. 4 is not the fun page.

Then the second piece can't be an ad since it says there is an ad. So the second piece is an article. Since there must be at least one ad, the first is an ad and false.

Case 2: No. 4 is the fun page.

If the first piece is true then the second is false since the pieces can't both be true. And if the first isn't true, then "There is an ad on this page." is false so both pieces are articles and again the first piece is false.

Chapter Six

6.1 Predicate   (p.138)

1. If Daryl reads romance novels, Daryl knows Mao.
3. "Astrid knows Mao or Daryl knows Mao." OR "Astrid knows Mao or Daryl does."
5. No one knows everyone.
7. false
9. false
11. true
13. true
15. false
17. true
19. true
21. false
23. false
25. $\neg \forall x Px$
27. $\forall x Px$

6.2 English to Predicate   (p.144)

1. $\exists x(Nx \land Ux)$
3. $\exists x Sxa$
5. $\forall y(Ny \Rightarrow Sya)$
7. $\exists x(Px \land \forall y((Uy \land Ny) \Rightarrow Syx))$
9. $\exists x((Ux \land Px) \land \forall y((Uy \land Ny) \Rightarrow Sxy))$
11. $\neg \forall x(Nx \Rightarrow Ux)$ OR $\exists x(Nx \land \neg Ux)$
13. Oedipus
15. $\forall x((Bx \land \forall z(Bz \Rightarrow Izx)) \Rightarrow \exists y(By \land Ixy))$
17. $\forall x(Bx \Rightarrow \forall y((By \land \forall z(Bz \Rightarrow Izx)) \Rightarrow Ixy))$

6.3 Reading Between the Lines (p.150)

1.

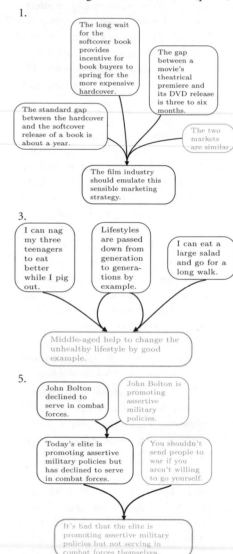

7.

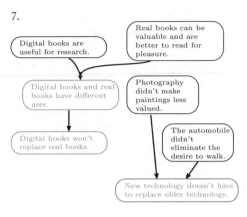

6.4 Multi-valued Logic (p.160)

1. 1
3. 0
5. 1
7. 1
9. Designated values: {1}.
11. Designated values: all probabilities greater than 0.
13. No designated values.

Chapter Seven

7.1 Universes (p.165)

1. True in the universe of people alive today, where *a* is Bill Clinton, *b* is Hillary Clinton, *Px* and *Qx* both mean *x* is male. False in the same universe except that *Px* and *Qx* both mean *x* is female.

3. True in the universe of people alive today, where *Px* means *x* is American and *Qx* means *x* is male. False in the same universe except that *Px* and *Qx* both mean *x* is female.

5. True in the universe of people alive today, where *Rxy* means *x* and *y* have the same birthday. False in the same universe except that *Rxy* means *x*'s birthday is later in the year than *y*'s birthday.

7. This is a contradiction. It is always false.

9. True in the universe of people alive today, where *a* is Bill Clinton and *Qx* means *x* is

male. False in the same universe except that *Qx* means *x* is female.

11. This is a contradiction. It is false in all universes.

13. **Y**
15. **N**
17. **Y**
19. **Y**
21. **I**
23. {∅} is not the empty set. It's a set with one member, the empty set.

7.2 Syllogisms (p.170)

1. a. $\neg\exists x(Dx \land Cx)$
       $\underline{\exists x(Cx \land Ix)}$
       $\therefore \forall x(Dx \Rightarrow \neg Ix)$

b. Invalid

c. Suppose our universe is all students in the world and *Dx* means "*x* is a college student." Let *Cx* mean "*x* is in second grade." Let *Ix* mean "*x* is female."

3. a. $\forall x(Lx \Rightarrow Gx)$
       $\underline{\exists x(Lx \land \neg Cx)}$
       $\therefore \exists x(Cx \land \neg Gx)$

b. Invalid

c. Suppose our universe is people alive today. Let *Cx* mean "*x* is a college student." Let *Lx* mean "*x* is a U.S. citizen," and *Gx* mean "*x* is human."

5. a. $\forall x(Px \Rightarrow Sx)$
       $\underline{\exists x(Px \land \neg Ax)}$
       $\therefore \exists x(Sx \land \neg Ax)$

b. Valid

Texts   Tedious

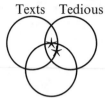

Exercises

7. a. $\forall x(Cx \Rightarrow Rx)$
          $\exists x(Cx \wedge Bx)$
          $\therefore \exists x(Rx \wedge Bx)$

    b. Valid

Sequels   Bonanzas

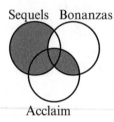

Acclaim

9. a. $\forall x(Px \Rightarrow (Sx \vee Cx))$
          $\forall x(Sx \Rightarrow Cx)$
          $\therefore \forall x(Px \Rightarrow Cx)$

    b. Valid

Glitters   Gold

Bucket

7.3 Validity   (p.173)

1. Let's take the set of living people and let P be "___ is a mammal." Then $\exists xPx$ is true. However the conclusion is false because in fact all people are mammals.

3. Let's take the set of flowers. let P be "___ is a wild flower" and let Q be "___ is a garden flower". Then the premise $\forall x(Px \vee Qx)$ is true as every flower is either a wild flower or a garden flower. The conclusion is false, however, because $\forall xPx$ is false (since there exists a flower that is not a wild flower)

and $\forall xQx$ is false (since there exists a flower that is not a garden flower).

5. Let's look at the universe of all healthy squirrels. Let P be "is a mammal" and let Q be "has a mouth." The first premise, $\forall x(Px \vee Qx)$, is true as all healthy squirrels are either mammals or have a mouth. The second premise, $\forall xPx$ is also true as all squirrels are indeed mammals. The conclusion, however, is false because it isn't true that there exists a healthy squirrel that doesn't have a mouth.

7. valid

9. valid

11. invalid

13.

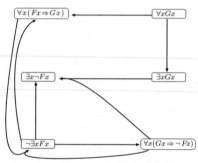

15. We can't tell if this is the fun edition or not but we can figure out that the first piece is false and the second is true.

7.4 Diagramming Your Argument (p.185)

1. a. My school should offer a major in logic.
    b. Logic majors are in demand in the workplace.
    c. Logic is a marketable skill.
    d. The college wants students to learn marketable skills.
    e. Many students are interested in logic.
    f. It is important for the college to cater to students' interests.
    g. Logic is a very popular course.
    h. Few schools offer a major in logic.
    i. Offering a major in logic would attract applicants to the college.

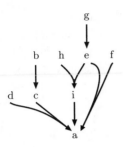

3. a. Cloning of human beings should be illegal.
    b. Sexual reproduction leads to greater biological diversity than asexual reproduction.
    c. Cloning is asexual reproduction.
    d. Cloning will result in decreased biological diversity.
    e. Biological diversity is important.
    f. Cloned individuals will be different from non-cloned individuals.
    g. People fear and hate those who are different.
    h. People will fear and hate cloned individuals.
    i. Cloning will result in human rights issues.

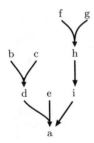

5. a. The United States should abolish the death penalty.
    b. Forensic evidence has shown many people to be wrongfully sentenced to death.
    c. In many cases, there is inadequate consideration of forensic evidence.
    d. In some cases, people might be executed whom adequate evidence would show are not guilty.
    e. A system in which people who are not guilty are executed is unjust.

    f. Most of the other nations which have the death penalty are also guilty of numerous human rights violations.
    g. We do not want to be like these other countries that have capital punishment.
    h. The death penalty is not effective as a deterrent.
    i. Places with the death penalty do not generally experience less violent crime than places without.

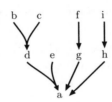

7. a. My school should have a quantitative skills requirement.
    b. Quantitative skills help people make good decisions when voting.
    c. Quantitative skills are necessary for good citizenship.
    d. The college wants its students to be good citizens.
    e. Quantitative skills are useful in the workplace.
    f. Our school wants to prepare students for the workplace.
    g. Quantitative skills have applications in many academic areas.
    h. Learning quantitative skills will help students become better in their chosen areas of study.
    i. Many students are uncomfortable taking courses involving quantitative skills.
    j. It is important for students to step outside of their comfort zone.

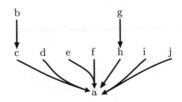

9. Christopher Robin goes hoppity hoppity. There are three reasons to support this conclusion. The first reason is that Buffalo buffalo buffalo. The second reason is that $2 + 2 = 4$ and this is because the swimming and diving team finished 2nd at the Betty Spears Relays and because it was a dark and stormy night.

The third and last reason that Christopher Robin goes hoppity hoppity is that since all mankind loves a lover, it follows that laboratory tests show that Chemtreats is not the best-tasting cereal.

For all the reasons above, Christopher Robin definitely goes hoppity hoppity.

Chapter Eight

8.1 Predicate Wffs   (p.194)

1. closed wff
3. open wff
5. closed wff
7. $\exists x \exists y (Lx \wedge Ly \wedge x \neq y)$
9. $\wedge x \wedge y (Lx \wedge Ly \Rightarrow \forall y (Ly \Rightarrow x = y)$
11. True.
13. True.
15. False.
17. contingent
19. tautology
21. false
23. true
25. true
27. false
29. $\Sigma x Px$ means that all or all but one have property P.

8.2 Outlining Your Argument
(p.203)

Again, these are outlines of imperfect arguments. In the next chapter they will improve significantly.

1. I. Introduction
   A. We claim that my school should offer a major in logic.
   B. We have three main reasons for this: marketability, student interest, and applicant draw.
   II. Body
   A. Paragraph
      i. We claim that offering a major in logic will help students learn marketable skills.
      ii. Here's why:
         a. Logic majors are in demand in the workplace.
         b. That means that the logic skills they learn are marketable.
         c. The college wants its students to learn marketable skills.
      iii. So the college should offer a major in logic.
   B. Paragraph
      i. We claim that logic should be offered because of student interest.
      ii. Here's why:
         a. Logic is a very popular course.
         b. That means that many students are interested in logic.
         c. It is important for the college to cater to students' interests.
      iii. Since student interest is important and students want logic, the college should offer it.
   C. Paragraph
      i. We claim that a logic major would attract students to the college.
      ii. Here's why:
         a. As we said, many students are interested in logic.
         b. Few schools offer a major in logic.

c. Thus, the students who are interested in logic will be attracted to the college.

    iii. Since logic attracts students to the college, the college should offer logic.

III. Conclusion

In conclusion, the college should offer logic because it provides students with marketable skills, students are interested in the course, and it will attract applicants to the college.

3. I. Introduction

  A. We claim that cloning of human beings should be made illegal.

  B. We have two main reasons for this: biological diversity and human rights.

II. Body

  A. Paragraph

    i. We claim that cloning will decrease biological diversity, which is important for our success as a species.

    ii. Here's why:

      a. Sexual reproduction leads to greater biological diversity than asexual reproduction.

      b. Cloning is asexual reproduction.

      c. That means allowing human cloning will result in decreased biological diversity.

      d. Biological diversity is important for our success as a species.

    iii. So there you have it. Human cloning should be made illegal because it will result in decreased biological diversity, which is important to our success as a species.

B. Paragraph

  i. We claim that human cloning will result in human rights issues.

  ii. Here's why:

    a. Cloned individuals will be different from non-cloned individuals.

    b. Historically, people tend to fear and hate those who are different.

    c. Therefore, people will fear and hate cloned individuals.

    d. Fear and hatred results in human rights issues.

  iii. There you go. Because cloned individuals will be different, non-cloned individuals will fear and hate them, resulting in human rights issues.

III. Conclusion

That's our argument. Human cloning will result in decreased biological diversity and human rights issues, and that's why it should be made illegal.

5. I. Introduction

  A. We claim that the United States should abolish the death penalty.

  B. There are three main reasons for this: the findings of forensic evidence, the fact that we don't want to be like the other countries with capital punishment, and the fact that the death penalty is not effective as a deterrent.

II. Body

  A. Paragraph

    i. We claim that forensic science shows that the death penalty is applied unjustly.

    ii. Here's why:

      a. Forensic evidence often shows people have been wrongfully sentenced to death.

b. Due to cost, forensic evidence is not always considered.

c. Therefore, it is likely that sometimes people are executed whom forensic evidence might show to be not guilty.

d. A system in which people who are not guilty are executed is unjust.

iii. That's the argument: forensic evidence suggests that people are sometimes wrongfully executed, which means the system is unjust.

B. Paragraph

i. We claim that because the other countries that currently enforce the death penalty have a record of human rights abuses, we should try not to be like those countries.

ii. Here's why:

a. Almost all of the countries that enforce the death penalty are third-world nations with a record of human rights abuses.

b. The United States does not want to be like those countries that have the death penalty.

iii. So that's the argument. The United States does not want to be like the countries that have human rights abuses, so it should abolish the death penalty.

C. Paragraph

i. We claim that the death penalty is not effective as a deterrent.

ii. Here's why:

a. Places that enforce the death penalty do not have less violent crime than places that don't.

b. Therefore, the death penalty is not effective as a deterrent.

iii. There you have it. The death penalty is not effective as a deterrent, so it should be abolished.

III. Conclusion

That's the argument. The death penalty should be abolished because forensic evidence has shown the system is unjust, because we do not want to emulate the other countries that enforce it, and because it is not effective as a deterrent.

7. I. Introduction

A. We claim that my school should have a quantitative skills requirement.

B. There are four main reasons for this: good citizenship, success in the workplace, success in academics, and challenging students to move outside their comfort zones.

II. Body

A. Paragraph

i. We claim that quantitative skills are essential to good citizenship.

ii. Here's why:

a. Quantitative skills help people make good decisions when voting on issues of economics, healthcare, etc.

b. Making good voting decisions is essential to good citizenship.

c. The college wants its graduates to be good citizens.

iii. That's one reason why the college should have a quantitative skills requirement: to better educate the nation's citizens.

B. Paragraph

    i. We claim that a quantitative skills requirement would help students be successful in the workplace.

    ii. Here's why:

        a. Quantitative skills are useful in the workplace.

        b. The school wants to prepare students for the workplace.

    iii. That's another reason for a quantitative skills requirement: it would help students succeed in the workplace, which is something the college wants to do.

C. Paragraph

    i. We claim that a quantitative skills requirement will help students do better in all fields of study.

    ii. Here's why:

        a. Quantitative skills have applications in all academic areas.

        b. Therefore, developing quantitative skills will help students do better in their areas of study.

    iii. That's why a quantitative skills requirement would make the student body better at all academic subjects: because quantitative skills have applications in all fields of study.

D. Paragraph

    i. We claim that a quantitative skills requirement will challenge students to move outside their comfort zones.

    ii. Here's why:

        a. Many students are uncomfortable taking courses involving quantitative skills.

        b. The college should challenge students to move outside their comfort zones.

    iii. That's another reason why the college should make students fulfil a quantitative skills requirement: to challenge them intellectually and force them to step outside of their comfort zones.

III. Conclusion

That's why the college should have a quantitative skills requirement: to educate responsible future citizens, to help students develop marketable skills, to help students become better academics, and to challenge students intellectually.

9.

8.3 The Logic of Chance   (p.210)

1. $\frac{1}{3}$

3. $\frac{1}{6}$

5. $\frac{1}{6}$

7. $\frac{1}{36}$

9. $\frac{1}{12}$

11. 0

red die
1 2 3 4 5 6

blue die
1 2 3 4 5 6

13. $\frac{1}{6}$, yes

15. $\frac{1}{3}$, no

17. A represents regions *i* and *j*. ¬A represents regions *k* and *l*. Together, they represent all possible outcomes. The truth value of all possible outcomes is 1. The probability that there is *some* outcome is 1.

19. $A \lor B$ represents the regions *i*, *j*, and *k*. $\neg(A \land B)$ represents region *l*. ¬A represents *k* and *l*. ¬B represents *i* and *l*. Thus $\neg A \land \neg B$ represents region *l*, the same as $\neg(A \lor B)$, so they have the same probability.

21. The first piece (read it carefully) has to be true. The second piece has to be an article. But it's not possible to tell from this edition whether or not it is the fun page.

3. $P \lor R$ premise
4. $\neg\neg(P \Rightarrow Q)$ ¬In, 1
5. $P \Rightarrow Q$ ¬Out, 4
6. $\neg\neg(R \Rightarrow Q)$ ¬In, 2
7. $R \Rightarrow Q$ ¬Out, 6
8. Q ∨Out, 3, 5, 7

7.

1. $(P \lor Q) \Rightarrow R$ premise
2. $(S \land U) \Rightarrow R$ premise
3. $(A \lor B) \Rightarrow (H \land P)$ premise
4. $(J \Leftrightarrow K) \Rightarrow (H \land P)$ premise
5. B premise
6. $A \lor B$ ∨In, 5
7. $(A \lor B) \lor (J \Leftrightarrow K)$ ∨In, 6
8. $H \land P$ ∨Out, 3, 4, 7
9. P ∧Out, 8
10. $P \lor Q$ ∨In, 9
11. $(P \lor Q) \lor (S \land U)$ ∨In, 10
12. R ∨Out, 1, 2, 11
13. $R \land P$ ∧In, 9, 12

9.

Chapter Nine

9.1 Simple Deduction   (p.219)

1.
1. $P \land Q$ premise
2. P ∧Out, 1
3. $P \lor Q$ ∨In, 2

3.
1. $P \Rightarrow ((Q \Rightarrow R) \land (P \Rightarrow R))$ premise
2. $Q \Rightarrow ((Q \Rightarrow R) \land (P \Rightarrow R))$ premise
3. $P \lor Q$ premise
4. $(Q \Rightarrow R) \land (P \Rightarrow R)$ ∨Out, 1, 2, 3
5. $Q \Rightarrow R$ ∧Out, 4
6. $P \Rightarrow R$ ∧Out, 4
7. R ∨Out, 3, 5, 6

5.
1. $\neg(P \Rightarrow Q) \Rightarrow ((P \Rightarrow Q)$ premise
     $\land \neg(P \Rightarrow Q))$
2. $\neg(R \Rightarrow Q) \Rightarrow ((Q \Rightarrow P)$ premise
     $\land \neg(Q \Rightarrow P))$

9.2 Simple Strategy   (p.225)

1. $P \Rightarrow R$ premise
2. $Q \Rightarrow R$ premise

1.
3. $P \lor Q$ premise
4. R ∨Out, 1, 2, 3
5. $R \lor S$ ∨In, 4

3.
1. $P \land Q$ premise
2. Q ∧Out, 1
3. $Q \lor R$ ∨In, 2

5.
1. $P \land Q$ premise
2. $P \Rightarrow R$ premise
3. $Q \Rightarrow R$ premise
4. P ∧Out, 1
5. $P \lor Q$ ∨In, 4
6. R ∨Out, 2, 3, 5

7.
1. $((P \Rightarrow Q) \land (R \Rightarrow Q)) \land (P \lor R)$ premise
2. $P \lor R$ ∧Out, 1
3. $(P \Rightarrow Q) \land (R \Rightarrow Q)$ ∧Out, 1

4. $P \Rightarrow Q$ ∧Out, 3
5. $R \Rightarrow Q$ ∧Out, 3
6. Q ∨Out, 2, 4, 5

9. Valid.

Formalization:

$$R \lor N$$
$$R \Rightarrow M$$
$$N \Rightarrow S$$
$$N \Rightarrow M$$
$$\therefore M$$

Deduction:
1. $R \lor N$ premise
2. $R \Rightarrow M$ premise
3. $N \Rightarrow S$ premise
4. $N \Rightarrow M$ premise
5. M ∨Out, 1, 2, 4

11. Invalid.

Formalization:

$$\neg F$$
$$\therefore F \lor C$$

One counterexample: Penguins can't fly. Therefore, either penguins can fly or ostriches are insects.

13. This dish isn't wholesome.

15. Eggs of the Great Auk can't be had for a song.

9.3 Writing Your Argument (p.232)

1. I believe that my school should offer a major in logic. There are three main reasons for this: marketability, student interest, and applicant draw.

For one thing, logic majors are in demand in the workplace. The skills logic majors develop through their academic program – critical thinking, abstract reasoning, and persuasive arguing – are highly applicable to many professional fields, including but not limited to law, business, and marketing. My school wants students to learn marketable skills, so my school should allow students to major in logic.

For another thing, many students are interested in logic, as you can see by looking at how popular logic is. It is important for the school to cater to the students' interests. If a logic major were offered, many students would jump at the chance to learn more logic.

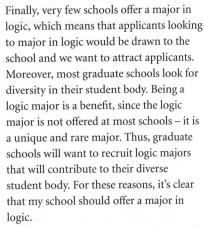

Finally, very few schools offer a major in logic, which means that applicants looking to major in logic would be drawn to the school and we want to attract applicants. Moreover, most graduate schools look for diversity in their student body. Being a logic major is a benefit, since the logic major is not offered at most schools – it is a unique and rare major. Thus, graduate schools will want to recruit logic majors that will contribute to their diverse student body. For these reasons, it's clear that my school should offer a major in logic.

3. Cloning of human beings should be made illegal. There are two main reasons for this: biological success and human rights.

First of all, cloning does not make sense as a reproductive strategy. As everyone knows, sexual reproduction is a more successful strategy than asexual reproduction because it leads to greater biological diversity. Cloning is, essentially, asexual reproduction. Therefore, allowing human cloning will result in decreased biological diversity. Biological diversity is important for our success as a species. Therefore, human cloning should be made illegal.

Second, cloned individuals will be different from non-cloned individuals. History has shown us that people fear and hate those who are different. Therefore, people will fear and hate cloned individuals. This fear and hatred will result in human rights issues regarding cloned individuals. Let's stop this problem before it starts! Human cloning should be made illegal!

5. The time has come for the United States to abolish the death penalty. Of the myriad reasons for this bold move, I shall dwell upon three: the impact of forensic

evidence, the nature of those few countries which have the death penalty, and the ineffectiveness of the death penalty as a deterrent.

In recent years, the development of forensic science has shown that in many cases, people have been wrongfully condemned to death. On several occasions the condemned has been mere weeks away from excecution when new evidence proved their innocence. Unfortunately, due to expense, many prisoners do not have adequate consideration of forensic evidence. Therefore it is likely that people are wrongfully executed. A system in which people are wrongfully executed is unjust. Therefore, the death penalty should be abolished.

Worldwide, almost all of the countries that currently enforce the death penalty are nonindustrialized nations, many of which – China, Iraq, North Korea, and many others – have a well-documented record of human rights violations. We are judged by the company we keep. Far better we should strive to emulate the United Kingdom, Sweden, France, Canada, Norway, Australia, Switzerland, and the many other first-world nations which have abolished the death penalty.

Finally, the death penalty is not effective as a deterrent. Places with the death penalty do not generally experience less violent crime than places without it. For these reasons, the choice is clear. The United States should abolish the death penalty.

7. In these modern times, it is essential that students develop quantitative skills. These skills are essential to good citizenship; they are essential in the workplace and in their chosen academic fields. Also, it is important to push students out of their "comfort zone" and into challenging arenas. That's why my school should have a quantitative skills requirement.

Quantitative skills are invaluable when it comes to making decisions at the polls, understanding statistics and advertisements, and making personal healthcare decisions. In short, development of quantitative skills is a necessary part of being a good citizen. The college wants its students to be good citizens; therefore, it should have a quantitative skills requirement.

Furthermore, quantitative skills are useful in the workplace, in fields from accounting to marketing. Our school wants to prepare students for the workplace, so we should require that students take courses emphasizing quantitative skills so they will be successful in later life.

Quantitative skills also have applications in all academic arenas. Women's Studies and Anthropology students, for example, would benefit from learning Statistics. Pre-Law and Literature students would benefit from taking Logic, which would help them become better writers and reasoners. The student body would be well-served all around by developing their quantitative skills.

Finally, many students are uncomfortable taking courses involving quantitative skills. This is all the more reason why they should! What is the point of an education which does not challenge students to move outside of their comfort zone? The college should see to it that students are adequately challenged, so they should be required to fulfil a quantitative skills requirement.

For these reasons, my school should have a quantitative skills requirement.

9. Maria and Cassandra have four arguments for voting. The first is that millions of soldiers died to preserve our freedom to vote. Cathy attacks the inference by saying that we also have the freedom not to vote, that's part of a free country. The second

reason was that voting was a duty. Cathy attacked the premise saying instead that our moral duty was to boycott a corrupt voting system. The third reason was that others can't vote. Cathy attacked the inference here arguing that her vote wouldn't help those who are unable to vote to vote. The last reason was that Cathy was well-informed and so would be an intelligent voter. Cathy attacked the inference but her attack had a logical flaw. Maria and Cassandra's argument form was $P \Rightarrow Q$. Cathy said that if that were true then $\neg P \Rightarrow \neg Q$, but

$$\frac{P \Rightarrow Q}{\therefore \neg P \Rightarrow \neg Q} \quad \text{isn't valid (check!).}$$

Cathy, you should vote. You should vote for two important reasons: it's your duty as a citizen, and your vote will make this a better, stronger country. Let's take these reasons one at a time.

You are a citizen of the United States. In a sense, you have an unwritten contract with the country. You receive as benefits shelter from foreign enemies. You receive protection from criminals, from fire and from other disasters. You have the advantage of a strong economic environment with job opportunities and entrepreneurial opportunities, all protected by United States Law. You enjoy a rich cultural environment subsidized by the government and enriched by diverse fellow citizens. You have all this and in exchange you pay taxes and you vote. Your vote is not required by law, but it is a token of your acceptance of the contract. It is an important part of your participation in the life of this country.

The other reason you should vote is the difference it makes. Your vote, every vote makes this country stronger and better. Democracy is not about good government. I know that sounds strange, but the strength of democracy is that it

produces popular government. That makes for a stable country, a country with less discontent, a country where revolution, violent or not, is not a threat. The votes of millions of citizens makes government popular. Now I know it seems to you that a single vote, your vote, makes no difference. But clearly there is something wrong with that argument because otherwise we could apply it to all voters and we would have the nonsensical conclusion that it wouldn't matter if no one voted. There have been elections won by a single vote. And even votes in a losing cause matter. President Johnson won the New Hampshire primary in 1968. The small margin of victory, however, was part of what convinced him to withdraw from the race.

In short, you owe it to the country that protects you, nurtures you, and offers you so much. And your vote isn't an empty gesture. The country needs your vote and is empowered by it.

Note: In Chapter Ten we discuss how to deal with potential rebuttals. This argument would be strengthened by some discussion of Cathy's point about the sliminess of elections.

9.4 Basic Modal Logic   (p.237)

1. $\Box P$ implies $\Diamond P$.
3. The first implies the second.
5. Equivalent.
7. The first implies the second.
9. Both Bob's columns contradict Alice's first column. Thus, Bob's column is not a feature. Thus, his column is an ad (it says it's a feature). That means that Bob didn't go to Swank Plank. So Alice's first column is true. But her second column is false (it refers to Bob's column as a feature). So Alice's column is a feature.

Chapter Ten

10.1 Sentential Deduction   (p.248)

1.

1. $(N \wedge R) \Rightarrow (N \vee R)$

1.1.	$N \wedge R$	assumption
1.2.	N	$\wedge$Out 1.1
1.3.	$N \vee R$	$\vee$In 1.2

3.

1. $\neg P \Rightarrow Q$ premise
2. $\neg Q \Rightarrow P$

2.1.	$\neg Q$	assumption
2.2.	$\neg P \Rightarrow (Q \wedge \neg Q)$	
2.3.	$\neg \neg P$	$\neg$In 2.2
2.4.	P	$\neg$Out 2.3

2.2.1.	$\neg P$	assumption
2.2.2.	Q	$\Rightarrow$ Out 1, 2.2.1
2.2.3.	$Q \wedge \neg Q$	$\wedge$In 2.1, 2.2.2

5.

1. $(P \vee Q) \Rightarrow R$ premise
2. P premise
3. $P \vee Q$ $\vee$In 2
4. R $\Rightarrow$ Out 1, 3

7.

1. $P \Rightarrow Q$ premise
2. $(P \wedge R) \Rightarrow Q$

2.1.	$P \wedge R$	assumption
2.2.	P	$\wedge$Out 2.1
2.3.	Q	$\Rightarrow$ Out 1, 2.2

9.

1. $P \Rightarrow P$

1.1.	P	assumption
1.2.	P	1.1

11.

1. $P \Leftrightarrow Q$ premise
2. $P \vee Q$ premise
3. $P \Rightarrow Q$ $\Leftrightarrow$ Out 1
4. $Q \Rightarrow Q$

4.1.	Q	assumption
4.2.	Q	4.1

5. Q $\vee$Out 2, 3, 4
6. $Q \Rightarrow P$ $\Leftrightarrow$ Out 1
7. $P \Rightarrow P$

7.1.	P	assumption
7.2.	P	7.1

8. P $\vee$Out 2, 6, 7
9. $P \wedge Q$ $\wedge$In 5, 8

13.

1. P premise
2. $W \vee \neg W$ premise
3. $(P \wedge W) \Rightarrow R$ premise
4. $(P \wedge \neg W) \Rightarrow R$ premise
5. $W \Rightarrow R$
6. $\neg W \Rightarrow R$
7. R $\vee$Out 2, 5, 6

5.1.	W	assumption
5.2.	$P \wedge W$	$\wedge$In 1, 5.1
5.3.	R	$\Rightarrow$ Out 3, 5.2
6.1.	$\neg W$	assumption
6.2.	$P \wedge \neg W$	$\wedge$In 1, 6.1
6.3.	R	$\Rightarrow$ Out 4, 6.2

10.2 Sentential Strategy (p.261)

1.

1.	P	premise
2.	$\neg P \Rightarrow (P \wedge \neg P)$	
3.	$\neg\neg P$	$\neg$In 2

2.1.	$\neg P$	assumption
2.2.	$P \wedge \neg P$	$\wedge$In 1, 2.1

3.

1.	$P \Rightarrow Q$	premise
2.	$\neg Q \Rightarrow \neg P$	

2.1.	$\neg Q$	assumption
2.2.	$P \Rightarrow (Q \wedge \neg Q)$	
2.3.	$\neg P$	$\neg$In 2.2

2.2.1.	P	assumption
2.2.2.	Q	$\Rightarrow$Out 1, 2.2.1
2.2.3.	$Q \wedge \neg Q$	$\wedge$In 2.1, 2.2.2

5.

1.	$A \vee B$	premise
2.	$\neg A$	premise
3.	$B \Rightarrow B$	

3.1.	B	assumption

4.	$A \Rightarrow B$	
5.	B	$\vee$Out 1, 3, 4

4.1.	A	assumption
4.2.	$\neg B \Rightarrow (A \wedge \neg A)$	
4.3.	$\neg\neg B$	$\neg$In 4.2
4.4.	B	$\neg$Out 4.3

4.2.1.	$\neg B$	assumption
4.2.2.	$A \wedge \neg A$	$\wedge$In 2, 3.1

7.

1.	$P \wedge \neg P$	premise
2.	$\neg Q \Rightarrow (P \wedge \neg P)$	
3.	$\neg\neg Q$	$\neg$In 2
4.	Q	$\neg$Out 3

2.1.	$\neg Q$	assumption
2.2.	$P \wedge \neg P$	line 1

1.	$(P \wedge Q) \vee (P \wedge R)$	premise
2.	$(P \wedge Q) \Rightarrow [P \wedge (Q \vee R)]$	

2.1.	$P \wedge Q$	assumption
2.2.	P	$\wedge$Out 2.1
2.3.	Q	$\wedge$Out 2.1
2.4.	$Q \vee R$	$\vee$In 2.3
2.5.	$P \wedge (Q \vee R)$	$\wedge$In 2.2, 2.4

9.

3.	$(P \wedge R) \Rightarrow [P \wedge (Q \vee R)]$	
4.	$P \wedge (Q \vee R)$	$\vee$Out 1, 2, 3

3.1.	$P \wedge R$	assumption
3.2.	P	$\wedge$Out 3.1
3.3.	R	$\wedge$Out 3.1
3.4.	$Q \vee R$	$\vee$In 3.3
3.5.	$P \wedge (Q \vee R)$	$\wedge$In 3.2, 3.4

11.

1.	$\neg P \vee \neg Q$	premise
2.	$\neg P \Rightarrow \neg(P \wedge Q)$	

2.1.	$\neg P$	assumption
2.2.	$(P \wedge Q) \Rightarrow (P \wedge \neg P)$	
2.3.	$\neg(P \wedge Q)$	$\neg$In 2.2

2.2.1.	$P \wedge Q$	assumption
2.2.2.	P	$\wedge$Out 2.2.1
2.2.3.	$P \wedge \neg P$	$\wedge$In 2.1, 2.2.2

1. $\neg Q \Rightarrow \neg(P \wedge Q)$
2. $\neg(P \wedge Q)$ $\vee$Out 1, 2, 3

1.1.	$\neg Q$	assumption
1.2.	$(P \wedge Q) \Rightarrow (Q \wedge \neg Q)$	
1.3.	$\neg(P \wedge Q)$	$\neg$In 3.2

1.2.1.	$P \wedge Q$	assumption
1.2.2.	Q	$\wedge$Out 3.2.1
1.2.3.	$Q \wedge \neg Q$	$\wedge$In 3.1, 3.2.2

13.

$$\frac{P \circlearrowleft Q}{\therefore P \wedge \neg Q} \quad \text{or} \quad \frac{P \circlearrowleft Q}{\therefore \neg(P \Rightarrow Q)}$$

15.

1. $P \circlearrowleft Q$ premise
2. $P \wedge \neg Q$ $\circlearrowleft$ Out 1
3. P $\wedge$Out 2
4. $Q \Rightarrow P$

| 4.1. | Q | assumption |
| 4.2. | P | line 3 |

17.

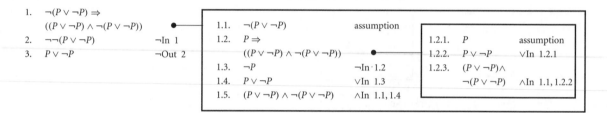

1. $\neg(P \vee \neg P) \Rightarrow$
    $((P \vee \neg P) \wedge \neg(P \vee \neg P))$
2. $\neg\neg(P \vee \neg P)$ $\neg$In 1
3. $P \vee \neg P$ $\neg$Out 2

1.1.	$\neg(P \vee \neg P)$	assumption
1.2.	$P \Rightarrow$	
	$((P \vee \neg P) \wedge \neg(P \vee \neg P))$	
1.3.	$\neg P$	$\neg$In 1.2
1.4.	$P \vee \neg P$	$\vee$In 1.3
1.5.	$(P \vee \neg P) \wedge \neg(P \vee \neg P)$	$\wedge$In 1.1, 1.4

1.2.1.	P	assumption
1.2.2.	$P \vee \neg P$	$\vee$In 1.2.1
1.2.3.	$(P \vee \neg P) \wedge$	
	$\neg(P \vee \neg P)$	$\wedge$In 1.1, 1.2.2

10.3 Arguing with Yourself (p.277)

1. This is pretty challenging! It's hard to imagine any politician today arguing for a return to prohibition. But let's adopt the conventions of parliamentary-style debating (see Chapter 12) where the person beginning the debate can define terms. That allows us to shape our own particular form of prohibition. We could, for example, take "prohibition" to mean that the sale of alcoholic beverages is forbidden. That would permit a government monopoly on alcohol sales. The government could then sell only by prescription and then only in generic form. You could make an argument for that. We'll put one on the web.

3. You could modify this and support limited suffrage for citizens 14–17, allowing them to vote in local elections only. These elections will have the issues of most immediate importance to teens. You could argue that it's unfair to deny representation to obviously capable citizens. You could argue that of all citizens, teens are the least likely to be corrupted and may be more sensitive to long-range planning issues. An outline and argument are on the web.

5. There are two very different arguments for a draft. One appeals to those who favor a muscular foreign policy. The argument is that a draft will make it easier to maintain a sizeable military, enabling us to project power across the globe. The other argument appeals to those who don't want the country to go to war. You can argue that voters are less likely to support military action if their children may be summoned to give their lives.

    You can also define "draft" to mean a system of universal service where all citizens must give two years to the country, either serving in the armed forces or in some other way, AmeriCorps, the Peace

Corps, etc. An outline and argument for at least one of these can be found on the web.

7. The policy might be no policy, that is, no speech is out of bounds. Then this must be defended. You could argue that you can't prepare students for the real world by shielding them from ugliness and meanness. You could argue that defining "hate" speech is problematic. And of course you can cite constitutional guarantees of free speech.

If you choose to ban hate speech, you will need to have some mechanism for deciding what hate speech is. This could be a faculty committee or a committee of students and faculty. You can argue that a university is like a greenhouse, sheltering students from the outside world while they grow strong enough to cope with it. You can argue that forbidding hate speech on campus doesn't violate the constitution (which only forbids the government from regulating speech). A sample policy and argument are on the web.

10.4 Sophisticated Modal Logic
(p.285)

1. Modal tautology
3. Not a modal tautology. Set B true in **G** which can access **U** where A is true and B is false.
5. Modal tautology

3.

1.	$\forall x \exists y (Qxy \wedge Pxy)$	premise
2.	$\forall x \exists y (Pxy \wedge Qxy)$	

7. Not a modal tautology. Set B true and A false in **G** which can access **U** where A is true and B is false.
9. Modal tautology
11. Set A true but B and C false in **G** which can access only itself and **U**, where B is true but A and C are false. $(A \wedge B) \rightarrowtail C$ is true in **G** (because in no accessible world is $A \wedge B$ true). But $(A \rightarrowtail C) \vee (B \rightarrowtail C)$ is false.
13. The first is an article and the second is an ad. Let A be that the first is an article and let B be that the second is an article. The first says $\Diamond(\neg A \vee \neg B)$. If the first is an ad $(\neg A)$ then $\Diamond(\neg A \vee \neg B)$ is true since every world can access itself. So A. The second says $\Diamond\Diamond\Diamond\neg A$. That's not true. A must be true in all worlds, so $\Diamond\neg A$ is false in all worlds, and so on.

Chapter Eleven

11.1 Predicate Deduction   (p.294)

1.

1.	$\forall x (Px \Rightarrow Qx)$	premise
2.	$\exists x Px$	premise
3.	c exists	$\exists$Out 2
4.	Pc	$\exists$Out 2
5.	$Pc \Rightarrow Qc$	$\forall$Out 1, 3
6.	Qc	$\Rightarrow$ Out 4, 5
7.	$\exists x Qx$	$\exists$In 6

2.1.	c exists	assumption
2.2.	$\exists y (Qcy \wedge Pcy)$	$\forall$Out 1, 2.1
2.3.	d exists	$\exists$Out 2.2
2.4.	$Qcd \wedge Pcd$	$\exists$Out 2.2
2.5.	Pcd	$\wedge$Out 2.4
2.6.	Qcd	$\wedge$Out 2.4
2.7.	$Pcd \wedge Qcd$	$\wedge$In 2.5, 2.6
2.8.	$\exists y (Pcy \wedge Qcy)$	$\exists$In 2.7

5. (a) You can't apply ∃ In unless there is a constant in the wff. (b) In the empty universe, ∀xRx is true and ∃y∀xRx is false.

7. (a) Line 3.1—you must have a new constant when using ∀In. (b) Ux means x was president of the United States, a is George Washington. In the universe of people, living and dead, Ua is true but ∀xUx is not.

9. (a) Line 4—You can't use the constant d outside the box. (b) In the empty universe, ∀xVx is true and ∃xVx is false.

11.

1.	∃x(Px ∧ Qx)	Premise
2.	a exists	∃Out 1
3.	Pa ∧ Qa	∃Out 1
4.	Pa	∧Out 3
5.	Qa	∧Out 3
6.	∃xPx	∃In 4
7.	∃xQx	∃In 5
8.	∃xPx ∧ ∃xQx	∧In 6, 7

13.

1.	∃x∀yPxy	premise
2.	a exists	∃Out 1
3.	∀yPay	∃Out 1
4.	∀y∃xPxy	

4.1.	b exists	assumption
4.2.	Pab	∀Out 3, 4.1
4.3.	∃xPxb	∃In 4.2

15.

1.	∃x(Px ∧ Qx)	premise
2.	a exists	∃Out 1
3.	Pa ∧ Qa	∃Out 1
4.	Pa	∧Out 3
5.	Qa	∧Out 3
6.	Qa ∧ Pa	∧In 4, 5
7.	∃x(Qx ∧ Px)	∃In 6

11.2 Predicate Strategy   (p.304)

1.

1.	∀x(Px ∧ Qx)	premise
2.	∃xPx ⇒ ∃xQx	

2.1.	∃xPx	assumption
2.2.	a exists	∃Out 2.1
2.3.	Pa	∃Out 2.1
2.4.	Pa ∧ Qa	∀Out 1, 2.2
2.5.	Qa	∧Out 2.4
2.6.	∃xQx	∃In 2.5

3.

1.	∀x(Px ⇒ ¬Qx)	premise
2.	∃x(Qx ∧ Rx)	premise
3.	a exists	∃Out 2
4.	Qa ∧ Ra	∃Out 2
5.	Qa	∧Out 4
6.	Pa ⇒ (Qa ∧ ¬Qa)	
7.	¬Pa	¬In 6
8.	¬Pa ∧ Qa	∧In 5, 7
9.	∃x(¬Px ∧ Qx)	∃In 8

6.1.	Pa	assumption
6.2.	Pa ⇒ ¬Qa	∀Out 1, 3
6.3.	¬Qa	⇒ Out 6.1, 6.2
6.4.	Qa ∧ ¬Qa	∧In 5, 6.3

5.

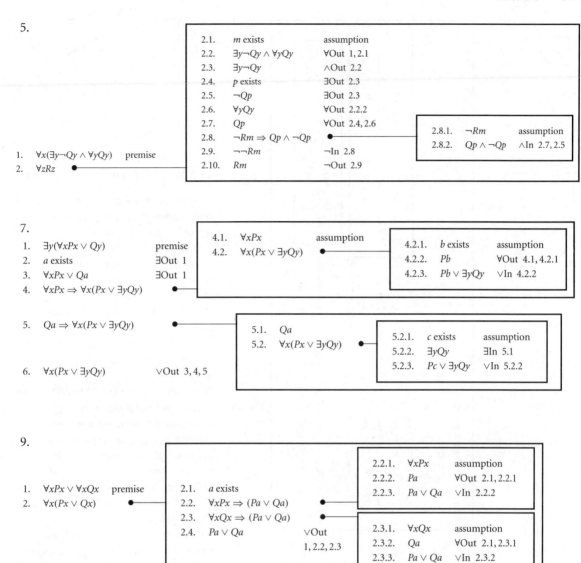

1. ∀x(∃y¬Qy ∧ ∀yQy)   premise
2. ∀zRz

2.1.	*m* exists	assumption
2.2.	∃y¬Qy ∧ ∀yQy	∀Out 1, 2.1
2.3.	∃y¬Qy	∧Out 2.2
2.4.	*p* exists	∃Out 2.3
2.5.	¬Qp	∃Out 2.3
2.6.	∀yQy	∀Out 2.2.2
2.7.	Qp	∀Out 2.4, 2.6
2.8.	¬Rm ⇒ Qp ∧ ¬Qp	
2.9.	¬¬Rm	¬In 2.8
2.10.	Rm	¬Out 2.9

2.8.1.	¬Rm	assumption
2.8.2.	Qp ∧ ¬Qp	∧In 2.7, 2.5

7.

1. ∃y(∀xPx ∨ Qy)   premise
2. *a* exists   ∃Out 1
3. ∀xPx ∨ Qa   ∃Out 1
4. ∀xPx ⇒ ∀x(Px ∨ ∃yQy)
5. Qa ⇒ ∀x(Px ∨ ∃yQy)
6. ∀x(Px ∨ ∃yQy)   ∨Out 3, 4, 5

4.1.	∀xPx	assumption
4.2.	∀x(Px ∨ ∃yQy)	

4.2.1.	*b* exists	assumption
4.2.2.	Pb	∀Out 4.1, 4.2.1
4.2.3.	Pb ∨ ∃yQy	∨In 4.2.2

5.1.	Qa	
5.2.	∀x(Px ∨ ∃yQy)	

5.2.1.	*c* exists	assumption
5.2.2.	∃yQy	∃In 5.1
5.2.3.	Pc ∨ ∃yQy	∨In 5.2.2

9.

1. ∀xPx ∨ ∀xQx   premise
2. ∀x(Px ∨ Qx)

2.1.	*a* exists	
2.2.	∀xPx ⇒ (Pa ∨ Qa)	
2.3.	∀xQx ⇒ (Pa ∨ Qa)	
2.4.	Pa ∨ Qa	∨Out 1, 2.2, 2.3

2.2.1.	∀xPx	assumption
2.2.2.	Pa	∀Out 2.1, 2.2.1
2.2.3.	Pa ∨ Qa	∨In 2.2.2

2.3.1.	∀xQx	assumption
2.3.2.	Qa	∀Out 2.1, 2.3.1
2.3.3.	Pa ∨ Qa	∨In 2.3.2

11.   ¬∃x∀y(Sxy ⇔ ¬Syy).

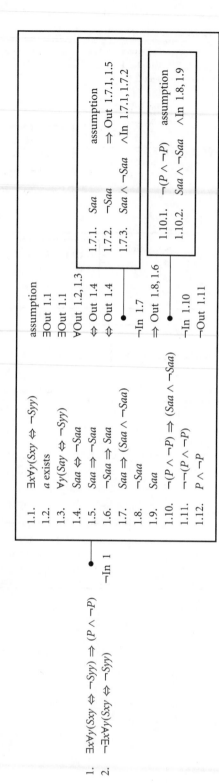

1.
$$\exists x \forall y(Sxy \Leftrightarrow \neg Syy) \Rightarrow (P \land \neg P)$$

2.
$$\neg \exists x \forall y(Sxy \Leftrightarrow \neg Syy)$$

1.1.	$\exists x \forall y(Sxy \Leftrightarrow \neg Syy)$	assumption
1.2.	a exists	$\exists$Out 1.1
1.3.	$\forall y(Say \Leftrightarrow \neg Syy)$	$\exists$Out 1.1
1.4.	$Saa \Leftrightarrow \neg Saa$	$\forall$Out 1.2,1.3
1.5.	$Saa \Rightarrow \neg Saa$	$\Leftrightarrow$Out 1.4
1.6.	$\neg Saa \Rightarrow Saa$	$\Leftrightarrow$Out 1.4
1.7.	$Saa \Rightarrow (Saa \land \neg Saa)$	
1.7.1.	Saa	assumption
1.7.2.	$\neg Saa$	$\Rightarrow$Out 1.7.1,1.5
1.7.3.	$Saa \land \neg Saa$	$\land$In 1.7.1,1.7.2
1.8.	$\neg Saa$	$\neg$In 1.7
1.9.	Saa	$\Rightarrow$Out 1.8,1.6
1.10.	$\neg(P \land \neg P) \Rightarrow (Saa \land \neg Saa)$	assumption
1.10.1.	$\neg(P \land \neg P)$	assumption
1.10.2.	$Saa \land \neg Saa$	$\land$In 1.8,1.9
1.11.	$\neg\neg(P \land \neg P)$	$\neg$In 1.10
1.12.	$P \land \neg P$	$\neg$Out 1.11

¬In 1

13.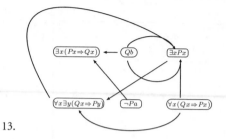

11.3 Why We Argue (p.308)

1. Hint: Focus on the goals a curriculum could achieve if a language requirement was implemented, or on the reasons why every student in a school would benefit from a language requirement.

3. Hint: Discuss the context for the passing of the amendment: have times changed enough to void the original reasoning behind it? Or emphasize the dangers of civilians having guns, weigh the risks with the reasons behind the amendment.

5. Hint: Focus on the need for budget cuts in different areas of government; is public broadcasting more important than, for example, college grants, special education, or health care programs? Or emphasize the use of taxpayers' money to create something that many conservatives have begun to view as having liberal bias.

7. Hint: If your policy allows for surrogate motherhood, it will have to make the rights of all concerned clear, including the those of the child.

11.5 The Logic of Paradox (p.324)

1. False in all worlds, true in **V** and **W**.
3. False in all worlds, true in all but **G**.
5. **G**: verified
   U: verified
   V: verified
   W: verified and falsified

7. **G**: verified
   U: verified and falsified
   V: verified
   W: verified and falsified
9. **G**: true and false
   U: true and false
   V: true
   W: true and false
11. **G**: true and false
   U: true and false
   V: true

W: true and false
13. **G**: true and false
   U: true and false
   V: true
   W: true and false
15. Yes it can.
17. They agree
19. C is a knave.

Chapter Twelve

12.1 Deduction with Identity (p.330)

1.
1. $a = b$ premise
2. $\forall x(x = x)$ = In
3. $a = a$ $\forall$Out 2, 1
4. $b = a$ = Out 1, 3

3.
1. a exists   premise
2. b exists   premise
3. $\forall x(Px \lor x = a)$ premise
4. $\neg Pb$ premise
5. $Pb \lor (b = a)$ $\forall$Out 2, 3
6. $Pb \Rightarrow (b = a)$

6.1. Pb assumption
6.2. $(b \neq a) \Rightarrow (Pb \land \neg Pb)$

6.2.1. $(b \neq a)$ assumption
6.2.2. $Pb \land \neg Pb$ $\land$In 4, 6.1

6.3. $\neg\neg(b = a)$ $\neg$In 6.2
6.4. $b = a$ $\neg$Out 6.3

7. $(b = a) \Rightarrow (b = a)$

7.1. $b = a$ assumption

8. $b = a$ $\lor$Out 5, 6, 7

5.
1. $\exists xPx$ premise
2. a exists $\exists$Out 1
3. $\forall x(x = x)$ = In
4. $a = a$ $\forall$Out 2, 3
5. $\exists y(a = y)$ $\exists$In 4
6. $\exists x\exists y(x = y)$ $\exists$In 5

7.
1. $\exists y\forall x(x = y)$ premise
2. a exists $\exists$Out 1
3. $\forall x(x = a)$ $\exists$Out 1
4. $\forall y\forall x(x = y)$

4.1. b exists   assumption
4.2. $b = a$ $\forall$Out 3, 4.1
4.3. $\forall x(x = b)$

4.3.1. c exists   assumption
4.3.2. $c = a$ $\forall$Out 3, 4.3.1
4.3.3. $\forall x\, x = x$ = In
4.3.4. $b = b$ $\forall$Out 4.1, 4.3.3
4.3.5. $a = b$ = Out 4.2, 4.3.4
4.3.6. $c = b$ = Out 4.3.5, 4.3.2

9.

$$\frac{\complement v \mathcal{H} v}{\therefore \exists x \exists y ((\mathcal{H}x \land \mathcal{H}y) \land x \neq y)}$$

11.

1.	$\neg \complement xx = x$		premise
2.	$\complement xPx \Rightarrow (\complement xx = x \land \neg \complement xx = x)$		
3.	$\neg \complement xPx$		$\neg$In 2

2.1.	$\complement xPx$	assumption
2.2.	$\exists x \exists y ((Px \land Py) \land x \neq y)$	$\complement$Out 2.1
2.3.	a exists	$\exists$Out 2.2
2.4.	$\exists y ((Pa \land Py) \land a \neq y)$	$\exists$Out 2.2
2.5.	b exists	$\exists$Out 2.4
2.6.	$(Pa \land Pb) \land a \neq b$	$\exists$Out 2.4
2.7.	$\forall xx = x$	$=$ In
2.8.	$a = a$	$\forall$Out 2.3, 2.7
2.9.	$b = b$	$\forall$Out 2.5, 2.7
2.10.	$a = a \land b = b$	$\land$In 2.8, 2.9
2.11.	$a \neq b$	$\land$Out 2.6
2.12.	$(a = a \land b = b) \land a \neq b$	$\land$In 2.10, 2.11
2.13.	$\exists y ((a = a \land y = y) \land a \neq y)$	$\exists$In 2.12
2.14.	$\exists x \exists y ((x = x \land y = y) \land x \neq y)$	$\exists$In 2.13
2.15.	$\complement xx = x$	$\complement$ In 2.14
2.16.	$\complement xx = x \land \neg \complement xx = x$	$\land$In 1, 2.15

13. $Ga \land \exists w \exists z \exists t \exists u ((Rwzt \land Rtub \land Rwza) \lor \exists s (Rwzs \land Mas))$

12.2 Deduction, FMTYEWTK (p.334)

1.

1.	W	premise
2.	$\neg\neg W$	$\neg\neg 1$
3.	$\neg\neg\neg\neg W$	$\neg\neg 2$

3.

1.	$A \Rightarrow B$	premise
2.	$\neg A \lor B$	$M \equiv, 1$
3.	$B \lor \neg A$	OS, 2

5.

1.	$\neg (C \land D)$	premise
2.	$\neg C \lor \neg D$	DeM, 1
3.	$\neg D \lor \neg C$	OS, 2
4.	$D \Rightarrow \neg C$	$M \equiv, 3$

7.

1.	$\neg \forall x \neg Px$	premise
2.	$\exists x \neg\neg Px$	QE, 1
3.	a exists	$\exists$Out 2
4.	$\neg\neg Pa$	$\exists$Out 2
5.	Pa	$\neg$Out 46. $\exists xPx$ $\exists$In 5

9.

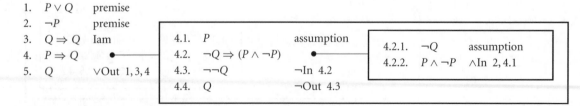

1.	$P \lor Q$	premise
2.	$\neg P$	premise
3.	$Q \Rightarrow Q$	Iam
4.	$P \Rightarrow Q$	
5.	Q	$\lor$Out 1, 3, 4

4.1.	P	assumption
4.2.	$\neg Q \Rightarrow (P \land \neg P)$	
4.3.	$\neg\neg Q$	$\neg$In 4.2
4.4.	Q	$\neg$Out 4.3

4.2.1.	$\neg Q$	assumption
4.2.2.	$P \land \neg P$	$\land$In 2, 4.1

11.

1. $A \Rightarrow B$ premise
2. $C \vee \neg C$ LEM
3. $C \Rightarrow ((A \Rightarrow C) \vee (C \Rightarrow B))$
4. $\neg C \Rightarrow ((A \Rightarrow C) \vee (C \Rightarrow B))$
5. $(A \Rightarrow C) \vee (C \Rightarrow B)$ $\vee$Out 2, 3, 4

3.1.	C	assumption
3.2.	$A \Rightarrow C$	
3.3.	$(A \Rightarrow C) \vee (C \Rightarrow B)$	$\vee$In 3.2

| 3.2.1. | A | assumption |
| 3.2.2. | C | line 3.1 |

4.1.	$\neg C$	assumption
4.2.	$C \Rightarrow B$	
4.3.	$(A \Rightarrow C) \vee (C \Rightarrow B)$	$\vee$In 4.2

| 4.2.1. | C | assumption |
| 4.2.2. | B | Exp 4.1, 4.2.1 |

13.

1. $\forall x Px \Rightarrow \exists x \neg Qx$ premise
2. $\forall x Qx \Rightarrow \exists x \neg Px$

  2.1. $\forall x Qx$ assumption
  2.2. $\neg(\exists x \neg Px) \Rightarrow$
      $(\forall x Qx \wedge \neg \forall x Qx)$

    2.2.1. $\neg \exists x \neg Px$ assumption
    2.2.2. $\forall x \neg \neg Px$ QE, 2.2.1
    2.2.3. $\forall x Px$ $\neg$Out 2.2.2
    2.2.4. $\exists x \neg Qx$ $\Rightarrow$Out 1, 2.2.3
    2.2.5. c exists $\exists$Out 2.2.4
    2.2.6. $\neg Qc$ $\exists$Out 2.2.4
    2.2.7. $\forall x Qx \Rightarrow$
        $(Qc \wedge \neg Qc)$

      2.2.7.1. $\forall x Qx$ assumption
      2.2.7.2. Qc $\forall$Out 2.2.5, 2.2.7.1
      2.2.7.3. $Qc \wedge \neg Qc$ $\wedge$In 2.2.6, 2.2.7.2

    2.2.8. $\neg \forall x Qx$ $-$In 2.2.7
    2.2.9. $\forall x Qx \wedge \neg \forall x Qx$ $\wedge$In 2.1, 2.2.8

  2.3. $\neg\neg(\exists x \neg Px)$ $-$In 2.2
  2.4. $\exists x \neg Px$ $\neg$Out 2.3

15.

1. $\forall x \forall y (Pxy \Leftrightarrow \neg Pyx)$ premise
2. $\forall z Qz$

  2.1. b exists   assumption
  2.2. $\forall y (Pby \Leftrightarrow \neg Pyb)$ $\forall$Out 1, 2.1
  2.3. $Pbb \Leftrightarrow \neg Pbb$ $\forall$Out 2.1, 2.2
  2.4. $Pbb \Rightarrow \neg Pbb$ $\Leftrightarrow$Out 2.3
  2.5. $\neg Pbb \Rightarrow Pbb$ $\Leftrightarrow$Out 2.3
  2.6. $\neg Qb \Rightarrow$
      $(Pbb \wedge \neg Pbb)$

    2.6.1. $\neg Qb$ assumption
    2.6.2. $Pbb \Rightarrow$
        $(Pbb \wedge \neg Pbb)$

      2.6.2.1. Pbb assumption
      2.6.2.2. $\neg Pbb$ $\Rightarrow$Out 2.4, 2.6.2.1
      2.6.2.3. $Pbb \wedge \neg Pbb$ $\wedge$In 2.6.2.1, 2.6.2.2

    2.6.3. $\neg Pbb$ $-$In 2.6.2
    2.6.4. Pbb $\Rightarrow$Out 2.6.3, 2.5
    2.6.5. $Pbb \wedge \neg Pbb$ $\wedge$In 2.6.3, 2.6.4

  2.7. $\neg\neg Qb$ $-$In 2.6
  2.8. Qb $\neg$Out 2.7

17. $\forall x(Rx \Leftrightarrow \forall y(Pxy \Rightarrow Ry))$

19. In the previous problem you proved that anyone with no children is a real sweetie. If h has no grandchildren, then all of his children are real sweeties. Therefore h is a real sweetie.

12.5 Incomplete Logic   (p.346)

1. It can be determined that this is the fun page. It is not possible, though, to determine whether either piece is an article or an ad.

Index